# Options for Britain

A Strategic Policy Review

Edited by
David Halpern
Stewart Wood
Stuart White
& Gavin Cameron

# Dartmouth

Aldershot • Brookfield USA • Singapore • Sydney

Published by
Dartmouth Publishing Company Limited
Gower House
Croft Road
Aldershot
Hants GU11 3HR
England

Dartmouth Publishing Company
Old Post Road
Brookfield
Vermont 05036
USA

**British Library Cataloguing in Publication Data**
A catalogue record for this book is available from the British Library.

**Library of Congress Cataloging-in-Publication Data**
Library of Congress Catalog Card Number: 95-83406

ISBN 1 85521 715 5 (hbk)
ISBN 1 85521 831 3 (pbk)

# Contents

# Notes on contributors

**Richard Best**
Director of the Joseph Rowntree Foundation, York, and Director of the Joseph Rowntree Housing Trust. He is also a Commissioner on the Rural Development Commission and Chair of the United Kingdom National Council for the United Nations Conference on Human Settlements. He was previously the Director of the National Federation of Housing Associations and Secretary to the Duke of Edinburgh's Inquiry into British Housing, and has published widely on the topic of housing and housing policy.

**Vernon Bogdanor**
Reader in Government, Oxford University and Fellow of Brasenose College, Oxford. He is also a constitutional advisor to a number of governments including Hungary, Slovenia and Israel. His recent books include *Monarchy and the Constitution* (1995) and *Essays on Politics* (1996).

**George Brock**
European Editor of the Times. He covered European issues from Brussels from 1991-1995. He has been the Op-ed Page Editor and Foreign Editor. He broadcasts frequently on the BBC.

**Gavin Cameron**
Research Officer at Nuffield College, Oxford. The main focus of his research is the econometric modelling of consumer expenditure, housing markets, and economic growth. He was previously an Economist at the Department of Trade and Industry.

**David Currie**
Professor of Economics at London Business School, and formerly Deputy Principal and Director of the Centre of Economic Forecasting (1988-95). He

has held visiting appointments at the International Monetary Fund, the Bank of England and the University of Manchester. His research interests include international macroeconomics and policy, and government regulation of industry. He sits on a variety of government advisory bodies including the Treasury's Panel of Independent Forecasters (the "wise men") and the Retail Price Index Advisory Committee. Recent publications include *Policy Rules, Credibility and International Macroeconomic Policy* (1994) and *North-South Linkages and International Macroeconomic Policy* (1995).

## David Faulkner

Fellow of St. John's College and Senior Research Associate at the Centre for Criminological Research, University of Oxford. He was previously at the Home Office, where he was Deputy Under Secretary of State in charge of the Research and Statistics Department and later the Principal Establishment Officer.

## David Halpern

Prize Research Fellow at Nuffield College, Oxford. He was previously a Research Fellow at the Policy Studies Institute, London. He will be taking up a University Lecturer post at the Faculty of Social and Political Sciences, Cambridge from early 1996. He has wide-ranging research interests that encompass social policy, psychology, and the policy-making process.

## Josh Hillman

Research Fellow at the Institute for Public Policy Research. He was Research Officer at the National Commission on Education throughout its existence, and has also worked at the University of London Institute of Education and the then Department of Education and Science. He recently co-edited, with Margaret Maden, the National Commission's book on effective schools in disadvantaged areas, entitled *Success Against the Odds*, published by Routledge.

## John Hills

Reader in Economics and Social Policy at the London School of Economics, where he is also Co-director of the Welfare State Programme. He is Programme Adviser on Income and Wealth to the Joseph Rowntree Foundation, and was Secretary to its Income and Wealth Inquiry, the report of which was published in February 1995. Recent books includes *The Dynamic of Welfare* (co-editor, 1995), *Beveridge and Social Security* (co-editor, 1994), and *The Future of Welfare: a Guide to the Debate* (1993).

## Michael Hough

Professor of Social Policy at South Bank University, London, where he is Director of the Criminal Policy Research Unit. He was previously the Deputy Director of the Home Office Research Unit.

## Kathleen Kiernan

Reader in Social Policy and Demography in the Department of Social Policy and Administration at the London School of Economics and Political Science. She has published widely on topics relating to families and households in

Britain and other European countries. Her current research is on the changing demography of partnership and its implications for the private and public domains of life.

## Ruth Lister
Professor of Social Policy and Administration at Loughborough University and was a member of the Commission on Social Justice. She has published widely on the issues of poverty and income maintenance and is currently writing a book on feminist perspectives on citizenship for Macmillan.

## Iain McLean
Official Fellow in Politics, Nuffield College, Oxford, and co-editor of *Electoral Studies*. He was previously Professor of Politics, University of Warwick.

## Stephen Nickell
Professor of Economics at Nuffield College, Oxford and Director of the Oxford Institute of Economics and Statistics, 1984. Previously Professor of the Economics Society, 1980; Fellow of the British Academy, 1993. Numerous publications on unemployment, wage determination, productivity and corporate performance.

## Raymond Plant
Master of St. Catherine's College, Oxford and a Labour spokesman on Home Affairs in the House of Lords. He was previously Professor of Politics at Southampton University. His many books include *Political Philosophy and Social Welfare* (1981), *Philosophy, Politics and Citizenship* (1984), and *Conservative Capitalism* (1989).

## Sally Prentice
Associate Fellow at the King's Fund in London. She is a non-executive member of the Lambeth, Southwark and Lewisham Health Commission and a Lambeth Councillor.

## Bridget Taylor
Research Officer for the ESRC Centre for Research into Elections and Social Trends (CREST) and at Nuffield College, Oxford. She was previously at Social and Community Planning Research where she worked on the British Election Studies and co-directed the British Social Attitudes team.

## Stuart Taylor
Gwilym Gibbon Fellow, 1994-95 at Nuffield College, Oxford. His main research interests concern the environmental effects of transport and the possible policy responses. He has published work on topics ranging from problems associated with sparse populations to climatic change. He is currently completing a book entitled *Pathways to Greener Transport: transport and environment policy across the world*.

**Stuart White**
Gwilym Gibbon Prize Research Fellow in Politics at Nuffield College, Oxford.
He has previously worked at the Institute for Fiscal Studies, London and
recently completed his doctorate at Princeton University. His research
interests encompass political theory and social policy, and is currently writing
a book entitled *Egalitarianism after Socialism*.

**Stewart Wood**
Research Fellow at St. John's College, Oxford. He is at present completing a
doctorate in political science at Harvard University. His main research
interests concern cross-national comparisons of the institutional foundations of
aspects of ecomomic performance, with particular reference to Germany and
Great Britain, and neo-liberal governments' attempts at institutional reform in
Western Europe since the early 1980s.

# Preface and acknowledgements

The *Options for Britain* project is an attempt to have a hard look at the long-term policy options available to Britain as we approach the twenty-first century. In the relatively short-term, we hope that this book, or report, will be used to inform debate in the run-up to the next general election and the activity that follows it. In the longer term, we hope that the book will provide an accessible source of ideas and information to both policy-makers and to wider audiences, and will serve to increase the honesty and imagination in political debate in Britain.

All too often, pre-election debates become captured by one or two 'key' issues that in retrospect don't seem very 'key' at all. For example, the 1992 election involved considerable debate about the resources available to the National Health Service, yet the fact is that the objective commitments made by the parties differed very little. Similarly, promises about tax were considered to be a major issue at the time, but in retrospect now look rather flat. Unfortunately, such false debates tend to obscure the very real policy options that are available and that need to be discussed. It has also become fashionable, and perhaps too convenient, to believe that governments are powerless to make real changes to the economy or society, and all that they can do is to try and ride the tides of global and social forces in the least obtrusive fashion possible. The most that can be done, it is often argued, is to tinker with the slimmest margins of change.

Yet cross-national, econometric and sociological analyses suggest that governments can do a great deal. As this volume shows, the main constraints are generally political, and sometimes psychological, rather than 'structural' or economic. If politicians have the imagination and the nerve to present the ideas, and the public are prepared to vote and pay for them, then the choices available to us are very wide indeed. Generally speaking, the question is not whether we *can* affect our social and economic future, but whether we have the imagination and the political will to do so.

Many people made contributions to the *Options for Britain* project. The idea
for the project arose out of number of informal conversations with friends and
colleagues in 1993 and onwards, including Joni Lovenduski, Desmond King,
Alan Ware, and several of my old colleagues from the Policy Studies Institute
such as David Smith, Michael White and Peter John. The idea was encouraged
and made possible by a number of people at Nuffield College, Oxford
including Avner Offer, Anthony Heath, Sir David Cox, Anthony Atkinson,
Iain McLean, Chelea Halsey, Simon Porter and David Butler. I am also very
grateful to the Economic and Social Research Council for providing a core
grant for the project and to Nuffield College for providing additional support.

A major component of the *Options* project was a three day conference and
discussions held in December 1994. Many thanks are owed to many people for
making this such a successful event, not least to the staff of the College who
really rose to the occasion, especially Oliver Gibbs, and to all my colleagues
who had to run around arranging rooms, picking up keys and even making
beds. Thanks go to the contributors of papers and to the discussants, who are
listed below, for their thoughtful, good humoured and valuable contributions.
Particular thanks go to those people who provided papers at very short notice,
such as Dawn Oliver and Sally Prentice. The papers and presentations at the
December conference provided the starting point for the current book.

In the time since the conference there have been further meetings and a great
deal of work in order to move the ideas raised at the conference forward, and
to draw out conflicts and contradictions into a coherent whole. New people
came forward to fill gaps that were identified through the discussions - such as
Stuart Taylor and Bridget Taylor on the transport and the environment, and
Richard Best on housing. Meanwhile, existing contributors worked to
incorporate ideas and conflicts raised into their own analyses and papers, and
others read drafts and sent in comments. Special thanks should go my co-
editors in this process - Stewart Wood, Stuart White, Gavin Cameron and, at
an earlier stage, Chris Clifford. This project would have been completely
impossible without their extremely hard work and considerable expertise.
There are also a large number of credits that should go to the individuals, from
government ministers to junior officials, who contributed to the development
of particular policy ideas and analyses contained in this volume but who are
not necessarily individually credited. Some are listed below, but others remain
anonymous, especially with respect to the controversial aspects of the 'policy-
making process' (Chapter 1).

Finally, I would like to thank those who turned the draft documents into the
camera-ready copy before you, and especially Lis Box, and those at Dartmouth
and BPC Books who assisted with the task of ensuring that copies of the book
arrived on the right desks at the right times.

D.S.H., Nuffield College, October 1995

## Contributors to the *Options for Britain* project

Anthony Atkinson, Warden, Nuffield College
Jenny Bacon, Director General, Health and Safety Executive
David Beetham, Professor of Politics, Leeds University
Brian Bell, Prize Research Fellow, Nuffield College
Samuel Bentolila, Centro de Estudios Monetarios y Financieros (CEMFI), Madrid
Richard Best, Director, Joseph Rowntree Foundation
Richard Berthoud, Head of Social Security Group, Policy Studies Institute
Vernon Bogdanor, Brasenose College, Oxford
Derek Bok, Kennedy School of Government, Harvard University
Stephen Bond, Institute for Fiscal Studies and Nuffield College
Anthony Bottoms, Professor, Institute of Criminology, Cambridge
Lis Box, Social and Community Planning Research
David Butler, Emeritus Fellow, Nuffield College
George Brock, The Times
Michael Brock, Honary Fellow, Nuffield College
Ken Burgin, ex-Department for Education
Sir Terence Burns, Permanent Secretary, H.M. Treasury
Camilla Bustani, New College, Oxford
Bill Callaghan, Head, Economic and Social Affairs Department, Trades Union Congress
Gavin Cameron, Research Officer, Nuffield College
Christopher Clifford, Research Officer, Nuffield College
Sir David Cox, Honarary Fellow, Nuffield College
David Currie, Professor, London Business School
Sir Ralph Dahrendorf, Warden, St. Anthony's College, Oxford
Colin Darracott, Charter 88
Andrew Dilnot, Institute for Fiscal Studies, London
Mark Egan, University College, Oxford
David Faulkner, Centre for Criminological Research, Oxford
David Finegold, Rand Organisation, California
Duncan Gallie, Official Fellow, Nuffield College
Norman Glass, Chief Economist, Department of the Environment
Alistair Graham, Chief Executive, Calderdale and Kirklees Training and Enterprise Council
Peter Hall, Center for European Studies, Harvard University
David Halpern, Prize Research Fellow, Nuffield College
A.H. Halsey, Emeritus Fellow, Nuffield College
Timothy Hames, Research Officer, Nuffield College
Anthony Heath, Official Fellow, Nuffield College
Marion Headicar, Gwilyn Gibbon Fellow, Nuffield College
Josh Hillman, Institute for Public Policy Research, London
John Hills, Reader, London School of Economics and Political Science
Gerald Holtham, Director, Institute for Public Policy Research
David Howell, Member of Parliament
Mike Hough, Professor, South Bank University
Carolyn Hoyle, Centre for Crimiological Research, Oxford

Will Hutton, Economics Editor, The Guardian
Nevil Johnson, Official Fellow, Nuffield College
Kathleen Kiernan, Reader, London School of Economics and Political
        Science
Desmond King, Fellow in Politics, St.John's College, Oxford
Martin Linton, Guardian Research Fellow, Nuffield College, Oxford
Ruth Lister, Professor of Social Policy and Administration, Loughborough
        University
Joni Lovenduski, Professor of Politics, Southampton University
Ben Lucas, Assistant to Jack Straw, Westminster
Geoffrey Marshall, Master, Queen's College, Oxford
Graham Mather, President, European Policy Forum; Member of the
        European Parliament
Iain McLean, Official Fellow, Nuffield College
Mavis Maclean, Socio-legal Studies, Oxford
Anand Menon, Socio-legal Studies, Oxford
Michael Moran, Professor, Department of Government, Manchester
        University
Stephen Nickell, Professor, Economics and Statistics, Oxford
Daphne Nicolitsas, Economics and Statistics, Oxford
Lord Raymond Plant, Master, St. Catherine's College, Oxford; Labour
        Home Affairs Spokesperson, House of Lords
Sally Prentice, Associate, The King's Fund Institute, London
Avner Offer, Professorial Fellow, Nuffield College
Dawn Oliver, Professor, University College London
David Raffe, Professor, University of Edinburgh
Jennifer Rubin, Anglia Polytechnic University, Cambridge
Sarah Stewart-Brown, Director, Health Services Research Unit, Public
        Health, University of Oxford
William Solesbury, Secretary, The Economic and Social Research
        Council
Mary Southcott, Chair of the Labour Party Campaign for Electoral Reform
Bridget Taylor, Research Officer, Nuffield College
Roger Taylor, Birmingham City Council
Stuart Taylor, Gwilyn Gibbon Fellow, Nuffield College
Helen Wallace, Professor, Sussex European Institute, Sussex University
Alan Ware, Worcester College, Oxford
Michael White, Head of Work and Employment Group, The Policy Studies
        Institute
Stuart White, Prize Research Fellow, Nuffield College
David Willetts, Member of Parliament
Tony Wright, Member of Parliament
Stewart Wood, Research Fellow, St. John's College, Oxford

# 1 Introduction: the policy-making process

*David Halpern and Stewart Wood* [*]

policy n., pl. -cies. **1.** Any plan or course of action adopted by a government, political party, business organisation, or the like, designed to influence and determine decisions, actions, and other matters: *British foreign policy.* **2.a.** A course of action, guiding principle, or procedure considered to be expedient, prudent, or advantageous: *Honesty is the best policy.* **b.** Prudence, shrewdness, or sagacity in practical matters. [Adapted from Morris, W., The Heritage Dictionary, 1973]

Policy is concerned with purposive action, or action that is designed to carry out certain objectives (Hogwood, 1987). Today, in an industrialised country such as the United Kingdom, government and public policy is a massive and integral party of our economy and our society, and its effects are felt in almost every aspect of life. However, despite the constant stream of newspaper headlines, news bulletins and talk-shows, it is relatively rare for us to sit back and try to see the bigger picture. Where is this juggernaut of public policy taking us? Is it where we want to go? And what, if any, are our choices?

This book, or report, is an attempt to look at the bigger picture of where we are going as a society and the kinds of choices that we have. It is a review of the policy options available to us across a range of areas, and especially concerning the longer term. Each chapter has been written by a leading expert in the area concerned, but in consultation with the other authors and discussants (these are listed in the appendix). We have also sought to draw out the interrelationships between the policy areas. However, the simple fact that

---

[*] David Halpern is a Prize Research Fellow at Nuffield College, Oxford, and Stewart Wood is a Research Fellow at St. John's College, Oxford.

this report needed to be written raises questions about the current policy-making process itself. Who is it who actually makes current policy? What institutions check its progress or direction? Or in terms of the juggernaut analogy, who is at the wheel and, perhaps more importantly, who is doing the navigation - is anyone looking at the map? The answers to these questions, as this chapter shows, give serious cause for concern. Current institutional arrangements for providing policy that serves the long-term interests of the British public are woefully inadequate and in need of major re-thinking. This chapter offers some proposals for how such improvements could be made.

## How is long-term and strategic policy made?

Long-term, or 'strategic', policy concerns issues that are either very broad in their scope, such as the goal of economic growth or the distribution of power, or issues that will take many years to come to fruition, such as pensions or increasing the skills of the population. As a consequence, these types of policies have two distinctive characteristics. First, they tend to cut across specific policy areas and across government departments. Second, their implementation and eventual impacts tend to take decades rather than a few years or months and therefore typically extend across Parliamentary cycles. As we shall see, these properties sit uneasily alongside the political and institutional pressures on governments and their agencies.

### The idealised model of policy-making

There is something that we might call the 'text-book' model of how government operates and how policy is made. In this model, democratic processes, the media, and the occasional crisis serve to bring a range of issues to the attention of Parliament and the government. Through the votes that people cast in elections, the weight of letters that Members of Parliament receive, and through the concerns and requests expressed to government by various interest groups, a policy agenda or set of priorities is formed. In addition, the government itself may seek to achieve certain political objectives.

   In this text-book model, agenda setting is followed by a search for possible policy solutions to address the issues raised. This process of developing policy options is primarily thought of as being the responsibility of the civil service and of the various government departments, but also involves some input from interest groups and the political parties. Hence, if the issue is to do with health then the Department of Health will consider what the options are, and if it is to do with transport then the Department of Transport will consider it, and so on, with interest groups offering their particular views and the Opposition throwing in a few suggestions and criticisms from the sidelines.

   Third, the process of developing possible policy solutions is followed by a process of choosing between the options by the government and, to a lesser extent, by Parliament. This stage is normally described in terms of 'rational actors' weighing the evidence and deciding on the best option for 'the nation', at least according to their own viewpoint. After choices have been made and the details have been debated and agreed upon by the House of Commons, the House of Lords, and so on, the policy is then implemented by whichever government agencies it concerns.

Seeing the policy-making process written out in this form, many commentators might remark on its unrealistic simplification of the reality. However, this classical model is of importance because many figures in the media, Parliament and even government talk of policy-making *as if* the text-book model was true. Also, in some very real sense, it is the 'official model' of how things are supposed to happen (see Box 1.1). However, as we shall see, the reality is very different.

### Box 1.1 Steps in policy appraisal*

> → **Summarise the policy issue:** seek expert advice to augment your own knowledge as necessary.
>
> → **List the objectives:** give them priorities, and identify any conflicts and trade-offs between them.
>
> → **Identify the constraints:** indicate how binding these are, and whether they might be expected to change over time or be negotiable.
>
> → **Specify the options:** seek a wide range of options, including the do-nothing or do-minimum options; continue to look at new options as the policy develops.
>
> → **Identify the costs and benefits:** do not disregard likely costs or benefits simply because they are not easily quantifiable.
>
> → **Weigh up the costs and benefits,** concentrating on those impacts that are material to the decision.
>
> → **Test the sensitivity of the options** to possible changes in conditions, or to the use of different assumptions.
>
> → **Suggest the preferred option,** if any, identifying the main factors affecting the choice.
>
> → **Set up any monitoring necessary** so that the effects of the policy may be observed, and identify any further analysis needed at project level.
>
> → **Evaluate the policy at a later stage,** and use the evaluation to inform future decision making.

* Adapted from: Department of the Environment, 1991, p.2

*The reality of the policy-making process*

Turning first to the setting of the policy agenda, we can see that the way in which issues get to be on the agenda is considerably messier and less democratic than the text-book model implies. First, there are well known concerns about the differential ability of groups to express their views and mobilise action. This helps to account for why some issues of apparently similar importance may attract very different priorities on the policy agenda. For example, the mental disorder of schizophrenia, which afflicts approximately one per cent of the population, is both extremely debilitating to those who suffer from it and extremely expensive in financial terms to society. Despite the immense cost of the disease to society, remarkably little is spent on schizophrenia research - about one twentieth of that which is spent per patient on cancer research (though the financial cost of schizophrenia to society has been estimated to exceed that of all the cancers combined).[1] Of course, the basic political problem is that people suffering from schizophrenia have, for obvious reasons, been less able either to campaign or, rather unfairly, to attract public sympathy. Consequently, research into this disorder has never been particularly high on the political agenda.

The process of agenda setting is also distorted by the weight of existing policies and institutional structures. There tends to be a bias towards considering the problems of existing policies and institutions rather than the potential of new or future issues. This is largely because policies create their own communities of beneficiaries, both within and outside government. Government departments and people involved in existing programmes tend to be at the head of the queue in the fight for more resources, and issues that have no clear departmental champion tend to be at a disadvantage. Finally, there tends to be a weighting in favour of problems that are more immediately pressing, and issues that have a long time run often get a lower priority.

Many of the same distorting factors can be seen operating in the development of policy options. There are serious disincentives for politicians to pursue issues that require long-term solutions, and especially if the costs fall early and the benefits fall late. Where the salience of an issue demands that *something* be done, there will be considerable pressures on politicians to opt for the 'quick-fix' that will bear fruit before, rather than after, the next general election, even if this solution is less efficient in the longer term. The weight of previous policies and decisions is also a major factor. In general, people complain far more about the loss of a benefit than they give credit for the gain of a new one, as Rose and Davies (1994) note, 'a decision to abolish a programme usually stirs up more political controversy than a decision to carry on with inherited measures' (p.238). These pressures are especially marked for the service providers themselves, as status and influence within organisations often flow from the 'winning' or 'saving' of resources regardless of the actual merits of the case.

The battle over resources between specialist government departments, despite the claims of the flow-diagrams in civil service literature, introduce considerable distortions into the process of reviewing policy alternatives. For example, if a government department can find a policy that it thinks will give it a greater degree of leverage over the Treasury or, better still, that will allow it to capture or effectively hypothecate funds, then the department may be tempted to pursue this solution even if there are other solutions that might be more efficient or effective. Even more seriously than this, however, is the way that inter-departmental competition can undermine effective strategic policy-making. For example, imagine that research showed that high-quality pre-school education could lead to lower rates of criminal offending in later life. An objective appraisal might suggest that the Home Office should therefore spend less money on, say, prisons and instead put money into such pre-school programmes. However, this expenditure and expertise would be unlikely to fall inside the official remit of the Home Office, and would imply the transfer of resources to some other department such as Education (or, curiously in this case, Environment). This 'loss' of resources would not be welcomed by officials in the Home Office, and consequently they might be less than enthusiastic to pursue it as a policy option - unless, of course, some other department would have to pay for it.

The process of developing policy options, and eventually choosing between them, tends to be presented by politicians in terms of careful cost-benefit analysis and well-defined objectives. This is what academics call the 'rational actor model'. However, this popular model of policy-making has been shown to have little correspondence with the reality of the process. In a series of case-studies of policy development and decision-making in Britain, Greenaway *et al* (1992) found that:

> ...*in every case, politicians used the rational model to explain and justify their actions.* They presented their choices as ways of achieving clear goals, as based on the 'facts', often ones that we, the public, could not know or comprehend, and as being almost a matter of technical assessment rather than politics (that is to say, values). In each case, politicians justified their actions very much along the lines of 'we've considered the options, weighed up the costs and benefits of each, and the only way to proceed is as follows'. Our case-studies show that this was never the way in which it worked, and yet this is the picture you would get from watching the *Nine O'Clock News* or *News at Ten* (Greenaway, J. *et al*, 1992; p.218; emphasis in original).

In practice, the distinction between developing policy options and making a final choice between them is rather poorly defined. Particular policy options can be eliminated at an early stage by bureaucratic politics, or their cases can be poorly prepared in order to damage their chances of selection. Greenaway *et al*, as others before them, found that factors such as bureaucratic politics and the influence of small specialist policy networks were far more important in determining policy choices than the 'rational' actions of politicians or the activity of Parliament. And even when choices have been made, they can be effectively overridden by a reluctance to implement them. As Greenaway *et al* concluded:

> The popular official picture of decision-making in British politics is a very poor guide to how decisions get made in practice... The emphasis placed on the role of Parliament in many institutional, media and academic accounts seems particularly unrealistic (*ibid.*, p.239).

This raises serious questions about how policy really does get made and who, if anyone, actually thinks it through. This is an especially serious concern with regard to strategic policy given that it cross-cuts departments and specialist policy groups.

## Who makes strategic policy?

Before considering how the strategic policy-making process might be improved, it is useful to consider briefly who the 'major players' presently are, and what their particular interests may be.

### The interests of the government

Formally speaking, the government comes to power after having been elected on the basis of a set of policy promises described in their party manifesto, and once elected they set about implementing these policies. However, as mentioned above, there is an enormous dead-hand on the role of government in the form of existing or inherited policies. This can be seen, for example, in the division of expenditure between different types of programme. As some researchers have noted, even by 'the beginning of the 1990s, 74 per cent of expenditure was devoted to programmes that had been inherited from half a century ago or longer' (Rose and Davies, 1994; p.226). Furthermore, manifestos are primarily designed to help a party win elections, and their proposals are rarely 'costed' or evaluated in great detail. After the election is over, the pressures of day-to-day government crowd out a good deal of the policy ambitions expressed within the manifestos and they receive little further attention.

Looking in from the outside, the part of government that one might have thought would be responsible for developing and coordinating strategic policy is the Cabinet. However, given that ministers must also represent the interests of their respective departments, and that their reputations and future careers are often seen to depend on how well they do this, it is not clear that the Cabinet is necessarily the place from where strategic policy will arise. There is jealous competition between government departments, and this is reflected at Cabinet level where 'the reputation and political future of ministers has traditionally depended on spending, even if the public policy or government requires restraint' (Hogwood, 1992; p.206).

An alternative institutional base that springs to mind for the development of strategic policy is the Cabinet Office, which is staffed by civil servants rather than politicians. The Cabinet Office has a close relationship with both the Cabinet and Prime Minister and stands outside of the specialist government ministries. It is subdivided into various broad areas (such as Defence, Health, and so on) and it is staffed by people who are brought in for a few years at a time from other areas in the civil service. However, the Cabinet Office is actually very small and its role relatively limited. Its secretariat numbers no more than around 150 people (including domestic staff) compared with the thousands or tens of thousands in each of the specialist ministries, and each subdivision consists of no more than fifteen to twenty people. The Cabinet Office has no formal power and does not attempt to develop or coordinate strategic policy, though it will sometimes invite officials together from different departments in order to help to resolve conflicts.

The third possible institutional base for the development of strategic policy inside the government, and perhaps the most obvious one, is within Number 10 Downing Street. The Prime Minister is in a unique position to obtain an overview across policy areas and government departments in order to direct overall strategic policy, just as a conductor directs an orchestra. However, the resources available to the Prime Minister to do this are relatively limited. Individual specialist government ministries have far greater numbers of personnel and budgets than the Prime Minister's office. Nonetheless, having 'the ear of the Prime Minister' is clearly a very important credential in the policy-making world. It is unsurprising then, that in recent years, the Policy Unit, established in 1974 by Wilson and which advises the Prime Minister directly, has often been seen to be very influential in the formation of the government's strategic policy thinking. However, relatively little is known about the specific role or influence of the Policy Unit outside a small group of political insiders, and many people are astonished to discover how small it is. At the time of writing, the Policy Unit is described by a junior minister as being 'back up to full strength of around "*seven to eight*" people.'[2]

Two striking features begin to emerge about strategic policy-making inside the government. First, at present there appears to be no clear institutional base for the development and coordination of long-term strategic policy. This was not always the case, and there have been some experiments within the government to create an institutional base for the development and analysis of strategic policy, the most notable being the establishment of the Central Policy Review Staff (CPRS, see below). Second, and related, is that remarkably few people appear to be involved in the process. This stands in some contrast, for example, to the USA where government appears laced with policy analysts and special advisors, where policy analysis has been seen as a distinct discipline for some time and where policy analysts appear to be a 'recognised category in the civil service' (Kleine, 1980; Hogwood and Gunn, 1984).[3]

Strategic policy-making in Britain is also affected by the nature of the electoral system, based as it is on a 'first past the post' principle. This principle has historically tended to generate a two-party system with (until recently) relatively frequent oscillations of power between the Labour and Conservative parties and governments of one party only, rather than two or more parties in coalition. As a result, the development of long-term policies has tended to be further undermined, as parties have usually marked their coming to power by ending the policies and institutional innovations of their predecessor. The absence of coalitions similarly tends to undermine the quest for continuity and consensus. This contrasts, for example, with the Federal

Republic of Germany where the small Free Democratic Party has been a coalition partner continuously for over 25 years, first with the Social Democrats and then with the Christian Democrats. They have undoubtedly exerted a 'centrist' pull on both administrations that has moderated the potentially disruptive effects on policy of an electoral swing from 'left' to 'right'.

However, arguably the biggest question that hangs over strategic policy-making in government is the relationship between the desire of the government to win the next election and the long-term issue of 'what is best for the nation'. Of course, it has become a distinctive paradox of democracy that it is the same mechanism - the electoral process - that both gives governments their legitimacy and yet also tends to undermine it as politicians seek to bribe and promise their way to their next victory. Electoral systems can also introduce other more specific distortions and incentives to governments. In particular, it can be argued that in the UK, a government that is rationally attempting to get itself re-elected should concentrate not on the interests of the nation *per se*, but on the interests of the floating voter in geographically specific marginal constituencies. In terms of strategic policy, the tension arises both from the relative shortness of the electoral cycle compared to the time needed to implement long-term policies and from any potential differences in the interests of marginal voters compared to the rest of the electorate. The standard response to this problem is to point to the role of civil service as a source of continuity and consistency. It is certainly empirically true that the continuities across governments, even where their political complexion appears to have changed, are far greater than the differences (Hogwood, 1992; Rose and Davies, 1994). However, this immediately raises questions about the source of this consistency: is it the wisdom of considered experience or blind inertia?

*The civil service and government departments*

The structure of government departments has been fairly stable over time (Cope and Atkinson, 1994), and government departments are clearly a major source of continuity in policy (Hogwood, 1992). Formally speaking, it is not the role of the civil servants to initiate government policies, rather their role is to respond to the ideas of government ministers and ensure the smooth day-to-day running of the existing machinery and policies of state.

As mentioned above, government ministries have far more resources and manpower than the Prime Minister, so it is unsurprising that empirical studies have found that bureaucratic politics between the ministries are a very powerful explanation of policy decision-making. Greenaway *et al* (1992) noted that their case-studies were 'literally full of examples of where decisions resulted from the bargaining between bureaucracies, with the Cabinet often being the political setting where these battles were fought out' (p.223). However, the departmental structure of government is potentially strongly in tension with the needs of strategic policy-making. While on occasion, government ministries may attempt to conduct strategic policy-making internally, many long-term and strategic policy issues do not fall neatly within the remit of any one particular department.

A good example of a government ministry attempting to develop its own internal strategic policy is the Department of Health's *Health of the Nation* report (DoH, 1991). The *Health of the Nation* was a discussion document which set out 'the Government's proposals for the development of a health strategy for England'. It was written in a readable form and presented wide ranging objectives and targets for the health of the population and the organisation of services. This document has been used, with some success, to coordinate policy across the many arms of the Department of Health and the health service itself, and to inject some long-term and strategic thinking into health policy decisions. However, the shortcomings, as well as the strengths, of the *Health of the Nation* initiative illustrate the problems of organising strategic policy across government departments. It can be argued that many of the factors that affect health, and especially that lead to variations in health across the population, fall in the responsibility of other government departments. For example, socio-economic differences in health are very large (see Chapter 7), but the types of policy that might affect the underlying mediators of these differentials, such as housing conditions or employment prospects, fall outside the remit of the Department of Health. Apart from the question of formal responsibility, other departments might well be hostile to the Department of Health telling them what to do and second, Department of Health officials might feel that it would be a mistake, in terms of bureaucratic politics, to draw attention to issues that could imply the transfer of resources from their own budgets.

However, at least an issue like health can be said to roughly coincide with the interests of a government department. Unfortunately, many issues of long-term or strategic importance inherently cut across departmental interests. The problem then arises that the issue may be 'nobody's baby' and will fall between the concerns of individual departments. A good example of this, and one that will be returned to in a number of the chapters of this book, is the work incentives structure that emerges out of the activities and policies of many government departments but that is coordinated by none. The so-called 'poverty trap' is not a government policy, yet it emerges as a direct consequence of many different, often well-intentioned, government policies on various issues such as benefits, taxation, housing and so on. In addition to the fragmentation of issues across government departments, fragmentation also occurs 'vertically' though layers of government such that issues and policies can be pursued in contradictory ways by local government, Westminster and, more recently, by European institutions.

Recent developments inside Whitehall have raised still further questions about the ability of the civil service and government departments to develop and coordinate strategic policy. Stemming from the Ibbs Report (Jenkins *et al*, 1988), many of the functions of government departments have now been transferred to new specialist agencies under the so-called 'Next Steps' programme. By August 1993, around 100 agencies had been established and they represented about 60 per cent of the civil service's manpower (Cope and Atkinson, 1994). Whether the creation of all these agencies will improve the quality of strategic policy-making remains to be seen. On the one hand, it could be argued that the further fragmenting of government, and the creation of specialist services promoting their own needs and policies without reference to wider policies or context, could be disastrous. On the other hand, if the creation of agencies acts to break down the rigid hierarchies of Whitehall and the artificial boundaries between government departments, then this reorganisation might actually open the door to major improvements in strategic policy-making. Also, if agencies come to be seen as more loosely attached to individual ministries, then it may become more possible for politicians and policy-makers to make less partial and short-term judgements about which activities to promote and if necessary, which to cut.

*Parliament and the committee system*

In the idealised model of how policy is developed and selected, Parliament looms large. However, as we have seen, the reality is very different, and in practice Parliament has a very much more limited role in strategic policy-making than the government or even individual ministries. Indeed, cynics might say that every time you hear a government minister telling the general public not to worry because they are 'accountable to Parliament' or that 'the issues will be presented for the House to decide', then that is the very time to start worrying. Parliament has little capacity, nor opportunity, to discuss, test or develop strategic policy.

There are occasional dramatic debates on subjects over which the government and political parties have no clear line, such as the heated debate over abortion or big foreign policy events such as over Bosnia, but these are relatively rare and tend to be restricted to very specific non-strategic issues. Less dramatic, but arguably of greater importance, however, has been the emerging role of the Select Committees. Committee structures have a long history in the UK Parliament, but the present Select Committee structure dates largely from the recommendations of the Procedure Committee of 1977-78 and the subsequent motion put forward by Norman St John Stevas, and passed by the House, soon after the May 1979 election (Garrett, 1992). The role of the Select Committees is to 'shadow' the activities of government departments. The Committees, now around fifteen in number, meet at least once a week for a session of two hours or more in order to examine some particular activity of the department that they shadow. Their meetings are open to the public and involve the examination of witnesses who may be experts, officials or even ministers. The committees produce a steady stream of reports - many hundreds have been produced since 1979 - and the direct reporting of the proceedings themselves often attract considerable media attention.

Nonetheless, although the Select Committees do much worthy work, their present impact on strategic policy-making is quite limited. First, the effectiveness of the Committees is seriously compromised by the existence of the 'Osmotherly Rules' which govern the behaviour of civil servants giving evidence. These rules are extremely restrictive, leading one well-known commentator to describe them as being 'an outrage' and parts of which 'should enrage all decent Parliamentarians' (Hennessy, Memorandum of Evidence to Select Committee on Procedure, 2nd Report Session 1989-90; quoted in Garrett, 1992). On occasion, the government has even intervened to stop civil servants appearing at all. Second, the Select Committees have very little institutional back-up. Most Select Committees have no more than three or four staff to support them, and even when the reports are produced, there is no clear institutional framework within which to respond to them. Only a handful of their many hundreds of reports have ever led to a debate or motion in the House, and there is no fixed time limit within which the government must respond to their work. Third, the Select Committee system shares the weakness of the structure of government departments that it shadows. As Garrett (1992) noted:

> A structure which mirrors government departments, though probably the best way of organising the committees, also has the weakness of giving inadequate attention to government policies which cross departmental boundaries. It is surprising that the committees have never made arrangements for joint sessions for enquiries into such topics or for networking to mobilise the resources of several committees for an enquiry into a group of related policies - especially as the House of Lords have proved to be very successful in considering such policies (Garrett, 1992; p.87).

The fourth weakness of the Select Committees is that their briefs are essentially retrospective rather than prospective. If strategic policy is to be made or commented on effectively, then the analysis must be forward-looking and it must be possible to have an input into the formation of policy at an early stage of the process, not after all the decisions have already been taken. Finally, one must also consider the more subtle ways in which the government may take the teeth out of troublesome Parliamentary committees. Until recently, the Select Committees have been known as sites of vigorous questioning of witnesses, and places where Parliament was seen to work particularly effectively and openly. Expert witnesses and advisors to the Committees often noted with some surprise that Select Committee members were often especially sharp in their questioning of people from inside their own party. The reason given for this was that the Select Committees were composed of those troublesome Parliamentarians who had given up hope of, or been passed over for, higher office either inside the government or their party. However, one recent development has been that John Major has let it be known that Select Committee posts will, from now on, be viewed as stepping stones to government office. Sadly, this may have the effect of making the Committees altogether more tame, and also potentially more divided, as government hopefuls seek favour through loyalty on the committees.

## The role and interests of political parties

It is said by some politicians and commentators that Parliament and the political parties have a see-saw relationship: when the power of the parties is strong, the power of Parliament is reduced, and when the power of the parties wanes, Parliament grows stronger. The source of this relationship is the dominance of the political parties within British political life. Strong party discipline within the main political parties tends to undermine the supposedly independent activities of Parliament in a number of ways. One important effect is on the incentives that individual representatives face once elected to Parliament. The selection process for electoral candidates, which takes place within and is controlled by the party machines, tends to encourage MPs to be first and foremost party loyalists and only secondarily constituency representatives. If an MP is at all ambitious, she faces strong incentives to promote herself through adversarial point-scoring and towing the party line, rather than participating in the formation of strategic policy-making.

Nonetheless, it is the political parties, not Parliament, that attempt to develop coherent sets of policy programmes, and it is the parties that present sets of proposed plans to the electorate in the form of their election manifestos. Arguably, of all public documents, it is the party political manifestos that come closest to a written statement of strategic policy. In one relatively short document, each political party attempts to state what its overall objectives are and what types of policies it intends to implement over the next few years if elected. This still may not seem very impressive in terms of long-term policy such as for pensions or education, but it is certainly more long-term in its orientation than, say, the budget or the Queen's Speech. Manifestos also have the major advantage of being structured around policy issues rather than around government departments.

Leaving aside the issue of whether promises made in elections actually get implemented once a party is elected, the manifestos raise the question of how policies are developed within the parties and how they end up in such documents. Analyses of the British Social Attitude surveys suggest that party policies both shape, and are shaped by, public opinion (Heath and McMahon, 1992). This is an important piece of evidence as it suggests that the parties, to some extent at least, can innovate and develop new ideas rather than simply respond to current public fashion.

The manifestos, in some literal sense, are generally written by just two or three people, but officially the process of developing and choosing between policies involves the whole party. Nowadays, much of the drafting is done by an individual from an internal party 'think-tank'. In 1992, for example, the Conservative manifesto was said to have been largely drafted by Sarah Hogg, Head of the P.M.'s Policy Unit, and the Labour manifesto by Patricia Hewitt, the Deputy Head of the Institute for Public Policy Research (Butler and Kavanagh, 1992). The Prime Minister or leader of the party also normally takes a strong interest. John Major, when asked who wrote the 1992 election, replied 'It's all me', and Thatcher and Kinnock were each responsible for the dramatic shortening of the 1979 Conservative and 1987 Labour manifestos respectively (Butler and Kavanagh, 1992; Topf, 1994). Does the manifesto, therefore, offer the party an opportunity to develop and present its strategic policy?

The business of developing and choosing between policy ideas varies according to whether the party is in government or not. When in power, a political party can utilise the massive machinery and full information of government to develop policies, though given the fragmentary nature of government departments, this may be something of a mixed blessing in terms of strategic, as opposed to specific, policy (see above).

Party members are officially supposed to be a fertile source of ideas and vigorous but constructive debate, as well as being a source of political legitimacy. However, when in power, the party is presented with a serious dilemma. If the party conducts too lively and public a debate, then it risks being seen as in conflict with its own government. As one senior figure explained, 'the official party machine must say that the government is wonderful, otherwise it would be a major political story... once in government, party research becomes propaganda'. Imagine the embarrassment if, as occasionally happens, a Conservative Central Office document that discusses some new and radical policy at variance with official government policy is leaked to the press. This danger perhaps helps to explain why the Conservative party machine, in terms of policy-making, appears to be relatively dormant at present. Despite this, things are not quite as quiet as they seem, especially as we now move closer to a general election. Every month, Conservative Central Office sends out an issue or question for discussion and response from the local Conservative parties. The views of the parties are then collated by Central Office and circulated. This does not, of course, imply that any of these views will necessarily be taken on board, especially given that the incumbent administration has so many other sources to draw upon (not least of which are the relatively influential right-wing 'think-tanks'; see below).

The Labour and Liberal Democrat parties have more of a reputation of attending to their members than the Conservative party, though this may partly reflect their current opposition status and their consequent lack of access to the machinery of State. The Labour party, in recent years, has developed a framework for policy development that, on the face of it at least, appears to be well suited for the development of strategic policy. It also bears some similarities to Liberal Democrat procedures for the development of policy. After the 1992 election defeat, the Labour party set up a small number of 'standing policy commissions', each being responsible for a broad, but relatively well-defined policy area. The most famous of these so far has been the 'Social Justice Commission', the report of which attracted considerable academic and press interest when released in 1994. Each Commission has representatives from the shadow cabinet, the National Executive Committee (NEC), the Trades Unions and the constituency parties. Both outsiders and party members are allowed, and can be invited, to present evidence to the Commissions. Drafts of documents written by the policy commissions are referred to the 'National Policy Forum', which consists of representatives from constituency Labour parties, councillors, the NEC, Trade Unions, the Parliamentary Labour Party, and shadow ministers in their areas of responsibility. Amendments are made in the light of comments and a second draft is referred to the Policy Forum. Documents are then referred to the 'Joint Policy Committee', which is effectively a clearing body composed of the NEC, the shadow cabinet and some Policy Forum members. The Joint Policy Committee decides whether to publish a document, though it does not necessarily get published as 'official policy'; it may just be described as a consultative document. Once it is published as an official document, the policy proposal then has to be passed by the party conference (the Labour party is unusual in formally constraining the leadership in this way). If the document is passed by two thirds or more, then it normally goes into the manifesto. Of course, this is the official picture, and it remains to be seen how much of this process would remain in place if the Labour party were elected into government. Historically, once in power, the Party has tended to act with considerable autonomy from the multiple and competing interests within the Party machinery, and there is evidence that Blair is preparing to do the same.[4]

Having identified the parties and manifestos as a possible site and opportunity for strategic policy-making, we should also recognise the various shortcomings of this process. Even the elaborate machinery of the present Labour Party belies the fact that it allows a number of competing interests within the Party to pursue their own chosen causes without detailed reference to one another. The result is that the Conference, which is formally the sovereign legislative body within the Labour Party constitution, adopts a patchwork of policy proposals as official Party policy. Furthermore, across the parties, the manifestos have inevitably become largely promotional devices. Because of this, they must capitalise on relatively dramatic issues that will catch media and public attention, and they must respond to the relatively immediate and short-term concerns of the electorate. This is reflected in the relative sensitivity of the electoral promises to the short-term condition of the economy. It is striking, for example, that the Labour party manifesto and campaign of 1992 appeared to have been wrong-footed by the relatively early preparation of its policy documents. Party insiders describe the 1992 manifesto as having been, in effect, largely written by 1990. However, by 1992 there was a serious recession and many of the party's policy promises had come to look unrealistic. It can be argued that well-considered strategic policy should not be so vulnerable to short-term changes in the economy as it should set long-term priorities and formulae rather than short-term goals.

More generally, the day-to-day battles of the political parties, and especially in the context of a combative two (to three) party system, tends to squeeze out the consideration of long-term policy concerns. So-called 'Punch and Judy' politics is ill-suited to the needs of strategic policy as it perpetually breaks up consensus and minimises the search for the common ground on which long-term planning and policy development must be based. The struggle for political and electoral advantage has also proved a poor medium for well-rounded debate about the inter-relationships between policy areas. Political parties, especially when in opposition, are always tempted to call for more spending on everything while avoiding the issue of the trade-offs between areas. Similarly, general arguments about reducing (or increasing) tax often become divorced from arguments about the benefits (and disadvantages) of specific public spending and provision.

The pressures of public life and inter-party competition can lead to a separation between the public and private debate. Public debate becomes about 'fire-fighting' on the issue of the day, and long-term and strategic policy development - if it occurs at all - takes place in private. In government, this may largely mean delegating such policy development to the civil service and, to some extent, to various 'think-tanks'. In opposition, the resources to conduct such policy reviews are far more limited and depend to a large extent on the relatively informal and voluntary resources that the party can muster. This tends to result in policy documents drafted on kitchen tables with the assistance of a skeleton party staff and a few academic volunteers, a situation that had led some people, such as the ex-mandarin Sir Douglas Wass (1984), to suggest that the opposition should be served by a special civil service department (Kingdom, 1991).

## The think-tanks and the policy networks

The policy-making community in the UK can be described as small, relatively amateur and ruthless. During research for this project, one member of the government when asked about how many people were involved in strategic policy-making in a given area replied that it was 'about the number of like-minded people who could sit around a table...about seven or eight'.

Academic studies have generally shown that, like bureaucratic politics, the 'policy networks' or 'policy community' model of policy-making has considerably more validity than the text-book Parliamentary or rational actor models of policy-making (Hogwood, 1987; Greenaway, Smith and Street, 1992). These models suggest that small and closely-knit groups of individuals with the right mix of expertise and political favour can have an enormous influence over policy-making. Until relatively recently, these networks were typically composed of politicians, high-ranking civil servants, selected interest group representatives and specialist academics, but the last twenty years has seen the expansion of influence of a new layer of individuals based at the so-called 'think-tanks' and specialist policy units. The emergence of this new layer of policy specialists has, to some extent, displaced the influence of academics and even politicians inside the policy community. There are probably a number of reasons for this latter effect, but the two most notable seem to be the greatly increased pressures on the time of politicians combined with the increased complexity of policy-relevant research and the expertise required to analyse it.

Contrary to popular opinion, the idea of 'think-tanks' is not a new one in the UK, and their existence certainly pre-dates their prominence of the late 70s. For example, the PEP (Political and Economic Planning), which produced many interesting pieces of work over its long history, was established in 1931. The PEP was merged, in 1978, with the Centre for Studies in Social Research (CSSP, established in 1972) to form the Policy Studies Institute (PSI) which is still active today. However, it was the activity and influence of think-tanks on the political right in the late 1970s and into the 1980s which really launched them into their current prominence. Units such as the Centre for Policy Studies (CPS), though small in size, are generally acknowledged as having been extremely influential in the development of the Conservative policies that characterised 'Thatcherism'. These small but influential think-tanks on the political right did not engage in primary research, but were instead 'magpies' freely importing ideas and material from the USA and from a variety of other sources. Even if one disagrees with the conclusions to which these right-wing think-tanks came, one would have to admit that they were enormously successful in their attempts to influence strategic policy. The small size but broad vision of the think-tanks enabled them to develop an overview across policy areas and over time that the machinery of both government departments and conventional political party structures had failed to do.

Since then the number of think-tanks and specialist policy institutes has continued to grow, though the total numbers of people employed by these institutions still remains relatively small, remaining in the low hundreds at most, as compared to the hundreds of thousands in the civil service and in the political parties. On the right, there continues to be a collection of small but very vocal units including the Centre for Policy Studies (CPS), the Institute of Economic Affairs (IEA), the European Policy Forum (EPF), the Adam Smith Institute (described as 'the brashest kids on the block') and the current flavour of the month, the Social Market Foundation.

In terms of think-tanks, the Left is still trailing, but it does now have the Institute for Public Policy Research (IPPR). In some ways, it looks like the IPPR is serving the Left with new ideas in much the same way that the CPS served the Right in the late 70s and early 80s. It is noteworthy, for example, that the current Head of Policy in Tony Blair's office is David Miliband, a figure transferred directly from the IPPR. However, the IPPR has had a more academic and research oriented profile than did the CPS. It is not yet clear whether this relatively academic orientation will assist or reduce its political impact.

In the political centre, there are a cluster of other so-called 'independent' policy research units. The quotation marks around the word independent are appropriate because the independence of these units varies according to the research involved and, more specifically, according to the funding arrangements of the institution. For example, the PSI describes itself as 'Britain's leading independent research organisation' (PSI, 1993), and it is certainly Britain's largest institution of its type. It has grown fairly steadily over recent years and now has around 50 researchers. This compares to a typical figure of around 7 to 15 full-time staff in most of the openly political think-tanks. However, the PSI has almost no core funding (in other words, funding that the institution can use according to its own judgement) and its finance comes almost entirely from specific funders and for specific projects. In fact, a very large proportion of the PSI's funding, and therefore the direction and content of its research activity, comes from government departments. This compromises the independence of the organisation not so much because of the direct involvement of government departments in the conducting and reporting of research, though this does happen on occasion, but because the organisation is not able to determine its own research programme. In other words, the funders are able to set much of the research agenda. In recent years this has become more and more of a problem as the research projects requested by funders, and especially by government departments, have become ever more highly specified and short-term.

These funding arrangements mean that an organisation such as the PSI finds it extremely difficult to pursue strategic policy research. First, as funding is too closely tied to highly specified projects, it is very difficult for researchers to step back and get the overview necessary to explore inter-relationships across policy areas or project into the longer term. On the rare occasions when the PSI has tried to do this, as in its *Britain in 2010* report (Northcott, 1991), it has run into severe funding difficulties and has had to heavily cross-subsidise the project. Secondly, researchers must always be concerned with not offending their present and future funders. Unfortunately, policy matters tend to be controversial, so even with the best will in the world it is difficult to conduct systematic reviews of policy without offending someone - and especially in government departments. Hence, despite its name, the PSI is not really in a very good position to look at 'policy' per se. Instead, PSI researchers must content themselves with 'establishing the facts' - but not the facts that funders do not wish them to establish.

In the light of the above, it is noteworthy that the (independent) policy organisations that have entered the fray of political controversy around government policies have tended to be either very small, or have had some kind of security to their funding. A good example of a small but surprisingly high profile think-tank has been the relatively recently created 'Demos'. Demos appears to have been successful by keeping its size, and therefore its funding requirements, small, and by a very effective engagement with the media. However, given its uncertain funding base and its risky engagement with wide-ranging policy issues, many people suspect that its life may be relatively short.

Examples of prominent policy organisations with relatively long histories and secure funding bases include: the Institute of Fiscal Studies (IFS), which has a strong reputation for work on taxation, social security, costing spending commitments and analysing economic policy; the Joseph Rowntree Foundation, which has tended to concentrate on housing policy and poverty; and the King's Fund, which mainly examines health issues, such as the re-organisation of health care in London. The first, IFS, currently holds a substantial core grant from the Economic and Social Research Council (ESRC) in the form of research centre funding, and before this it held a large grant from the American Gatsby Foundation. The latter two organisations have substantial endowments of their own. However, even such organisations as these cannot always be said to be engaged in strategic policy research, for to do so one has to consider the competing demands of many policy areas simultaneously. If the organisation tends to specialise in just one particular policy area, then how can it comment on the relative merits of, say, spending more on the health service *versus* spending more on education? These types of organisations make valuable contributions to many specialist debates, but their ability to initiate or widen strategic policy debates is more limited.

Finally, there is the question of political influence. It is all very well having expertise, but if no-one is listening - if you can't get a seat around the table with the key decision makers - then your impact will be relatively limited. There appear to be three factors that determine the influence of any given policy organisation on a particular topic. These are, roughly in order: perceived political viewpoint, expertise and proximity to Westminster. Given the very small size of the policy network in the UK and the conflictual style of our party politics, if you are viewed as having the wrong sort of political sympathies, then you are unlikely to get 'a seat at the table'. The second factor is expertise - obviously, you are more likely to have an impact if you are seen as knowing what you are talking about. The third factor is perhaps less obvious - for an institution or individual to have much of an impact on policy, they really need to be based close to Westminster. This again indicates the small and informal nature of the policy networks in the UK. One of the ways in which 'think-tanks' such as the CPS were able to influence significant policy-makers was simply to invite them round for lunch or for an informal seminar. In contrast, one of the reasons why the PSI is seen to have lost political influence is, according to a number of policy-makers, because they moved from their base within a few minutes walk of the House of Commons to a more distant site in Camden. PSI research continues to be highly respected among academics, yet its impact on policy-makers is now relatively weak.

To sum up, the size of a policy organisation is no guarantee of political influence in the policy networks of the UK, and especially if not tied to secure funding. Many of the small think-tanks have become quite important in the development of strategic policy ideas, though to be really influential they need to be seen as having the right political sympathies (or at least not the wrong ones) and generally need to be close the policy-makers (and to the press) at Westminster. This means that, in terms of long-term strategic policy-making, the number of people engaged in developing, reviewing and influencing ideas at any one point in time is actually very small. Many people might regard this as a surprising, even bizarre, state of affairs.


*Other external pressure groups*

It is generally acknowledged that special interest pressure groups are an important part of the policy-making process. Not only do they draw attention to the needs of particular groups, but they are also used by politicians as a source of information and in the refining of policy. Prominent examples include the Trades Unions, environmental pressure groups such as Greenpeace, third world aid agencies and campaign groups such as Oxfam or the World Development Movement (WDM), and many others. Less prominent but probably more influential are various commercial interest groups such as the National Farmers Union (NFU), the British Roads Federation (BRF), the Confederation of British Industry (CBI) and various large companies. Pressure groups, and especially the latter type, often have a very close relationship with particular government departments, sometimes in the form of 'consultative status', and can plug directly into the policy-making network in their own area of interest (Burch and Wood, 1990).

However, by their very nature, these specialist interest groups are not concerned with strategic policy. Though they may be interested in long-term issues in their own area of interest, these groups do not address the trade-offs that their demands might require in other areas. The British Roads Federation is not in existence in order to develop a balanced and environmentally friendly transport policy, and Greenpeace would not see its role to campaign for the protection of jobs in industry. Similarly, Oxfam has relatively little interest in domestic economic policy and the CBI has little interest in offering proposals for which programmes should be cut in order to pay for the tax cuts it might like to see. Strategic policy is centrally concerned with exactly such inter-relationships and trade-offs. Should we spend less on roads and more on health? What would the consequences be of reducing spending on social security in order to cut taxes on business? It is clear that, although special interest groups may have an important role to play in highlighting some issues, by themselves they are quite incapable of developing strategic policy. Indeed, they may often be rather unhelpful: the group that shouts loudest is not necessarily the group with the greatest need or the strongest case.

There is one particular class of 'pressure group' which would claim to concern itself with the whole range of policy issues rather than just a single interest. It is, of course, the media. The media does cover a very wide range of issues, and there are some senior figures in the media who believe that they have a very major influence over policy decisions. This belief was illustrated, and some might argue proven, by the tabloid newspaper campaigns running up to the 1992 election as, for example, in the notorious front page of *The Sun* newspaper immediately before the election showing a light-bulb with Kinnock's face inside it, and the headline 'If Kinnock wins today, will the last person to leave Britain turn out the lights'. Even more notoriously, of course, was the headline immediately after Kinnock's shock defeat that proclaimed 'It was the Sun wot done it!' (for which public assertion the editor was later reprimanded by Murdoch). On a slightly more cerebral level, other broadsheet editors, such as the ex-editor of *The Times*, Andrew Neil, have made it perfectly clear that they believe that the press can determine the outcome of policy in government and, equally importantly, can determine which issues get on to the political agenda in the first place.

These claims are almost certainly overstated, though it is clearly true that the press can have a significant impact (though not an exclusive one) on the policy-making process. Many important policy initiatives are developed quite independently and invisibly inside Britain's small policy networks well away from the prying eyes of the press. Part of the reason for this is simply because such issues are generally not seen as very 'sexy' by the press. For example, the issue of electoral or constitutional reform, though potentially of immense importance and capable of having a major impact on the nature of government and the policy-making process, is not seen by the press as of much interest. On the other hand, a minister having an affair, especially after the government has made comments that appear to relate to personal morality, provides an excellent story for the media.

This illustrates the fundamental weakness and potential irrelevance of the press to the process of strategic policy-making. By its nature, strategic policy is complex and slow moving. It concerns the subtle inter-relationships between policy areas and the impacts that these policies may have next year, or even over the next decade, but rarely next week. The vast majority of the media is too fickle, and its attention span too low, to be able to conduct debates about such issues. However, some might argue that this criticism is also true of politics and politicians (see above). It is an open question, therefore, as to how the media would respond to improvements in the quality of strategic policy-making at a political and formal institutional level.

## Improving the policy-making process

Having examined how strategic policy is currently made in the UK, we now turn to a brief examination of past efforts to improve the policy-making process and how it might be improved in the future.

### Past efforts to improve strategic policy-making

The overwhelming message that emerges from the examination of the strategic policy-making process in the UK is that it is fragmented, small scale and often barely occurs at all. This is not a new finding, and there have been periodic attempts to improve the quality of the process.

The traditional method used to strengthen the process of policy-making has been the formation of *ad hoc* commissions and inquiries. In recent years, the establishment of Royal Commissions and committees of inquiry have acquired a reputation as being a way for the government to kick difficult political 'footballs' out of play. Establishing a Commission could give the appearance that something was being done, but by the time its report was finally produced the political storm that gave rise to its creation would long since have passed. However, this was not always the case. The Select Committee on Procedure (1970-71), when reviewing this issue, recorded that since 1900 nearly half of pre-legislative Committees had given rise to identifiable legislation. However, the use of Royal Commissions and similar committees of inquiry fell out of favour after 1979, not least because Mrs. Thatcher disapproved of them (Garrett, 1992).

As mentioned earlier, some people think of the Select Committees as having a role in the review of strategic policy but, as we saw, this is not really the case. This is not to say that the Select Committees could not help to fulfil such a role, and there is nothing formally to stop them doing so. At present, however, the Select Committees focus their activities on the relatively narrow role of shadowing of government departments and they do not tend to concern themselves either with the potential conflicts between departments or with the prospective review of future policy concerns.

Perhaps of greater potential than the Select Committees, in terms of the review of strategic policy, was the proposal of the Procedure Committee of 1977-78 to allow the committee that was to consider a bill to examine the factual and technical background to the proposed legislation before proceeding to debate its clauses:

> In order to achieve this the committee should be free directly to question those who have drafted the proposed legislation and those who implement it as to the purpose of the legislation, the evidence on which clauses are based, the degree and content of any prior consultation with outside interests, the effects which the legislation is expected to produce and the problems which will be involved in its implementation. They should also be free to consult those who will be principally affected by the legislation (Select Committee on Procedure 1977-78, 1st Report, HC 588, para.2.19).

The unusual point about this proposal was that it was designed to stimulate constructive critical debate before, rather than after, a policy proposal had become hardened into specific legislation. In principle, this process would encourage a higher quality of debate and introduce the opportunity to consider the wider strategic context and ramifications of a particular policy before it was too late to change it. The procedure was accepted by the government on a sessional basis from 1980-81 to 1983-84 and was incorporated in the standing orders of the House in 1984 (Garrett, 1992). It was used for five bills, three in 1980-81, one in 1982-83 and one in 1983-84, but has not been used since.

The failure to use the Special Standing Committee procedure since 1984 is very disappointing and somewhat puzzling. The Procedure Committee in 1985 reported very favourably on the performance and effectiveness of the procedure. One witness, the Solicitor-General, reported that, '...here at least the House of Commons is permitting itself to do important work in a mature manner, and is doing it well' (Public Procedure Bill, Select Committee on Procedure 1984-85, 2nd Report, HC 49, para. 12). Unfortunately, it would seem that ministers were less than enthusiastic about their legislation being examined so carefully. As Garrett concluded:

> The most likely explanation is that ministers know that much of the legislation they bring forward is so inadequately prepared that they could not explain, let alone defend, it under cross-examination and that outside experts would make their proposals untenable. The thought of public demolition of a government bill, perhaps televised, is more than they can stand (Garrett, 1992; p.71).

The less public alternative for strengthening the quality of strategic policy-making is to consider issues more carefully before legislation is proposed. It can be argued that this is exactly what the Heath government had in mind when it established the internal think-tank known as the Central Policy Review Staff (CPRS) in 1970. The role of the CPRS, outlined in the White Paper on *Reorganisation of Central Government* (Cmnd 4506, 1970), was to help ministers access 'policies and projects in relation to strategic objectives'. Heath briefed the staff of the newly formed CPRS in the garden of 10 Downing Street saying that he intended the unit to address the weakness of 'Cabinets which all the time seemed to be dealing with the day-to-day problems' and which 'never [had] a real opportunity to deal with strategy' (Heath, 1972; p.5 - quoted in Kingdom, 1991). The CPRS was to be based in the Cabinet Office. In this respect it was unlike the Policy Unit, formed in 1974 by Wilson (and later strengthened when the CPRS was disbanded by Thatcher), the role of which was to advise the Prime Minister only (Cope and Atkinson, 1994).

Clearly, the CPRS was not a great political success in that it was axed by Thatcher in 1983, but, as we saw from the experience of the Special Standing Committee procedure, this does not indicate that it did not improve the quality of policy and debate. Issues raised and explored by the CPRS included the implications of demographic analysis for social policy, the implications of microprocessors for society and policy, and the projection of long-term trends in public expenditure (Hogwood and Gunn, 1984). Its analysis of future trends in the structure of the population, for example, threw up a wide range of implications for the social services and economy such as fluctuations in the number of school children, the size of the wage-earning (and therefore taxable) population, and the size of various categories of households (CPRS, 1977). However, a series of selective leaks of a report by the CPRS in Autumn 1982 that discussed the spending cuts necessary to contain public expenditure within specified limits led to considerable political embarrassment. The Cabinet disowned the report and did not publish it. Similarly, a leaked CPRS report on the future of the NHS under private insurance forced Thatcher to her fervent conference declaration in 1982 that the service was 'safe with us' (Kingdom, 1991). The subsequent axing of the CPRS was thus no great surprise, and its demise raised few protests from the Ministers and government departments long suspicious of its role.

There have been a number of other attempts to strengthen the quality of strategic policy-making. Most of these innovations attempted to increase the 'rationality' of how resources are allocated to spending programmes by encouraging longer term analysis, by replacing the competitive in-fighting between government ministries with greater coordination, and by reducing the tendency of the Treasury to force reductions in spending regardless of the merits of particular policies. One such attempt was the formation of the Public Expenditure Survey Committee (PESC) following a critical report of Treasury control over expenditure by Lord Plowden (Plowden, 1961). PESC was given the task of making annual five-year projections of future expenditure needs, including those of the nationalised industries and local government, in the light of forecasts of economic growth. It was composed of senior officials from various departments (including the Treasury) and it soon became an integrated part of public finance, producing a White Paper around February to assist Parliament in its deliberations. However, the original character of the PESC process was gradually eroded as the time scales for its analysis became shorter and competitive bargaining between departments replaced the more cooperative approach envisaged in the Plowden report. By the late 1980s, the Treasury was routinely holding separate meetings (termed 'bilaterals') with each department (Kingdom, 1991).

There have also been attempts to increase the quality of strategic planning through the introduction of techniques such as 'programme budget systems' (PBS) and 'policy analysis review' (PAR). These techniques were intended to test whether the particular policies being pursued by individual departments made sense in the context of wider strategic objectives and whether they provided good value for money. However, as with PESC, such techniques were gradually absorbed into the Whitehall 'game' and simply became seen as other tools to be used in the battles between departments (Kavanagh, 1990).

This depressing catalogue of the dominance of short-term departmental thinking and thwarted attempts at reform has led to recurring criticisms of policy-making in the UK. Such criticisms have come from inside, as well as outside, the establishment. Sir Douglas Wass, a former head of the Civil Service, argued in his 1983 Reith lecture that the Cabinet, as a collectivity, had lost the capacity to think strategically (Wass, 1984). He recommended that government should be more open, that policies should be evaluated by a standing policy commission and that something along the lines of the old CPRS should be re-established. Similarly, Sir John Hoskyns, a former head of Mrs. Thatcher's Policy Unit, complained that for Ministers:

> ... questions of policy analysis and formulation are ... of secondary interest, until it is too late. Politicians not only fail to think about the long term but there is no strategic planning capacity at the centre of government (Hoskyns, 1984; p.8).

In sum, it is clear that, despite previous efforts at reform, our institutions of state continue to have very little capacity to develop or review strategic policy and, consequently, the quality of such policy-making in the UK remains poor.


*Present options*

Considerations of present influences on the policy-making process and of past efforts at reform suggest a number of morals for future reformers. The common thread throughout these is that a very fine balance has to be achieved between integrating any reforms with existing structures and yet not being overwhelmed by them. Also, for any reform to be successful (and for it to be accepted in the first place), it needs to build smoothly upon existing political and administrative structures.

The first moral, therefore, is that any future reforms, or new institutions for the development of strategic policy, need to be carefully protected from the hostile and competitive actions of existing government departments. There is a long history of attempted reforms being 'largely absorbed or deflected by the people on whom they were designed to operate' (Kavanagh, 1990; p.312). This does not mean cutting off any such new institutions from government departments entirely; any successful reform is also likely to need to draw on the personnel and expertise of existing departments and organisations. Second, any new institution must be placed close to the centre of power, and yet must also be sufficiently at 'arm's length' from Ministers in order not to cause severe political embarrassment at the publication of its first controversial work such as to be wound up at the next available opportunity. Third, any new institution should be kept relatively small, should directly connect with the policy network and should have direct access to the sources of information on which policy is made (and especially, therefore, to the Central Statistical Office). Fourth, any new institution or reform needs to have a secure funding base if it is to have any true independence, yet that independence should not be so great as to allow the institution to pursue its own goals regardless of its original brief or wider public needs.

With these morals or conclusions in mind, we suggest that the following options for reform should be considered. First, the capabilities of Parliament to analyse strategic policy should be strengthened:

1. **Future bills should be reviewed by Special Standing Committees.** Provision for this procedure already exists, having been incorporated in the standing orders of the House in 1984, but Parliament should insist

that this Special Bill Procedure is actually used. This would allow the intentions behind legislation, and its likely effects, to be tested at an early stage through the calling of witnesses from both inside and outside the government. There is no guarantee that the use of this procedure would, by itself, lead to greater consensus, but there is every reason to think that it would improve the quality of debate and any subsequent legislation. It is important that the parties commit themselves to using this procedure before the general election, as all parties in government will face strong incentives from within not to go ahead with such an administrative innovation once in power. One of the benefits of adopting this procedure would be that it will encourage MPs to develop a number of skills that we would want our representatives to possess but that are not normally cultivated by the current Westminster system, such as deliberative skills, independence of mind (from party whips) and an involvement in longer-term policy thinking.

2. **Select Committees should be encouraged to cooperate, and hold joint sittings, over matters that cut across departmental boundaries.** Again, provision for this already exists, but at present it is a very rare occurrence as the Committees concentrate on a relatively narrow shadowing of departments. However, in the context of a package of other innovations to improve strategic policy-making, it would be hoped that the Select Committees would be keen to broaden their vision. Select Committees should also be encouraged to enquire about the longer-term objectives of government departments, and could provide a suitable forum for the airing of tentative proposals (in closed session if necessary) in front of a range of interested parties.

3. **A specialist research unit should be created and attached to Parliament to review, on an ongoing basis, the strategic policy options in public policy.** This unit should have direct links with the Central Statistical Office and with the House of Commons Library. The unit would be funded via Parliament rather than the government in order that it would not be vulnerable to absorbtion by other government departments. The role of the unit would be to serve Parliament and the Committee system both with information in response to specific inquiries and also with more general ideas and strategic reviews in order to inform and improve debate. The establishment of the unit should not be used as an excuse to restrict any other current rights of MPs to inquire for information. The role of the unit would not be to offer definitive answers to policy debates - this is a matter for Parliament and the government to decide - but would be to provide analyses of the range and probable outcomes of the options available to achieve a given set of objectives. The unit should be free to consult external experts where necessary.

Second, there should be a strengthening of the capability of the government, and particularly the Cabinet, to develop, review and coordinate strategic policy:

4.  **Some reorganisation of the Cabinet should occur around strategic policy objectives rather than just ministries.** The simplest way to do this might be to give a senior minister responsibility for certain cross-departmental policy objectives. The obvious person to do this might be, if not the Prime Minister, then the 'First Secretary of State' or Deputy Prime Minister, a role that has previously been rather vague in its terms of reference. In addition, junior ministers within each department could be allocated specific responsibility for particular legislative initiatives in order to improve the chances of the initiatives being seen through to the end.

5.  **The Cabinet Office should be charged with the responsibility of translating the winning party's manifesto into a strategic policy plan after general elections.** The Cabinet Office could then be used to assist with the coordination of its implementation, presumably in conjunction with the First Secretary of State. If necessary, the Cabinet Office should form a small research unit to assist with this task, though this should probably be more focused and integrated than the earlier CPRS. A deadline should be set for the production of the plan so as to reduce likelihood of the civil service paralysing the process and preventing the plan from being produced.

Third, there are a number of broader and longer term options that should be considered for improving the quality of strategic policy-making:

6.  **The structures of the Civil Service should be encouraged to become more flexible and less departmentalised.** The development of the Next Steps agencies provides the opportunity to do this. The smaller and less specialised 'core functions' of the civil service that now remain should utilise this new freedom to become more strategically orientated and more cooperative with other departments. For certain phases of policy development, the possibility should be considered of setting up small competing teams to develop alternative solutions to the same problem in order to ensure a full range of options are explored.

7.  **The possibility should be considered of some state funding of policy research inside the political parties, and especially when in opposition.** The intention of this would be to increase the quality of debate and generate a better 'market' of potential policy options. The National Audit Office should keep track of how this money was being spent. The possibility should be considered of creating a civil service 'Department of the Opposition', or at least improving the access of the Opposition to data and information at present reserved for the exclusive use of the government. At present, the Opposition parties' policy proposals are based on informed guesses about the incumbent government's policy and expenditure commitments, projected revenues, and so on. This means that the Opposition's policies may often be artificially unrealistic and their ability to contribute to debate reduced. Furthermore, when they do eventually get into power there is a 'rude awakening' effect that may

undermine their commitments and proposed policies, and can also be used as an excuse to renege on manifesto pledges.

Most of these policy options would have almost no cost attached to them. Even the most expensive options, the establishment of a research unit to serve Parliament and the funding of policy research inside the political parties, would be extremely modest compared to the potential savings that they might produce in the form of improved public policy. For example, a fully equipped research unit with a staff of 50 researchers would cost around £2.5 million per year to run. This spending would represent less than 0.001 per cent of the £273 billion of general government expenditure that the unit would be seeking to improve the social and economic return on.

Improving the quality of the strategic policy-making process will not, by itself, guarantee solutions to all of our social or economic solutions, nor guarantee that we would be any more likely to reach a consensus about any particular policy issue. However, what it should do is increase the quality of our political debates, improve the level and quality of coordination across policies and government departments and, ultimately, enrich the 'market' of policy ideas and eventual policy itself.

## Notes

1.  In the USA, the annual cost of schizophrenia has been estimated at around two per cent of the gross national product, about one fifth of this figure being from the cost of treatment and the remaining being from the loss in productive capacity and the costs of hospitalisation (Kaplan and Sadock, 1988).
2.  Of course, it was through the Policy Unit that John Redwood (then under Thatcher and before becoming an MP) rose to power.
3.  This is not to say, however, that the policy-making process in the USA is to be preferred. A large policy community per se certainly does not guarantee 'better quality' policy.
4.  It is interesting to note that it was the perceived distance of the Callaghan government from the rank-and-file that was the main reason why the 'Labour Left' sought to introduce constitutional change in the early 1980s in order to bring the leadership back into line.

## References

Burch, M. and Wood, B. (1990), *Public Policy in Britain; Second edition,* Oxford: Blackwell.

Butler, D. and Kavanagh, D. (1992), *The British General Election of 1992,* London: MacMillan Press.

Central Policy Review Staff (1977), *Population and the Social Services,* London: HMSO.

Cmnd 4506 (1970), *The Reorganisation of Central Government,* London: HMSO.

Cope, S. and Atkinson, R. (1994), 'The structures of governance in Britain', in Savage, S.P., Atkinson, R. and Robins, L. (eds.), *Public Policy in Britain,* Basingstoke: MacMillan Press.

Department of Health (1991), *The Health of the Nation,* London: HMSO.

Department of the Environment (1991), *Policy Appraisal and the Environment: a Guide for Government Departments,* London: HMSO.

Garrett, J. (1992), *Westminster: Does Parliament Work?* London: Victor Golancz.

Greenaway, J., Smith, S. and Street, J. (1992), *Deciding Factors in British Politics: a Case-studies Approach,* London: Routledge.

Heath, A. and McMahon, D. (1992), 'Changes in values', in Jowell, R., Brook, L., Prior, G. and Taylor, B. (eds.), *British Social Attitudes: the 9th Report,* Aldershot: Dartmouth.

Heath, E. (1972), *My Style of Government,* London: Evening Standard Publications.

Hogwood, B. (1992), *Trends in British Public Policy: Do Governments Make Any Difference?* Buckingham: Open University Press.

Hogwood, B. (1987), *From Crisis to Complacency? Shaping Public Policy in Britain,* Oxford: Oxford University Press.

Hogwood, B. and Gunn, L. (1984), *Policy Analysis for the Real World,* Oxford: Oxford University Press.

Hoskyns, Sir J. (1984), 'Conservatism is not enough', *Political Quarterly,* **55** (1), pp.3-16.

Jenkins, K., Caines, K. and Jackson, A. (1988), *Improving Management in Government: the Next Steps,* London: HMSO.

Kaplan, H. and Sadock, B. (1988), *Synopsis of Psychiatry* (5th edition), London: Williams and Wilkins.

Kavanagh, D. (1990), *British Politics: Continuities and Change; Second Edition,* Oxford: Oxford University Press.

Kingdom, J. (1991), *Government and Politics in Britain,* Cambridge: Polity Press.

Klein, R. (1980), 'Creating problems', (review of Aaron Wildavsky, *The Art and Craft of Policy Analysis*), *New Society,* **53,** p.141.

Morris, W. (1973), *The Heritage Dictionary of the English Language,* Boston: McGraw-Hill.

Northcott, J. (1991), *Britain in 2010: The PSI Report,* London: PSI Publishing.

Plowden, Lord (chairman) (1961), *The Control of Public Expenditure,* Cmnd 7797, London: HMSO.

Policy Studies Institute (1993), *Annual Report*, London: Policy Studies Institute.

Rose, R. and Davies P. L. (1994), *Inheritance in Public Policy: Change Without Choice in Britain*, London: Yale University Press.

*Select Committee on Procedure (1984-85) Public Bill Procedure, 2nd Report*, HC 49.

*Select Committee on Procedure (1977-78) 1st Report*, HC 588.

Topf, R. (1994), 'Party manifestos', in Heath, A., Jowell, R. and Curtice, J. (eds.), *Labour's Last Chance? The 1992 Election and Beyond*, Aldershot: Dartmouth.

Wass, Sir D. (1984), *Government and the Governed*, (BBC Reith lectures), London: Routledge and Kegan Paul.

# 2 Prospects and strategies for UK economic growth

*David Currie* *

This chapter examines the short and long term prospects for UK economic growth, in the light of both domestic and international trends.

It starts by examining the immediate prospects for growth over the next two to three years. It argues that the immediate prospects for growth are good, and that continued growth at a 2.5 - 3 per cent rate should be feasible without running into significant capacity or inflation constraints or balance of payments difficulties. This is not surprising in view of the severity of the recent recession and the fact that output growth did not grow for the four years between 1990 and 1994, with output only exceeding its 1990 peak towards the end of 1994. Indeed data on capacity utilisation and inflation expectations suggest that the surprise is in the relatively small scope for above trend growth, despite the severity of the recession from which the UK economy is recovering. A key element in the recovery has been the competitive level of the pound, which has encouraged exports and investment, and its maintenance will be important to continued sustainable growth. If a competitive exchange rate is not to result in inflationary pressures, there is a need to maintain tight control over the government deficit, so that the bias of the macroeconomic policy stance is towards tight fiscal and loose monetary policy. This limits the Chancellor's scope to cut taxes, or for a new government to meet spending priorities through increased borrowing (see also Chapter 4 on taxation).

There are a number of reasons why the sense of well-being (the 'feel-good' factor) may not recover as much as the economy. Personal disposable income is being squeezed by tax increases, and may well fall over the coming year for

---

* Professor, London Business School.

those in work. This is the necessary counterpart to the shift of resources into exports and investment, and of the reduction in public borrowing. Moreover, much of the rise in employment appears to be in the form of part-time jobs, where remuneration and security may be limited. More generally, the shift by many companies to more flexible forms of contractual arrangements without long term commitment has led to more job insecurity. Increased profitability and income inequality also reduces the gainers at the lower end of the income distribution. Moreover, the housing market, which has generated major capital gains for house-owners over the past three decades, is in the doldrums, and is widely expected to remain so.

The chapter then moves on to consider underlying growth performance. It notes that, after several decades of slow UK productivity growth relative to the major industrial countries, the UK's underlying growth performance over the last decade or so has broadly been in line. This has not resulted from an increase in the UK's underlying growth performance, for which there is no evidence, but rather from a slow-down in other countries' growth rates. However, it also notes the appreciable differences in the level of productivity and per-capita GDP between the UK and other major European economies, and even more so between the UK and the US and Japan. Thus there is scope for the UK to grow more quickly to catch up. But the evidence that this is happening is not strong. Productivity in manufacturing and some key service sectors is rising fast, but this is largely being offset in terms of overall whole-economy productivity performance by the creation of jobs in low productivity service sectors.

The chapter analyses a number of factors that may influence longer run growth rates. It considers, but rejects, the view that low inflation is a necessary condition for high sustainable growth, though it accepts that fluctuations in inflation rates, which are damaging to growth, tend to be associated with high inflation. It notes the low levels of savings and investment in the UK as a factor inhibiting growth, but questions the causation: while small and medium sized enterprises may be inhibited by the availability of domestic finance, this is increasingly not true of major companies. It also examines and questions whether a deregulated labour market is essential for high growth, noting that a more flexible labour market may not improve growth performance but merely increase the sensitivity of prices to demand conditions.

The chapter concludes by considering the case for an active industrial policy. It notes that government intervention of a market-friendly kind has been a key element in the growth of the high performance economies. But it questions the capacity of the UK government system to avoid the dangers inherent in an active industrial policy of this kind. It emphasises instead investment in knowledge and skills, in which the UK is in danger of lagging, and essential infrastructure. It also emphasises the importance of openness to inward investment as an important force for competition, restructuring and the transformation of work practices. It concludes by examining the risk that the UK's stance towards Europe will make it a less attractive location for inward investment, and thereby weaken its growth prospects.

## Prospects for growth in the short term

We start by examining the immediate prospects for growth over the next two to three years, and considering how well-founded the current UK recovery is.

As Figure 2.1 shows, the last recession started in the third quarter of 1990, and recovery started in the second quarter of 1992. Initially this recovery was tentative, with output growing at an annual rate of less than 2 per cent, well below the trend growth of the UK economy. But from the middle of 1993, growth rose to more than 3 per cent, then to around 4 per cent, before slowing to a more sustainable 2.5 per cent rate. At the time of writing, there are concerns about renewed recession. In our view, it seems unlikely that there will be a major interruption to growth, and that growth is set to proceed at a sustainable 2.5 - 3 per cent rate into the medium term (see London Business School, 1995).

Figure 2.1

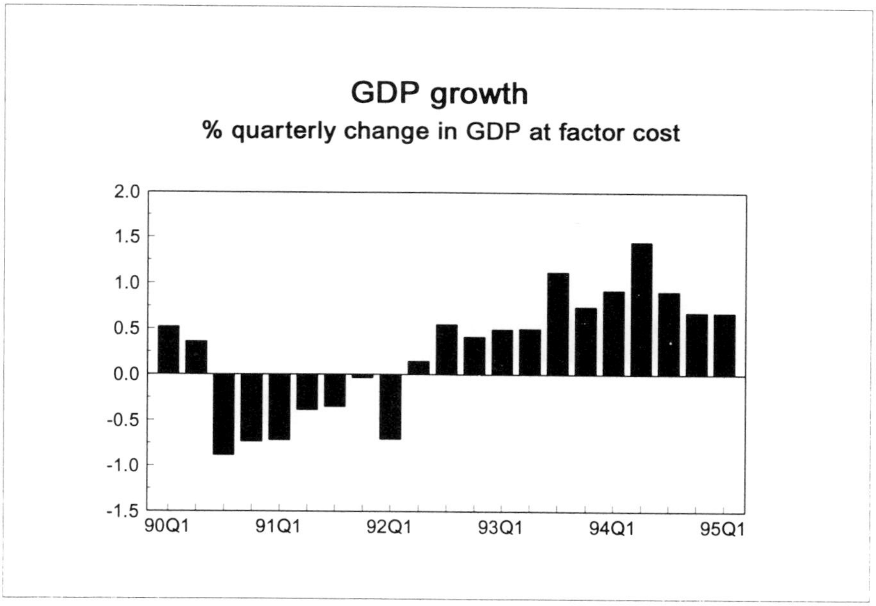

GDP growth
% quarterly change in GDP at factor cost

The sources of this growth are several. Consumer spending has been growing slowly but steadily, led by growing incomes and a greater level of confidence that has allowed consumers to reduce the amount of income that they save. But tax increases have meant that consumer spending has grown slowly over the recent past, not perhaps surprisingly since real disposable income grew more slowly in the recent years of recovery (1993-94) than in the years of recession (1990-92). Trade performance has been very strong following the 1992 ERM exit and devaluation, with exports growing much more quickly than imports despite recession in Europe. Moreover, investment and stock-

building have been picking up, and can be expected to grow faster. Recovery
has brought sustained falls in unemployment since early 1993 (Figure 2.2).

**Figure 2.2**

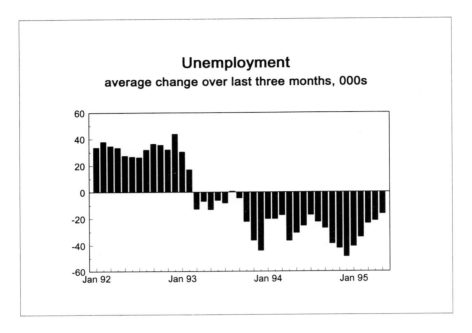

Continued growth and falling unemployment have also gone together with
favourable trends on two other key indicators: inflation and the balance of
payments. Inflation at the turn of the year was at its lowest level since the
1960s, measured in terms of the underlying measure excluding mortgage
interest payments (RPIX) on which the Government defines its target (though
it has risen a little since; Figure 2.3). After years of large deficits in the late
1980s and early 1990s, the current account of the balance of payments has most
recently moved into surplus (Figure 2.4). Some forecasters are predicting
continued surpluses, which would represent a useful consolidation after the
large deficits of the late 1980s and early 1990s. But even if deficits do re-
emerge, the balance of payments is most unlikely to represent any constraint
on UK economic growth in the foreseeable future.

Figure 2.3

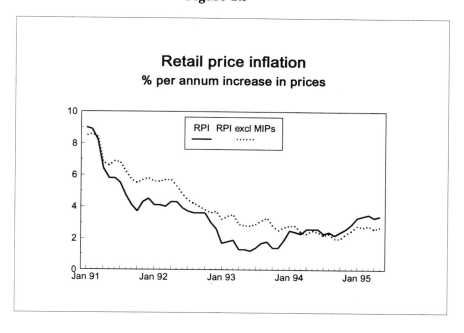

Figure 2.4

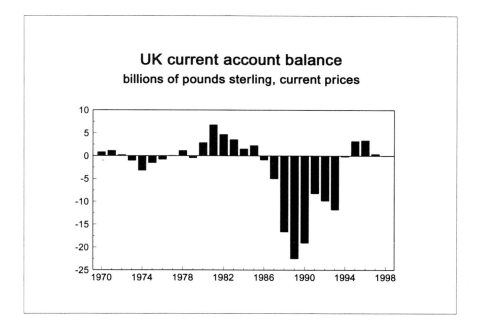

The success of this recovery owes much to the stance of monetary and fiscal policy. Since leaving the Exchange Rate Mechanism in September 1992, the balance of monetary and fiscal policy has shifted markedly. Monetary policy has loosened, with a fall in both nominal and real interest rates, while fiscal policy has been sharply tightened as a consequence of the two 1993 budgets. The fiscal tightening continued in 1994, with a further £6.5bn (or about one per cent of GDP) of tax increases in the pipeline, about half from the Spring 1993 Budget and the other half from the autumn Budget. This shift in policy has been helpful in dealing with three significant imbalances in the UK economy. First, it has helped to reduce the high level of public sector borrowing. Second, it is helping to reduce the excessive level of consumption, both public and private, in the UK economy (a point that is discussed further below). Third, the combination of lower interest rates and tight fiscal policy offers the best prospect of maintaining a competitive exchange rate without inflationary pressures, and thereby maintaining the improvement in the balance of payments (see Figure 2.5).

**Figure 2.5**

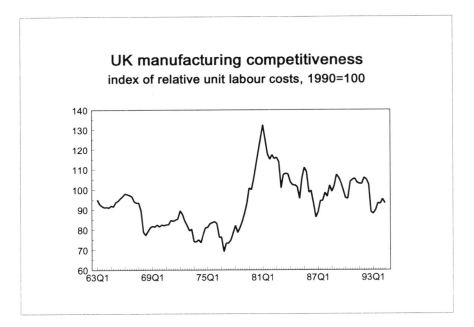

It is therefore to be hoped that the Government will maintain its tight grip on public finances since this is the key to a competitive exchange rate and sustainable growth without a re-run of the Lawson boom. Two forces may make this difficult. First, there will be the usual temptation to cut taxes and relax control on public spending ahead of the election. Second, there are the very considerable pressures to increase spending in health, education, welfare and other areas of political sensitivity. The need to maintain a competitive exchange rate and low inflation would also limit the scope for a new government to meet spending priorities through an increase in borrowing.

The exit from the Exchange Rate Mechanism and the resulting shift in policy stance has therefore created a most unusual phenomenon for the British economy, but one that economists have long called for: an export-led boom. But so far, the export-led boom has generated a two-speed economy, in which the tradeable sector is booming but the domestic sheltered sector is weak. The key question is whether the boom is sustainable, so that there will be time for growth in exports to spill over into the domestic sector, and that depends on two factors: inflation and investment.

## Inflation: dead or reviving?

Does all this good news mean that the economy is now set for continued growth with low inflation? It is probably too early to say. It is quite normal, on UK and international experience, for the first few years of economic expansion to be benign, with low inflation, rising output, falling unemployment and rising profitability. But the favourable phase of expansion often gives way after two or three years to a period of increasing prices, leading to a tightening of policy that brings the expansion to an end. This was the experience of the UK and Germany in the late 1980s and early 1990s. It is important to be aware of the appreciable lags inherent in the inflation process and not to be misled by early favourable signs. Two signals of potential concern are provided in Figures 2.6 and 2.7.

**Figure 2.6**

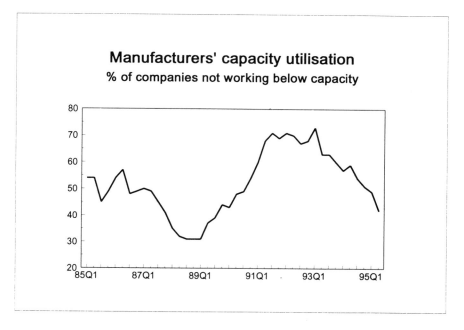

### Manufacturers' capacity utilisation
#### % of companies not working below capacity

Figure 2.6 plots the percentage of firms reported by the CBI survey to be working at capacity. This has risen appreciably over the past two years of recovery, though it remains well below its 1988 peak. But it should be noted that it is at the level of early 1987, and rising quickly. In so far as capacity bottlenecks contributed to the inflation of 1988/89, this Figure highlights the potential for a resurgence of inflationary pressure over the next two years. This is confirmed by price and cost inflation expectations, plotted in Figure 2.7. This again shows an index that is around the level of end-1986 and early 1987, suggesting inflationary pressures ahead.

**Figure 2.7**

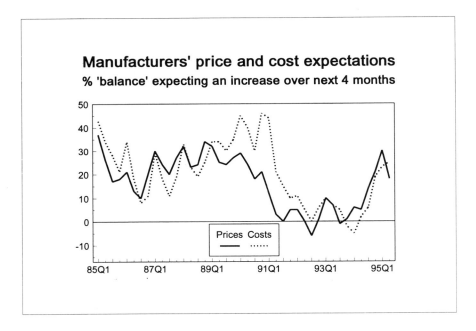

These concerns should not be overstated. The UK economy looks set for a period of good growth over the next few years. Although some inflationary pressures may appear, these are likely to be quite mild, and easily offset by a moderate rise in interest rates. Provided the fiscal deficit is kept low and the exchange rate competitive, expansion at the 2.5 - 3 per cent rate should be sustainable. Figure 2.8 gives the latest London Business School (1995) forecasts for growth through to 1998; Figure 2.9 shows that this forecast implies a five year growth performance for UK manufacturing comparable to the last best period of postwar growth between 1964-68.

**Figure 2.8**

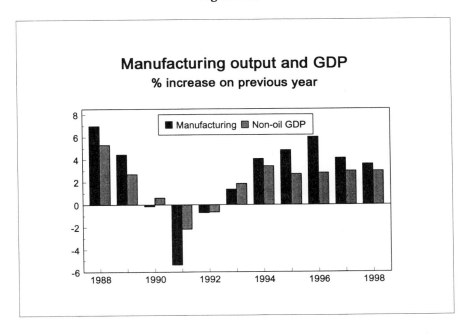

**Figure 2.9**

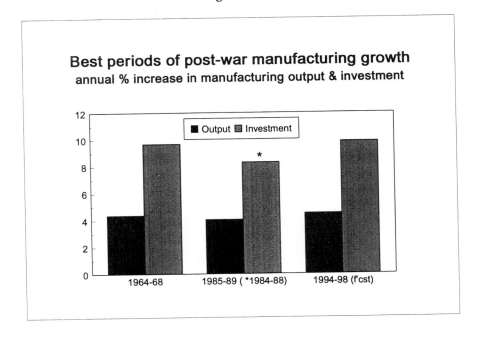

This favourable growth performance is mainly attributable to cyclical recovery from the preceding recession: it should not be difficult for an economy to grow quickly after the depth of the recession that the UK experienced in the early 1990s. Thus it was only in the second quarter of 1994 that output exceeded its previous peak in the second quarter of 1990: the UK economy experienced four years of no growth, first going down one side of the chasm and then up the other. In the rest of this chapter we focus on the longer term, or underlying, growth performance of the economy. But before doing so, we briefly examine why a sense of well-being, or the 'feel-good' factor has been absent so far from this recovery.

### The joyless recovery?

This favourable economic recovery has not been matched by a similar recovery in the sense of well-being or the 'feel-good' factor. There are a number of reasons why this has been so. Personal disposable income is being squeezed by tax increases: indeed real disposable income of the personal sector has recently risen more slowly with recovery than it did in 1992, a year of recession (Figure 2.10).

**Figure 2.10**

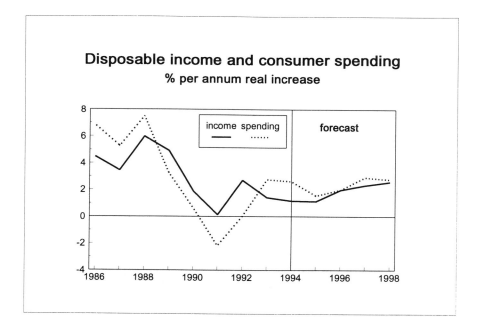

This squeeze was the necessary counterpart to the shift of resources into exports and investment, and of the reduction in public borrowing and the improvement in corporate profitability. To improve the balance of payments and to restore government and corporate finances, the household sector had to bear the strain. What this demonstrates is the obvious: that export-led growth, for which we have long hankered, does not give the quick returns to households of the UK's normal consumer boom.  It remains to be seen whether the expected longer term benefits of a more sustainable recovery will lead in due course to more household well-being.  But with the consumption share of GDP (whether private or public) at its highest level in recent years since the 1950s (Figure 2.11) the need for this adjustment is unquestionable.

Figure 2.11

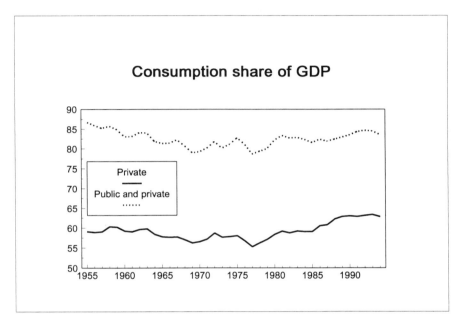

A further reason for the absence of 'feel-good' is that much of the rise in employment appears to have been in the form of part-time jobs, where remuneration and security may be limited.  More generally, the shift by many companies to more flexible forms of contractual arrangements without long term commitment may have led to increased job insecurity.  Although as yet this does not appear to have led to a reduction in length of job tenure, the widespread perception that it may do so has affected household confidence and the 'feel-good factor'.  The well-being of home-owners has been dented by the collapse of the housing market and the perception that the years of easy capital gains on houses are in the past.  Increased profitability and greater income inequality both also act to reduce the gainers at the lower end of the income distribution (see Hills, 1993, and Chapter 4 of this book).  So far, the recovery has been a joyless one, though not altogether a jobless one, although there is a puzzle as to how little recorded employment has risen despite falling unemployment (see Panel of Independent Forecasters, 1995).

## Underlying growth performance

So far, we have considered the prospects for growth over the next few years, and noted that these are dominated by cyclical factors with the recovery from recession. We now move on to consider longer term, underlying growth performance.

It should be noted that, after several decades of slow UK productivity growth relative to the major industrial countries, the UK's underlying growth performance over the last decade or so has broadly been in line (see Tables 2.1 - 2.3 for further detail). This has not resulted from an increase in the UK's underlying growth performance, for which there is no evidence, but rather from a slow-down in other countries' growth rates. The exception to this is the US which has been a sluggard in terms of productivity growth for most of the postwar period.

The general slow-down in the growth of other countries outside the US can be attributed to three main factors. First, many countries achieved high growth in the two decades after the war by drawing reserves of labour into manufacturing, either from unemployment or from low productivity agriculture. As these reserves became exhausted, so growth rates slowed. Second, many countries were able to grow by emulating the productivity performance of the US (which, unable to imitate, was forced to grow by genuine innovation, and therefore grew more slowly). As the gap between the US and other countries closed, so the gains from catch-up fell and overall growth rates slowed. Third, the major engine of productivity growth was the manufacturing sector, encouraged by the postwar opening up of international trade in manufactures through GATT. But growth increasingly shifted demand to services, where productivity growth was slower. The result was a general slowing of overall growth rates.

### Table 2.1 Real GDP, annual average % change

|                | 1960-90 | 1960-68 | 1968-73 | 1973-79 | 1979-90 | 1990-94 |
|----------------|---------|---------|---------|---------|---------|---------|
| United States  | 3.2     | 4.5     | 3.2     | 2.4     | 2.6     | 2.2     |
| Japan          | 6.3     | 10.2    | 8.6     | 3.6     | 4.1     | 1.6     |
| West Germany   | 3.1     | 4.0     | 4.9     | 2.3     | 2.0     | 2.2     |
| France         | 3.7     | 5.4     | 5.4     | 2.8     | 2.1     | 0.8     |
| Italy          | 3.9     | 5.7     | 4.5     | 3.7     | 2.4     | 0.8     |
| United Kingdom | 2.4     | 3.0     | 3.4     | 1.5     | 2.1     | 0.8     |
| Canada         | 4.2     | 5.5     | 5.4     | 4.2     | 2.8     | 1.3     |
| G7             | 3.6     | 5.0     | 4.5     | 2.7     | 2.7     | 1.8     |
| European Union | 3.4     | 4.7     | 4.9     | 2.5     | 2.2     | 1.3     |
| OECD           | 3.6     | 5.1     | 4.6     | 2.7     | 2.7     | 1.7     |

Source: OECD historical statistics 1960-90 and OECD Economic Outlook

Table 2.2  Real value added by industry 1960-90,
annual average % change

| | Agri-culture | Industry | Manufac-turing | Services | GDP total | GDP per head |
|---|---|---|---|---|---|---|
| United States | 1.4 | 2.6 | 3.4 | 3.6 | 3.2 | 2.0 |
| Japan | 0.3 | 7.7 | 8.7 | 6.2 | 6.3 | 5.3 |
| Germany | 1.7 | 2.5 | 2.9 | 3.5 | 3.1 | 2.6 |
| France | 1.5 | 3.8 | 4.1 | 4.1 | 3.7 | 2.9 |
| Italy | 1.1 | 4.2 | 5.3 | 4.0 | 3.9 | 3.4 |
| United Kingdom | 2.6 | 1.5 | 1.4 | 3.2 | 2.4 | 2.1 |
| Canada | 2.0 | 3.4 | 3.7 | 4.8 | 4.2 | 2.9 |
| G7 | 1.2 | 3.4 | 4.0 | 4.0 | 3.6 | 2.8 |
| European Community | 1.7 | 3.1 | 3.5 | 3.7 | 3.4 | 2.8 |
| OECD | 1.5 | 3.5 | 4.1 | 4.0 | 3.6 | 2.7 |

Source:  OECD historical statistics 1960-90

Table 2.3  Real value added per person employed 1960-90,
annual average % change

| | Agri-culture | Industry | Manufac-turing | Services | GDP total |
|---|---|---|---|---|---|
| United States | 3.1 | 1.6 | 2.7 | 0.9 | 1.2 |
| Japan | 4.0 | 5.9 | 7.1 | 3.8 | 5.1 |
| Germany | 6.3 | 2.8 | 2.9 | 2.0 | 2.8 |
| France | 5.5 | 4.0 | 4.4 | 2.2 | 3.2 |
| Italy | 5.4 | 4.2 | 5.4 | 2.0 | 3.7 |
| United Kingdom | 4.9 | 2.8 | 3.1 | 1.6 | 2.1 |
| Canada | 3.4 | 1.9 | 2.7 | 1.4 | 1.8 |
| G7 | 4.6 | 2.9 | 3.7 | 1.6 | 2.4 |
| European Community | n.a. | 3.4 | 3.8 | 1.9 | 3.0 |
| OECD | n.a. | 2.9 | 3.7 | 1.6 | 2.5 |

Source:  OECD historical statistics 1960-90

Compared with this general experience, the UK has experienced generally low growth throughout the postwar period, but has not exhibited the recent relative decline in growth rates of most other OECD countries. The absence of a relative decline may reflect the slowness of UK growth itself, but it may also have reflected the supply side reforms in the 1980s. The result is that, after several decades of slow UK productivity growth relative to the major industrial countries, the UK's underlying growth performance over the last decade or so has broadly been in line. However, as already noted, this is due to a relative slowdown abroad rather than an increase in the UK's underlying growth performance.

The data so far show that the productivity growth performance of the UK has converged over the last decade or so on the average of our major industrial competitors. This is a creditable performance after many decades of poorer performance, but many years of slow growth mean that convergence in terms of growth rates still leaves us lagging seriously in terms of levels of productivity and output per head. This is illustrated in Table 2.4.

### Table 2.4  OECD countries:  per capita PPP comparisons, OECD = 100

|  | GDP | | Total consumption | | Investment | |
|---|---|---|---|---|---|---|
|  | Index | Ranking | Index | Ranking | Index | Ranking |
| Canada | 108 | 8 | 116 | 4 | 98 | 10 |
| Mexico | 38 | 24 | 39 | 24 | 39 | 24 |
| United States | 136 | 2 | 144 | 1 | 111 | 7 |
| Japan | 115 | 4 | 97 | 15 | 175 | 2 |
| Australia | 96 | 15 | 96 | 16 | 94 | 12 |
| New Zealand | 87 | 19 | 82 | 19 | 81 | 16 |
| Austria | 107 | 10 | 99 | 12 | 131 | 4 |
| Belgium | 109 | 5 | 105 | 7 | 98 | 9 |
| Denmark | 108 | 7 | 106 | 6 | 80 | 17 |
| Finland | 87 | 18 | 87 | 18 | 65 | 21 |
| France | 105 | 11 | 105 | 8 | 100 | 8 |
| Germany | 103 | 12 | 101 | 10 | 116 | 6 |
| Greece | 49 | 23 | 56 | 23 | 43 | 23 |
| Iceland | 107 | 9 | 109 | 5 | 86 | 15 |
| Ireland | 77 | 20 | 70 | 21 | 59 | 22 |
| Italy | 100 | 13 | 99 | 13 | 86 | 14 |
| Luxembourg | 159 | 1 | 134 | 2 | 196 | 1 |
| Netherlands | 98 | 14 | 93 | 17 | 98 | 11 |
| Norway | 109 | 6 | 100 | 11 | 121 | 5 |
| Portugal | 67 | 22 | 68 | 22 | 87 | 13 |
| Spain | 74 | 21 | 75 | 20 | 74 | 18 |
| Sweden | 94 | 17 | 97 | 14 | 68 | 20 |
| Switzerland | 130 | 3 | 119 | 3 | 147 | 3 |
| Turkey | 30 | 25 | 31 | 25 | 39 | 25 |
| United Kingdom | 95 | 16 | 103 | 9 | 73 | 19 |
| European Union | 96 |  | 96 |  | 91 |  |
| OECD | 100 |  | 100 |  | 100 |  |

Source:  OECD National Accounts and Consensus Forecasts

Table 2.5 shows Gross Domestic Product (GDP) per capita for a range of countries. GDP per capita is compared in two ways: in the second column of the Table in terms of current market exchange rates; and in the first column, in terms of exchange rates adjusted for differences in purchasing power (as calculated by the OECD). The aim of the purchasing power adjustment is to take account of two factors: first that current exchange rates may be out of equilibrium; and second that substantial differences in prices, notably for non-traded prices, may not be reflected in exchange rates.

On the basis of the purchasing power parity adjustment, the US has the highest per capita living standard. On this basis, the UK lies 16th, behind most of our main OECD industrial competitors. If the range of countries is expanded to include non-OECD countries, as in Table 2.5, the UK slips to 17th, with Hong Kong entering high up the ranking in 5th place (World Bank, 1994).

### Table 2.5  High income countries: relative GDP, 1992

| | PPP comparison | Index ranking | Current exchange rates | Index ranking | Per capita consumption | Index ranking |
|---|---|---|---|---|---|---|
| United States | 100.0 | 1 | 100.0 | 6 | 100.0 | 1 |
| Switzerland | 95.6 | 2 | 155.2 | 1 | 82.1 | 3 |
| Germany * | 89.1 | 3 | 99.1 | 7 | 75.5 | 5 |
| Japan | 87.2 | 4 | 121.3 | 2 | 67.8 | 15 |
| Hong Kong | 86.7 | 5 | 66.1 | 17 | 71.4 | 11 |
| Canada | 85.3 | 6 | 89.1 | 12 | 82.2 | 2 |
| France | 83.0 | 7 | 95.8 | 9 | 77.2 | 4 |
| Denmark | 80.7 | 8 | 111.9 | 4 | 73.1 | 8 |
| Austria | 79.4 | 9 | 96.3 | 8 | 68.9 | 13 |
| Belgium | 78.5 | 10 | 89.8 | 11 | 71.1 | 12 |
| Norway | 78.0 | 11 | 111.1 | 5 | 67.9 | 14 |
| Italy | 76.7 | 12 | 88.0 | 14 | 72.2 | 9 |
| Sweden | 76.2 | 13 | 116.2 | 3 | 73.5 | 6 |
| Netherlands | 76.0 | 14 | 88.1 | 13 | 67.1 | 16 |
| Australia | 75.0 | 15 | 74.3 | 16 | 71.5 | 10 |
| United Kingdom | 72.4 | 16 | 76.5 | 15 | 73.3 | 7 |
| Finland | 69.1 | 17 | 94.5 | 10 | 65.9 | 17 |
| Israel | 63.1 | 18 | 56.9 | 19 | 62.4 | 18 |
| New Zealand | 62.3 | 19 | 52.9 | 20 | 85.6 | 19 |
| Spain | 57.0 | 20 | 60.1 | 18 | 53.7 | 20 |
| Ireland | 52.2 | 21 | 52.5 | 21 | 44.2 | 21 |
| Greece | 34.6 | 22 | 31.4 | 22 | 37.1 | 22 |

* Former West Germany
Source: World Bank, World Development Report 1994

The group of countries with lower per capita GDP on this basis are not ones with which the UK normally compares herself. At current exchange rates, the ordering of countries is rather different, with high price countries such as Switzerland, Japan and the Nordic countries rising in the ordering, while the fast growing developing countries fall back. But the UK's position relative to the US is not very different, and its position in the overall ranking is largely unchanged. Indeed on this basis, the comparison with our major continental competitors is less good.

These numbers emphasise the degree to which the UK has slipped behind our main competitors in terms of per capita income level: about 30 per cent or so below the US and some 5 - 15 per cent below the major economies of continental Europe. (The World Bank numbers give a somewhat smaller disparity with the US, and a somewhat larger disparity with Europe. In comparing these numbers, it is important to bear in mind that the OECD numbers refer to the whole of Germany, while the World Bank numbers refer to West Germany alone. Given the uncertainties in PPP estimates, an average of the two estimates may provide the best guide). This impression is confirmed by productivity comparisons between UK, US and German manufacturing industry, shown in Figures 2.12 - 2.14. The comparison with the US (Figure 2.12) suggests that UK productivity per hour worked is less than 60 per cent of the US level, while joint factor productivity (including capital input) is estimated to be a little more than 60 per cent. Interestingly, relative productivity in the UK rose from 1977 to 1982, and has been largely flat since then.

**Figure 2.12**

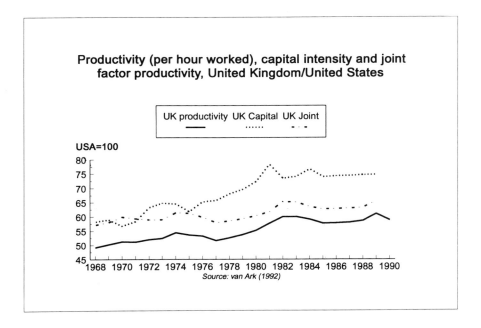

Relative to Germany (Figures 2.13 and 2.14), the improvement in productivity performance started later, after a steady worsening in the 1970s, and continued through the 1980s, though with signs of tailing off at the end. (The year-to-year movements in these series partly reflect cyclical differences, and should be treated with caution). Output per worker was 10 - 12 per cent higher in Germany compared to the UK; while output per hour worked was 20 per cent higher, reflecting longer hours worked in the UK.

The rise in manufacturing productivity growth in the 1980s (Figure 2.13) is often attributed to the impact of the Thatcher administration in changing the balance of power in industrial relations, giving the power to manage back to managers, and introducing a more competitive environment in which business had to operate. Most studies conclude that this effect was a one-off increase in productivity, though it took a number of years to come through, rather than a shift to a permanently higher growth rate (see Crafts, 1992; Layard and Nickell, 1989; and Muellbauer, 1991). Gordon (1992) expresses doubts as to whether this manufacturing productivity breakthrough was really a product of the Thatcher Government's policies, asking why the supply side benefits were limited to manufacturing: the incentive effects of lower taxes and other supply side policies should have been felt throughout the economy, not just in manufacturing, and better industrial relations and privatisation should also have had wider effects. A possible response is that there were comparable productivity gains in parts of services, but that the effects on overall service sector productivity performance were masked by induced absorption of labour into labour intensive services.

**Figure 2.13**

Source: O'Mahoney (1992)

**Figure 2.14**

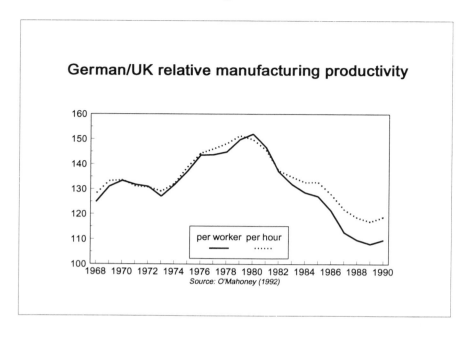

German/UK relative manufacturing productivity

Source: O'Mahoney (1992)

Whatever the source, these more detailed comparisons show that even after the 1980s improvement, the UK still has considerable scope for growth by catch-up, certainly relative to the US and probably also to continental Europe. An underlying growth performance that merely matches that of our major competitors leaves a performance gap measured in levels. There is some evidence that the recent recession, which in contrast to the 1980/81 recession fell on services as well as manufacturing, has led to an increased drive for cost-cutting and productivity gains in key sectors of services. But this will not necessarily lead to higher productivity growth in the economy as a whole. This is because the release of labour from service sector jobs may simply result in the creation of more low paid, low productivity jobs in other parts of the service sector. This has been the experience in the United States, where rapid productivity growth in some service sectors where information technology has impacted on productivity has led to a growth in low productivity, labour intensive services, so that overall service sector productivity has grown only slowly. This is an almost inevitable result. Since manufacturing and agriculture are unlikely to absorb much labour, labour shed from those parts of the service sector where rapid productivity is possible is likely to result in higher employment in other parts of the service sector. Otherwise it must be reflected in lower participation in the labour force, higher unemployment, increased criminal activity or some combination of these three.

Casual observation suggests that the British people are not fully aware of just how far productivity and per capita income has declined in the UK relative to other countries. One possible explanation for this lies in the third and fourth columns of Table 2.4, which gives an index of relative consumption (both private and public) per head measured on a PPP basis. What it shows is that, on this basis, the UK lies in 9th place amongst OECD countries, ahead of Japan, Germany and Italy, and just behind France. But in this comparison, low savings and therefore high consumption are merely masking a low level of income. And this problem is likely to grow as low investment leads to a further decline in the UK's fundamental position. This is highlighted by the last two columns of Table 2.4, which provide an index of per capita investment levels, again on a PPP basis. On this index, the UK ranks 19th and falls well below continental levels.

## Factors conducive to growth

One commonly held view is that low inflation is conducive to economic growth. This is encouraging for the UK economy in view of the current inflation performance, but it would be foolish to rely on it. The empirical evidence for a link between inflation and growth is, at best, rather weak: indeed many fast growing economies experience quite high inflation without impairing growth performance. The high priests of monetary orthodoxy, Friedman and Schwartz (1982), in their monetary history of the US and the UK have a little-read concluding chapter in which they note that long booms in economic activity (over twenty or thirty years) have been associated with rising, not stable, prices. Nor is there any strong theoretical reason why low inflation should help growth. The most that can be said is that very rapid, hyper-inflation damages growth as everyone focuses on the management of cash, not production; and that there is some tendency for volatile inflation to be associated with high inflation. This is not to say that low inflation is undesirable. It is helpful on other grounds, including stability and equity, but low inflation alone is not a major spur to growth. This view is supported by the recent empirical work of Barro (1995).

Of more relevance to growth is the low level of savings and investment in the UK economy (see Table 2.6). The UK economy consumes more (in both private and public consumption) and saves less than our main competitors except for the US (which with much higher living standards can perhaps enjoy the luxury of lower growth). There is a clear association empirically between high investment and high growth, though of course the direction of causation is unclear: the UK may grow slowly because it invests less, but it may also invest less because it lacks good growth prospects. What is clear is that public consumption has tended to be higher than our main competitors (Table 2.6); and that total consumption has recently been higher as a proportion of GDP than at any time over the past three decades. An orientation more to saving and less to consumption will be important for future growth.

Table 2.6  Consumption and saving in G7 countries, 1980-90

| | Private consump- tion | Government consumption | Total consump- tion | Total saving | Total fixed investment |
|---|---|---|---|---|---|
| Japan | 58.7 | 9.6 | 68.3 | 31.7 | 29.4 |
| West Germany | 56.2 | 19.9 | 76.1 | 23.9 | 20.4 |
| Canada | 57.0 | 19.8 | 76.8 | 23.2 | 21.5 |
| Italy | 61.4 | 16.3 | 77.7 | 22.3 | 21.2 |
| France | 60.4 | 18.8 | 79.2 | 20.8 | 20.6 |
| United Kingdom | 61.9 | 20.8 | 82.7 | 17.3 | 17.6 |
| United States | 65.9 | 18.2 | 74.1 | 15.9 | 17.6 |

Source:  OECD historical statistics 1960-1990

A further factor that is frequently cited as a constraint on UK growth is the cost of capital, which is alleged to be higher in the UK because of short-termism in financial markets (see, for example, Hutton, 1995). It is possible that this was an important factor in earlier decades when international financial markets were less well integrated.  But in a world of very high capital mobility, there are no major national differences in the cost of capital for major international companies, not least because they can raise funds in many forms and in many markets around the world.  It remains possible that differences in the cost of finance continue to prevail for small and medium sized companies, and this represents some constraint on growth performance, though even for such companies international financial market integration is likely increasingly to erode such differentials over time.  This is not to dismiss the charge of short-termism, which may indeed be prevalent in the UK.  But it is much more likely to be the product of behaviour in both companies and financial markets jointly than in financial markets alone (as, for example, in the analysis of Holmstrom and Ricart I Costa, 1986; see also Marsh, 1991).  As Nickell (1995) discusses, such short-term behaviour is likely to be linked to deeper issues of corporate governance, and is not susceptible to superficial policy interventions. However, as the globalisation of business increases, so we may well see growing convergence in structures of corporate governance across the major industrial countries, so that in time such factors will become increasingly irrelevant in explaining differences in growth performance.

A further factor frequently cited as conducive to economic growth is flexibility of the labour market.  It is clear that the set of factors helpful to growth is wider than the labour market. But many would argue that flexibility in the labour market is an essential element in a dynamic economy and hence for growth.  The OECD Jobs Study (1994) emphasises this point, but also points to the distinction between deregulation and flexibility. An active labour market strategy to promote skills and mobility may help flexibility.  Increased competition and deregulation of the UK labour market has certainly increased flexibility in the sense of increasing the responsiveness of wages to demand conditions, and that has been helpful in containing costs in recession.

But it remains to be seen how far this labour market deregulation has enhanced overall supply performance and increased the underlying rate of growth of the UK economy. This may have happened; but it is also possible that the changes in labour market structure will merely increase the responsiveness of wages and prices to demand when the economy moves into a boom phase. The remarkable fact about the boom of the late 1980s is the relatively sluggish response of wages: had wages responded more flexibly to the rapid surge in demand, the resulting inflationary surge would have been even greater. Reforms may not have improved underlying performance: and the jury must still be out. If instead the labour market has been made more responsive to demand, then this is a mixed benefit for growth performance: it is a common experience to find keen builders willing to undertake a job at a competitive price when times are hard, only to find that they disappear as better opportunities arise, leaving the client to find other, and usually more expensive, ways of completing the job. There are signs that smart companies are finding ways of sourcing key inputs from outside the company in ways that cut costs and increase flexibility, but do this within a long-term relationship that gives better guarantees of supply. This may represent a small shift in the direction of Japanese styles of management.

## International competition: threats from the Asian Pacific rim?

A common perception is that a major factor holding back growth prospects in the UK is competition from the low-cost producers of East Asia. A popular view is that the only way to withstand such pressure is to resort to protection.

It is true that competition from East Asia is forcing significant restructuring in the old industrial countries. The strategy of these countries of targeting particular sectors results in intense competition in traditional sectors, imposing considerable adjustment costs in the form of job losses and unemployment. This makes it appear that standard international trade theory, which emphasises the gains from international trade, is wrong. However, it is important to appreciate that these economies are not, on the whole, black holes in the world economy which destroy demand without recreating it. These economies are increasing exports very rapidly, but imports are growing as quickly: indeed, as a group they are a source of net demand as capital importers in the world economy.

## Box 2.1  Modern Theories of Economic Growth

In the traditional theory of economic growth, output grows because of increases in the quality or quantity of labour and physical capital or because of technological progress. However, only the growth rate of physical capital is explained by the model, and other sources of growth are assumed to be exogenous (that is, unexplained). Dissatisfaction with this approach led to the recent interest in endogenous growth theory, which tries fully to make the growth of output per capita endogenous. Four main sources of growth have been considered - learning by doing; human capital accumulation; public infrastructure investment; and research and development (R&D).

In the paper that reawakened interest in growth theory, Romer (1986) argued that the investment process has the by-product of increasing knowledge about production, so that a firm that invests in new equipment learns how to produce more efficiently. This process is called learning by doing. The knowledge that the firm acquires through the investment is able to spill over through the movement of ideas and workers through the economy, and so benefits other firms. In another strand of the literature, Lucas (1988), argued that investments in human capital drive the growth process. Highly skilled workers are able to use more sophisticated capital equipment; are more flexible in their approach to problems; and are more likely to think of ways in which production can be organised more efficiently.

A wide-range of government provided services are also thought to have an impact on the efficiency of production - such as transport networks and utilities. Barro (1990) argued that these services could be seen as inputs to the production process, and that there are externalities to their provision. Furthermore, government assurance of property rights through investment in police services, courts, and defence may also raise the incentive to accumulate private capital.

Lastly, firms in the UK devote a significant proportion of their profits to the development of new products and processes. Endogenous growth theory has attempted to model the R&D process as one in which firms make intentional investments in R&D, and these may produce new varieties of goods or raise the quality of existing goods (see Aghion & Howitt, 1992). An important feature of some of these models is known as creative destruction - the discovery of new goods makes old products obsolete and so firms go bankrupt and their capital equipment is also made obsolete.

Cross-sectional evidence suggests that countries with high rates of economic growth tend to have high levels of human capital and high levels of physical investment. These studies are not usually able to distinguish cause and effect. Indeed, it is possible that causality is reversed, and that a high level of growth causes high investment. Another interpretation is that innovative countries invest more in physical capital because the returns to doing so are higher, and that their physical capital is more advanced than elsewhere, and so more productive.

Empirical work on human capital has suggested that highly-qualified workers can be up to twice as productive as those with no qualifications. The evidence also suggests that there are significant benefits to R&D spending, and that these benefits spill over to other firms and industries. Some studies have also found significant relationships between public sector capital formation (such as infrastructure investment) and private sector productivity.

In terms of policy conclusions for the UK, endogenous growth theory does not offer any panaceas. There is substantial evidence that investments in new technologies and in people will lead to faster economic growth, or at least help the UK catch up with international levels of best practice. When a country has a highly skilled workforce and is innovative, it is likely that physical investment will also be high. But attempts to raise physical investment (say, through tax breaks) are unlikely to have significant effects. Instead, government policy should attempt to produce a skilled and innovative workforce and to create an environment that encourages firms to invent and to adopt new technologies and ideas.

*Gavin Cameron*

The key point is that the trade that these economies are generating represents an increase in the international division of labour, increasing economies of scale and scope and raising efficiency in the world economy. An implication is that the dynamic economies represent both a threat and an opportunity. Those countries that are slow to restructure their production and reallocate resources will lose out on the opportunities, thereby bearing the brunt of adjustment costs. But those countries that are quick to move to meet the demands of this fast growing region will secure major gains. The increased competitive pressure represents an important catalyst for change. In the face of this, disparities of performance between countries will reflect differences in their supply side performance. This will sound to some as a gloomy message for the UK. However, it is worth noting that in 1994 the UK ran a trade surplus with two regions of the world: North America, and the developing world - including the Asian tigers.

**Figure 2.15**

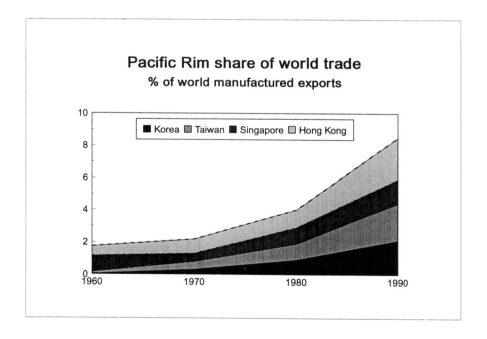

It is possible to argue that this is merely one manifestation of a general intensification of competitive pressures in all parts of the world economy, from which there will be gainers and losers depending on capacity for change. The phenomenon is one that Krugman describes as 'fractal' in nature: as one disaggregates, by country, by sector, by company, by type of job, and by individuals within jobs, so one observes a widening differential of reward. Intensified competition may well have put a much higher premium on performance in all aspects of economic life. If this is right, it emphasises the need to improve performance generally and widely in the UK economy.

## Do we need an active industrial policy? Lessons from the Asian Pacific rim

In considering ways of enhancing the UK's growth performance, it is clearly sensible to draw on international experience. However, with many countries experiencing low growth, the range of models from which to draw lessons is limited. The US has low productivity growth, coupled with the problem of a large pool of unskilled workers on poverty wages, with attendant social problems. Continental Europe now faces similar productivity issues to the UK in terms of growth, though performs somewhat better in terms of productivity levels, and shares the problem of high and persistent unemployment. Much of the developing world faces the same challenge of achieving sustainable growth. The obvious examples of success are the high performance economies of the Asian Pacific Rim.

The success of this part of the world has been in achieving rapid and continuing growth with increased economic equality: what the World Bank (1993) describes as the East Asian miracle. There are several different explanations of this phenomena. One explanation runs in terms of historical and cultural factors, that are not readily copied or transferred. The factors are several: the influence of Confucianism, with its emphasis on group structures, loyalty, hard work and education; the impact of the colonial inheritance and strategic US aid; and the unusual combination of autocratic political structures and a sense of political purpose. Another essentially neo-classical explanation emphasises the fact that these countries have got the basics right. These basics include: high savings and investment (though causation is problematic here); high investment in education, focused particularly on basic education, possibly the key to growth with equality; the primacy of orthodox macroeconomic policies; a strong export orientation; low price distortions despite protection; flexible labour markets; and a government friendly to business. Another explanation emphasises the interventionist nature of East Asian industrial policies: heavy government influence on the allocation of finance and credit; aggressive and targeted export promotion; and the fostering, with state aid, of specific industries.

The East Asian economies, of course, exhibit differences amongst themselves, from the more market oriented Taiwan to the more interventionist South Korea. But in surveying the evidence, the World Bank (1993) concludes that East Asia does represent a case of successful intervention, the success of which has depended on 'market-friendly' intervention. The evidence does support a *prima facie* case that intervention can help supply-side performance and growth (though we must keep firmly in mind the cases, such as Latin America, where intervention has gone disastrously wrong). Neo-classical economics recognises the case for supporting 'infant industries', particularly in a world of increasing returns and barriers to entry, though it also points to the problems of getting the grown-up infant to leave home. The effectiveness of the East Asian economies may well owe much to success in handling this problem. It is less a question of picking winners, the terms in which the case for industrial strategy is usually posed and dismissed in the UK. It is instead to recognise that, just as talented individuals cannot do all that is in their potential capacity to achieve, so small countries must make choices over the sectors on which to focus, and that market forces alone may not be adequate to guide such choices.

This argument notwithstanding, there must be major doubts as to the capacity of the UK to draw usefully on this model. The ability of our state machinery to make effective industrial decisions is, on past performance, quite lamentable. In part, this may result from rivalry and division between the different ministries and arms of government in the UK (see Chapter 1). It may also be related to the educational background of our civil service, and the tradition, only now under pressure, for lack of two-way mobility between civil service and industry and commerce. Indeed in the fields of innovation, the lack of interchange with research institutions may also matter. Those countries with a freer interchange between different spheres of life may be more able to run an active industrial policy to good effect, but the UK may be unwise to attempt it again.

An alternative emphasis is on getting the basics right. This is not equivalent to leaving matters to the market alone, because the absence of key markets and/or the absence of effective competition in some markets means that market forces, left to themselves, will deliver undesirable outcomes. Hence there is a case for government intervention, provided that the problems of government failure are not too great. This provides a potentially wide range for government intervention, certainly wider than it has been conventional to draw the role of government over the past one and a half decades in the UK. The key areas where externalities mean that the market, left to itself, may be severely suboptimal include: education and investment in skills; provision of infrastructure; and support of innovation and R&D, especially the knowledge networks emphasised in the work of Porter (1991) and in the new endogenous growth literature. These aspects have not been well handled by UK policy over the post-war period, and getting them right may help to create the conditions for a better growth performance.

## Box 2.2  Tax Credits for Research & Development

UK manufacturing productivity grew relatively fast in the 1980s compared with its major competitors, but the *level* of productivity remains relatively low.  The evidence on UK technological performance is fairly clear-cut.  R&D data suggest that the UK has tended to under-invest in innovation compared with its major competitors, and other data on the innovative performance of the UK support this conclusion.  The UK needs to improve its technological performance if it is to catch-up on international levels of productivity, and to raise its growth rate in the long run.

There are a number of likely reasons that the UK may have under-spent on R&D over the past twenty or so years, such as problems in financial markets, labour markets, and lack of competition in product markets.  There are no easy solutions to these problems.  Although the social returns to R&D are thought to be around three times the private returns (see Griliches, 1991, for example), any government intervention could potentially make the situation worse by distorting incentives and encouraging 'rent-seeking' behaviour.

In 1981, the USA introduced a 25 per cent tax credit for spending on R&D.  Because of the way it was targeted, the credit originally had very little impact on the cost of R&D and so had little effect on the amount of R&D performed by industry.  In 1990, the US system for calculating the tax credit was changed significantly, so that credits were linked to changes in the ratio of R&D to sales.  These changes to the structure of the credit raised the average effective reduction in the cost of R&D from around 3% in the late 1980s to around 7½% in 1990.

In 1985, Mansfield conducted a survey of R&D executives to find out their responses to the tax credit.  His results suggested that for a 1% reduction in the cost of R&D, firms would increase their R&D spending by about 0.3%.  Mansfield argued that this was not cost-effective, because the amount of additional R&D stimulated by the credit was less than the tax revenue forgone.

More recent work, however, by Hall (1993) has taken the recent changes in the system into account and concludes that previous estimates of the effect of the tax credit on R&D have been underestimates.  She estimates that a 1% reduction in the cost of R&D leads to an increase in spending in the short-run of between 0.84% and 1.5%.  Although the exact size of the long run effect is rather more difficult to calculate precisely, it is likely to be larger.  These estimates suggest that the price elasticity of R&D is significantly higher than previously thought.

To put these percentage figures into more concrete form, Hall estimates that the US tax credit stimulated additional R&D spending in the short-run of about $2 billion 1982 dollars per year, while the forgone tax revenue was about $1 billion 1982 dollars per year.

The evidence, therefore, now seems to suggest that the US tax credit has been a successful and cost-effective way of stimulating additional R&D spending.  Whether the US experience can be used to draw conclusions for UK policy is a difficult question (see Griffith et al., 1995).  The structure of industry in the US is quite different and there are far more significant R&D spenders.  It is also likely that an R&D tax credit would encourage firms to reclassify expenditure as R&D.  However, as Hall argues for the US, incentives to reclassify other spending as R&D have always existed to some extent, and tax officials are well-placed to check on such reclassification.  Lastly, it is not clear that improving the technological performance of the UK will necessarily lead to improved productivity growth unless steps are taken to solve many other supply side problems and to solve other problems in the UK corporate tax system, such as surplus advanced corporation tax (ACT).

*Gavin Cameron*

## Inward direct investment: an engine for growth?

The absence of an active industrial strategy leaves hanging the question of what provides the catalyst for dynamism and change in the UK economy on which growth depends. One plausible answer is provided by inward direct investment. Foreign investment can bring with it access to new technology and production techniques, new management techniques, and changes in work practice. The transformation of the car industry from a low to high productivity sector under foreign management is a good example, as is the consumer electronics industry. Associated with the former has been the turn-around in the UK's trade position in cars, with a move from large and increasing deficit back towards balance, with a trebling of car exports from the UK since 1988. Higher productivity has risen not just in new plants financed from overseas, but also in competitors forced to compete against keener competition. The transformation of the car components industry, forced to adapt to the requirements of the Japanese management of the car industry, shows that the impact is also felt upstream. Many would point to the high levels of Japanese inward investment in the UK as an important force for industrial transformation. At the same time, it is also an important source of tension within Europe. Some other European countries, notably France, continue to prefer an industrial strategy based on national, or failing that European, champions, they are suspicious of the UK's strategy of welcoming foreign capital irrespective of origin, and moreover of accepting, if not welcoming, foreign take-overs of long-established UK companies. It is this difference of perspective on issues of industrial policy that leads the French sometimes to view the UK with suspicion as a Japanese battleship moored off the coast of Europe.

It is certainly the case that inward direct investment has forced British management to seek to compete more effectively, and the current cost-cutting in British industry, which is leading to falling unit labour costs, is a tribute to that. It is, of course, the case that the UK has always been very open to inward investment, but its importance has risen over time with its ratio to total investment rising from 7.3 per cent in 1971-75 to 12.3 per cent in 1986-90. Moreover, as the UK has slipped further behind the productivity performance of our main competitors, so there is increasing scope for foreign investment to act as a force for catch-up.

There are important questions to be asked of this strategy of relying on direct foreign investment as a catalyst for change. One issue concerns how far the UK benefits from such investment since the profits are repatriated. However, since the bulk of value-added remains at home in higher incomes or taxes, and a substantial part of profits are reinvested, not repatriated, the UK is a substantial beneficiary. Another issue concerns the commitment of such investment to the UK, to which the answer is that overseas companies investing in the UK are as committed to their investment as comparable UK owned companies, many of which show no reluctance to invest overseas. Indeed, it is more pertinent to ask what significance attaches to the formal nationality of companies, conventionally defined in terms of where the company's headquarters are located, when other dimensions of the company's activities (production, sales, labour force, share ownership, and even board membership and corporate culture) may be highly internationally diversified and not identifiable with the supposed home country (see Reich, 1992).

More subtle questions concern the effective transfer of skills and knowledge through the process of investment, and whether the R&D functions, where the high value-added end of the business may lie, move from the company headquarters. The answer here is that there is increasing evidence that multinational companies, including the Japanese, are dispersing key R&D functions, so that there is the potential for the UK to attract these parts of the business.

Realising this potential, however, may not be straightforward. The factors determining success in attracting the R&D and knowledge-based parts of multinational business come back to the issues discussed above: getting the basics right. This especially includes investment in human capital (i.e. education and training) where UK performance looks increasingly weak when measured against our international rivals, including the East Asian dynamic economies. But there is also a question that must be posed about the UK's European policy. If the UK finds itself increasingly sidelined in Europe, as currently seems possible as a consequence of the present Government's ambivalence towards Europe, it may be relegated to a slow lane of Europe. In this case, the advantages of the UK as a low cost location for inward investment may be dented, exemption from the Social Chapter notwithstanding. If the strategy is to use inward investment as the catalyst for change in the UK economy, then the present government's European strategy may well prove ill-advised.

## References

Aghion, P. and Howitt, P. (1992) 'A model of Growth through Creative Destruction', *Econometrica*, Vol. **60** (2), pp. 323-51.

van Ark, B. (1990), 'Comparative levels of manufacturing productivity in post-war Europe: measurement and comparison', *Oxford Bulletin of Economics and Statistics*, November.

van Ark, B. (November, 1992), 'Comparative productivity in British and American manufacturing', *National Institute Economic Review*.

Barro, R .J. (May, 1995), 'Inflation and economic growth', *Bank of England Quarterly Bulletin*, Vol. **35** (2).

Barro, R. (1990) 'Government Spending in a Simple Model of Endogenous Growth', *Journal of Political Economy*, Vol. **82** (6), pp. 1095-1117.

Cowling, K. and Sugden, R. (1993), 'Industrial strategy: a missing link in British economic policy', *Oxford Review of Economic Policy*, Vol. **9** (3), pp.83-100.

Crafts, N. (October, 1992), 'Productivity growth reconsidered', *Economic Policy*, Vol. 0 (15), pp.387-414.

De Long, B. and Summers, L. (1991), 'Equipment investment and economic growth', *Quarterly Journal of Economics*.

Friedman, M. and Schwartz, A. J. (1982), *Monetary Trends in the United States and the United Kingdom, 1867-1975*, National Bureau of Economic Research, Chicago: University of Chicago Press.

Gordon, R. J. (November, 1992), 'Comment on crafts', *Economic Policy*, No. **15**.

Griffith, R., Sandler, D. and Van Reenan, J. (1995) 'Tax Incentives for R&D', *Fiscal Studies*, Vol. **16**, pp. 21-44.

Griliches, Z. (1991) 'The Search for R&D Spillovers', National Bureau of Economic Research Working Paper, No. 3768.

Hall, B. (1993) 'R&D Tax Policy During the 1980s: Success of Failure?' *University of California Working Paper in Economics:* 93-208.

Hills, J. (1993), *The Future of Welfare: A Guide to the Debate*, York: Joseph Rowntree Foundation, York.

Holmstrom, B. and Ricart i Costa, J. (1986), 'Managerial incentives and capital management', *Quarterly Journal of Economics*, Vol. **101**, pp.835-60.

Hutton, W. (1995) *The State We're In* , London: Cape.

Layard, R. and Nickell, S. (1989), 'The Thatcher miracle?', *CEPR Discussion Paper*, No. **315**.

London Business School (August, 1995), *Economic Outlook*, Oxford: Blackwells.

Lucas, R. (1988) 'On the Mechanics of Economic Development' *Journal of Monetary Economics*, Vol. **22**, pp. 3-42.

Mansfield, E. (1985) 'Public Policy toward Industrial Innovation: An International Study of Direct Tax Incentives for R&D'. In Clark, K., Hayes, R., and Lorenz, C., (eds.) *The Uneasy Alliance.* Cambridge, MA: Harvard Press.

Marsh, P. (1991), *Short-Termism on Trial*, London: IFMA.

Muellbauer, J. (1991), 'Productivity and competitiveness', *Oxford Review of Economic Policy*, Vol **73** (3), pp.99-117.

Nickell, S. (1995), *The Performance of Companies*, Oxford: Blackwells.

OECD (1994), *The Jobs Study*, Paris: OECD.

O'Mahoney, M. (1992), 'Productivity levels in British and German manufacturing industry', *National Institute Economic Review*.

O'Mahoney, M. (August, 1993), 'Capital stocks and productivity in industrial nations'; *National Institute Economic Review*.

Panel of Independent Forecasters (May, 1995), *Report*, HM Treasury.

Porter, M. (1990), *The Competitive Advantage of Nations*, London: Macmillan.

Reich, R.(1991), *The Work of Nations;* New York: Basic Books.

Romer, P. (1990) 'Endogenous Technological Change', *Journal of Political Economy* Vol. **98**, pp. S71-S102.

United Nations (1992), *World Investment Report: Transnational Corporations as Engines of Growth*, New York: United Nations.

World Bank (1993), *The East Asian Miracle*, Oxford: Oxford University Press.

World Bank (1994), *World Development Report*, Oxford: Oxford University Press.

# 3 Can unemployment in the UK be reduced?

*Stephen Nickell* *

## Why do we have unemployment?

The recent history of the British economy indicates that it is not difficult to generate substantial reductions in unemployment. Using the 'headline' definition (benefit recipients), unemployment fell from 11.1 per cent in 1986 to 5.8 per cent in 1990, so it was almost cut in half.[1] This dramatic fall was produced in part by expansionary fiscal and monetary policy, in part by an international boom and in part by a large fall in commodity prices in the mid 1980s. In the light of this, it is clear that unemployment can be reduced simply by inducing a demand expansion at the appropriate level (e.g. cut interest rates, raise government expenditure). So what is the problem? The answer lies in the fact that over the same period, headline inflation (RPI) rose from 3.4 to 7.8 per cent per annum and the trade deficit (including so called invisibles) rose to around four per cent of GDP. Indeed, for one month, retail price inflation got into double figures. As a consequence, monetary policy went into reverse, followed shortly thereafter by the economy. By 1993, unemployment was over 10 per cent and 'headline' RPI inflation had fallen to around two per cent.

This pattern of rising inflation in booms and falling inflation in slumps is typical throughout the OECD (see Figure 3.1) and this, along with the UK experience we have described, suggests the following. During any particular period, there is some baseline level of unemployment such that if actual unemployment moves too far below it, then inflation starts rising and the trade

---

* Professor of Economics at Nuffield College, Oxford and Director of the Oxford Institute of Economics and Statistics.

balance deteriorates. This continues until macroeconomic policy is reversed, unemployment moves well above the baseline level, inflation falls and the trade balance improves. This baseline level of unemployment is generally known as the equilibrium rate or the natural rate or the NAIRU (non-accelerating inflation rate of unemployment).

Despite these titles, the equilibrium rate changes quite significantly from one decade to the next. How and why it has changed in Britain we shall discuss below. What is important to understand here is that, broadly speaking, it cannot be changed by messing around with monetary, fiscal and exchange rate policy. Cunning ploys like joining the ERM, leaving the ERM or giving independence to the Central Bank cannot be expected to shift the equilibrium unemployment rate. What they can do is change the way the economy cycles around this rate, by reducing or increasing the size of the fluctuations, for example. This is important but not the focus of the present investigation.

Finally, then, to answer the question posed by the title of this section, we have unemployment to hold down inflation and the trade deficit. It may not be a price worth paying but it is the price we do in fact pay. The next question is why do we need to pay so much?

## Figure 3.1
### Employment fluctuations and changes in inflation in the OECD

### (a) Employment rate

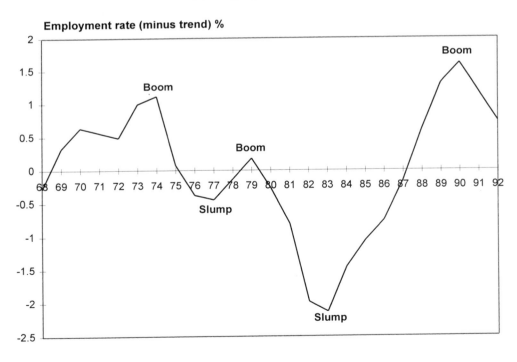

### (b) Inflation

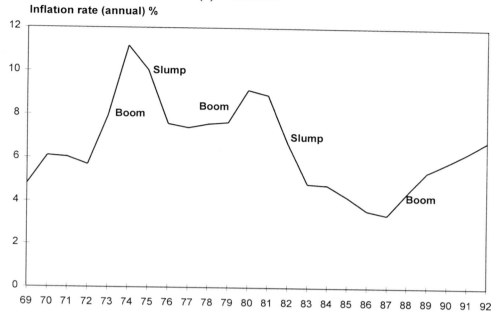

### (c) Employment rate and change in inflation

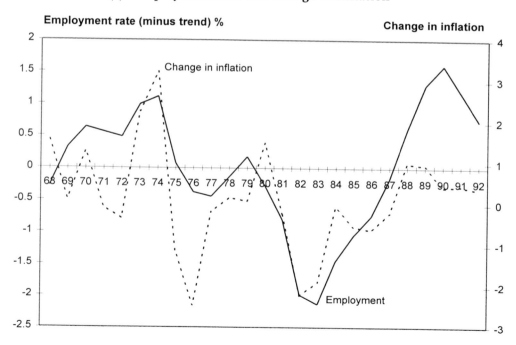

Note:     Inflation refers to the GDP deflator. The employment rate is the deviation from trend. These data refer to the OECD countries as a whole.

Source:   Layard *et al* (1994), Figure 5.

## Why is unemployment so high?

The first question we must ask is whether unemployment is, in fact, very high. Broadly speaking, when thinking about unemployment, we can divide the last 140 years into four periods, namely 1855-1914, 1920-1939, 1945-1974, 1975-1994. During the first period, unemployment probably fluctuated around five per cent (or more), during the second it fluctuated around nine per cent, during the third it fluctuated around 2.5 per cent and during the last it fluctuated around seven to nine per cent.[2] It is clear from this that the third period is quite exceptional and is the one on which we can expect economic historians to focus.

In order to see what happened during the post-war period, we present in Table 3.1 some estimates of equilibrium and actual unemployment, and the relevant measures of the trade deficit (including invisibles) and *changes* in inflation. We can see first how equilibrium unemployment started rising in the late 60s and, broadly speaking, had reached its current level by the early 80s. Then, as actual unemployment fluctuates around this level, inflation alternately rises and falls. During the most recent period the trade deficit remains positive except at the end but this is offset by the rapid fall in inflation.[3]

**Table 3.1  Unemployment, changes in inflation and the trade deficit**

|  | 1956-59 | 1960-68 | 1969-73 | 1974-80 | 1981-87 | 1988-90 | 1991-95 |
|---|---|---|---|---|---|---|---|
| Actual unemployment (%) | 2.24 | 2.62 | 3.39 | 5.23 | 11.14 | 7.27 | 9.30 |
| Equilibrium unemployment (%) | 2.2 | 2.5 | 3.6 | 7.3 | 8.7 | 8.7 | 8.9 |
| Change in inflation (% points p.a.) | 0.58 | -0.11 | 1.00 | 1.51 | -1.45 | 1.03 | -1.12 |
| Trade deficit (% potential GDP) | -0.57 | -0.22 | -0.81 | 1.06 | -1.39 | 1.44 | 0.8 |

Notes:  Unemployment is the OECD standardised rate, the change in inflation refers to the GDP deflator and is lagged 1 period, the trade deficit is lagged two periods except for the 1991-95 period. The lags take account of the time taken for the effects to feed through into unemployment. In the recent past the reaction of unemployment to general economic conditions appears to be more rapid.

Source:  1994-95 data is derived from forecasts published in the Goldman Sachs UK Economics Analyst, October 1994.

The key issue we must address is why equilibrium unemployment has risen so dramatically over the period and why it has not fallen back recently despite all the 'supply-side' measures enacted by the government during the 1980s. All we can do here is summarise what we know while making clear that we do not know everything.

The first point to notice is that unemployment has not risen dramatically because of any substantial increase in turnover. In Figure 3.2 we show the average probability of a person in work entering unemployment in any given month. This average probability in the 1980s and 90s is around 25 per cent higher than in the late 1960s but given that unemployment has risen by at least 300 per cent over the same period, the contribution of the increase in inflow rates to the overall rise in unemployment is very small. What this means is that the average employee is only slightly more likely to become unemployed now than twenty five to thirty years ago. However, once they enter unemployment, they remain without a job for nearly three times as long. So while job loss is only a bit more common than it was in the 1960s, it is a much more serious event because it takes so much longer, on average, to get back into work.

Looking now at the specific factors underlying the rise in equilibrium unemployment, the increase from the mid 60s to the early 70s is probably due to a marked increase in the generosity of the unemployment benefit system over this period allied to a sharp rise in trade union pressure on wages. This latter appears to have been part of an international shift which saw the number of industrial conflicts per employee in the OECD almost double in the period from 1967 to 1974. (Incidentally, this number has declined continuously since 1974 to less than half its 1967 level!)

The period from the early 70s to the early 80s saw an enormous rise in commodity prices (from 1972 to 1980, they rose by around 3 times relative to OECD output prices) and this was the major force behind the rise in equilibrium unemployment during this period despite the offset due to North Sea oil. Other factors which have been discussed include the introduction of employment protection legislation and the rise in payroll taxes, but these played only a very small role. It is worth noting, for those who are taken with the payroll tax explanation, that Denmark has no payroll taxes whatever and has unemployment around the EC average. The reason why payroll taxes are not very important is that, in the long run, they are shifted onto employees. As for employment protection, there is no evidence that it has any impact on the equilibrium rate although it may reduce adjustment speeds.

The most difficult thing to explain is why the equilibrium rate has shown no sign of falling back in recent years despite the fact that many of the original causes of the rise in the equilibrium rate have gone into reverse. First, commodity prices are, in real terms, back where they were at the end of the 1960s. Second, the unemployment benefit system appears to have been substantially toughened up over the last decade with lower replacement rates and stiffer work testing. Third, the power exercised by unions over wage determination has been weakened, although by how much it is hard to say. So what has offset these changes?

First, it is not clear that shifts in the benefit system are all one way. In particular, it is worth noting that housing benefit (which pays the rent) represents a very substantial part of total benefits for single persons when they are unemployed and is withdrawn at a rapid rate (65p for every £1 of net income) when they are employed. In high rent areas (such as London), this substantially reduces the incentive to work. Second, after the very deep recession of the early 1980s and encouraged by the indefinite availability of benefits, the proportion of long-term unemployed was very high (more than 40 per cent over 1 year). This markedly increases the persistence of high unemployment because, for a variety of reasons, the long-term unemployed find it very difficult to get back into work. Third, the decline in the value of North Sea oil production since the mid 1980s has put pressure on the trade balance and this has, in turn, tended to raise equilibrium unemployment.

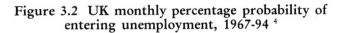

**Figure 3.2  UK monthly percentage probability of entering unemployment, 1967-94** [4]

However, perhaps the most important factor has been the collapse in demand for unskilled workers over the last two decades caused both by technical change (e.g. computers) and by competition from the Newly Industrialized Countries (NICs). There has also been a substantial fall in the supply of unskilled workers over the same period but in the 1980s this has not kept pace with the fall in demand. On the other side of the coin, of course, the *rise* in demand for *skilled* workers appears to have outpaced supply over the same period.[5] This has a significant impact on the equilibrium unemployment rate because skill shortages can generate inflationary pressure in the labour market even at historically high levels of unemployment. To see what has happened since the early 1970s we set out, in Table 3.2, the unemployment rates for high and low skill men and women, and also the male non-employment rates (i.e. unemployed plus non-participants divided by population).

Table 3.2  UK unemployment rates by education

| | Females Unemployment rates by education | | | | | | |
|---|---|---|---|---|---|---|---|
| | 1973-74 | 1975-78 | 1979-82 | 1983-86 | 1987-90 | 1991 | 1992 |
| Total | 2.7 | 4.6 | 6.7 | 8.7 | 5.9 | 6.8 | 7.2 |
| High ed. | 3.1 | 3.6 | 4.2 | 6.4 | 4.3 | 4.5 | 6.4 |
| Low ed. | 2.6 | 4.8 | 7.3 | 9.4 | 6.8 | 7.9 | 7.5 |
| Ratio | 0.8 | 1.3 | 1.7 | 1.5 | 1.6 | 1.8 | 1.2 |

| | Males Unemployment rates 16-64 | | | | | | |
|---|---|---|---|---|---|---|---|
| | 1973-74 | 1975-78 | 1979-82 | 1983-86 | 1987-90 | 1991 | 1992 |
| Total | 2.9 | 4.4 | 7.7 | 10.5 | 7.5 | 10.0 | 11.5 |
| High ed. | 1.4 | 2.0 | 3.9 | 4.7 | 4.0 | .7 | 6.6 |
| Low ed. | 4.0 | 6.4 | 12.2 | 18.2 | 13.5 | 17.4 | 16.9 |
| Ratio | 2.9 | 3.2 | 3.1 | 3.9 | 3.4 | 3.1 | 2.6 |

| | Males Unemployment rates 25-54 | | | | | | |
|---|---|---|---|---|---|---|---|
| | 1973-74 | 1975-78 | 1979-82 | 1983-86 | 1987-90 | 1991 | 1992 |
| Total | 2.4 | 3.7 | 63.7 | 9.1 | 6.6 | 8.5 | 10.2 |
| High ed. | 0.8 | 1.5 | 2.6 | 3.4 | 2.9 | 4.4 | 5.7 |
| Low ed. | 3.4 | 5.3 | 10.1 | 15.6 | 12.3 | 15.2 | 15.7 |
| Ratio | 4.3 | 3.5 | 3.9 | 4.6 | 4.2 | 3.5 | 2.8 |

| | Males Non-employment rates 25-54 | | | | | | |
|---|---|---|---|---|---|---|---|
| | 1973-74 | 1975-78 | 1979-82 | 1983-86 | 1987-90 | 1991 | 1992 |
| Total | 4.4 | 6.0 | 9.7 | 12.9 | 11.2 | 13.9 | 15.7 |
| High ed. | 2.0 | 3.2 | 4.4 | 5.6 | 5.1 | 7.5 | 9.3 |
| Low ed. | 5.7 | 8.3 | 14.1 | 21.3 | 20.3 | 23.5 | 25.1 |
| Ratio | 2.9 | 2.6 | 3.2 | 3.8 | 4.0 | 3.1 | 2.7 |

Source:  General Household Survey Tapes (thanks to Jane Roberts).  The unemployment rates are based on standard ILO definitions (i.e. unemployed are seeking work).  They are *not* based on claimant counts.

Definitions: High ed.  =  A levels or better.
Low ed.  =  No qualifications.
Ratio  =  Low ed. u rate/High ed. u rate.

Note:  Some 40 per cent of the working population is between high ed. and low ed.

There are several points worth noting about these numbers. First, unemployment rates have risen substantially across *both* high and low education groups. Second, up to the mid to late 1980s, unemployment in the low education group was increasing faster. Third, in the 1991-2 recession, high education unemployment rates rose *more* rapidly than low education rates, indicating that in this particular recession, higher education workers were unusually badly hit. All these points apply equally to women and men whose unemployment rates by education exhibit very similar patterns despite the substantial increase in women's participation over the period. The only important difference is the fact that women without qualifications have far lower unemployment rates than their male counterparts. Thus the sheer scale of the increase in unemployment rates *and* non-employment rates among men without qualifications is startling. Notably, that fact that a quarter of prime age (25-54) men without qualifications are currently not working reveals an economic and social problem of considerable magnitude.[6]

What do these three points reveal about the impact of the collapse in demand for the unskilled on overall unemployment? It is clear from the numbers in Table 3.2 that, up to the late 1980s, we have seen a relative shift in demand against the unskilled superimposed on an overall reduction in demand which is neutral as between skill groups. The important question is how much the total change in unemployment can be allocated to the relative demand shift and how much to neutral shocks? This will clearly depend on whether neutral demand shifts generate changes in unemployment rates by skill group which are closer to *equal percentage point* increases in the unemployment rate (e.g. skilled rates go from 1 to 4, unskilled rates go from 4 to 7) or are closer to equal proportionate increases in unemployment (e.g. skilled rates go from 1 to 4, unskilled rates go from 4 to 16). In fact our best estimates indicate they are somewhere in between, and this implies that around 15 to 25 per cent of the overall increase in equilibrium unemployment can be explained by the relative demand shift against the unskilled (see Nickell and Bell, 1995, for more details).

To summarise therefore, despite the supply-side changes induced by government policy and the significant decline in commodity prices during the 1980s, equilibrium unemployment in Britain remains high for a number of reasons. First certain aspects of the benefit system still encourage unemployment in general and long-term unemployment in particular (notably the housing benefit system, particularly its impact on single people, and indefinite benefit availability with no serious changes in regime). Second, the decline in the value of North Sea oil production has tended to raise equilibrium unemployment by putting pressure on the trade balance. Third, the substantial shift in demand against the unskilled and in favour of the skilled has outpaced the changes in relative supply. This means that even when unemployment is at an historically high level, inflationary pressure tends to appear in the labour market because of shortages of labour with the right kinds of skill. Finally, it must be emphasised that this is not an exhaustive list. There are undoubtedly other important causes of the persistence of high unemployment which remain to be identified.

## What can we do about high unemployment?

It is most important to recognise that policies to combat high unemployment over the long term are unlikely to work rapidly. What is required is a consistent strategy.

### *Where **not** to look for the answer*

*Cunning demand-side policies.* For example, instituting an independent Bank of England, joining the EMS, staying out of the EMS etc. These policies may be of value in their own right by helping to reduce economic fluctuations, but they will not have much impact on the average level of unemployment about which the economy fluctuates.

*Reducing labour supply.* For example, job sharing, *imposed* cuts in working hours, early retirement, persuading women that their place is in the home etc. Policies of this type increase inflationary pressure at any given level of labour demand unless they are precisely targeted on workers whom nobody wishes to employ. Since the rise in inflationary pressure must be combated, labour demand is reduced and we typically end up with similar levels of unemployment, lower employment and lower output. So unemployment is the same and the country is poorer. Note that we refer to *imposed* cuts in working hours to distinguish them from cuts which are freely chosen or negotiated. The latter are simply part of the process of getting richer and taking some of the increased wealth in the form of leisure.

*Cutting employment protection.* There is no evidence that employment protection legislation has any impact on levels of unemployment although it slows down the speed at which the economy responds to shocks, thereby increasing the persistence of unemployment. Thus it may encourage the persistence of high unemployment after an adverse shock although the effect is not large.

*Profit sharing and related pay structures.* It is sometimes argued, notably by Weitzman (1984) that profit sharing tends to reduce unemployment, on average, by making total remuneration more flexible over the business cycle. There is no evidence that this is correct. However, there may be other reasons for introducing profit sharing, notably to improve productivity.

### *Where to look for the answer*

*Programmes targeted on the long-term unemployed.* A typical example would be job subsidies for the long-term unemployed which increase with unemployment duration as in the Snower plan (1990). These may help because the long-term unemployed tend to become discouraged and are often discriminated against by employers. Consequently, they play little role in holding down inflation. However, proponents of these schemes tend to overstate their impact because employers are typically less responsive to such subsidies than might be imagined, in part because if they see someone coming to them for a job carrying a subsidy, they imagine that there must be something wrong with them. Potentially more valuable and more dramatic is simply to prevent long-term unemployment by substantially reducing benefits after one year, say, thereby forcing individuals to come off unemployment. At this point, the government must provide training programmes or employment of last resort, as in Sweden. Such a programme can only operate on the flow, and during the transition the existing stock of long-term unemployed will eventually wither away. The existing situation in Sweden is, in a sense, a grand experiment to see whether or not such a programme can survive when confronted with a massive adverse shock. Currently, things are not looking good. However, the lesson from Sweden is not that the whole system is bad. After all it helped to eliminate poverty and to keep unemployment below three per cent throughout the 1970s and 80s. The important lesson is not to run macro and monetary policy in such a way that the economy is subjected to an enormous and rapid reduction in aggregate demand.[7]

*Programmes targeted on the unskilled.* The general idea is to raise the returns to work for those with low skills as well as reducing the cost of employing them. Possibilities include cutting payroll taxes for the unskilled, perhaps introduced simultaneously with the introduction of a minimum wage for prime age workers. An alternative to the latter is to extend the family credit scheme which does not have the demand side problems associated with the minimum wage. However, evidence suggests that the adverse employment consequences of the minimum wage are minimal so long as the level is low and it does not apply to teenagers. Thus, a recent rise in the US minimum wage (to around £3.20 per hour) appeared actually to raise employment in fast food outlets (see Card and Krueger, 1994 and 1995) presumably because it enabled them to recruit and retain their employees more readily. More generally it is worth bearing in mind that policies focused on getting the unskilled into reasonably paid work are of vital importance. As time goes on, the market rewards for unskilled work are likely to decline substantially, particularly relative to the market rewards for crime and other anti-social activities. Basic policies to counteract this involve either subsidising unskilled work or, in the longer term, reducing the supply of unskilled workers in order to raise their market rewards. This leads on to the next topic.

*Education and training.* As we have already seen, the shift in demand against the unskilled seems to have outpaced the shift in supply in the same direction with adverse consequences. Over the longer term, this suggests that we must focus on improving the quality and quantity of education and training for the bottom half of the ability range. Many ways of doing this have been proposed but any reasonable costing of such an activity will include the transfer of resources away from the top 30 per cent of the ability range. For example, it must be right to transfer resources from higher education to nursery education and the obvious way to do this is to impose some form of graduate tax. In the long run, of course, the benefits in the form of reduced expenditure on crime prevention, prisons, unemployment benefit and so on will substantially offset the increased education and training costs.

*Reform the benefit system.* The overriding principle must always be to maintain the rewards of working relative to not-working while sustaining the well-being of those without work. Thus, wherever possible, it is best to avoid providing benefits which depend solely upon an individual not working. Just as important is to avoid benefit structures which discourage spouses from working. This points in the direction of an insurance based rather than a welfare based system. Unfortunately, the new Job Seekers Allowance moves in the opposite direction, reducing the insurance element (from 12 months to 6 months) and raising the welfare element. I am also in favour of raising the level of unemployment benefit for a limited period (say six months) from its current miserable level, since I feel there is little to be gained from plunging families into poverty the instant they become unemployed. Allied to this, there should be a time-limit on benefits of the type described under the long-term unemployment heading.

*Encourage employer co-ordination.* Evidence suggests that there are distinct advantages in terms of lower unemployment accruing in those economies where there is some degree of employer co-ordination in wage setting and in other labour market activities (see Soskice, 1990, for example). While the notion of a 'going rate' is decidedly unpopular in establishment circles in Britain, where flexibility (and hence pay leapfrogging) is all, it can be very helpful in holding down inflation when the labour market is tight. However, if companies are opposed to it, there seems little that can be done other than to persuade them otherwise.

## Conclusions

Unemployment in Britain is high by historical standards and can be reduced by the introduction of a long-term strategy. Some ideas on what should be included in such a strategy are programmes targeted on the long-term unemployed and on the unskilled, improving education and training for the bottom half of the ability range and reforming the benefit system. However, even with an effective strategy in place, it is hard to imagine that we could ever return to the exceptionally low rates of the immediate post-war period. Reducing the equilibrium unemployment rate to five per cent would be a very significant achievement.

## Notes

1.  On the OECD standardised definition, the unemployment rate fell from 11.1 to 6.5 per cent over the same period. Meanwhile, employment rose by 8.4 per cent, that is around 2.1 million jobs.
2.  The published figures have been adjusted in an attempt to make them comparable.

3. This analysis can only be undertaken over periods of three or more years in order to smooth out the year on year fluctuations and cope with the significant lags in the system.

4. These data represent the standardised monthly inflow into unemployment excluding school-leavers normalised on the workforce in employment. The former are currently published monthly in the Employment Gazette (Table 2.19) and were first published in the Gazette of September 1976 (Table 117) going back to 1967. Various revisions were made in 1980 (exclude self-service), 1982 (move from registration to claimant count) and 1983 (GB to UK), and the data have been adjusted to the most recent definition (i.e. UK Claimant Count).

5. This is part of the explanation for the dramatic rise in the pay of skilled workers relative to the unskilled since 1980.

6. At least half of the increase in non-participation is due to the rise in the numbers on invalidity benefit since the early 1970s. The increase is equivalent to around four per cent of the labour force.

7. As in most of Scandinavia, the collapse of the enormous credit boom of the late 1980s was so severe that the banking system had to be supported by the government in order to prevent its complete demise.

## References

Card, D. and Krueger, A. (1994), 'Minimum wages and employment: a case study of the fast-food industry in New Jersey and Pennsylvania', *American Economic Review*, Vol. **84**, (4), pp.772-793.

Card, D. and Krueger, A. (1995), *Myth and Measurement: The New Economics of the Minimum Wage*, Princeton: Princeton University Press.

Nickell, S. and Bell, B. (Spring, 1995), 'The collapse in demand for the unskilled and unemployment across the OECD', *The Oxford Review of Economic Policy*.

Layard, R., Nickell, S. and Jackman, R. (1994), *The Unemployment Crisis*, Oxford: Oxford University Press.

Snower, D. (1994), 'Converting unemployment benefits into employment subsidies', *American Economic Review*, Vol. **84**, (2), pp.65-70.

Soskice, D. (Winter, 1990), 'Wage determination: the changing role of institutions in advanced industrialized countries', *Oxford Review of Economic Policy*, Vol. **6**, (4), pp.36-61.

Weitzman, M.L. (1984), *The Share Economy*, Cambridge, Mass.: Harvard University Press.

## Acknowledgements

I am grateful to the ESRC for funding, to Daphne Nicolitsas, Brian Bell and Jane Roberts for help with the data and to Samuel Bentolila, Bill Callaghan, Gavin Cameron and participants at the Conference for helpful comments on an earlier draft.

# 4 Tax policy: are there still choices?

*John Hills* [*]

Taxation - its level and structure - is central to public policy on four counts. Firstly, the balance between total tax revenues and total government spending (the 'fiscal stance') is crucial to macroeconomic policy. Secondly, once the level of borrowing (or surplus) is set, the overall level of taxation determines how much can be spent on public services or cash transfer programmes. Thirdly, the structure of taxation is a key part of what determines the distribution of net income between individuals. Finally, the structure of taxation may have important effects - positive as well as negative - on individual behaviour, and on the efficiency of the economy.

In this context it is surprising that tax - or rather options for tax policy - are not *more* central to the political debate. At present there appears to be a consensus on both sides of the political divide that the only important question is whether there will be scope for the Government to announce cuts in income tax rates in advance of the next election, and, if it does so, how the Opposition should respond. However, as will be argued below, this level of debate does justice neither to the range of options available, nor to what the population as a whole say they would like to happen.

The chapter first discusses the background in terms of the overall level of taxation and the state of government finances - which is where the main constraints may lie - then explores questions concerned with the shape of the system - which is where many of the options are - and finally, it discusses potential policy directions.

---

[*] Reader in Economics and Social Policy and Co-Director of the Welfare State Programme at the London School of Economics.

## Revenue and the public finances

*Medium-term trends in the tax ratio*

Figure 4.1 shows the movements in the overall (non-North Sea) tax ratio (tax as a share of national income) in the UK over the last thirty years. Since 1967-68 the ratio has never been below 33 per cent, and never higher than 39.25 per cent.[1]  Looking back over the medium-term past (i.e. since the late 1960s), political choices for the tax take from the economy have been made within the relatively narrow range of around six percentage points of GDP. The increase in taxation over the two years 1993-94 to 1995-96 from 34 to 37 per cent of GDP traverses half of the range within which policy has operated.

There is no clear trend in either direction in the ratio, and no obvious link to which party is in government. In the 1970s and early 1980s, one could point to fluctuations in the ratio in relation to the state of the economic cycle, with low points in the booms of the early and late 1970s, and a peak in the recession of the early 1980s. However, the most recent pattern has moved in the opposite direction relative to the economic cycle.

**Figure 4.1**
**Tax burden (excluding North Sea)**

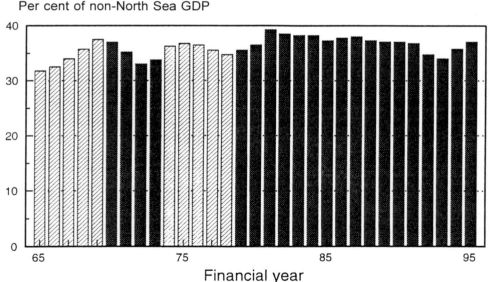

Per cent of non-North Sea GDP

Financial year

Source:  HM Treasury (1994), Table 4A.9

*International comparisons*

Given the rather limited change in the tax ratio in the UK over this period, one might suppose that there were really quite tight boundaries within which the size of the public sector had to operate, but international evidence suggests that the potential freedom of action for countries to choose is a great deal wider. Figure 4.2 compares tax ratios (calculated on a different basis to the above to give comparability) in nineteen OECD countries in 1990.

**Figure 4.2**
**Tax ratios 1990**

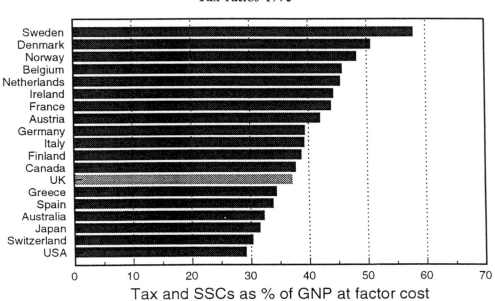

Tax and SSCs as % of GNP at factor cost

Source: CSO (1994a); based on OECD statistics

Taxes and social security contributions ranged from seven percentage points of GNP *below* the UK in Switzerland and the USA to eleven or more percentage points *above* it in three of the Scandinavian countries. The tax ratio in the highest, Sweden, was very nearly twice that in the lowest, the USA. The range of three percentage points up or down which apparently represents the politically acceptable limits of tax policy in the UK in recent years encompasses the ratios in only five of the other eighteen countries.

Figure 4.3 shows the trend in the UK since the mid-1970s in relation to the international range (again, on a different basis to give comparability over time). What is most striking in this figure is the way in which the comparatively stable ratio in the UK has implied a shift from being a country just above the mid-point of the range to being one clearly below it. The ratio for the lowest country (Spain in 1975, but the USA by 1989) rose by almost ten percentage points, while that for the highest (Norway in 1975 and Sweden in 1989) rose by twelve points. The comparable rise in the UK was just under three points.

**Figure 4.3**
**International range of tax ratios**

Tax and Social Security Contributions as % of GNP at factor cost

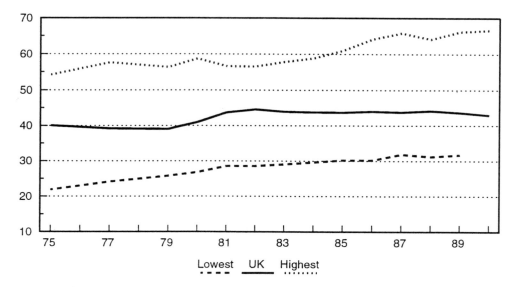

Lowest     UK     Highest

Source: CSO (1992) and earlier equivalents

By contrast to the limits within which UK policy has actually operated, whether for reasons of tight Treasury control or political preference, there is nothing in the experience of other countries which suggests that different choices would be *infeasible*, or that the UK is anywhere near an upper bound above which it would be in danger of provoking a 'New York City' flight to lower tax neighbours.


*Government finances: cash flow*

The main determinant of tax revenues is the need to cover spending. Figure 4.4 shows how the level of tax revenues over the last thirty years has been related to other parts of government finances. The diagram shows in its different 'strata' the ways in which general (central and local) government expenditure has been financed, starting with non-North Sea taxes and national insurance contributions, followed by North Sea revenues, privatisation proceeds, other receipts, and borrowing (though for two short periods, total revenues exceeded spending so there was a surplus). The figures are shown in relation to total GDP, rather than excluding the North Sea as in Figure 4.1.

**Figure 4.4**
**Government receipts and spending**

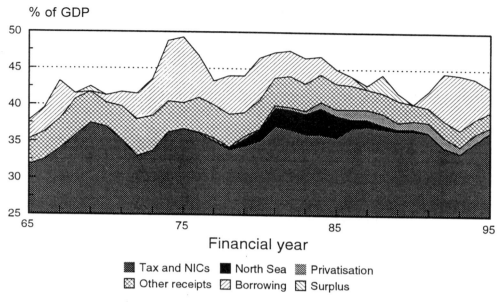

Source: HM Treasury (1994); earlier equivalents

The figure shows the much greater scale of the movements in spending than in tax revenues, with general government expenditure (without deducting privatisation receipts) ranging from under 38 per cent of GDP in 1965-66 to over 49 per cent ten years later. It makes clear the background to the recent rises in the tax ratio. Firstly, this does not reflect a general trend towards higher government spending. Indeed, comparing either recession years or boom years, the trend in spending has been downwards since the mid-1970s. Secondly, borrowing is intended to fall from 7.5 to 3.25 per cent of GDP between 1993-94 and 1995-96, with the larger part (3 per cent of GDP) of this reduction being accounted for by rising tax revenues. Thirdly, non-North Sea taxes and national insurance are having to replace revenues from other sources. In each year between 1984-85 and 1988-89 government revenues from the North Sea and privatisation receipts exceeded 4 per cent of GDP. In 1995-96 they are forecast to be under 1 per cent of GDP. *All* of the recent increases in general taxation could be described as a (belated) move to fill this gap. Finally, the miscellaneous category of 'other receipts' has also been dwindling, falling from 4.25 per cent of GDP in 1983-84 to 2 per cent by 1994-95. This includes items like interest and dividend receipts from outside general government, and an element reflecting the assumed value of the depreciation of government assets during the year (which is imputed as both a revenue and spending item). Part of the fall is an important consequence of privatisation - which generates sales revenue in the short-term, but reduces potential interest, dividends or surpluses later. Another part of it reflects the falling value of government capital assets in relation to GDP.

In political terms, the difference in trends between the bottom stratum (non-North Sea taxes and national insurance contributions (NICs)) and total spending is crucial. Over the medium term, the non-North Sea tax ratio has been fairly constant, while spending has been falling. Over the immediate past, taxes have been rising, but spending has been falling in relation to national income. Whether this represents virtuous behaviour by government in controlling borrowing or the response to the loss of a previous unsustainable windfall may matter little for the unpopularity resulting from the fact that, in effect, people have been paying more for less. However, reactions to tax rises which do not produce better public services do not necessarily reflect people's general preferences for the size of the public sector, as is discussed below.

### Government finances: balance sheet

This discussion raises the question of the extent to which current revenue levels are sustainable in relation to spending. Here it is not simply the flow of government borrowing which is important, but also the stock of government debt. One potential constraint on both would be the Maastricht limits, if membership of a European Monetary Union was being kept as an option. Public debt is still below the Maastricht limit of 60 per cent of GDP, and should stay below it in the short term unless growth is very low (HM Treasury, 1994, Chart 4.2). Looking at what level of borrowing would be consistent with long-term stability in the debt: GDP ratio at around 50 per cent, the Institute for Fiscal Studies has suggested that a PSBR of around 3 per cent of GDP would be sustainable (Davies et al, 1994, p.39). With a forecast 1995-96 PSBR at this level in what - according to Treasury forecasts - is still the middle of an upswing and with PSBRs projected to be significantly lower in coming years (HM Treasury, 1994, Table 4.2), the implication is that the pain of raising revenue in return for no extra spending may be over.

However, this is still a one-dimensional view of fiscal prudence and virtue. Debt is, after all, only one side of a balance sheet, and not many businesses would be regarded as a success if they had only managed to reduce their debts at the cost of a greater fall in assets. Table 4.1 gives a very different impression of the last thirty years from that given by concentration on annual borrowing figures.

First, the upper part of the table shows the relationship between the public sector's net financial balance (financial assets minus financial liabilities) and its physical assets. Despite the borrowing illustrated in Figure 4.4, the net financial balance *improved* in real terms between 1957 and 1979.[2] Relative to GDP, net financial liabilities fell substantially.

At the same time, the value of publicly owned physical assets was growing substantially, as significant parts of public spending were on capital investment in excess of depreciation of existing assets. By 1979 physical assets exceeded net financial liabilities to the extent of a year's GDP. Since 1979, the picture has changed. Net investment collapsed between 1974 and 1982 as government capital spending bore the brunt of cuts (Hills, 1989, Figure 3); assets have been sold through privatisation; but net financial liabilities grew slightly in real terms between 1979 and 1992. As a result, the physical/financial balance has deteriorated markedly, with the net advantage falling below 50 per cent of a year's GDP.

### Table 4.1
### UK public sector balance sheet
(all items as % of GDP)

|  | 1957 | 1966 | 1975 | 1979 | 1987 | 1992 |
|---|---|---|---|---|---|---|
| Net financial balance | -103 | -74 | -39 | -32 | -31 | -30 |
| Physical assets[1] | 83 | 105 | 131 | 131 | 106 | 75 |
| *Physical/financial balance* | -21 | 31 | 92 | 99 | 76 | 45 |
| Basic pension[2] | -109 | -130 | -155 | -153 | -116 | -114 |
| SERPS | - | - | - | -4 | -22 | -23 |
| Public service pensions | -15 | -15 | -39 | -38 | -41 | -47 |
| Deferred tax liability[3] | 7 | 9 | 20 | 17 | 28 | 43 |
| *Balance including pensions* | -136 | -106 | -83 | -80 | -77 | -96 |
| Future oil revenues | - | - | 29 | 38 | 7 | 2 |
| *Overall balance* | -136 | -106 | -54 | -42 | -70 | -94 |

Notes:   1  Including dwellings at current market value.
2  Assuming future earnings-linking up to 1979, but price-linking in later years.
3  Mainly reflecting future taxation of pensions in payment.

Sources:  1957-1987 figures from Hills (1989). 1992 figures based on same methodology, using more recent editions of source documents. All figures in lower part of table subject to substantial margins of error.

The deterioration between 1979 and 1992 is much the same if one takes a broader view of what should be included in public assets and liabilities, as the lower part of the table shows (some of its items being subject to very wide margins of error).[3] For instance, the implications of unfunded state pension rights for future generations of taxpayers may, on some arguments, not be so different from those of an equivalent amount of public sector debt. Similarly, the windfall ability of the state to extract rents from oil and gas reserves in the North Sea might best be regarded as a wasting asset. Allowing for such factors, the public sector had overall net liabilities equivalent to 42 per cent of GDP in 1979, rising to 94 per cent by 1992. Whether one looks at the narrower physical/financial balance or at the wider definition, the net position of the public sector appears to have deteriorated by roughly 4 percentage points of GDP per year between 1979 and 1992, with a rather faster deterioration in the years since 1987. Much of this is another way of looking at the problem of replacing oil and gas revenues and privatisation receipts which has already been discussed. Given the government borrowing of the early 1990s shown in Figure 4.4, the net financial balance at least will have deteriorated further between 1992 and 1995.

A deterioration continuing at the sort of rate shown in the table would in the long run be unsustainable or would have expensive consequences: sooner or later taxes would to have to rise to service growing debts, renew public infrastructure, pay for services which were once but are no longer available from public assets, or to cover the costs of pensions. However, changes in all items in the table might be expected to be much slower now than before 1992. With the rise in the general tax ratio, public borrowing appears to have fallen to the point where the debt to GDP ratio is stable or falling. Major asset sales may now be over, and the years of lucrative oil revenues are already past. Price-linking of state pensions appears to have ended the growth in accrued liabilities in relation to national income (as well as causing a very large one-off reduction in accrued liabilities after 1979). While the table tarnishes the view of the 1980s as a time of fiscal virtue, measures already taken may have brought the situation under control.

## Future spending trends

It is easy - and sometimes politically convenient - to overstate the upward pressures on public spending and to suggest that the prospect of a future 'demographic time-bomb' makes some kind of case for lower public spending now. Nonetheless, the pressures clearly *are* upwards, at least so far as some of the major spending areas are concerned, particularly as a result of the ageing of the population:

- **Health** spending is likely to rise as a share of national income, not just because the health needs of an elderly population tend to be greater than those of younger people, but also because health care appears to be a 'luxury' good - as people become richer, they want more spent on it. In addition, recent experience has been that the cost of delivering health services has risen faster than other prices. The financing and provision of long-term care for the elderly is emerging as a crucial issue for the future balance between public and private sectors.

- On demographic grounds, one might expect a long-term fall in **education** spending as a share of national income, but the increasing importance of education and training to international competitiveness suggests that one way or another the country will have to invest more rather than less in education in future (National Commission on Education, 1993; Barclay, 1995; see also Chapter 6). Some of this might be financed privately (for instance through income-contingent loans for higher education, or through higher company spending on training). However, for pre-school education and compulsory schooling it is hard to see how some form of public spending increase could be avoided while maintaining equity in access (Glennerster, 1995).

- **Social security** spending will depend critically on two things. First, with a continued policy of price-linking benefits, spending would eventually *fall* as a share of national income, other things being equal, despite the ageing of the population. However, it must be questioned whether this policy is sustainable indefinitely. Will it really be acceptable for the real living standards of all those dependent on pensions and other benefits to be fixed indefinitely while, say, other living standards double? A return to income-linking benefits in some form, combined with ageing, would imply a rising share of national income going to pensions and other benefits for the elderly.[4] Second, however, other things will not be equal, particularly the level of unemployment: economic performance may be more important to overall welfare spending than factors like ageing.

None of these factors implies infeasible increases of spending, even looking a considerable period ahead (Hills, 1993: 11-14). But they do not offer much scope for painless spending *reductions* to allow a fall in the tax ratio, short of rapid economic growth coming to the rescue, radical welfare restructuring of a kind which even recent governments have shied away from (and which in many cases simply shift an equivalent cost onto people through private alternatives), or substantial savings in other areas of Government spending such as defence, housing or transport. As a corollary, reconciling such upward pressures with an aim of keeping the tax ratio fixed would imply cuts in spending in relation to rising demands, either visibly through removing certain programmes altogether or less visibly through the continued erosion of relative benefit levels.

*Implications*

Summarising all of this, together with the continuing lack of evidence for significant microeconomic ill-effects from tax rates anywhere near current levels for most people,[5] the limits to taxation appear to be largely political rather than economic. We could spend more if we were prepared to tax more. We could tax less if we were prepared to spend less.

Here the current political debate seems to lead to a straightforward conclusion. Labour is perceived, in part at least, to have lost the last election because of worries about tax, while the Conservatives are currently unpopular partly because of the recent tax rises. By implication, the route to political popularity is seen to be about ensuring cuts in tax.

However, the picture is not quite so straightforward. First, 54 per cent of the electorate voted at the last election for parties promising in one way or another to increase public spending paid for through higher taxes, either in the shape of Labour's 'Shadow Budget' or through the Liberal Democrat's 'penny on income tax for education'.

Second, using detailed analysis of voting behaviour in the 1992 election Heath, Jowell and Curtice find very little evidence in their surveys to back the argument that it was tax which led to Labour's defeat (1994: 292). Looking at those who originally said they would support Labour at the start of the campaign, but in the end failed to do so, 'there is no evidence that they were people particularly adverse to high taxation; rather they seemed to be people who had relatively little faith in Labour's ability to improve services like health and education' (*ibid*: 292).

More strangely, given the current political debate, when people are actually asked what they want, there is a large and growing majority who say they want higher spending and higher taxes, and very few who say they want lower spending and lower taxes, as can be seen from the results of the *British Social Attitudes Survey* shown in Table 4.2. When people are asked about the linked choice between spending and taxes that largely determines the size of the public sector, they appear to want a larger, rather than a smaller public sector. Whereas in 1983, rather more opted for the *status quo* than for an increase, by 1993, 63 per cent of the population favoured higher taxes and spending (on health, education and social benefits). Even in 1983 fewer than 10 per cent actually wanted cuts in both; ten years later, only 4 per cent did so. Even allowing for the fact that the latest round of questioning was in 1993, before the recent rise in taxation, the swing against lower spending and lower taxes since the early 1980s seems decisive.[6] Table 4.2 shows that when it comes to services like health, education and pensions, the majority in favour of higher tax-financed spending is now overwhelming. Cuts in spending on the arts might be less unpopular, but the amounts of money involved are much smaller than in areas where people say they want more spent publicly.

How is one to reconcile the difference between politicians' perceptions of the salience of low taxes as a vote-winner and the consistent results of attitude surveys? First, people may be telling the surveyors what they would like, *if* it could be guaranteed that the money would be spent on the services they would like. When it comes to a vote, they may not, however, trust the politicians enough to give them a mandate to increase taxation when there is no guarantee of this kind. As Heath, Jowell and Curtice conclude, 'it is of no conceivable value to be seen as a high tax party unless voters are convinced that the high taxes will yield effective returns' (1994: 294).

**Table 4.2**
**Public attitudes to tax and spending trade-off**

**(a)  General trade-off**

|  | Percentage saying government should: | | |
|---|---|---|---|
|  | Reduce taxes and spending[1] | Keep taxes and spending at same level | Increase taxes and spending |
| 1983 | 9 | 54 | 32 |
| 1986 | 5 | 44 | 46 |
| 1990 | 3 | 37 | 54 |
| 1993 | 4 | 29 | 63 |

Note:  1  On health, education and social benefits.

**(b)  Specific spending programmes (1993)**

| | Percentage wanting government to spend: | | |
| --- | --- | --- | --- |
| | Less | Same as now | More |
| Health | 1 | 9 | 87 |
| Education | 1 | 16 | 79 |
| Pensions | 1 | 17 | 78 |
| Police, etc. | 3 | 25 | 68 |
| Environment | 3 | 36 | 54 |
| Unemployment benefits | 8 | 39 | 48 |
| Defence | 33 | 40 | 21 |
| Arts | 44 | 38 | 10 |

Source:   Lipsey (1994).

Second, the *BSAS* questions do not pin down what kind of taxation is involved: what people may have in mind is taxation on someone else, rather than on themselves.  Finally, the politicians may simply be wrong, confusing the unsurprising unpopularity of recent tax rises which were neither promised nor linked to more extensive services with underlying views on the tax-spending trade-off.  Tax cuts paid for by spending cuts could be *even more* unpopular.

## The shape of the tax system

So far the discussion has been about the overall tax burden and the constraints on it.  But even within a completely fixed tax ratio there remain considerable options for the structure of the system, both in terms of the balance between different taxes and in terms of their distributional effect, as determined by features like income tax rates and allowances.

Table 4.3 shows the broad changes in the balance between different taxes between 1978-79 and 1994-95.  The biggest changes are the fall of the contribution of the main personal direct taxes - income tax and NICs - from 54 to 45 per cent of all tax revenues, and the rise of the contribution of VAT from 9 to 18 per cent of the total.  Looking at intervening years, the year to year changes are gradual rather than sudden, with the exception of the switch between income tax and VAT in 1979-80, when the contribution from indirect taxes as a whole rose by 3.6 percentage points in a single year (Twigger, 1994, Table 3.2).

**Table 4.3**
**Tax composition 1978-79 and 1994-95**

|                                             | Share of total tax revenue (%) | |
| ------------------------------------------- | :-----: | :-----: |
|                                             | 1978-79 | 1994-95 |
| Income tax                                  | 32.9    | 27.2    |
| National insurance contributions[1]         | 21.1    | 18.0    |
| Corporation Tax[2]                          | 6.9     | 8.5     |
| Capital taxes[3]                            | 2.0     | 1.7     |
| VAT                                         | 8.6     | 18.3    |
| Other indirect                              | 17.6    | 14.3    |
| Rates/Council Tax[4]                        | 10.1    | 8.9     |
| Oil royalties/Petroleum Revenue Tax         | 0.9     | 0.5     |
| Other                                       | -       | 2.5     |
| All                                         | 100     | 100     |

Notes:   1 Includes National Insurance Surcharge in 1978-79.
         2 Includes Advance Corporation Tax.
         3 Includes Development Land Tax in 1978-79.
         4 Includes Uniform Business Rate in 1995-96.

Sources: Kay and King (1980), Table 1; Twigger (1994), Table 3.2; HM Treasury (1994),
         Table 4A.1.

The changes in composition combined with those in the overall tax ratio are
reflected in the Treasury figures for the tax burden on a hypothetical family
shown in Figure 4.5. While a family of this kind, with a single earner and a
man earning male average earnings is not necessarily representative of a very
large proportion of the population, its income, adjusted for family size as the
DSS does when examining income distribution (e.g. DSS, 1994) is close to the
median for the population as a whole, and the tax burden and its composition
move in roughly the ways one might expect from Figure 4.1 and Table 4.3.
The total tax burden for 1995-96 is higher than in any year apart from the
early 1980s, and the major increase has come from rising VAT, together with
some rise in NICs (only employee NICs are shown in this series and local tax
is estimated for 1993-94 to 1995-96).

**Figure 4.5**
**Tax burden on hypothetical family**
**One earner couple (100% male average) 2 children**

Tax as % of gross earnings

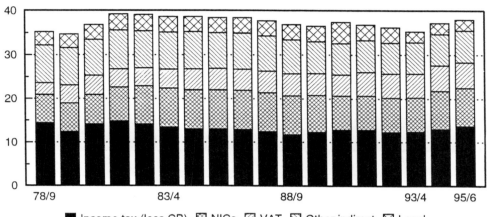

Source:   Official Report 19 December 1994, col. WA944-50 and 1 February 1995, col 667-
670 and Twigger (1994)

The positions of other hypothetical families of the same kind, but with
different earnings in relation to the male average, are compared with this case
in Figure 4.6 (data on local taxes are not available in this form).

**Figure 4.6**
**Tax burdens on hypothetical one earner couple**

**(a) 1978-79**

Tax as % of gross earnings

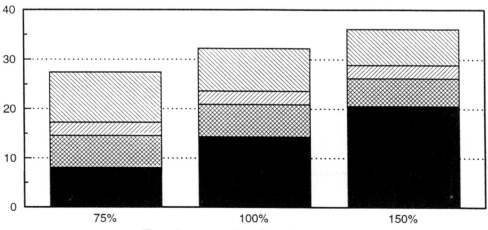

Earnings as % of male average

**(b) 1994-95**

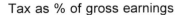

Tax as % of gross earnings

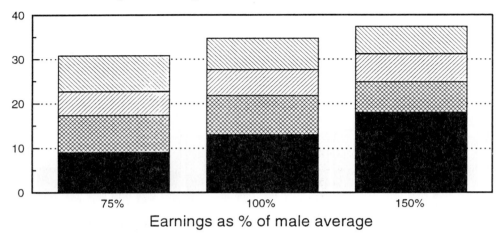

Earnings as % of male average

■ Income tax (less CB) ⊠ NICs ⧄ VAT ◩ Other indirect

Source: Official report 19 December 1994, col. WA944-50 and 1 February 1995, col 667-670 and Twigger (1994)

Again, the proportion of the population corresponding to each precise case may be small, but the 'tilt' in the tax burden towards those with lower and middle incomes is clear. As earnings double from 75 to 150 per cent of the male average the total tax burden rises from 27.4 to 36.1 per cent, a rise of 8.7 percentage points in 1978-79. The equivalent rise in 1994-95 was from 30.9 to 37.4 per cent, a rise of only 6.5 percentage points.

Redmond and Sutherland (1995) looked in more detail at the effects of changes in tax structure between 1978-79 and 1994-95 on a representative sample of households, divided into tenths according to income in 1994-95. They compared the 1994-95 tax system with what would have been in place, if the 1978-79 and other intervening tax systems had been maintained (but with features like tax allowances and thresholds indexed either with inflation or with income growth). Part of their findings are shown in Figure 4.7, which shows tax (direct and indirect, but not intermediate taxes) as a percentage of gross household income.[7] Whether the comparison is with the 'old' system uprated for price inflation only or uprated with income growth (to eliminate the 'fiscal drag' effect of a rising proportion of income being taxable if tax thresholds are fixed while real incomes grow), the pattern shown in Figure 4.6 is confirmed: the bottom seven tenths of the distribution are paying more tax than under the old system, and only the top tenth is paying less.

**Figure 4.7**
**Total tax burdens in 1994/95 and 1978/79**

(households ranked by income, adjusted for household size)

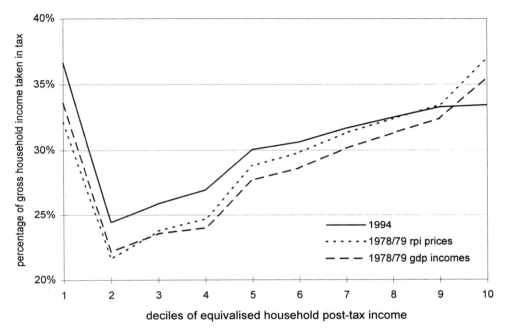

Source: Redmond and Sutherland (1995)

In a similar study of tax changes in the period between 1985 and 1995, Giles and Johnson (1994) found that those in the poorest half of the population - particularly those in the poorest fifth - were paying more tax than they would have done under the 'old' system (price-uprated), while those in the top half were paying less, particularly those in the richest tenth. This resulted from the fact that, in the period when the tax burden was falling, the tax burden fell most for those with high incomes, but when taxes were increasing, the effects were more evenly spread.

Calculations of this kind refer to the change in tax burden between two tax systems applied to the *same* population, with market incomes estimated at the same levels in each case. In reality, the population changed in various ways between the two years, notably with a large increase in the inequality of market incomes. Rising market income inequality, by itself, might have been expected to increase the proportion of the overall tax burden borne by those with higher incomes, as they were carried into higher income tax brackets and so on. The reduced tax burden on someone with an income at a fixed level above the average does not therefore mean that those with high incomes are necessarily paying a smaller proportion of the tax burden overall. In fact, looking over the 1980s as a whole, it appears that this kind of *automatic* effect of rising inequality has been cancelled out by the *discretionary* changes of the kind examined by Redmond and Sutherland (Hills, 1995: 59-61).

As with other aspects of tax policy, change in the relative burden carried by different groups is generally glacial - the cumulative effect of small discretionary changes each year - rather than seismic. The eventual effects of glaciation can, however, be substantial. Given a long enough period of time, a government which follows a consistent bias in the direction of the incremental changes introduced each year can make a significant difference to tax structure, as Figures 4.6 and 4.7 illustrate, without having to resort to major shifts of the kind represented by the introduction of the Poll Tax, which may be too much for people to swallow all at once.

*Constraints on the tax structure*

Some of the economic constraints on tax structure are harder than they were in the past. The top rate of income tax on investment income exceeded 88 per cent under both Conservative and Labour governments for the entire period from 1948 to 1978, reaching a theoretical maximum of 98 per cent between 1974-75 and 1978-79 (theoretical because alternative investment returns like capital gains were only taxed at 30 per cent, opening up opportunities for avoidance by the well-advised). With the ending of exchange controls, completion of the internal European market, and much more sophisticated international financial markets, attempts to tax investment income at anything like these rates would be doomed to failure. Mobility of financial assets does now represent a hard constraint on the rates of tax which could be imposed on investment income at the margin, although the current maximum rate of 40 per cent is probably still well below any such constraint. Similarly, company tax structures have to take account of operations across borders and the ability of accountants to move the place at which taxable profits accrue just as much as that of managers to move the physical location of investment.

A similar, but weaker, constraint is given by the ability of people themselves to move internationally. As the labour market becomes more global, or at least European, those with sought-after skills have more options about where to live, especially as information technology widens choices as to where to work. However, the proportion of the population affected should not be exaggerated, and the current top marginal income tax rate of 40 per cent is still at the lower end of the international range. Further, tax is also only one part, minor for many, of what determines where people choose to live.

Within the EU's internal market there are also some constraints on the rates of indirect tax which can be imposed without provoking 'cross-border shopping' and hence loss of revenue. However, even for the most heavily taxed items - like spirits - the reaction of UK demand to price increases is still well below the point at which higher taxes would imply *lower* revenue (Davies *et al*, 1994, Table 6.12).

Summarising such effects, the constraints on policy-makers as they consider rates of tax on particular items or activities are harder than they were in the past, particularly for easily transferable investment income. A return to the kinds of tax rates imposed on some activities and income sources in the 1940s or 1950s would be impossible, but there is little evidence to suggest that the constraints imposed by international tax competition are binding at anywhere near current levels.

## Options for future tax structure

Against this background, much of the range for feasible tax reform is as open (or as closed) as ever. This section sketches some of the options which are, or could be, on the agenda, starting with the most fundamental (but perhaps the least likely).

### Fundamental reforms

There are three areas where the case for fundamental reforms has been argued in recent years. The first is the relationship between the direct tax and social security systems, where two main strains of reform can be identified. Under **social dividend** (or basic income or citizens' income) schemes, social security payments and tax allowances would be replaced by a universal flat rate amount paid to all (analogous to Child Benefit, but paid to adults) and all, or nearly all, income would be taxable. Worries about the marginal tax rates which would be needed if the social dividend was set high enough to replace the main benefits for those with no other income source have led to modified proposals for 'partial basic incomes' (Parker, 1989). Worries about the public acceptability of entirely unconditional payments have led to the suggestion of 'participation incomes', which would be a conditional addition to, rather than replacement for, social insurance benefits, but would still allow a considerable reduction in means-testing (Atkinson, 1993; Commission on Social Justice, 1994; see also Chapter 5).

An alternative direction for reform would be towards tax-benefit integration under some form of **negative income tax** arrangement (see, for instance, Dilnot, Kay and Morris, 1984), combining means-tested benefits and direct taxation in a single income assessment resulting in a net payment or receipt administered through the tax system. Whereas social dividend schemes attempt to avoid the 'poverty trap' at the cost of relatively high marginal tax rates on all income, negative income tax schemes try to rationalise the confusion of overlapping income assessments for those with low incomes, but preserve high effective marginal tax rates at the bottom end to keep down marginal rates for the majority of taxpayers.

A second area canvassed for fundamental reform is the taxation of savings, and the idea of moving to some kind of **expenditure tax** (Meade Committee, 1978; Kay and King, 1990). Instead of the base for direct taxes being a measure of an individual's income, it would become income less net saving (or plus net dis-saving). This could have advantages in terms of rationalising the current wide variations in the tax treatment of different kinds of saving, produce a system which was more robust to inflation, and might, according to some proponents, have beneficial effects on incentives to save.

The third area is that of **local taxation**. The end result of the poll tax debacle has been a structure of local government finance in which only a small proportion of local government spending is financed by locally variable taxes (the council tax) and where small variations in spending result in large variations in tax rates (Hills and Sutherland, 1991). Broadening the local tax base in some way - perhaps through a local income tax of some kind - remains an option for some.

This last area illustrates, however, the problems with proposals for sweeping fundamental reforms. Replacing domestic rates with the poll tax was a reform of this kind, and was not an experience that many would want to repeat. Fundamental reforms imply both major administrative upheaval and significant changes in individual tax liabilities. Both threaten revenue, the first because of the teething problems of getting a new system into place, the second because of the almost inevitable need to try to compensate 'losers' at least temporarily to make the change politically acceptable (see also the introduction to this volume). Lost revenue implies higher taxes elsewhere (higher VAT in the case of the transition from rates to poll tax to council tax) or lower spending, so the advantages of reform have to be substantial to be worthwhile.

Nonetheless, the ideas behind the more sweeping variants of such reforms may provide the engine for incremental changes going in the same direction. Full-blown tax-benefit integration may not be a realistic option (Clinton *et al*, 1994), but some kind of integration of benefits, pensions and direct taxes for pensioners may be (Dilnot and Johnson, 1992). We may not get a social dividend, but proposals for making the transition from 'welfare-to-work' easier embrace some of its principles (Commission on Social Justice, 1994; Barclay, 1995; see also Chapter 5). An expenditure tax may be on no party political agenda, but the introduction of tax-free forms of saving like Personal Equity Plans (PEPs) and Tax Exempt Special Saving Accounts (TESSAs) can be described (with important provisos) as moves in that direction, and proposals for their extension have been made on similar grounds (Freeman, 1992).

### Taxing 'bads'

Given the unpopularity of raising the rates of existing taxes when revenue is needed, there is an understandable attraction in the ideas for new taxes, particularly if they can be represented as 'taxes on bads' rather than 'taxes on goods'. Work is a good thing, so taxing it is self-evidently a mistake, it is argued, while pollution is a bad thing, so taxing it must be a good idea. As we (mostly) think of ourselves as engaged in 'good' activities, 'taxing bads' is a politically appealing slogan. Candidates of this kind recently proposed include a 'landfill' levy (to be implemented from 1996), a Carbon Tax (to discourage carbon dioxide emissions), various kinds of pollution taxes (or tradeable licences for particular discharges), road pricing (either for new motorways or for congested urban roads), and differential vehicle excise duties depending on fuel efficiency and other characteristics of a car (see also Chapter 10). Popular existing stand-bys for hard-pressed Chancellors include taxes on petrol, tobacco and alcohol.

There may indeed be compelling microeconomic efficiency reasons for any of these taxes on the grounds that the market does not give producers and consumers the right signals, so that imposing a tax 'internalises' what would otherwise be an external cost or benefit. But it is a great mistake to think that they constitute painless ways of boosting government revenues or substituting for other taxes. If they are really successful in curbing some undesirable activity, they raise no revenue. In order to sell them politically, they may have to be tied to compensation (as with VAT on domestic fuel) or an equivalent reduction in some other tax on the same group (as with the landfill levy), so again, little net revenue may result. If only some people or businesses change behaviour, revenue is raised, but the history of the extension of VAT to domestic fuel should disabuse people of the idea that taxing bads is going to be painless.

Further, changing relative prices is only one effect of the tax system: such taxes are unlikely to be neutral in their distributional effects. Tobacco tax is the classic example of a tax on vice which is highly regressive (Marsh, 1994), but the overall impact of some other suggestions would also be regressive (see, for instance, Smith, 1992, Table 4.2 for the regressive impact of a Carbon Tax). It is always possible, of course, to devise 'compensation' packages which would offset in broad terms such distributional effects, but only at three costs. First, as with any compensation system, revenue is sacrificed. Second, while one can demonstrate that, for instance, the poorest part of the population *as a whole* is protected from any net loss, there will usually be individuals or households within it who remain net losers. Third, compensation mechanisms 'use up' available devices for redistribution like social security spending or tax allowances. In later years what was once specific compensation becomes subsumed into the general discussion of uprating or the cost of particular spending items. When real pension levels are discussed in five years time, will the 'VAT on fuel' compensation element always be deducted? When people discuss the public expenditure cost of Child Benefit, do they always allow for the savings on Child Tax Allowances which accompanied its introduction?

All of these arguments can be seen in the case of the extension of VAT to domestic fuel (and would also arise with a more general extension of VAT to currently zero-rated items like food).

*Reforming existing taxes*

Whatever the attractions of new areas where Chancellors can both raise revenue and claim virtue, the big questions will continue to relate to familiar features of existing taxes:

- The balance between direct and indirect taxation;
- The structure of income tax rates;
- The range of tax allowances and concessions for particular kinds of saving or income, especially the future of the Married Couples Allowance and of mortgage interest tax relief now that their values have been restricted to 15 per cent;
- Abolition or phasing out of the Upper Earnings Limit for employee NICs;
- Integration of income tax and employee NICs (national insurance contributions);
- The structure of employer NICs for the low paid;

- The tax and NIC treatment of the self-employed;
- The range of items zero-rated for VAT;
- Annual uprating of specific duties and excises in relation to the rate of inflation;
- The taxation (or lack of it) of inheritance;
- Corporation Tax and the treatment of dividends, borrowing, investment, research and development, and training costs.

Many of the arguments surrounding these areas are much the same as they have always been, and the trade-offs they involve have been discussed in detail elsewhere (see, for instance: Kay and King, 1990; Hills, 1988; Davis, 1992). There is, however, one particular feature of the context in which they are debated which has changed dramatically since the late 1970s. This was highlighted by the recent Joseph Rowntree Foundation *Income and Wealth* report (Barclay, 1995). Part of its findings are reproduced in Figure 4.8. This compares the growth in real net incomes of those at the mid-points of successive tenths of the population over two periods, 1961 to 1979, and from then until 1991/92.[8] The difference between the two panels is dramatic. In the earlier period all income groups benefited from generally rising living standards, but in the more recent period those at the bottom have failed to do so. This remains the case even after allowing for potential distortions to the trends shown, like misreporting of incomes by the self-employed.

### Figure 4.8
### Change in real net income by income group

#### (a) 1961 to 1979

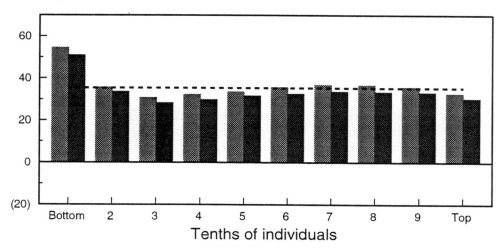

Change in income (%)

Tenths of individuals

Before housing costs   After housing costs   Overall mean (BHC)

Source: Goodman and Webb (1994)

**(b) 1979 to 1991/92**

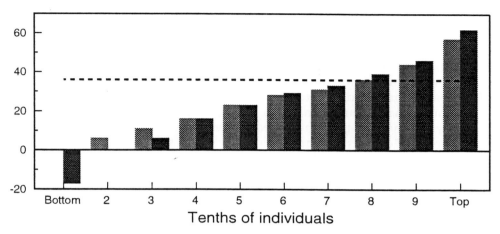

Change in income (%)

Tenths of individuals

Before housing costs   After housing costs   Overall mean (BHC)

Source: DSS (1994), Table A1 and Appendix 10

The Rowntree Inquiry Group - echoing many of the concerns of the politically more narrowly based Social Justice Commission - argued that the exclusion of a substantial minority of the population from the benefits of economic growth was a major social and economic problem. The effects of discretionary changes to taxation of the kind illustrated in Figure 4.7 were only one part of the causes of the picture shown in the lower panel of Figure 4.8. The Group's recommendations were very wide ranging: from emphasising the need for improved education and training, to action to support the residents of increasingly marginalised low income council estates and other neighbourhoods. However, tax is part of the picture, and the Group recommended that in future the balance of incremental decisions about tax structure 'should be to reduce the share of the tax burden (whatever level that is) borne by those with lower incomes' (Barclay, 1995, p.51).

To put this another way, in contrast to the changes of recent years, if taxes are rising, they should rise least at the bottom, but if they are falling, the cuts should have the greatest effects there. Self-evidently, the main tax change currently discussed as a possibility before the next election - cuts in the basic rate of income tax - would not meet such a criterion.

*Better 'marketing'*

A paradox discussed above is that people consistently report that they would like public spending increases even at the cost of higher tax, but the political debate focuses almost entirely on the idea of tax cuts. One explanation advanced for this is the way in which tax and spending decisions have been 'disconnected' (Mulgan and Murray, 1993).  By implication, if they were better connected the paradox could be resolved.  Specifically, if more taxes were earmarked or 'hypothecated', voters could put more trust in politicians to spend money in the way they would like.  Interestingly, the recent Commission on Social Justice (1994) rejected one of the main ideas for a major extension of hypothecation, an 'NHS tax' substituting for part of income tax, on the grounds that it would lead to an increase in health spending of which the Commission disapproved (but which voters appear to want).  There also remain powerful economic arguments against hypothecation (see Wilkinson, 1994), mostly coming down to the problem that satisfactory matching of revenue sources and spending needs is impossible.  Some services end up with more buoyant revenues than they need, others with fixed revenues in the face of rising need.  Mechanisms which bridge such gaps subvert hypothecation by allowing the Treasury control over 'equalisation' payments, reducing the link between revenue and spending to one of form only (as can be argued to be the case for National Insurance Contributions, the main existing example of hypothecation).

Nonetheless, whatever the technical merits of unified revenue and spending accounts, some forms of hypothecation may prove the only way to reconcile pressures for spending increases with the taxes needed to finance them.  If, as Mulgan and Murray argue, part of the problem is that tax and spending decisions have become disconnected, the 'marketing' advantages of linking changes in the two at the margin may become irresistible.  Specific cases of this kind might include the following:

(a) **Long term care insurance**, paid for through a premium on national insurance payments (as recently implemented in Germany);

(b) An income-contingent **student loan scheme**, under which expanded spending on higher education would be recouped through later repayments linked to future earnings through the national insurance system (Barr, Glennerster and Falkingham, 1995);

(c) A **training levy** on firms with low direct spending on training, aimed at reducing the 'free rider' problem which leads to sub-optimal spending on training (possibly linked to the income-contingent loan idea to create a kind of revolving fund for higher education and training through a 'Learning Bank' as proposed by the Commission on Social Justice and discussed in Chapter 6).

(d) A locally-administered **transport levy** on business under which a percentage of wage bills (or an addition to business rates) would be used to improve local transport or other infrastructure (as with the long-standing 'one per cent' or 'patronal' in France used mainly for subsidising housing).  Crucially the receipts from such a levy would be used locally, rather than absorbed into the equalisation system of local government finance.

Ideas like these have three things in common: they involve the provision of new or additional services; they are areas where private benefits are involved (rather than pure redistribution) but where communal or pooled provision may be more efficient than purely private arrangements; and the extra tax levied comes from a group which can also broadly be identified as beneficiaries. In such cases the 'connecting' advantages of earmarking may allow services to develop, while under a purer system of unified revenues this simply would might not occur.

## Conclusion

In one sense the conclusion of this review is that the options for tax policy remain wide open, both in terms of the overall level of tax and spending as a share of national income, and in terms of the structure of the tax system. This does not mean, however, that tax policy changes are easy. Changes in the balance of taxation tend to come incrementally; historically, the British tax ratio has been kept within a narrow band; and any major reform is liable to need expensive 'compensation' or transitional arrangements to smooth its path. Crucially, discussion of tax options needs to be less divorced from the reason why taxation is there - the need to raise revenue to finance public spending in the fairest and most efficient way. As a corollary, proposals for changes in the tax burden have to be linked to their consequences - positive or negative - for spending. In the last two years, the Opposition has been very successful in drawing public attention to the scale of tax increases being implemented by a Government which had appeared to promise the opposite. The danger in such success is that it leaves behind the message that taxation *per se* is a bad thing. But tax is a price, and like any other price it can only be evaluated in terms of what one buys with it. If people value the things financed through taxation - health, education, pensions, defence, redistribution towards those otherwise excluded from the mainstream - highly enough, the 'price' may be seen as a bargain, particularly if the private supply of the same items, such as health, would be more expensive. By implication, to discuss tax without mentioning spending may be as irresponsible as to promise spending without saying where the money is going to come from.

There is, however, a final catch for those trying to formulate policy options from outside government. Table 4.4 shows the result of comparing Treasury forecasts for general government tax revenue (including NICs) made in March Budgets for the coming financial year (i.e. for 1982-83 in the 1982 Budget) and for the following year (i.e. 1983-84 in 1982) with the eventual outcomes given the March after the financial year end.[9]

Table 4.4
Treasury Forecasting Errors[1]
(£ billion)

| Forecast made in: | March forecast for coming financial year | March forecast for subsequent financial year[2] |
|---|---|---|
| 1982 | -1 | 0 |
| 1983 | -2 | -2 |
| 1984 | -1 | -4 |
| 1985 | -1 | -1 |
| 1986 | -3 | -13 |
| 1987 | -6 | -16 |
| 1988 | -5 | -9 |
| 1989 | -1 | -6 |
| 1990 | 0 | +6 |
| 1991 | +5 | +18 |
| 1992 | +11 | +25 |
| 1993 | +1 | +2[3] |

Notes:   1  Red Book forecasts of general government taxes and NICs compared to out-
             turn one year after financial year end.   Under-estimates negative; over-
             estimates positive.
         2  Adjusted for impact of tax changes made after Budget (using Red Book figures
             for impact compared to indexed base).
         3  Compared to estimated out-turn in November 1994 (forecast for 1994-95).
Source:   HM Treasury (1994) and earlier equivalents.

The results for the forecasts made between 1982 and 1989 are reassuring and
perhaps unsurprising. For the coming financial year, as one would expect from
a cautious Treasury constantly negotiating with spending departments, the
forecasts consistently *under*-estimate tax revenue, by an amount averaging £2-3
billion. For the forecast for following years the error is greater - an under-
estimate averaging £6-7 billion.
   The forecasts made after this become considerably worse, however, especially
in 1991 and 1992, before returning to comparative accuracy in March 1993.
The March 1992 Budget *over*-estimated 1992-93 tax revenue by £11 billion, and
1993-94 revenue by £25 billion (adjusted for subsequent tax increases). In other
words, the March 1992 tax cuts were made, and the 1992 General Election
campaign was fought, against a forecast for tax revenue which was wrong by
1.8 per cent of GDP for 1992-93 - equivalent to 5 pence on the basic and lower
rates of income tax. Looking ahead to 1993-94, the March 1992 over-estimate
was nearly 4 per cent of GDP, astonishing by comparison with Treasury
forecasts made in the 1980s, and which has, of course, a great deal to do with
subsequent tax increases and government unpopularity.

Against such a background, Opposition politicians might be forgiven for taking the rather hackneyed line that, 'nothing can be decided until we've seen the books'. There certainly *are* options for tax policy, but there is also a strong case for keeping those options open.

## Notes

1. The meaning of this ratio has changed slightly over time as some policy changes have transformed what had been tax allowances into public spending, raising the tax ratio without necessarily affecting anything material (as when child tax allowances were subsumed into Child Benefit in the late 1970s), while others have had the opposite effect (as with the transformation of Statutory Sick Pay into amounts paid by employers, but offset by tax reductions).
2. The cash flows shown in Figure 4.4 are drawn up in nominal terms, which do not reflect the public sector's real position accurately if the real value of its debts is being eroded by inflation, or - to put it another way - if part of its spending on debt interest included in total spending represents compensation for this effect (Taylor and Threadgold, 1979).
3. For further discussion of the public sector balance sheet and of the methods used to derive the figures in Table 4.1, see Hills (1989).
4. This could be moderated if it was some form of minimum pension guarantee which was income-linked rather than all pensions. See Commission on Social Justice (1994: 267-272) for a discussion of the options (also outlined in Chapter 5, Box 5.2).
5. See Blundell (1992) for a survey of the literature of the effects of taxation on labour supply.
6. Even in April 1995, with most of the tax increases at least known about (even if some had not quite taken effect), a *Guardian*-ICM poll was still recording similar results. Sixty per cent of the sample agreed that government spending on 'services such as schools and hospitals' should rise, even if the basic rate of income tax had to rise from 25p to 30p in the pound, while only 26 per cent disagreed (*Guardian*, 13 April 1995). Conversely, only 15 per cent wanted the basic rate cut to 20p if this meant cutting such spending, with 76 per cent disagreeing. Compared to the 1993 *BSAS* results this suggests little change in the proportion wanting higher spending, but some increase in the minority wanting lower spending.
7. The CSO also produces estimates for the distribution of the tax burden, including intermediate taxes, between households arranged by decile group of disposable income (e.g. CSO, 1994b). In recent years these have suggested an almost proportional impact of the tax system, apart from a *higher* tax burden for the poorest group (partly distorted by the treatment of Council Tax benefit), and a *lower* tax burden for the richest tenth.
8. 1979 is taken as the break-point as it represents both the point at which the real after housing costs incomes of the poorest tenth stopped growing, and the point at which the official DSS series begins.
9. November 1993 for the out-turn for 1992-93 and November 1994 for the 1993-94 out-turn and forecast out-turn for 1994-95.

# References

Atkinson, A.B. (1993), *Beveridge, the National Minimum, and its Future in a European Context*, LSE Welfare State Programme Discussion Paper No. **85**.

Barclay, P. (chairman) (1995), *Income and Wealth*, Vol. **1**, York: Joseph Rowntree Foundation.

Barr, N., Falkingham, J. and Glennerster, H. (1995), 'Education funding, equity and the life cycle', in Falkingham, J. and Hills, J. (eds.), *The Dynamic of Welfare: the Welfare State and the Life Cycle*, Hemel Hempstead: Prentice Hall/Harvester Wheatsheaf.

Blundell, R. (1992), 'Labour supply and taxation: a survey', *Fiscal Studies*, **13** (3), pp.15-40.

Central Statistical Office (December, 1992), 'International comparisons of taxes and social security contributions in 20 OECD countries, 1980-1990', *Economic Trends*, No. **470**.

Central Statistical Office (February) (1994a), 'Taxes and social security contributions: an international comparison, 1981-1991', *Economic Trends*, No. **484**.

Central Statistical Office (December) 1994b), 'The effects of taxes and benefits on household income, 1993', *Economic Trends*, No. **494**.

Clinton, D., Yates, M. and Kang, D. (1994), *Integrating Taxes and Benefits?*, Commission on Social Justice issue paper, No.**8**, London: IPPR.

Commission on Social Justice (1994), *Social Justice: Strategies for National Renewal*, London: Vintage.

Davies, G., Dilnot, A., Giles, C. and Walton D. (1994), *Options for 1995: The Green Budget*, IFS Commentary, No.**46**, London: IFS.

Davis, E. (ed.) (1992), *Tax Reform for the Fourth Term*, IFS Commentary No.**32**, London: IFS.

Department of Social Security (1994), *Households Below Average Incomes: A Statistical Analysis 1979-1991/92*, London: HMSO.

Dilnot, A. and Johnson, P. (1992), 'What pension should the state provide?', *Fiscal Studies*, **13** (4), pp.1-20.

Dilnot, A., Kay, J. and Morris, N. (1984), *The Reform of Social Security*, Oxford: Oxford University Press.

Freeman, H. (1992), 'Towards a national investment tax', in Davis, E. (ed.), *Tax Reform for the Fourth Term*, IFS Commentary, No. **32**, London: IFS.

Giles, C. and Johnson, P. (1994), 'Tax reform in the UK and changes in the progressivity of the tax system', *Fiscal Studies*, **15** (3), pp.64-86.

Glennerster, H. (1995), 'Opportunity costs', *New Economy*, **2** (2), pp.110-114.

Goodman, A. and Webb, S. (1994), *For Richer, for Poorer: The Changing Distribution of Income in the UK 1961-91*, IFS Commentary, No. **42**, London: IFS.

Heath, A., Jowell, R. and Curtice, J. (eds.) (1994), *Labour's Last Chance? The 1992 Election and Beyond*, Aldershot: Dartmouth.

Hills, J. (1988), *Changing Tax: How the Tax System Works and How to Change it*, London: CPAG Ltd.

Hills, J. (1989), 'Counting the family silver: the public sector's balance sheet 1957 to 1987', *Fiscal Studies*, **10** (2), pp.66-85.

Hills, J. (1993), *The Future of Welfare: A Guide to the Debate*, York: Joseph Rowntree Foundation.

Hills, J. (1995), *Income and Wealth*, Vol. **2**, York: Joseph Rowntree Foundation.

Hills, J. and Sutherland, H. (1991), 'The proposed Council Tax', *Fiscal Studies* **12** (4), pp.1-21.

HM Treasury (1994), *Financial Statement and Budget Report 1995-96*, HC (94-95) 12, London: HMSO.

Kay, J. and King, M. (1980), *The British Tax System* (second edition), Oxford: Oxford University Press.

Kay, J. and King, M. (1990), *The British Tax System* (fifth edition), Oxford: Oxford University Press.

Lipsey, D. (1994), 'Do we really want more public spending?', in Jowell, R., Curtice, J., Brook, L. and Ahrendt, D. (eds.), *British Social Attitudes: the 11th report*, Aldershot: Dartmouth.

Marsh, A. (1994), *Poor Smokers*, London: Policy Studies Institute.

Meade Committee (1978), *The Structure and Reform of Direct Taxation*, London: George Allen and Unwin.

Mulgan, G. and Murray, R. (1993), *Reconnecting Taxation*, London: DEMOS.

National Commission on Education (1993), *Learning to Succeed: A Radical Look at Education Today and a Strategy for the Future*, London: Heinemann.

Parker, H. (1989), *Instead of the Dole*, London: Routledge.

Redmond, G. and Sutherland, H. (1995), *How has Tax and Social Security Policy Changed Since 1978? A Distributional Analysis*, Microsimulation Unit Discussion Paper (forthcoming), Cambridge: Department of Applied Economics.

Smith, S. (1992), 'Tax and the environment: the EC carbon tax proposals', in Davis, E. (ed.), *Tax Reform for the Fourth Term*, IFS Commentary, No. **32**, London: IFS.

Taylor, C.T. and Threadgold, A.R. (1979), *'Real' National Saving and its Sectoral Composition*, Bank of England Discussion Paper No.6, London: Bank of England.

Twigger, R. (1994), *The Burden of Taxation*, House of Commons Library Research Paper 94/66, London: House of Commons Library.

Wilkinson, M. (1994), 'Paying for public spending: is there a role for earmarked taxes?', *Fiscal Studies*, **15** (4), pp.119-35.

## Acknowledgements

The author is very grateful for comments and suggestions from Gavin Cameron, Andrew Dilnot, Howard Glennerster and Gerry Holtham, as well as from other participants in the 'Options for Britain' conference in December 1994. The author is particularly grateful to Philippe Legrain for research assistance and to the Yoko and Michio Morishima Fund for the financial support which allowed this paper to be written.

# 5 The welfare state: options against poverty

*Ruth Lister* [*]

This chapter will focus on income maintenance policy, leaving to later chapters the service and care elements of the welfare state. It is divided into four main sections which will:

- consider briefly the constraints which circumscribe any programme of reform;
- outline the key broad issues which underlie the more specific choices we face concerning the future of income maintenance policy;
- examine some of those specific choices; and, in particular,
- discuss the implications of the growing consensus around the central importance of an effective 'welfare-to-work' strategy.

In considering the policy options, I shall take as my reference point the reform programme outlined in *Social Justice: Strategies for National Renewal*, the report of the Borrie Commission on Social Justice (CSJ, 1994), drawing also on the more recent report of the Joseph Rowntree Inquiry into Income and Wealth (JRF, 1995). An income maintenance strategy akin to that outlined in the Borrie Report offers, I shall argue, both a feasible and (for those committed to the enhancement of social justice) attractive way forward for Britain.

## The parameters of reform

Economic growth, levels of unemployment and taxation policy constitute the key parameters constraining what governments are able to do in the field of

[*] Professor of Social Policy and Administration at Loughborough University.

welfare policy.    Since these parameters have been extensively discussed in earlier chapters, I will deal with the possible constraints facing welfare reformers only briefly here, under the headings of the notion of a welfare crisis and the implications of economic globalisation.

*Crisis, what crisis?*

The language of crisis, as applied to the welfare state, has surfaced at intervals over the past two decades.  As Christopher Pierson (1991) has noted, the notion of crisis has a broad range of meanings in this context.  The theme of financial crisis currently reflects the impact of high unemployment and demographic trends.    That of ideological crisis relates to a broader philosophical challenge to the role of the state and a reassertion of the centrality of the market, the family, and voluntary provision, in the name of promoting personal independence, as well as to an appeal to claims of public disaffection with welfare institutions.[1]  Even if the evidence for an actual crisis is rather thin, Pierson suggests that this may all add up to something of an intellectual crisis - a crisis which the report of the Commission on Social Justice (CSJ, 1994) has attempted to resolve.

Although he does not use the term 'crisis', the theme of financial crisis surfaces clearly in the present Social Security Secretary Peter Lilley's recent interventions in the debate over the future of social security.  Lilley's argument is premised on warnings about the implications of the continued 'remorseless growth' in social security expenditure (now checked by a series of measures which, according to Lilley (1995b), will cut the social security budget by £5 billion a year in current prices by the end of the century and by more than double that in the longer term).  However, the assumptions underlying the figures in the DSS document *The Growth of Social Security*, and the conclusions reached in it, have been challenged by Oppenheim (1994) among others. Indeed, the Government-appointed Social Security Advisory Committee began its contribution to Mr Lilley's debate by explicitly distancing itself from the idea that 'the cost of the social security system is out of control' (SSAC, 1993; p.43).  It also pointed out that part of the growth in social security expenditure in recent years is attributable to the government's own policies.  This is most notable in housing where a policy of increasing real rent levels has fed into a significant increase in expenditure on housing benefit, prompting a series of cutbacks in the benefit (see Chapter 11).

Perhaps the most thorough recent assessment of the level of British welfare spending has been that of John Hills (1993) for the Joseph Rowntree Foundation.  He notes that over the past 20 years or so, Britain's welfare spending has been fairly stable as a proportion of GDP and below that of most other industrialised countries.  While he accepts that welfare spending will come under pressure from demographic trends, he rejects the popular notion of a demographic time-bomb and of welfare policy being severely boxed in by fiscal constraints: there is still scope for real choices about the future of welfare, and the more so the lower the level of unemployment (see Chapter 4).

that across a large range of the political spectrum 'a consensus on how to redesign social security so that it promotes work rather than prevents it is starting to emerge'. (See Box 5.4 below for a summary of the main elements of welfare-to-work strategies of the kind contained in the reports of the Social Justice Commission and the Joseph Rowntree Inquiry into Income and Wealth.)

Despite this consensus, however, there remain very real differences revolving around two key issues. First, how should that work be rewarded? The present government appears to want to price the unemployed into low paid work, free of any minimum wages protection and with minimum employment rights, subsidised by means-tested benefits. This approach was spelt out by Peter Lilley (1994) in a recent lecture where he singled out 'the growing dispersion of earnings power' as 'probably the single most significant social change affecting the UK and most other Western countries', suggesting that 'it may play a major part in the break-up of families, the growth of lone parenthood, and a growing welfare dependency' (pp.4 and 6). He was adamant that a minimum wage did not form part of the solution which instead lies, he argued, in encouraging 'people looking for jobs to acquire the skills, training and education that make them attractive to employers and which mean that employers can afford to offer them higher wages' (p.9). He also emphasised the central importance of 'creating and maintaining incentives to work' which are endangered 'the closer benefits levels are to unskilled wages' (pp.9-10). As 'we do not want to reduce the level of existing benefits to the unemployed to reduce incentives', the answer lies in in-work means-tested benefits.

The CSJ on the other hand predicates its welfare-to-work strategy on a minimum wage, a Jobs, Education and Training Programme to raise the skills of the long-term unemployed and lone parents, higher child benefits and a child care strategy. These measures, taken together, should reduce, although not eliminate, reliance on means-tested benefits. A minimum wage is crucial to this strategy, for without it employers would be free to reduce the wages offered to low paid workers in the knowledge that the tax-payer can pick up the tab through the means-tested benefit system. The JRF inquiry was unable to reach agreement on the issue of a minimum wage.

Secondly, should claimants be encouraged into work by the 'carrot' or the 'stick'? The Government is increasingly reaching for the stick, tempered by a few carrots; the CSJ prioritises the carrots. These different approaches reflect different underlying assumptions about the motivations of benefit claimants and about whether the underlying problem is a growing 'dependency culture' (a thesis unproven by research, see, for instance, Taylor-Gooby and Dean, 1993; Kempson et al, 1994) or barriers in the benefits system itself. In fact, there is growing agreement as to the need to dismantle the barriers in the benefits system, as exemplified by some (though not all) of the measures in the 1994 Budget, while some Labour spokespersons have recently, and somewhat uncritically, deployed the notion of a 'dependency culture'.

**Box 5.4: Welfare-to-work: The main elements of the strategy**

The welfare-to-work (WTW) strategy may be said to have two basic objectives: (1) to maintain/increase *incentives* to work (reducing barriers to work created by the benefits system itself); and (2) to maintain/increase *capabilities* for employment. The two objectives are obviously closely related in that capabilities determine market opportunities and, therefore, incentives. Some elements on the WTW strategy are focused more immediately on incentives, others on capabilities. What follows is therefore a very rough breakdown. The various policy proposals are gleaned from the reports of the Social Justice Commission and the Joseph Rowntree Inquiry into Income and Wealth; there is much overlap between their respective policy recommendations, though there are inevitably some differences (e.g., the Social Justice Commission is more cautious about 'in-work' benefits, clearly wishing to relegate them to a residual role over the long-term).

a.   **Capability-promoting policies (improving employability)**

- Better access to childcare (especially for lone parents).
- Education and training programmes for those most lacking in job-related skills (perhaps on the model of the Social Justice Commission's proposed Jobs, Education and Training programme, already alluded to above). The question arises as to whether participation in such programmes should be voluntary or compulsory for benefit recipients.
- Direct or indirect state provision of employment. Either the state acts as employer of the last resort, employing the long-term unemployed on job guarantee schemes, or the state provides subsidies to other employers to take on the long-term unemployed (see Chapter 3). The question of voluntary or compulsory participation in such schemes arises once again.

b.   **Incentives-promoting policies (making sure that 'work pays', reducing 'barriers' within the benefits system)**

- All of the above in so far as they also increase the expected return on work.
- Some combination of a minimum wage and 'in-work' benefits. As far as the latter are concerned, one possibility would be to reform Family Credit, expanding its range of coverage to include childless couples and single people, and reducing rates of benefit withdrawal to lessen the poverty trap.
- Other incentives-promoting reforms of the benefits system:
  i.   Higher and more flexible earnings disregards for Income Support.
  ii.  Allowing people to keep Income Support after entering work while their Family Credit entitlement is calculated, and automatically re-entitling people to it if they lose their jobs within some specified period after coming off Income Support.
- Retention and improvement of individualised national insurance benefits where they exist (see Box 5.3). These should not be replaced with means-tested benefits which tend to reduce work incentives for the partners of the unemployed.

*Stuart White*

The growing consensus around the need for an effective welfare-to-work strategy is in many ways welcome. Nevertheless, it is not without its difficulties and tensions. First, and most obviously, its success depends on sufficient work being available. How realistic this assumption is is the subject of earlier chapters (see especially Chapters 2 and 3). But what if sufficient jobs do not materialise? The failure of the strategy because of insufficient jobs could simply serve to demoralise those looking for the jobs even further. If at the end of the day, we are not able to return to anything approaching full employment (for women as well as men), does the citizen's income approach then come into its own? Certainly it starts to become more viable politically in the sense that it could become accepted that paid work cannot provide an income for a significant section of the population. However, one must wonder whether the resources would be there to pay for it under this gloomier economic scenario.

A second problem is how to balance the imperative of an anti-poverty strategy through paid work with recognition of the value of unpaid caring work. Linked to this is the question of how best to ensure an independent income for those providing care (still mainly women) through the benefits system without at the same time reinforcing the sexual division of labour by effectively locking them out of the labour market (see Lister, 1992; 1994). The proposals for a modernised social insurance system and a participation income go some way towards resolving this tension, but they do not do so completely.

A further important tension is between an emphasis on getting people into paid work and the need to tackle the poverty of those who are not in a position to do so. The CSJ's report does acknowledge the existence and needs of the latter group. It notes the inadequacy of current benefit levels and it calls for government to commit itself to the principle of a benchmark 'minimum income standard', at a level 'considered sufficient to cover essential needs with regard to respect for human dignity' (a European Commission formulation), and to commission the necessary research for the purpose of reviewing benefit levels. It also recommends fundamental reform of the social fund. The JRF Inquiry recommends that benefits should be increased by more than inflation when living standards in general are rising so as to reduce the growing gap between those on benefit and the rest of the population and thereby give the former a share in rising living standards.

Of course, raising benefits costs money and the further the Labour Party moves from its traditional commitment to redistribution in its attempt to portray itself as the party of low taxation, the less money there will be to meet the immediate needs of those suffering poverty and deprivation. The failure to signal more clearly the need for significant redistribution back to the poor after 15 years in which income inequality has increased dramatically and poverty has grown to its present alarmingly high level (see Box 5.1 above) has been one of the criticisms levelled at the Commission's report.

While it was not for the Commission to propose short-term increases in particular benefits, and research suggests that claimants themselves would prefer jobs to benefit increases (see, for instance, Kempson *et al*, 1994), there are good arguments for why a future government of the centre-left should combine some immediate help for the less well-off with the kind of structural strategy proposed by the Commission. This might appear to offer more immediate choice - and hope - to those for whom the welfare-to-work strategy is not going to deliver the goods immediately, whilst also setting in place a longer term programme which will open up genuine opportunities for those currently trapped on benefit.

## Conclusion

This chapter has outlined some of the key choices for the reform of income maintenance which will face an incoming government. The position adopted has largely reflected that propounded in the report of the Commission on Social Justice and to a lesser extent in the report of the Joseph Rowntree Foundation Inquiry into Income and Wealth. In terms of the three main continuums which constitute the axes of policy choices, I have made the case for a more universalist position on the universal *versus* targeting continuum, the merits of public provision within a 'mixed economy of welfare' on the public-private continuum and for a middle point in the conditional *versus* unconditional continuum.

More specifically, I would argue that the main building blocks for the reform of income maintenance by a government committed to social justice should be on the one hand a modernised and strengthened social insurance scheme (which reflects women's as well as men's patterns of work - unpaid as well as paid) and on the other a clear 'welfare-to-work' strategy supported by a minimum wage and investment in child benefit and child care. In addition, action must be taken to tackle the poverty experienced by those who, either in the short or longer term, will be unable to cross the welfare-to-work bridge and to reduce the gap between their living standards and those of the wider population. The case for reform is urgent and compelling; whilst any programme of reform will take time to implement, it is essential that clear goals are established as soon as possible.

## Notes

1. Of course, the themes of financial and ideological crisis are interlinked for it is in the interests of those mounting an ideological challenge to the welfare state to be able to buttress their arguments with claims of a current or incipient financial crisis.
2. For a detailed exposition of the problems with private unemployment insurance see Barr, 1994.
3. The issue has been side-stepped to some extent by using the Child Support Act, coupled with benefit incentives to encourage 'full-time' work, to reduce lone parents' reliance on income support.

## References

Amin, K. with Oppenheim, C. (1992), *Poverty in Black and White*, London: Child Poverty Action Group/Runnymede Trust.

Atkinson, A. B. (1993), *Beveridge, the National Minimum, and its Future in a European Context*, London: STICERD.

Barr, N. (1994), 'Private unemployment insurance: myths and realities', *Benefits* **10**, pp.1-4.

*Benefits* (1994), Race, *Benefits* **9**, pp.1-15.

Beresford, P. and Croft, S. (1993), *Citizen Involvement*, Basingstoke: Macmillan.

Blank, R. (1994), 'Does a larger social safety net mean less economic flexibility?', in Freeman, R. B. (ed.), *Working under Different Rules*, New York: Russell Sage Foundation.

Bryson, A. and Jacobs, J. (1992), *Policing the Workshy*, Aldershot: Avebury.

Burkitt, B. and Baimbridge, M. (1994/95), 'The Maastricht Treaty's impact on the welfare state', *Critical Social Policy*, No. **42**, pp.100-11.

Carr, M. (1993), 'Women, pensions and the state', *Benefits*, No. **8**, pp.9-13.

Clinton, D., Yates, M. and Kang, D. (1994), *Integrating Taxes and Benefits?*, London: Commission on Social Justice/IPPR.

Cohen, S. (1993), 'Geo-economics and America's mistakes', in Carnoy, M., Castells, M., Cohen, S.S. and Cardoso, F.H. (eds.), *The New Global Economy in the Information Age*, Pennsylvania: Pennsylvania State University Press.

Corry, D. and Glyn, A. (1994), 'The macroeconomics of equality, stability and growth', in Glyn, A. and Miliband, D. (eds.), *Paying for Inequality: The Economic Costs of Social Injustice*, London: IPPR/Rivers Oram Press.

Crine, S. (1994), *Reforming Welfare: American Lessons*, London: Fabian Society.

Croft, S. and Beresford, P. (1989), 'User involvement: citizenship and social policy', *Critical Social Policy*, No. **26**, pp.5-18.

Commission on Social Justice (1994), *Social Justice: Strategies for National Renewal*, London: Vintage.

Dean, H. and Taylor-Gooby, P. (1992), *Dependency Culture*, Hemel Hempstead: Harvester Wheatsheaf.

DEG/DSS (1994), *Jobseeker's Allowance (White Paper)*, London: HMSO.

DSS (1993), *Containing the Cost of Social Security - the International Context*, London: HMSO.

Ellwood, D. (1988), *Poor Support: Poverty in the American Family*, New York: Basic Books.

Esam, P. and Berthoud, R. (1991), *Independent Benefits for Men and Women*, London: Policy Studies Institute.

Esping-Anderson, G. (1990), *The Three Worlds of Welfare Capitalism*, Cambridge: Polity Press.

Esping-Anderson, G. (1994), 'Equality and work in the Post-industrial Life-cycle', in Miliband, D. (ed.), *Reinventing the Left*, Cambridge: IPPR/Polity Press.

Falkingham, J. and Hills, J. (eds.) (1995), *The Dynamic of Welfare: The Welfare State and the Life Cycle*, Hemel Hempstead: Prentice Hall/Harvester Wheatsheaf.

Ford, J., Kempson, E. and Wilson, M. (1994), *Mortgage Arrears and Possessions; Perspectives from Borrowers, Lenders and the Courts*, London: HMSO/Department of the Environment.

Gray, J. (1994), *The Undoing of Conservatism*, London: Social Market Foundation.

Heath, A., Jowell, R. and Curtice, J. (1994), *Labour's Last Chance: The 1992 Election and Beyond*, Aldershot: Dartmouth.

Hills, J. (1993), *The Future of Welfare: A Guide to the Debate*, York: Joseph Rowntree Foundation.

JRF Inquiry (1995), *Joseph Rowntree Foundation Inquiry into Income and Wealth*, York: Joseph Rowntree Foundation.

Kempson, E., Bryson, A. and Rowlingson, K. (1994), *Hard Times?*, London: Policy Studies Institute.

King, D. (1995), *Actively Seeking Work*, Chicago and London: University of Chicago Press.

Kleinman, M. and Piachaud, D. (1993), 'European social policy: conceptions and choices', *Journal of European Social Policy*, **3** (1), pp.1-19.

Lilley, P. (1995a), *Speech to the Social Market Foundation*, 9 January: London.

Lilley, P. (1993), *Mais Lecture*, 23 June.

Lilley, P. (1994), *Widening Pay Differentials*, Northern Ireland: Conservative Political Centre in Northern Ireland.

Lilley, P. (1995b), Foreword, *Politics Today*, 1, London: Conservative Research Department.

Lister, R. (1990), *The Exclusive Society*, London: Child Poverty Action Group.

Lister, R. (1992), *Women's Economic Dependency and Social Security*, Manchester: Equal Opportunities Commission.

Lister, R. (1994), '"She has other duties" - women, citizenship and social security', in Baldwin, S. and Falkingham, J. (eds.), *Social Security and Social Change*, Hemel Hempstead: Harvester Wheatsheaf.

Lister, R. (1995a), 'Social Justice: radical plan or washout?', *Poverty* 90, pp. 10-11.

Lister, R. (1995b), 'Back to the family: family policies and politics under the Major government', in Jones, H. and Millar, J. (eds.), *The Politics of the Family*, Aldershot: Avebury.

Lister, R. (forthcoming), *Feminist Perspectives on Citizenship*, Basingstoke: Macmillan.

Luckhaus, L. (1994), 'Individualisation of social security benefits', in McCrudden, C. (ed.), *Equality of Treatment between Women and Men in Social Security*, London: Butterworths.

Mama, A. (1992), 'Black women and the British state', in Braham, P. (ed.), *Racism and Anti-Racism*, London: Sage.

Marshall, T. H. (1950), *Citizenship and Social Class*, Cambridge: Cambridge University Press.

Mead, L. (1986), *Beyond Entitlement: The Social Obligations of Citizenship*, New York: The Free Press.

Moore, J. (1988), *Speech to Conservative Party Conference*, 12 October.

NACAB (1991), *Barriers to Benefit*, London: National Association of Citizens Advice Bureaux.

NACAB (1993), *Dispossessed*, London: National Association of Citizens Advice Bureaux.

Novak, M. and Cogan, J. (1987), *The New Consensus on Family and Welfare*, Washington: American Enterprise Institute for Public Policy Research.

Oppenheim, C. (1994), *The Welfare State: Putting the Record Straight*, London: CPAG.

Pierson, C. (1991), *Beyond the Welfare State*, Cambridge: Polity.

Roll, J. (1991), *What is a Family?*, London: Family Policy Studies Centre.

SSAC (1994), *State Benefits and Private Provision*, Leeds: BA Publishing Services.

SSAC (1993), *Ninth Report*, London: HMSO.

The Sheffield Group (1989), *The Social Economy and the Democratic State*, London: Lawrence & Wishart.

Timmins, N. (1995a), 'A powerful indictment of the Eighties', *The Independent*, 10 February.

Timmins, N. (1995b), 'We can't all buy personal security', *The Independent*, 10 May.

Titmuss, R. (1968), 'The right to social security', in Lynes, T. (ed.), *Unequal Rights*, London: Child Poverty Action Group/London Co-operative Education Department.

Walker, R. (1991), *Thinking about Workfare: Evidence from the USA*, London: Social Policy Research Unit/HMSO.

White, S. (1995), 'Liberal equality, exploitation and the case for an unconditional basic income', in Lovenduski, J. and Stanyer, J. (eds.), *Contemporary Political Studies 1995*, Vol. 1, Exeter: Political Studies Association.

## Acknowledgements

I would like to thank Stuart White and the editorial group for their helpful comments on earlier drafts of this chapter.

# 6 Education and training

*Josh Hillman* [*]

## Introduction

The idea that we should progress towards a 'learning society' has become something of a mantra in statements on, and proposals for, the future of education and training, whether by political parties, industrialists, educationalists or think-tanks (Husen, 1974; Ranson, 1994; NCE, 1993; Labour Party, 1994). It would be difficult to argue against the concept as an ideal underlying a policy framework. However, even if we could agree on exactly what was meant by the term, it would be very difficult to measure, or to know when and whether it would have been achieved. First, because much learning takes place outside of educational institutions. Second, because the benefits of learning, whether relating to competitiveness or quality of life, are often subtle and slow-releasing. Third, because we learn not just as individuals, but also as families, organisations, associations and communities (Hayes *et al*, 1995).

Britain urgently requires an official, but independent, evaluation of education and training provision, and of progress towards a learning society. Such an evaluation could be carried out annually. The first section of this chapter attempts a more limited overview, based mainly on comparisons with other countries. The challenges for education and training posed now and in the decades to come are then briefly set out. The chapter outlines six areas of education and training in which Britain is failing to face up to these challenges. Responses to these challenges are then suggested such that government policy can have most impact on creating a learning society.

---

[*] Research Fellow at the Institute for Public Policy Research.

## How is Britain doing?

*Pre-school provision*

On average, British children start formal education later than their counterparts in other European countries. International comparisons of pre-school provision are notoriously difficult to compile, since definitions of appropriate services are disputed, children attend for different numbers of hours a day, and funding comes from a variety of sources, both public and private. Table 6.1 shows Britain to be well down the league table of participation rates for both three- and four-year-olds. Including private playgroups would move Britain up the table, but basing it on full-time equivalent places would bring Britain back down again.

#### Table 6.1  % of children attending publicly funded early childhood care and education services *

|          | Three-year-olds | Four-year-olds |
|----------|-----------------|----------------|
| France   | 98              | 100            |
| Belgium  | 97              | 99             |
| Denmark  | 76              | 81             |
| Sweden   | 63              | 67             |
| Norway   | 49              | 60             |
| Finland  | 44              | 49             |
| **Britain** | **41**       | **58**         |
| Spain    | 28              | 94             |
| Portugal | 28              | 44             |

\* 1992 for Scandinavian countries, 1991 for others
Source: Moss, 1994

Compulsory schooling starts at a relatively early age in Britain, but even looking at the three- to five-year-old age range as a whole, the 65 per cent of children in publicly funded services in Britain is well below other countries, including France (99 per cent), Italy (91 per cent) and Germany (77 per cent). There are also great variations in different parts of the country. In some local authorities in Britain there is de facto universal primary provision for four-year-olds, with over 90 per cent of under-fives in public sector classes and schools (DfE, 1995). In other authorities, less than 20 per cent of under-fives are covered by public provision.

*Achievement and basic skills at school*

In the fifty years since the war there has been little change in reading standards amongst eleven- and fifteen-year-olds, except for slight rises around 1950 and in the 1980s (Brooks *et al*, 1995). Researchers at the National Foundation for Educational Research, however, showed a fall in the average reading scores of seven- and eight-year-olds between 1987 and 1991 (Gorman and Fernandes, 1992).

Between 1982 and 1987, there was a fall in attainment amongst eleven- and fifteen-year-olds in arithmetic, and a rise in geometry and statistics (Brooks *et al*, 1995). This is reflected in recent international surveys of achievement in mathematics which show that thirteen-year-olds in England are below the international average in arithmetic and above average in geometry and statistics. Meanwhile top-ability English eighteen-year-olds are among the best performers in maths, while below-average younger students in Britain do worse than below-average performers in many other countries.

A 1991 study of achievement in science across twenty-three countries showed that England's eighteen-year-olds outperformed those of all other countries except for Hong Kong (Postlethwaite and Wiley, 1991). But in England, eighteen-year-olds studying science are not only an elite group, but they are also taking only three A-levels, instead of the nine or more subjects studied by their counterparts in most other countries. When fourteen-year-olds and ten-year-olds are similarly compared, England comes close to the bottom of the league table.

The message that emerges from this overview is that there is a large and internationally unusual disparity of achievement across children in the United Kingdom.

*School qualifications*

The consequences of shortfalls in skills and achievement are reflected in the numbers of sixteen- to eighteen-year-olds year olds failing to obtain formal qualifications. The findings of a study of qualifications and standards in four countries are shown in Table 6.2.

**Table 6.2  Attainment in four countries, 1990/91**

|  | Sixteen-year-olds reaching equivalent of GCSE grades A-C in maths, national language and one science | Young people obtaining a comparable upper secondary school qualification at 18+ |
|---|---|---|
| France | 66 | 48 |
| Germany | 62 | 68 |
| Japan | 50 | 80 |
| England | 27 | 29 |

Source: Green and Steedman, 1993

General Certificate of Secondary Education (GCSE) results are improving fairly steadily, but to reach the Government's 'national target' of 85 per cent of young people achieving five GCSEs grades A to C or their vocational equivalent by the year 2000, will require an unprecedented surge, since the current level is 63 per cent (NACETT, 1995). Another cause for concern is the huge discrepancies in GCSE performance between schools, and between local authorities. Schools in the Local Education Authorities (LEAs) forming the top quarter in terms of performance are now achieving results over 50 per cent better than those in the bottom quarter (Smith and Noble, 1995).

More than a third of young people now enroll in A-level courses, and the introduction of (General National Vocational Qualifications (GNVQs) may well raise overall attainment, with many of those pursuing the new courses likely to want to go on to higher education. However, a joint report from the Audit Commission and the Office of Standards in Education (OFSTED) concluded that between 30 and 40 per cent of those aged sixteen to nineteen were leaving schools and colleges without achieving the qualifications connected to completion of the courses for which they enrolled. Aside from the waste of these students' time, they estimate the cost of courses taken by failing students to be around £500 million a year (OFSTED/ Audit Commission, 1993).

*Staying on*

Examination results at sixteen are one of the most important influences on the student's decision of whether or not to remain in education. Increases in the proportion of sixteen-year-olds being entered for examinations and doing well, especially with the introduction of the GCSE which recognises a wider range of attainment, have encouraged staying on (Raffe and Surridge, 1995). Indeed there has been a remarkable improvement in participation in post-compulsory education in Britain (Government Statistical Service, 1995). In 1974, the proportion of sixteen- and seventeen-year-olds in full-time education was 35 per cent and 25 per cent respectively. By 1992 these figures had risen to 66 per cent and 48 per cent.

Despite this Britain remains extremely low in international league tables. Table 6.3 compares enrolment rates in post-compulsory education for sixteen- and seventeen-year-olds in OECD countries.

The average five-year-old in Britain can expect to have 13.4 more years of full-time education, 2.5 years less than five-year-olds in Germany and France (CERI, 1995). Again, only Turkey is lower.

Continuing the recent improvement in post-sixteen participation rates may help Britain catch up with competitors, but a recent study has reported that 'increases in levels of participation have, in general terms, been twice as great as increases in levels of attainment' (Richardson et al, 1994).[1] This would seem to suggest that some reform of the qualifications structure is necessary.

Table 6.3 Full-time enrolment
of sixteen- and seventeen-year-olds, 1992

|  | Sixteen-year-olds | Seventeen-year-olds |
|---|---|---|
| Netherlands | 97.3 | 90.8 |
| Belgium | 97.2 | 93.6 |
| Canada | 96.3 | 72.0 |
| Germany | 95.3 | 92.8 |
| Japan | 95.1 | 90.3 |
| Finland | 94.5 | 85.8 |
| Norway | 92.8 | 86.6 |
| Denmark | 92.4 | 80.1 |
| France | 92.1 | 87.2 |
| United States | 91.4 | 72.0 |
| Sweden | 89.2 | 87.0 |
| Greece | 88.4 | 62.1 |
| New Zealand | 87.8 | 65.7 |
| Ireland | 87.5 | 70.2 |
| Switzerland | 85.2 | 82.0 |
| Australia | 78.7 | 58.8 |
| Spain | 75.6 | 66.9 |
| **United Kingdom** | **75.3** | **55.3** |
| Turkey | 39.3 | 33.9 |

Source: CERI, 1995

*Entry into higher education (HE)*

The Government's rapid expansion of higher education since 1988 has been its biggest education success story. Nearly one in three eighteen-year-olds now goes on to higher education, as compared to around one in six in the early 1980s, and one in twelve in the early 1960s. International comparisons show that Britain still lags behind many other countries (see Figure 6.1; CERI, 1995). The United States, not shown, has higher rates of entry than any of these countries.

The figures for entry to higher education in the UK, and indeed in other countries, underplay the chances of particular individuals benefiting from higher education, given the large and growing numbers who choose to enroll later as mature students, either part-time or full-time. It has been suggested that as many as six in ten of today's eighteen-year-olds in Britain can now expect to enter higher education at some point in their lives (Smithers and Robinson, 1995).

The scale and speed of the expansion has caused serious strains, as the level of government funding has not nearly kept pace. Indeed, funding per student has fallen by a quarter in real terms over the past five years (Authers, 1995).

**Figure 6.1**
**Per cent of age group entering full-time education (HE) (1992)**

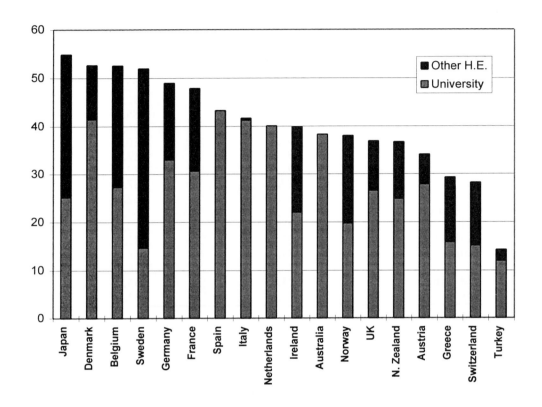

*Training*

Figure 6.2 shows the proportion of employees who had received some form of job-related training in the past four weeks for the ten years between 1984 and 1994 (Labour Force Survey, Employment Gazette [various years]). The level of training has increased significantly in the past ten years, and even held up well during the recession.

This trend is encouraging, and it is also worth noting that the training of women has now overtaken that of men. However, it might be of some concern that despite the ageing structure of the labour market, workers over the age of thirty are now only half as likely to have received training as younger workers. There is also little information on the quality of in-firm training.

**Figure 6.2**
**Per cent of employees receiving job related training in the UK (1984-94)**

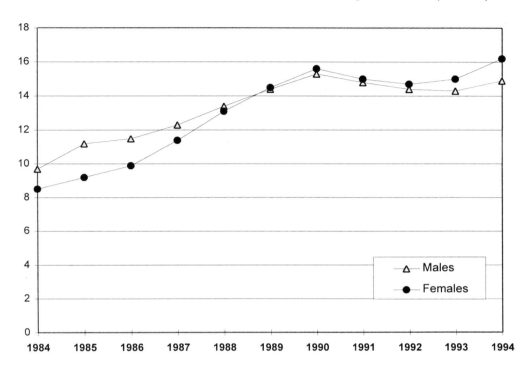

Evidence also suggests that the British workforce has a relatively low level of certified qualifications compared to most other countries (Green, 1994). Where Britain shows up worst is in terms of formal vocational qualifications for 'intermediate' skills and occupations in the labour market. This deficiency is shown in Table 6.4, and it partly explains why Britain has such a problem of skill shortages in times of economic growth.

**Table 6.4  Vocational qualifications in the workforce (%)**

|  | Degrees and higher vocational diplomas | Intermediate vocational | None |
|---|---|---|---|
| Germany (1989) | 18 | 56 | 26 |
| Netherlands (1985) | 18 | 44 | 38 |
| France (1988) | 14 | 33 | 53 |
| **Britain (1988)** | **17** | **20** | **63** |

Source:  Prais and Beadle, 1991

*Adult basic skills*

The Adult Literacy and Basic Skills Unit (ALBSU) estimates that there are around ten million adults who are functionally illiterate (Education, 1994). Their definition may be stricter than others, but research has shown that large numbers of adults have attained only low levels of literacy, with even more worrying findings for numeracy. A major survey of the basic skills of a representative group of twenty-one-year-olds revealed that 13 per cent had extremely low levels of literacy and 20 per cent had extremely low levels of numeracy (Ekinsmyth and Bynner, 1993). A much larger group required additional help in order to cope with the demands of everyday life and work; indeed 40 per cent themselves reported problems with writing and spelling. Another large study of students at further education colleges showed that 42 per cent would need some additional help with communication skills and 62 per cent with numeracy skills, to get a qualification at National Vocational Qualification (NVQ) Level 2 (ALBSU, 1993a). Nearly half of those adults who had difficulties with basic skills had never received special help of any kind at school (ALBSU, 1987). In one survey, nearly one in four employers reported that applicants' basic skills are only just adequate or worse (Atkinson and Spilsbury, 1993). The cost to industry of basic skills difficulties has been conservatively estimated at £5 billion (ALBSU, 1993b).

*Conclusion*

Two conclusions emerge from the foregoing analysis, and they are integrally linked. The first is that, despite some improvements, overall levels of participation and achievement in learning in Britain remain low in comparison with our competitors. The second is that opportunities to learn and achieve are unevenly distributed. Far too many children lack access to nursery provision, fail to learn the basics at primary school, and leave school without any qualifications. While a growing number of adults are benefiting from higher education, far too few of the remainder obtain intermediate-level vocational qualifications, and a significant proportion do not even have the basic skills for work and everyday life.

## What are the challenges?

Education currently occupies an extremely prominent position in public debate, but it is often misleadingly identified as a panacea for all social and economic problems. It is therefore important that our expectations of what education can achieve are both raised and linked to specific social and economic goals (Botkin, Elmandjra and Malitza, 1979). These include: civic goals, such as improving the quality of democratic deliberation; social and cultural goals, such as the enhancement of the quality of life; moral goals, such as greater awareness of the consequences of actions; and economic goals, such as building a more highly skilled and flexible workforce, and thus improving the competitive positions of companies. There may also be areas of tension between such goals that will require trade-offs and tough political choices. The challenges faced by this project are outlined briefly in this section.

*Work and the economy*

The structure of the world economy is changing rapidly because of the globalisation of production, the growth miracles of Southeast Asia, and because of accelerating technological change, especially in information-intensive industries. Britain cannot hope to compete with competitors from the less developed world on the basis of undercutting labour costs. There seems little option but to take more seriously the task of significantly improving the skills of the workforce, particularly in light of evidence that economic growth now depends unequivocally on the intelligence, abilities and creativity of workers (see Chapter 2). The long-term effects of increased competition on the structure of employment reinforces the need to focus on raising skill levels. Employment in professional, managerial, skill-intensive and knowledge-based occupations will continue to rise, and demand for unskilled labour will continue to fall as jobs are technologically upgraded. In short, more and more will be expected of every worker, and those who lack skills will continue to bear the majority of the adjustment costs (Hayes, Fonda and Hillman, 1995).

*Knowledge, skills and understanding*

A broader base of knowledge, skills and understanding will be required in most occupations, geared not to a narrow technical conception of jobs, but rather to a spectrum of competencies. Such competencies include:

- core skills such as communication and problem-solving;
- understanding of wider work processes;
- adaptability and flexibility;
- innovation and creativity;
- reaping the full benefits of developments in technology, especially information technology;
- standard-setting and quality assurance.

*Careers*

The concept of a career will continue to be transformed by changes in the labour market with:

- flatter organisational structures, with less scope for progression up a hierarchy;
- work taking place less often in large organisations, and more in small and medium sized organisations;
- more frequent changes of jobs and renegotiation of contracts, resulting in less job security and more fragmented patterns of work;

- increases in self-employment and work from home;
- a reduction in the number of core workers in organisations, and a growth in part-time, temporary and 'portfolio' workers, covered by more flexible work contracts.

## Lifelong learning

The British education system produces persistent patterns of achievement and under-achievement that are incompatible with flexibility. Education and training must respond better to regular and rapid change in markets and technology, and rather than being superseded by employment, must continue abreast of it. Individuals, as well as continuously learning new skills, will need to take more responsibility for their own careers, their self-development, and consequently their learning programmes, with enormous implications for guidance services.

A number of social changes also makes lifelong learning an imperative:

- the family is changing, creating new demands for more flexible work patterns, and for ways of combining family life, employment and education in different ways and at different times;
- people are living longer and having longer retirements, with more time for learning;
- due to the polarisation of society, the disadvantaged and unemployed are in most need of opportunities for lifelong learning, but are presently the least able to gain access to such opportunities.

## Six problems and ways forward

The last seven years have witnessed an unprecedented succession of reforms to almost every part of the British education system, and complaints of 'initiative overload' are rife. It is an unpopular time for new proposals, but there are many problems which have not been solved and which are holding us back. The rest of the chapter therefore focuses on six ways in which Britain is failing to face up to the challenges set out above, and sets out possible ways forward for policy.

## 1. Under-investment in the early years

Study after study has shown that high-quality pre-school provision leads to immediate gains in educational and social development, which persist through adolescence and adulthood (Sylva, 1994). Recent research in France can be added to the list: it shows that attendance at nursery school results in clear gains in progress at primary school (Jarousse, Mingat and Marc, 1995).

In 1972, Margaret Thatcher's White Paper promised nursery education for all, but since then, repeated calls for the fulfilment of this promise have been quashed largely (though not exclusively) by Treasury parsimony, despite evidence of high returns on the investment. Putting in place a statutory requirement on local authorities to ensure that sufficient high-quality, publicly funded nursery education places are available for all three- and four-year-olds whose parents wish it, remains an important aim. So does establishing national criteria to ensure its quality, in terms of the curriculum for the three- to five-age group, training and continuing the professional development of education and care workers, and increasing adult-to-child ratios in nursery classes. The National Commission on Education's goal of places on a half-time basis for three-year-olds and on a full-time basis for four-year-olds has been widely endorsed. Taking into account the fact that some parents do not wish to send their children to nursery school, the NCE estimated the recurrent annual cost of achieving their goal to be £860 million (NCE, 1993).

What should be done in the short- and medium-term? The Government is currently trying to introduce nursery vouchers, partly as a way of promoting parental choice and boosting private and voluntary provision (Lawlor, 1994). One objection to this is that unless they are means-tested, vouchers could constitute a subsidy for middle-class parents who would otherwise pay themselves. Using vouchers as a mechanism for targeting people in particular need (Glennerster, 1995) may get around this problem, but might contribute to the poverty trap, and anyway does not address the fact that vouchers do not themselves create places. As with all voucher and credit initiatives, unless a pilot scheme can show that nursery vouchers both motivate those who are not currently benefiting and stimulate providers to respond, they are not a sensible way forward. The final section of this chapter outlines more satisfactory financial arrangements for increasing access for targeted groups in the short-run, and for moving towards universal provision in the long-run.

Receiving less attention from politicians and the media than nursery expansion, though just as important, is the chronic under-funding of primary schools. Research has shown that the effect of primary school on pupils' progress is greater than that of secondary school (Mortimore, 1995). It is vital that high-quality learning take place throughout the years of primary school. By the age of eleven, many pupils have decided whether they consider themselves to be high or low achievers, and these self-perceptions become increasingly difficult to change. Furthermore, recent studies show that the quality of the primary school a child attends continues to influence his or her experience at secondary school, with a significant impact on attainment at GCSE (Sammons, 1994; Goldstein and Sammons, 1994).

These considerations make it absolutely essential that children in primary schools receive as much individual attention as possible. This is made very difficult by the inadequate allocation of the education budget, which was described by the National Commission on Education as:

> ... a pyramid turned upside down, with much more money being spent on each higher education student than on each secondary pupil, and in turn more on each secondary pupil than on each primary pupil (NCE, 1993).

The latest international comparisons show that this analysis still holds true (CERI, 1995). Britain spends far more on each student in tertiary education than does any other OECD country (two and a half times more than France and Germany, for example). This generosity is not extended to schoolchildren, particularly the younger ones. The differential in expenditure per pupil between primary and secondary school in the UK is 41 per cent, which compares poorly with the average differential for developed countries (24 per cent) and individual countries such as the USA (16 per cent) and Japan (10 per cent).

This poor treatment of primary schools is of course reflected in their class sizes. Class size is a particularly important factor for younger children (Mortimore and Blatchford, 1993), not least because they are more dependent on teachers than older children. It is disturbing, therefore, that the average class size in maintained primary schools is growing and now stands at 26.6, and that more than one in five classes have over thirty pupils (DfE, 1994). The great majority of teachers, parents and governors believe classes are too large, and that this is a very, if not the most, important educational issue (Bennett, 1994). The increases in the last few years are a worrying trend and are not mirrored in the independent sector, where overall there are 60 per cent fewer pupils per teacher than in the maintained sector (Mortimore and Blatchford, 1993), and many parents cite this as a major reason for paying twice for their children's education (MORI, 1989). Comparing the UK with other OECD countries shows that only Ireland and Turkey have as high a ratio of primary school pupils to teaching staff, and several countries have ratios of around half that of the UK (CERI, 1995).

The final section of this chapter sets out a way forward for redressing the imbalance of funding outlined above.


## 2. School performance

*Measuring school performance*

Variations between schools in Britain in terms of pupil achievement are greater than in most other OECD countries. A school where nearly all pupils achieve at least five good grades at GCSE may well be only down the road from another school where fewer than one in ten achieve this. Measuring and comparing school performance is highly problematic, however. Published examination results and league tables in newspapers show actual levels of attainment in schools, but variations will not mirror differences in effectiveness, because the 'raw' results partly reflect the pupils' abilities on entry to the school and their various backgrounds. These and other indices therefore measure the gross output of schools only, since they can not take account of inputs.

Of more interest, but more difficult to measure, is the relative boost to pupil performance - or the value added - for which the school is responsible. Determining the progress made by pupils during their time at a school requires information about the pupils' attainment at entry or their background. In that way, when comparing schools, the different challenges they face can be taken into account and like can be compared with like. Meanwhile, examining changes in school performance over time can give an indication of the extent to which the school is improving, and how consistent that improvement has been over time.

The measures and methods discussed above will give an indication of the effectiveness and improvement of the school as a whole. However, different parts of the school might not be equally effective, and it is important to consider the performance of different year groups, departments in secondary schools, or curriculum areas in primary schools. A school might also be more or less effective for different types of pupils, for example, according to their gender, ethnicity or level of ability. More information of this type will enable a more accurate understanding of the strengths and weaknesses of schools.

OFSTED and the School Curriculum and Assessment Authority (SCAA) have both taken an interest in and expressed concern over these issues, but league tables of raw examination results continue to be published without any warnings of the shortcomings of the information provided (Institute of Education, 1994; OFSTED, 1994). This practice has been particularly damaging for schools in disadvantaged areas, including many that are fostering remarkably good progress amongst their pupils in terms of 'adding value'.

## Effective schools

This last concern was the starting point for a major study of eleven effective schools in disadvantaged areas undertaken by the National Commission on Education (NCE, 1995a). The findings of this study are very much in line with those of the huge international body of research into the factors associated with school effectiveness, summarised for OFSTED in a comprehensive review (Sammons, Hillman and Mortimore, 1995). Much of school improvement must come from within the school itself. There are, however, a number of areas in which government can play a major role in levering up standards, not least in under-performing schools.

The most important factor in the effectiveness of schools is clearly the quality of teaching, and this is dealt with in the following section.

## Effective leadership

Headteachers in Britain have a particularly powerful role, and although recent reforms have resulted in a certain amount of confusion as to the borders of their responsibility, the demands upon headteachers have clearly increased. Yet the process by which potential headteachers are identified early in their careers, selected and prepared for the role, remains highly unsatisfactory. There is a huge diversity of practice, some of which is admittedly on the right track, but most of which is ad hoc to say the least. Responsibility for selecting headteachers has been transferred from local authorities to school governing bodies without the necessary guidance or training. Selection therefore tends to take place in an arbitrary manner, with patronage and highly subjective 'hunches' allowed to influence decisions. The provision of training before appointment is erratic and certainly not guaranteed by resources. Only one in four local authorities provides induction programmes for new headteachers. The following directions for policy are suggested:

- the establishment of an educational management development centre, responsible for management training for headteachers and deputies, providing initial and in-service teacher training modules, research, and interaction with management expertise outside the world of education;
- all deputy heads to be entitled to a programme of preparation for headship;
- a more professional system for the selection of headteachers, with professional advisers with voting rights included on selection panels, training for governors, and basic requirements for information going out about a post and coming in from candidates;
- new headteachers to be entitled to a comprehensive induction programme, with a well-trained headteacher mentor from another school;
- all headteachers to be entitled to a certain amount of ongoing training and development geared towards developing educational leadership skills.

*The physical environment*

Research shows that the physical environment of a school can have a significant effect on both the attitudes and achievement of pupils, yet two out of every five primary schools are judged by the inspectorate to have accommodation that is less than satisfactory. The message here is simple: no child should have his or her ability to learn hindered by leaking roofs, draughty windows and noisy pipes. The government must ensure that the physical environment of all schools can be judged to be adequate by the inspectorate.

*Learning the basics*

Unless children master the basic skills of literacy and numeracy, the rest of their education will be seriously hindered. Each year, the inspectorate identifies significant proportions of poor teaching of mathematics in primary schools, including teachers who are 'insecure in their grasp of its essential principles' (Mortimore, 1995). An urgent priority for both government and teacher training institutions is to ensure that this is remedied.

The government has recently withdrawn support for the Reading Recovery Programme on the grounds of cost-saving. It combats literacy problems by systematically identifying children who have had particular difficulties with reading and writing in their first year of primary school, and intervening by giving them a period of intensive individual help, not only to improve these skills but also to help them develop more efficient general learning strategies. In the pilot scheme, two-thirds of the children identified successfully achieved the target average level of literacy of the class and so could quit the programme and return to mainstream provision, thus reducing the need for expensive additional learning support at a later stage. The whole staff of a school also benefits from the skills, expertise, training and support of the specialist teacher, raising standards of literacy for all pupils. The Reading Recovery Programme should therefore be restored.

*Parental participation*

The basic skills problems amongst both school children and adults cited earlier in this chapter are not unrelated. The educational level of parents and their involvement in their children's schooling are powerful influences on children's early development and achievement. ALBSU has also reported a strong association between reading problems reported by adults and the reading scores of their children, which it describes as the 'inter-generational effect' whereby the children who most need help at home are the least likely to get it (ALBSU, 1993c; see also Chapter 8). ALBSU has set up a range of special schemes in which parents and children are educated in tandem, both separately and together. This is an exciting development in attacking the 'cycle of deprivation' which, if successful, should be followed through on a large scale.

## 3. Teaching quality

Another factor holding back improvement in the education system is the failure to face up to a painful truth: teaching is not viewed, as perhaps it once was, as a profession in the full sense of the word. This is not just an issue of status. It is an issue of quality, because until teaching is seen as a challenging, creative and satisfying career by the most talented of our young people, it will always be an uphill struggle to raise standards.

Evidence of the scope for improvement in the quality of teaching is not just anecdotal:

- nearly a quarter of lessons are judged by the inspectorate to be unsatisfactory or poor (OFSTED, 1995);
- over a quarter of tuition in secondary schools in England is undertaken by teachers not qualified in the subject (DfE, 1993);
- undergraduates expecting third class degrees are three times more likely than those expecting first class degrees to have chosen teaching as a career (Hillman, 1994);
- the inspectorate judges that only half of new teachers are well equipped for their posts in terms of their personal, professional and academic qualities, their ability to be self-critical and their performance in the classroom (OFSTED, 1993b);
- a national survey showed that 44 per cent of eleven-year-old pupils and 45 per cent of thirteen-year-old pupils never discuss their work with teachers (Keys and Fernandes, 1993).

How can the quality of teaching be improved, so as to prepare our children for the challenges of the twenty-first century? Raising the quality of teaching should be one of the main priorities for education: doing so will set in motion a virtuous spiral raising the standing of the profession.

### High-quality recruitment and retention

Teaching does not compete effectively with other professions and careers in attracting bright graduates. For the last eight years, attempts to promote and publicise teaching have centred on the 'Teaching as a Career Unit'. The experience of that unit has shown that good intentions and minimal financial backing can do no more than ensure that most teacher training places are filled. They have not succeeded in encouraging high numbers of applications which, coupled with tough entry requirements, are the key to high quality in recruitment. Entry requirements can be raised by initiatives to attract the many excellent teachers who have left teaching and have for various reasons declined to return. The new Teacher Training Agency, as a matter of urgency, must set up an ambitious, well-resourced, permanent body which will compete vigorously with other professions and the business world to fire the interest of our best graduates. The goal should be for every young person to ask: 'Am I good enough to become a teacher?'. In turn, poor teaching must cease to be a taboo subject. While incompetence, indolence and lack of control over pupils can in some cases be dealt with through intensive professional development, it is also essential that procedures for dismissal, while remaining scrupulously fair, must be made to work much more simply.

### Opening up the profession

One of the main drawbacks of teaching, from the point of view of many young graduates and, indeed, of mid-career teachers, is that long-term prospects are not particularly exciting. It would be of benefit to both the individual teacher and the school if secondments and sabbaticals were standard practice. For example, those about to become headteachers or deputy heads could gain a year of management experience outside the world of education. The practice should work in both directions with people being brought in from outside the teaching profession as visiting teachers. This might be encouraged by fostering the recognition that teaching skills are useful outside the profession, so that teaching qualifications will be held by people who may not occupy full-time posts within schools.

### Focused role for teachers

Teachers are currently obliged to spend too much of their time on tasks that do not require a qualified teacher to perform them. These tasks may be administrative, supervisory, or relate to the preparation of educational materials. Imaginative staffing practices to free up some of this time so as to allow teachers to focus on pupil learning have been piecemeal. But teamwork will become increasingly important for effective teaching, with teachers drawing on a range of support and expertise in different situations. What is needed is a coherent career structure for a new grade of specialist support staff driven by rigorous training and development, and worthwhile qualifications.

*Teachers as learners*

Reducing some of the unnecessary burdens on teachers will also give them more time to be life-long learners themselves. There should be a continuum of professional development starting with initial teacher training, passing through induction, and ongoing in-service training and appraisal, to management development. This formal foundation must be supplemented by innovation and evaluation, a willingness to keep up with developments in educational technology, an openness to outside expertise and a familiarity with the huge international body of research into effective teaching and learning which has until recently been poorly disseminated among practitioners. It is essential that personal development not be crowded out by externally set and short-term priorities.

*Exploiting new technologies*

Information technology is changing the practices of many teachers in schools, colleges and universities, but the potential for raising teaching quality through the use of new technologies has not yet even begun to be realised. Government must play a strategic role in facilitating innovation and diffusing good practice. Increasing the availability and development of hardware, educational software, multi-media and interactive technologies and integrated learning systems will facilitate:

- the enhancement of every subject area of the curriculum, including the learning of basic skills;
- greater independence for the learner, so that the role of the teacher is less one of instruction and imparting of knowledge, and more one of mediation, planning, review, individual guidance and feedback;
- the scope for more differentiated learning for individual pupils or students;
- increases in the motivation of pupils to learn, including those bored at school;
- new approaches to assessment, monitoring, records, administration and budgeting, freeing up teachers' time to teach more effectively;
- the opening up of schools, colleges and universities, and an increase in teachers' and learners' access to information, resources and people all around the world;
- a means of bringing the home (and hence parents) into new forms of communication with school;
- the development of computer facilities as support tools for teachers, e.g. internet groups to compile curricula in different subject areas.

*Full professional status*

In the United States, teaching has been described as 'one of the semi-professions' (Etzioni, 1969). This view would not be disputed by much of the British public and particularly by those considering their career options. Whether or not the concept of 'profession' is the most helpful one in assessing the condition and standing of teachers, it is to be deplored that the recognition and rewards accorded to teachers and lecturers fail to match the high and increasing demands made on them and the value of their work. Teachers' pay is currently two per cent above average non-manual earnings, compared with 37 per cent twenty years ago. Econometric analysis shows that raising teachers' pay by 25 per cent could double the proportion of graduates applying for teacher training (Court *et al*, 1995). Of course, professionalism is not just about money. Teachers should not be forced to put up with the poor condition of school buildings, noted year after year by the inspectorate. Nor should they be denied a professional body devoted to upholding and raising standards, such as those enjoyed by so many other professions (including teachers in Scotland). This would help to unify the six teacher unions, which currently spend far too much energy competing with each other. It is vital, however, that any such professional body should not become a special interest group oriented towards self-protection, and thus become just another institutional obstacle to change within the educational system.

## 4. A new qualifications structure

Britain (excluding Scotland) is the only advanced industrialised country with a formal school-leaving examination at age sixteen. From the age of fourteen, students work towards GCSEs, and as of 1995, some will supplement these with GNVQs at foundation level. After sixteen, those wishing to carry on learning can do so at school, in sixth-form colleges or in further education colleges. Qualification routes also diversify and the following three-track system is emerging in England, Wales and Northern Ireland:

- academic education leading to A-levels and AS-levels;
- vocational education leading to GNVQs in broad subject areas at foundation, intermediate or advanced level;
- work-based training leading to occupation-specific NVQs.

NVQs are replacing a Byzantine array of vocational qualifications, many of which had extremely complex award structures. NVQs differ in fundamental ways from traditional academic qualifications. Instead of formal examinations, the performance of students is assessed at work by their trainers or supervisors against centrally mandated written standards, laid down by the National Council for Vocational Qualifications, and portfolios of evidence are collected which may be externally verified. GNVQs, by contrast, are not as much of a new departure as is commonly believed. They have subsumed Business and Technology Education Council (BTEC) First and National Diplomas - letting two other awarding bodies in on the act - are modular in structure and again, grading depends on assessment of portfolios of evidence by the teacher.

In practice, the high-status academic track is for the most able students, and the vocational routes are for the less able. Despite the fact that GNVQs provide an alternative route to higher education, and despite claims that there could be 'parity of esteem' between academic and vocational qualifications, the Prime Minister has stressed that 'A-levels will remain the benchmark of academic excellence' (DES, 1991). This is recognised by students with good GCSE grades, the vast majority of whom choose the A-level route (Further Education Unit et al, 1994). GNVQs are displacing other vocational courses and GCSE re-sits, rather than A-levels. This is reflected in the large numbers of students with GCSE grades below those required for entry to higher education recruited to GNVQ courses.

Furthermore, in no other advanced industrial country do students at the age of sixteen choose only three subjects. In most systems (including Scotland) a wide range of subjects, usually between six and ten, is studied at this stage. The narrowness of A-levels is a sharp jolt for students after the breadth of the national curriculum. This is reflected in the increasing number of students following mixed A-level programmes, for example, including both arts and science, in an attempt to broaden their curriculum and delay specialisation. It is also reflected by students opting for the highly academic but broad International Baccalaureate courses in certain schools and colleges, and by the popularity of pilot schemes mixing components of different qualifications.

On the vocational side, NVQs are also too specific to prepare young people for open-ended futures. Because they offer training for narrow, occupationally specific, practical skills, with restrictive career choice, their status is low. The popularity of GNVQs partly stems from the fact that for less academically inclined young people they provide a desirable alternative to NVQs, retaking GCSEs or embarking on A-levels. However, while they are less narrow than NVQs, it could hardly be said that studying for a GNVQ in a particular sector of work for two or three years provides a broad education for a teenager.

The hasty introduction of GNVQs has resulted in other shortcomings: variable standards, lack of clarity about their content, an insufficiently rigorous core of knowledge and an over-reliance on performance-based assessment (OFSTED, 1994; Further Education Funding Council, 1994; Further Education Unit et al, 1994). Some of these may be teething problems, and it may be unfair to judge the new qualifications too harshly. However, students taking the GNVQ route generally intend to stay on in full-time (usually higher) education rather than enter the labour market, and so are competing with those opting for A-levels.

The qualifications debate is no longer A-levels versus Baccalaureate, or separate versus integrated academic and vocational streams. Three policy options can be identified. The first is to retain a multi-track system, but to erode some of the barriers between the tracks (Dearing, 1995). In a sense this is what is happening now on a small scale, with NVQ or GNVQ at Level 3 being deemed as equivalent to two A-levels, and with some students combining GNVQ with an A-level. The recent announcement that the University of London examinations board and BTEC will merge is a further step along those lines, as is the modularisation of syllabi. Such policies, if followed through, could allow greater transferability across qualifications, and break down some of the barriers between academic and vocational routes.

A second and much more comprehensive option is to create a unified system in which there is a single qualification. This would require all of the component qualifications to be credit-based and credit-transferable. No country in the world has ever actually developed and implemented a genuinely integrated single system. For example, in France, while there are several 'baccalaureates', they do not have equal status, and there is no credit transfer whatsoever between them. A unified framework is being attempted in Scotland, in the merging of academic Highers with the vocational National Certificate into a single modular system. Some English educationalists have suggested following this line (Finegold *et al*, 1995), and even extending a unified qualifications structure to the fourteen to sixteen age group (White, Pring and Brockington, 1995).

While such an ambitious approach is no doubt admirable, policy-makers should be cautious about pursuing an option on the grounds of administrative tidy-mindedness, and given the debacles surrounding the implementation of the national curriculum and NVQs there is widespread reluctance amongst teachers to face yet another huge change. It would also be a great risk to attempt to construct a credit-based system covering all types of studies. In a sense, there is already an embryonic credit-based system, in that a student can make up points for entry to higher education from combinations of A- and AS-levels. While some universities are happy to deal simply in points totals, others see the claim that all A-levels and AS-levels are equal as a heroic assumption. Extending equivalencies to vocational qualifications would not only be even more difficult, but would require a large central body to set these equivalencies by fiat. The effects on students' choices and on entry procedures for higher education are unknown. The messiness of the current system partly reflects the fact that it is responding to a great variety of demands and needs. Other countries may seem, at first sight, to have systems that are simpler, but their central core of qualifications is invariably surrounded by a fragmented periphery.

A third, halfway-house option, could achieve many of the social and educational aims of the option of a single qualification without immediately abolishing the three-track system. It would involve the integration of existing qualifications through a more evolutionary process. A portfolio of academic and vocational studies, conforming to a minimum requirement framework, could be accredited as a loose overarching diploma. Such a framework could prescribe combinations of modules which ensure greater breadth than current routes, and could also embody core skills such as communication, numerical skills, problem-solving and information technology. The diploma could be used for entry into HE and accepted by employers for selection into skilled jobs. It may be possible for employers in different industries to specify certain core requirements of modules that will be necessary for entry into different types of work. This option is less elegant from a policy point of view but it takes more notice of the interests and motivations of young people. Its value lies in leaving open to a young person whether to aim at early employment or HE. The features of their portfolios would be the same as those of a single qualification. Indeed there is no reason why it should not eventually become a single qualification for those aged fourteen to nineteen and also for adults who may have missed out the first time around.

## 5. Funding post-compulsory education and training

The main goal of post-compulsory education and training should be the encouragement of lifelong learning. Earlier in this chapter, it was argued that while under-investing in the education of young children, Britain is relatively generous in the funding of education for older age groups. In fact, the various arrangements through which post-compulsory education and training are funded result in an unfair and unsustainable distribution of public and private funding for those aged over eighteen.

The current system for funding higher education was, in the main, designed for an elite cadre of undergraduates. Recent rapid increases in participation are putting an immense strain on universities and colleges and are threatening the quality of the education delivered. Moreover, the funding of tuition fees and maintenance grants channels money to those with high lifetime incomes. For example, public expenditure on higher education for those in the top decile of lifetime income is over four times that for those below the average (Falkingham and Hills, 1995). There are two principal explanations for graduates having higher incomes than non-graduates. The first is that they benefit from an investment in human capital which increases their marketable skills. The second is that their qualifications act as a screening device for employers to identify more able or industrious recruits, regardless of the content of what they actually learned as students. In fact, there is more than an element of truth in both explanations, but either way, the implications are the same: public expenditure on higher education results in a regressive transfer from the worse off to the better off.

Meanwhile, part-time higher education students are not eligible for mandatory awards for tuition fees, means-tested maintenance grants or student loans. They may receive support through discretionary awards from local authorities, but total expenditure on these is low and falling, and now stands at around one twelfth of what is spent on mandatory awards. Discretionary awards are also one of the first things to go when local authorities are cutting expenditure, and several authorities no longer give out any such awards.

Fees are charged to many of the 1.6 million students aged over 18 enrolled in further education colleges. As with part-time higher education students, some may get discretionary awards, or access to a 'career development loan' from the small Employment Department fund. Others, if they are lucky, might have their fees remitted at the discretion of their college, or be helped out by their employers if the course is of immediate relevance to their job. Those studying for more general vocational qualifications will almost certainly have to find their own funds. A series of moves towards a more laissez-faire government policy for training coincides with growing inequalities in individuals' access to opportunities to update and re-equip their own skills throughout their working lives. However, changes in the labour market, discussed earlier, mean that responsibility increasingly falls on individuals to invest in learning. Meanwhile banks are generally reluctant to lend to students against the prospect of future earnings resulting from investments in vocational skills.

Government policy to improve Britain's training performance must also address the perennial problem of the weak incentives faced by employers to skill and re-skill workers. The poor record on industrial training in the UK is largely a result of the lack of organisational cohesion or co-ordination between employers compared to their north European counterparts. This organisational infrastructure is crucial both in order to align the training system with other features of the supply-side (for example, the wage bargaining system), and also to overcome the problem that, in the absence of co-ordination, each employer faces an incentive not to train workers but to 'poach' workers whose training costs have been borne by other firms. Britain's weak performance in industrial training in the post-war period is usually, perhaps excessively, attributed to the inability of British employer organisations to resolve this problem. However, it is important here to note the distinction between company-specific and general (or marketable) skills (Becker, 1964). In light of the problem of poaching, it is only in the interests of the company to train workers largely in the former type of skill. Responsibility for the provision of general skills therefore may have to be shared between employers, individuals and government.

Government policy relating to company-specific skills concerns a range of supply-side and macroeconomic policies which bear upon the incentives firms face to train more or fewer workers. In this connection, it can be argued that the Conservative government's success since 1979 in creating an economy geared towards low-cost production and services has further discouraged the training activities of British firms. Labour mobility and company profitability have been boosted by a number of measures - the weakening of Wage Councils and employment security, the subsidising of the creation of low-paid and temporary jobs through a variety of youth training schemes, legal attacks on the rights of trade unions, and the liberalisation of financial markets with the result of increasing the pressure on firms to maximise short-term profits. The result has been to encourage firms to compete by cutting costs (notably labour costs), rather than to invest in more flexible, high-technology, high-skill markets. Policy relating to general skills offers a more feasible alternative for improving the training record. In the 1980s, a plethora of youth training schemes basically served to provide employers with 'a cheap means of screening large numbers of low-skilled, but well-socialised young workers' (Finegold and Soskice, 1988). Training policy thus became in part a short-term measure for dealing with unemployment. After 1988, responsibility for the delivery of government training programmes was assumed by Training and Enterprise Councils (TECs), regional boards of nominated employers in a contractual relationship with central government. Though the contribution of these schemes should not be dismissed, it is unlikely that they will engender any significant change in the policies of companies towards training without further supporting measures.

It seems clear from this brief description that current arrangements whereby individuals, government and employers pay for post-compulsory learning are both unfair and unsustainable. The heart of the problem is the excessive targeting of public money on a narrow sub-group of post-compulsory learners -

full-time students in higher education. The majority of such people do not have savings which they can invest in education at the time that they wish to become students. However, such an investment usually results in continuous personal benefits later in life.

What is required is a mechanism for shifting the time-scale of the costs of education to align better with needs and ability to pay. The current Student Loan Scheme, introduced in 1990-1991 when grants were cut, is an attempt at such a mechanism, but it is limited to full-time higher education, has not succeeded in preventing student debt and hardship, and has been blighted by administrative problems. Various organisations have examined other ways of financing higher education. The National Commission on Education recommended student contributions to both maintenance and tuition via repayments through the national insurance system. The university vice-chancellors, the Confederation of British Industry, political parties and even the National Union of Students have examined similar ideas including a 'graduate tax'. Many American universities operate schemes whereby loans are issued for payment of tuition at advantageous rates of interest, subject to repayment over a fixed period beginning after the student has begun salaried employment.

More radical would be the creation of a unified system for funding all post-compulsory learning, putting individuals in control of their own investment in education and training. This is where the concept of the 'Learning Bank', proposed by the Commission on Social Justice, begins to look extremely attractive (Commission on Social Justice 1995; see also Chapters 4 and 5). The idea remains embryonic, but could potentially solve many of the problems described above. Everyone would have an Individual Learning Account (ILA) which they could use throughout their lives to fund any form of education and training. The Learning Bank would draw in government grants, individual payback for maintenance and tuition costs, and employers' contributions for training which would be compulsory if an ILA had been established by an employee. The concept builds on the ideas of learning vouchers and educational credits, funding individuals rather than institutions, but it goes further by allowing much greater mobility and choice across different types of provision.

While the Learning Bank could structure entitlements and demand for post-compulsory education and training, there is also a need on the supply-side to raise the efficiency and responsiveness of provision. Three policies could help to achieve this:

- a 'ladder of progression' or credit-based achievement structure across further education, higher education and vocational training (Robertson, 1994);
- the integration of strategic planning for all provision at a single level, preferably regional;
- establishing a 'University for Industry' to transfer high-quality learning materials through new technologies into the workplace (Brown, 1994).

## 6. Accountability and funding

There has been a rapid growth in the power of central government over
education in recent years.  While many of the responsibilities of local
education authorities, such as management and budgetary control, have been
transferred to individual institutions such as schools and colleges, much power
has accrued to centrally appointed quangos.  This shift has not been matched
by a willingness to accept greater responsibility at the centre for the
performance of the education system, or to be more accountable for the results
of decisions taken centrally (NCE, 1995b).[2]

This reluctance to accept responsibility is particularly apparent when it comes
to spending.  The gap between the rhetoric and reality of education
expenditure has always been wide.  Ministers trumpet figures showing real
spending increases year after year and claim that education is faring well.
Meanwhile, teachers and lecturers feel that cuts are being imposed, with class
sizes rising, buildings deteriorating and resources such as books being shared
amongst increasingly large groups of pupils and students.

Does money leak out as it passes through the various channels between the
Chancellor's allocation and the chalk face of the classroom or lecture theatre?
There is certainly room for greater efficiency in the administration and funding
of education institutions, both at the national and local level.  However, the
principal explanation for the conundrum lies in the fact that education is a
particularly labour-intensive industry, and only minor productivity gains
through technology have yet been achieved.  With salaries accounting for
nearly three-quarters of education expenditure, costs in education rise faster
than prices as a whole.  This means that to increase the number of teachers,
books or repairs - or indeed education's share of the budget - is to row
upstream against a powerful current.  If we take account of this, the 'real'
increase in education expenditure in the United Kingdom during the 1980s was
not 12.6 per cent but 0.4 per cent (NCE, 1993).

The recent progress of education up the political agenda resulted in a couple
of rounds of public expenditure allocations in the early 1990s which were a bit
more favourable.  It appeared that after a decade of strict rationing, the
education world was finally being invited to the table.  But the extra resources
were directed mainly at the non-compulsory sectors:  further and higher
education and also nursery education.  Most schools remained unaffected:  a
significant proportion of the increased spending in the compulsory sector was
taken up by the new inspection arrangements and by the extra funding for
grant-maintained schools.  This year saw the hatches being battened down
again, to the extent that protest and other forms of direct action have been
taken by school governors all round the country.  According to one observer,
'the 1995-96 finance settlement probably is the toughest ever for local
authorities and schools' (Travers, 1995).

Problems are raised not just by the level of resources for education but also
by their distribution.  The Audit Commission found huge disparities in
education spending among local authorities, and in particular in the funding

gap between primary and secondary schools (Audit Commission, 1995). Their analysis is compromised by the fact that some authorities have middle schools, and also that in some authorities post-sixteen education is concentrated in sixth-form colleges (funded separately) and not in school sixth forms. The fact that these figures are the best available for comparing the policies of different councils highlights the lack of accountability in the allocation of funds.

The wide differentials derive partly from differences in LEA policies and in their historic patterns of spending. They also derive from the government's standard spending assessments (SSAs), which are the amount the government assesses that local authorities need to provide a standard level of services, in determining the formula for allocation of block grants. SSAs are based mainly on the number of pupils of the relevant age in the area, although disadvantaged areas benefit from the Additional Educational Needs (AEN) element. A significant number of anomalies arises from this complex system, which favours some boroughs that have a relatively good educational performance, and works against others which have much poorer results. For example, Table 6.5 shows Harrow, with a low proportion of children from poor backgrounds and among the best GCSE results in the country, to have a higher AEN index than Barnsley (Smith and Noble, 1995). Meanwhile, Knowsley, with a high proportion of children from a poor background and one of the worst GCSE results in the country, has a lower AEN index than Wandsworth.

**Table 6.5  AEN, GCSE results and socio-economic background in four LEAs, 1992**

| LEA | AEN index (higher = more need) | % 16-year-olds with 5 or more GCSE grade A-C | % 0-15 from low socio-economic group | % 0-15 from high socio-economic group |
|---|---|---|---|---|
| Barnsley | 0.500 | 24.2 | 41.3 | 18.8 |
| Harrow | 0.562 | 46.7 | 20.0 | 43.5 |
| Knowsley | 0.904 | 16.9 | 51.3 | 13.1 |
| Wandsworth | 1.049 | 27.5 | 34.9 | 36.4 |

Differentials in allocations to LEAs are only part of the story. LEAs themselves have their own local management of schools (LMS) formulae for allocating resources to schools. Large variations in these formulae mean that under some authorities, chronically disadvantaged schools receive hardly any extra money. Meanwhile, grant-maintained schools are financed directly by a central government quango which has developed its own system of formulae funding. Finally, to add to these discrepancies, pupils in independent secondary schools have 66 per cent more spent on them than those in maintained schools, with a difference of 84 per cent at primary level (NCE, 1993).

In short, the regime under which funds reach schools is extremely fragmented, and it is no wonder that so few people have the remotest understanding of its operation. Even more seriously, the vagaries of the arrangement in practice mean that pupils in one school might have significantly more spent on them than those in another, for no justifiable reason.

These issues should be seen alongside the points raised in the section on 'Under-investment in the early years', concerning the inadequate provision of nursery places and the under-funding of primary schools. Responsibility should remain with elected local government, with a common and loose relationship with all schools, including those that are currently grant-maintained, roughly in line with the status currently enjoyed by voluntary-aided or voluntary-controlled schools. The six functions for a new style LEA proposed by the Audit Commission would provide a good starting point: leader, regulator and quality assurer, information provider, partner with local bodies, banker and planner (Audit Commission, 1989).

Some principles for a new funding system might be as follows:

- the Department for Education and Employment (DFEE), not, as currently, the Department of Environment, to distribute separate budgets to LEAs, for primary and secondary schools, according to a formula based on both pupil numbers and socio-economic factors;
- in the short-term, DFEE to distribute budgets to LEAs for nursery provision in such a way as to build upon existing provision, and target disadvantaged areas;
- all these budgets to be ring-fenced at the level of the LEA, but LEAs could top them up from local taxation;
- DFEE would set standards where necessary, for example for class sizes in primary schools, or for provision of nursery places.

The drawback of such a system from the point of view of LEAs would be that they would lose the discretion to, say, fund extra teachers in their secondary schools through cutting back nursery provision or increasing primary school class sizes. This is a small price to pay for the positive effects that would ensue in terms of transparency, equality of opportunity and entitlement for children in the years in which they have a lot to lose and little capacity to choose for themselves.

## Summary of recommendations

This chapter has identified six problems in the field of education and training in the UK. The table below summarises its key recommendations.

Table 6.6 Key problems and recommendations

| Problems | Ways forward |
| --- | --- |
| Under-investment in the early years | Shift of public investment to nursery and primary education |
| Wide differentials of school performance with large concentrations of low achievers | Rigorous headteacher selection and training, improvements to physical infrastructure, boost to literacy scheme |
| Failure to raise the status and quality of teaching | Teachers to have a more focused role, drawing on a wider range of skills and expertise, using new technologies, and engaged in continuous learning |
| Qualifications that promote early and inflexible specialisation for the 'academic', and low status options for the rest | Integration and broadening of post-16 qualifications |
| Unfair and unsustainable funding for post-compulsory education and training | Development of a system of entitlements for lifelong learning |
| Lack of accountability | Recasting of the funding regime for schools |

## Notes

1. This may reflect the increasing numbers of lower-than-average performers who have stayed on as a result of the recent high and sustained levels of unemployment.
2. This situation is not dissimilar to that found in the area of health care (see Chapter 7).

## References

Adult Literacy and Basic Skills Unit (ALBSU) (1987), *Literacy, Numeracy and Adults: Evidence from the National Child Development Study*, ALBSU.

ALBSU (1993a), *Basic Skills Support in Colleges: Assessing the Need*, ALBSU.

ALBSU (1993b), *The Cost to Industry: Basic Skills and the UK Workforce*, ALBSU.

ALBSU (1993c), *Parents and their Children: the Intergenerational Effect of Poor Basic Skills*, ALBSU.

Atkinson, J. and Spilsbury, M. (1993), *Basic Skills and Jobs*, ALBSU.

Audit Commission (1989), *Losing an Empire, Finding a Role*, London: HMSO.

Audit Commission (1995), *Local Authority Performance Indicators: Volume 1*, London: HMSO.

Authers, J. (1995), 'Expansion taxes higher education', *Financial Times*, 20.3.95.

Becker, G. (1964), *Human Capital: a Theoretical and Empirical Analysis, With Special Reference to Education*, New York: Columbia University Press.

Bennett, N. (1994), *Class Size in Primary Schools: Perceptions of Headteachers, Chairs of Governors, Teachers and Parents*, Exeter: University of Exeter.

Botkin, J., Elmandjra, M. and Malitza, M. (1979), *No Limits to Learning: Bridging the Human Gap*, Oxford: Pergamon.

Brooks, G. *et al* (1995), *Standards in Literacy and Numeracy, 1948-1994*, National Commission on Education Briefing New Series 7.

Brown, G. (1994), *University for Industry: Turning the Workplace into a Centre of Continuous Learning*, London: Labour Party.

Centre for Educational Research and Innovation (CERI) (1995), *Education at a Glance*, Organisation for Economic Cooperation and Development.

Commission on Social Justice (1995), *Social Justice: Strategies for National Renewal*, London: Vintage.

Court, G., Morris, S., Reilly, B. and Williams, M. (1995), *Teachers: Recruitment, and the Labour Market*, Brighton: Institute for Employment Studies.

Dearing, R. (1995), *Review of 16-19 Qualifications: Interim Report*, London: SCAA.

Department for Education (DfE) (1993), *1992 Secondary School Staffing Survey*, London: DfE.

DfE (1994), Statistics of Schools in England. *Statistical Bulletin*, August, 1994.

DfE (1995) Pupils Under Five Years of Age in Schools in England. *Statistical Bulletin*, February, 1995.

Department of Education and Science (DES) (1991), *Education and Training for the 21st Century*, London: HMSO.

*Education* (1994), The Right to Read has Become a Family Matter, 25 March 1994.

Ekinsmyth, C. and Bynner, J. (1993), *The Basic Skills of Young Adults: Some Findings from the 1970 British Cohort Study*, ALBSU.

*Employment Gazette* (various issues). Sheffield: Employment Department.

Etzioni, A. (1969), *The Semi-professions and their Organisation: Teachers, Nurses and Social Workers*, New York: Free Press.

Falkingham, J. and Hills, J. (1995), *The Dynamics of Welfare*, Hemel Hempstead: Prentice Hall/Harvester.

Finegold, D., Keep, E., Miliband, D., Raffe, D., Spours, K., Young, M. (1990), *A British 'Baccalaureate': Ending the Division Between Education and Training*, London: Institute for Public Policy Research.

Finegold, D. and Soskice, D. (1988), 'The failure of training in Britain: analysis and prescription', *Oxford Review of Economic Policy*, Vol. **4** (3), pp.30-7.

Further Education Funding Council (1994), *General National Vocational Qualifications in the Further Education Sector in England*, FEFC.

Further Education Unit, University of London Institute of Education and Nuffield Foundation (1994), *GNVQs 1993-94: a National Survey Report*, London: Further Education Unit.

Glennerster, H. (May, 1995), 'Opportunity costs', *New Economy*.

Goldstein, H. and Sammons, P. (1994), *The Influence of Secondary and Junior Schools on 16-year Examination Performance: a Cross-classified Multi-level Analysis*, London: Institute of Education.

Gorman, T. and Fernandes, C. (1992), *Reading in Recession*, National Foundation for Educational Research (NFER).

Government Statistical Service (1995), *Education Statistics for the United Kingdom*, HMSO.

Green, A. and Steedman, H. (1993), *Educational Provision, Educational Attainment and the Needs of Industry: a Review of Research for Germany, France, Japan, the USA and Britain*, National Institute of Economic and Social Research (NIESR).

Green, F. (1994), 'Training: inequality and inefficiency', in Glyn, A. and Miliband, D. (eds.), *Paying for Inequality: the Economic Cost of Social Injustice*, Rivers: Oram Press.

Hayes, C., Fonda, N. and Hillman, J. (1995), *Learning in the New Millennium*, National Commission on Education Briefing New Series 5.

Hillman, J. (1994), 'Undergraduate perceptions of teaching as a career', in National Commission on Education, *Insights into Education and Training*, London: Heinemann.

Husen, T. (1974) *The Learning Society*, London: Methuen.

Institute of Education (1994), *Assessing School Effectiveness: Developing Measures to Put School Performance in Context*, OFSTED.

Jarousse, J-P., Mingat, A. and Marc, R. (1995), 'Nursery education for two-year-olds: social and educational effects', in Moon, B. and Corbett, A. (eds.), *Education Reform in France: the Mitterrand years 1981-1995*, London: Routledge.

Keys, W. and Fernandes, C. (1993), *What Do Students Think About School?* NFER.

Labour Party (1994), *Opening Doors to a Learning Society.* The Labour Party.

Lawlor, S. (1994), *Nursery Choices.* London: Centre for Policy Studies.

MORI (1989), *How and Why Parents Choose an Independent School,* London: MORI.

Mortimore, P. (1995), *Effective Schools: Current Impact and Future Potential,* London: Institute of Education.

Mortimore, P. and Blatchford, P. (1993), 'The issue of class size', in *National Commission on Education Briefings,* London: Heinemann.

Moss, P. (1994), 'Statistics on early childhood services: placing Britain in an international context', in Ball, C. (ed.), *Start Right: The Importance of Early Learning,* London: RSA.

National Advisory Council for Education and Training Targets (NACETT) (1995), *Report on Progress Towards the National Targets,* London: NACETT.

National Commission on Education (NCE) (1993) *Learning to Succeed,* London: Heinemann.

National Commission on Education (NCE) (1995a), *Success Against the Odds: Effective Schools in Disadvantaged Areas,* London: Routledge.

National Commission on Education (NCE) (1995b), *Learning to Succeed: the Way Ahead,* London: National Commission on Education.

Office for Standards in Education (OFSTED)/Audit Commission (1993a), *Unfinished Business: Full-time Educational Courses for 16-19 Year Olds,* London: HMSO.

OFSTED (1993b), *The New Teacher in School,* London: HMSO.

OFSTED (1994), *GNVQs in Schools 1993/94,* London: HMSO.

OFSTED (1995), *The Annual Report of Her Majesty's Chief Inspector of Schools,* London: HMSO.

Postlethwaite, T. and Wiley, D. (1991), *Science Achievement in 23 Countries,* Oxford: Pergamon.

Prais, S. and Beadle, E. (1991), *Pre-vocational Schooling in Europe Today,* NIESR.

Raffe, D. and Surridge, P. (1995), *More of the Same? Participation of 16-18 Year Olds in Education,* National Commission on Education Briefing New Series No. **6**.

Ranson, S. (1994), *Towards a Learning Society,* London: Cassell.

Richardson, W., Spours, K., Woolhouse, J. and Young, M. (1994), *14-19 Education and Training: Changes and Challenges,* Learning for the Future Working Paper.

Table 7.1 British Health Policy 1948-95

| | Health care delivery | Population health | Accountability | NHS finance |
|---|---|---|---|---|
| **1948-78:**<br>**The era of planning** | 1962: Hospital Plan<br><br>1974: reorganisation of NHS<br><br>1974-76: disputes on private practice and pay beds | 1976: 'Priorities for Health and Social Services'<br><br>Improve services for neglected groups, e.g. elderly, people with disabilities | 1974: creation of Community Health Councils - regional and district health authorities | 1950s & 60s: rapid growth in NHS expenditure<br><br>1976: report of Guillebaud Committee on the cost of NHS<br><br>1976: RAWP report on allocation funding<br><br>1979: Royal Commission on NHS |
| **1979-88:**<br>**The growth of managerialism** | 1982: reorganisation of the NHS. Ninety AHAs replaced by 200 DHAs<br><br>1983: Griffiths Report on management in the NHS<br><br>1983: contracting out of non-clinical services | 1987: Promoting Better Health | 1982: new NHS structure<br><br>Reduction in local authority representation on DHAs | Tight public expenditure control<br><br>1987-88: financial crisis in the NHS |
| **1988-95:**<br>**The creation of an internal market** | 1990: NHS and Community Care Act<br><br>1993: Managing the New NHS (merger of DHAs and FHSAs)<br><br>1994: Developing NHS Purchasing and GP Fundholding | 1992: Health of the Nation | 1990: new governance structures for Trusts and health authorities. No local authority representation<br><br>1992: Patient's Charter | Generous public expenditure settlement in 1991-92 and 1992-93 |

**Table 7.2 An assessment of health policy 1948-95**

### 'Planning' 1948-78

**Strengths**

- Macro-efficient: tight control of NHS expenditure
- Macro-equitable: treatment based on clinical need (?)
- Macro-accountable: Ministerial accountability
- Management by consensus

**Deficiencies**

- Funding crisis in economic downturn
- Micro-inefficient: lengthening waiting lists
- Micro-inequitable: unresponsive, different waiting times, variable standards of service, e.g. GPs
- Dominance of acute hospital medicine: neglect of services for priority groups or population health
- Paternalistic bureaucracy: professional domination, neglect of users
- Lack of leadership

### 'Managerialism' 1979-88

**Strengths**

- Incentives to improve internal efficiency: performance review, contracting out
- General management: mobilising consent for change

**Deficiencies**

- Funding crisis: 1987-88
- Long waiting lists for elective surgery
- NHS agenda still dominated by acute hospitals

### 'Internal markets' 1989-94

**Strengths**

- Purchaser/provider split: free DHAs from management of services to focus on needs assessment and commissioning; devolved managerial responsibility to Trusts
- GPFHs shaken up inefficient hospital system
- Improved information (?)
- Emphasis on outcomes and appropriateness

**Deficiencies**

- Rising administrative and managerial costs
- Two-tier health service (?)
- Perceived lack of *local* accountability
- Organisational turbulence (?)

*1979-87: The growth of managerialism*

The new Conservative Government of 1979 carried out its manifesto pledge to decentralise the NHS. The main feature of the 1982 model NHS was to further streamline the organisational structure, with the middle tier - the Area Health Authorities - being replaced by smaller 'District Health Authorities'. The change in policy was partly a reaction against central planning but it was also a way of passing responsibility for allocating resources away from central government at a time of severe budgetary constraints.

The policy of 'small is beautiful' was short-lived. After the 1983 General Election, Patrick Jenkin was replaced as Secretary of State for Health and Social Security by Norman Fowler, who had a radically different approach. The policies he introduced, such as contracting out of non-clinical services, laid the foundations for the implementation of the internal market in the NHS. The Department of Health and Social Security adopted a system of performance review designed to monitor progress towards the achievement of very specific targets with a tighter system of control and central accountability than had ever existed in the previous history of the NHS (Butler, 1993). Norman Fowler unreservedly accepted the late Roy Griffith's managerialist diagnosis of the ills of the health service and enthusiastically implemented general management at all levels (House of Commons, 1983).

However, the introduction of general management in the NHS and the involvement of clinicians in the running of hospitals through the Resource Management Initiative (DHSS, 1986) did not resolve the underlying difficulties facing the health service, namely increased budgetary pressures and inefficiencies in the use of resources within the service. Substantial waiting lists for hospital care in some parts of Britain coexisted with under-utilised surgical facilities in others. Beds, staff, theatre time and revenue resources were not always distributed across districts to ensure their optimum use. Operating theatres were poorly managed, according to a report by the National Audit Office (NAO), such that only some 50-60 per cent of planned sessions actually occurred (Public Accounts Committee, 1988). In the winter of 1987-88 the NHS was engulfed in a financial crisis which prompted Mrs Thatcher to set up a fundamental review of the NHS.

*1989-95: the creation of an internal market in the NHS*

A striking feature of the NHS and the welfare state during the first two Thatcher administrations was that they remained largely unchanged. The vast majority of the population was still served by state-funded and state-provided systems of education, health care and social services. Yet there were many within the Conservative Government who saw in the very principles of the NHS and welfare services many of the manifestations of Britain's supposed post-war malaise: the heavy influence of central and local bureaucracies; the restrictive practices of powerful professions; the absence of real consumer choice; an indifference to the quality of what was provided; lack of incentives for innovation and efficiency; and a deadening reliance upon government funds (Butler, 1993). It was therefore not surprising that a major offensive against the bureaucratic structures of welfare provision was launched in 1988 and 1989, years that in retrospect may be seen as critical in the history of British social policy (Le Grand and Bartlett, 1993).

The reforms embodied in the 1990 NHS and Community Care Act and introduced on 1 April 1991 represented the greatest change in the organisation and management of the NHS since it was established. A form of market structure was created within the NHS in which the responsibility for purchasing services was separated from the responsibility for providing them. On the demand side of the market, the key decision-makers became the district health authorities (DHAs) and general practice (GP) fundholders. DHAs had major new responsibilities for assessing the health care needs of their resident populations and for commissioning secondary and community health services to meet those needs from a range of providers including the voluntary and private sectors. Between 1991 and 1994 there have been a number of amalgamations among DHAs, as they no longer manage hospitals, and several initiatives designed to integrate DHA functions with those of Family Health Service Authorities who are responsible for overseeing the development of primary care services. Operating along side health authorities are an increasing number of GP fundholders. These GPs receive budgets from district allocations with which they can purchase a range of diagnostic, out-patient and elective inpatient procedures for patients registered with them. On the supply side of the market, the key change has been the establishment of NHS trusts (Box 7.1). These are independent of the health authorities, but still part of the NHS, providing acute and community health services. They are directly accountable to the Secretary of State for Health. Trusts can set the pay and conditions of service of their workforce, decide upon the size and skill-mix of their staff and exercise some limited new freedoms in relation to capital expenditure.

It is worth noting that *Working for Patients* left the financing of the Health Service largely unchanged except for modest changes to the funding formula for district health authorities, despite the fact that it was financial difficulties that prompted the review of the NHS in the first instance. Initially the NHS review group did consider alternative methods of financing the health service such as private health insurance. However, a recognition of the difficulties of controlling health expenditure in insurance-based systems combined with the associated political sensitivities quickly forced a change of direction; instead the group considered proposals for increasing the efficiency with which *existing* resources were used and this formed the nucleus of *Working for Patients*. Although there was scope to improve internal efficiency within the NHS, the decision to ignore the resource constraint confronting the health service was to re-emerge as a critical issue as the impact of the reforms started to be felt.

## Figure 7.1  The changing administrative structure of the National Health Service (England)

### 1948 Model

### 1974 Model

### 1982 Model

## 1990 Model

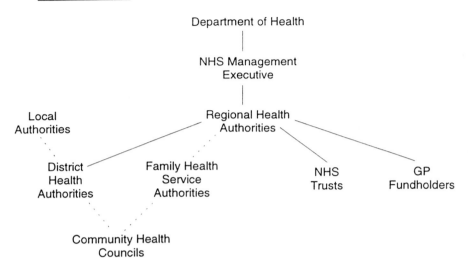

## 1996 Model

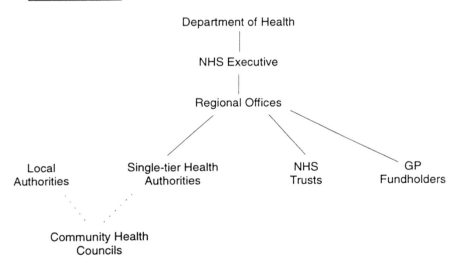

——————  Indicates line of direct managerial authority
- - - - - -  Indicates consultative/co-ordinating relationships

*Impact of the NHS reforms*

It is difficult to identify significant improvements arising from the implementation of the 1990 NHS and Community Care Act partly because there has been no system of monitoring and evaluation and also because it is difficult to isolate the impact of the reforms from other changes that have been happening. Resources going into the NHS increased in real terms by 6.1 per cent and 5.5 per cent respectively in 1991/92 and in 1992/93; it would therefore be astonishing if there had been no changes in waiting lists or improvements in the range of services offered quite independently of any changes in the delivery systems of health care (Le Grand and Robinson, 1993). Likewise the reorganisation of hospital services, which could involve the closure of some of Britain's best-known hospitals, would have been discussed regardless of the introduction of the internal market. Restructuring of acute hospitals would have been on the agenda in the old-style health authorities as changes would have been necessitated by the major advances in medical science and technology, combined with reductions in junior doctors' hours and the need for larger, more specialist clinical teams. In the future there are likely to be fewer but larger hospitals providing specialist services with a greater range of health care services provided in community and in primary care settings.

There is evidence to suggest that the reforms are working in a number of areas. Freed from the responsibility for managing health services, health authorities are now able to concentrate on assessing health care needs and commissioning services to meet those needs. The information requirements of a market system are requiring both purchasers and providers to improve their costing procedures and information systems. Cost sensitivity also seems to be increasing throughout the service, with a consequent reduction in wasteful procedures and increased resource savings (Le Grand, 1993).

However, the reforms are not without their problems. Costing and other aspects of running the market require extra administration. The accountability of both purchasers and providers to the local community as a whole is tenuous, and many patients will not know whether their GP is a fundholder or not. The contracting process has not necessarily resulted in a better use of resources. Some health authorities, particularly those in rural areas, have to accept an inefficient and expensive service because they cannot risk jeopardising their local hospital's financial position. In a study of the cost structures of the first and second waves of hospital trusts, it was found that in many areas of hospital activity, trusts had significantly lower costs than non-trusts. However, these could not be attributed to the reforms, since the data were taken from the period immediately before the reforms were implemented. The results showed that the first and, to a lesser extent, the second wave of trusts were a selected group of units that were *already* among the most efficient providers (Bartlett and Le Grand, 1993).

## Box 7.1  Key facts about the NHS

- Government spending on health has increased by around two-thirds in real terms since 1977-78 and is estimated at £39.3 billion for 1994-95. This is equivalent to an average growth of just under 3 per cent per year. Spending on health now represents around 14 per cent of government expenditure or 6 per cent of GDP. Staff costs account for around 70 per cent of these sums.

- In the decade following 1981, the average number of in-patient beds available in the NHS fell by just under a third (from 351,000 to 242,000 in 1991-92; the fall was especially marked for mental health hospital beds). However, over the same period, the number of patients treated (as measured by finished consultant episodes) increased by 35 per cent. From 1976 to 1994, day case attendances increased from 0.6 to 2.7 million, accidents and emergency attendances increased from 10.5 to 13.7 million, and other new out-patient attendances increased from 9.2 to 11.9 million.

- From April 1991, health authorities became responsible for purchasing health services and the concept of NHS Trusts was established. Hospitals that became NHS Trusts were allowed to advertise, raise their own funds and to bid for contracts to treat patients. By April 1994 there were 419 NHS Trusts in England delivering 96 per cent of NHS hospital and community health services, and there were 13 in Northern Ireland delivering 70 per cent of such services in the region.

- GP fundholding is a voluntary scheme allowing medical practices to manage sums of NHS money (see text). By April 1994, 8,800 GPs in over 2,000 practices in Great Britain had become fundholders; these covered 36 per cent of the population.

- The Patient's Charter (April 1992) states that patients must be given detailed information on the quality standards and maximum waiting times of local services, and admission for treatment is guaranteed no later than two years after being put on the waiting list. The proportion of patients who had waited for over twelve months was 6.3 per cent in 1994 compared with 18.3 per cent in 1991, but the total number of people on the waiting list increased. There are wide variations in waiting times across regions and specialities.

- There has been over a 20-fold increase in the number of NHS managers since the late 1980s, with the salary bill increasing from around £26 million to £500 million (or 1.4 per cent of health spending) over a six year period.

Sources:  Data from Central Statistical Office, 1994, 1995a and 1995b; Central Office of Information, 1995.

## Current major issues in health policy: the future of purchasing

Health care delivery systems across the industrialised world are undergoing far-reaching changes. Demographic change, rapid developments in medical science and technology and unrelenting pressure to contain costs are requiring managers, health care professionals and politicians to rethink how health services are organised and how they are financed.

In Britain, the major issue that will confront the government over the next few years is whether the internal market in the NHS should be retained, abolished or extended. The operation of the internal market has thrown up a range of issues:

- Trust boards and to a lesser extent, purchasing authorities, are viewed as unaccountable by local populations, particularly when such bodies have agreed to the closure of hospitals which have been strongly opposed by residents and patients;

- GP fundholding is thought to have created a 'two-tier' service in which some patients have preferential access to treatment and the extension of fundholding may exacerbate an inequitable pattern of care;

- A market in health care may make it more difficult to plan and deliver high quality services which are sensitive to the needs of patients and may increase administrative costs, because competition could impede effective collaboration between health and social care providers.

At a strategic level there are three options available to a future Secretary of State for Health. He or she could decide to abolish Trusts and GP fundholding and return to the pre-reforms structure of health authorities having both purchaser and provider functions. Alternatively the market could be extended by enabling Trusts to become independent bodies, outside the NHS, extending fundholding to all GPs and increasing the role of private finance. A third option would be to retain the purchaser-provider structure but to tackle the deficiencies of the internal market such as weak local accountability and rising administrative costs. A detailed discussion of these options is beyond the scope of this chapter, but one aspect of the internal market, the future of purchasing, is considered in detail.

## The organisation of purchasing

The NHS reforms created two different types of purchaser: District Health Authority (DHA) purchasers and GP fundholders. These represented two different, and arguably incompatible, models of purchasing. Whereas DHA purchasers are required to carry out needs assessments as the basis for their purchasing plans and to balance priorities for the complete range of health care needs in a large population (roughly 500,000), GP fundholders are expected to interpret their patients' demands by purchasing a selected range of services (hospital outpatient services, admissions for elective surgery, diagnostic tests and investigations, community health services) for a relatively small practice population (roughly 10,000 patients). DHA purchasing is similar to the traditional top-down planning model, whereas GP fundholding was to be bottom-up and demand-led, with responsiveness to patients as its key characteristic. Although GP fundholding represents a substantial transfer of resources to GPs, the fundholders have purchasing power over only about a quarter of the total hospital and community health care costs of their patients. The remaining services are the direct responsibility of the DHA purchasers who purchase accident and emergency services, general medical inpatient admissions, specialist services and some community services.

Since the implementation of *Working for Patients*, the structure of purchasing has become increasingly diverse. As districts have shed their provider functions, they have merged to form larger consortia to purchase health care. An increasing number of districts have formed health commissions with Family Health Service Authorities (FHSAs) in order to contain managerial costs, promote joint working with local authorities (boundaries are often coterminous) and foster an integrated approach to primary and secondary health care. Health commissions have the advantages of size and strategic capability, but they could become more remote from primary health care practitioners and residents. All DHAs and FHSAs will be required to merge to form new unitary health authorities by April 1996 (DoH, 1993). The take up of GP fundholding has been uneven. In some areas, such as Hertfordshire, between 80 and 90 per cent of GPs are in fundholding practices whereas in deprived urban communities, such as Lambeth, Southwark and Lewisham, the proportion of the population covered by fundholding practices is less than 15 per cent. The present Government is committed to extending fundholding further and has recently introduced community fundholding (for small practices with 3,000 or more patients) and pilot schemes for total fundholding. Hence, at a local level, a wide range of purchasing initiatives have developed involving fundholding and non-fundholding GPs.

Partly to counterbalance their increasing size, health authorities have sought to develop a local area perspective to commissioning in order to involve residents, voluntary groups and general practices. Locality purchasing is designed to ensure that purchasing is sensitive to local needs and views, typically by devolving purchasing decisions to a locality manager or group, or by reflecting a locality's needs and views in central purchasing decisions (Ovretveit, 1995). In some authorities, practices are given a shadow budget rather like a fundholder's budget but covering most hospital services. Although the benefits and drawbacks depend on the model used, in general, locality purchasing:

- allows GPs to influence the full range of hospital and community services purchased by a health authority, rather than the more limited range of the GP fundholding scheme;

- saves GPs the time, trouble and expense of fundholding, but gives some of the advantages, albeit shared with a larger number of GPs;

- retains the purchasing power of contracts for larger groups of patients, but allows GPs' and others' preferences to be built into contracts;

- makes the most efficient use of scarce commissioning staff expertise and contracting systems;

- counteracts the potential and perceived remoteness of larger commissioning authorities; and

- provides one way of integrating a variety of FHSA and DHA activities (Ovretveit, 1995).

The disadvantages of such arrangements are that while GPs may have greater involvement in contracting decisions, locality schemes do not give the clear financial sanctions and incentives of the kind that fundholding does (Glennerster, 1994). Locality schemes will involve additional administrative and support costs but, as non-fundholding practices do not qualify for additional financial support, these costs have to be borne by the district.

A more recent innovation is the creation of GP multi-funds. Multi-funds are a 'bottom-up' model in which a number of fundholding practices agree to set up their own purchasing organisation and employ their own contract managers, who are directly accountable to the multi-fund. The advantages of multi-funds are that they reduce management overheads and increase the leverage which GPs can exert over providers; GPs also have more control if they employ contract managers directly rather than having to rely on health authority managers as in schemes to involve GPs in purchasing which are organised by the health authority. Multi-funds are attractive to small practices who are reluctant to become single-handed fundholders, but are nevertheless interested in becoming part of a larger GP purchasing group. There are, however, several aspects of multi-funds which are problematic: they are not 'stable' organisations and are critically dependent on the commitment of a few GPs to oversee the running of the group and, as with fundholding practices, the accountability of multi-funds to patients and local residents is weak.

*An assessment of different types of purchasers*

It is difficult to draw conclusions on the relative successes and failures of alternative purchasing models partly because most of the studies of fundholding have been small scale projects and few have been comparative studies. The limited studies of GPs' impressions that have been conducted have found fundholders convinced that there have been quality improvements as a result of fundholding (Newton et al, 1993; Bain, 1994; Corney, 1994; Glennerster et al, 1994), whereas those involved in non-fundholding groups are less certain about what fundholding GPs have achieved (Grafty and Williams, 1994). Improved communication between GPs and hospital consultants and provider unit managers has been seen as one of the greatest benefits of the fundholding scheme (Newton et al, 1993; Bain, 1994; Corney, 1994; Glennerster et al, 1994). Reports from non-fundholders involved in purchasing groups have also reported greater contact with providers; and it is said that communication has improved because a competing system of decentralised purchasing has forced districts to improve their contracting skills and to invent new ways of involving GPs in the contracting process (Glennerster et al, 1994; Willis, 1992).

In theory, GPs ought to be more effective contractors than districts because GPs have the incentives and the information to seek better contracts. Unlike districts, GPs have personal contact with the patients before and after admission to hospital and so can directly assess the quality of care provided. The GPs are very aware of any delays and patient dissatisfaction. GPs have been able to diversify their providers, bring to bear a real threat of moving their business elsewhere, and provide their patients with choice and a speedier and better service (Glennerster, 1994). However, GPs' behaviour may be in part a function of the type of practices that were selected for inclusion fundholding; arguably these were among the more dynamic of GP practices. Furthermore, while DHA purchasers were explicitly required to maintain a 'steady state' in the first couple of years after organisational changes, fundholders were free to negotiate contracts with new providers if they were unhappy with the service provided by their local hospital even from the first year of the reforms. This makes it is difficult to compare the two models fairly. It is acknowledged that the costs of practice-based contracting are higher than district based contracting. However, Glennerster has speculated that these additional costs may be partly offset by improvements in cost-effectiveness stemming from the more individualised patient information and monitoring of hospital progress that can be achieved as a result of practice-based contracting. Also, contracting costs may be lower for GP fundholders who have set up consortia or multi-funds.

One of the criticisms of GP fundholding is that it fragments the system and makes it more difficult for health authorities to plan services for their populations. However, it could also be argued that 'a multitude of decisions made closer to users is more likely to reflect accurately their wants and needs than some overall view from a district planning office' (Bartlett and Le Grand, 1993). A balance needs to be struck between responding to individual patients' needs and meeting the overall population's needs. Many fundholders have reinvested savings in developing new practice-based services such as physiotherapy. These services have been very popular with patients, but have been criticised for not necessarily being 'cost effective' innovations in the sense that they could be more cheaply provided in a hospital setting (Coulter and Bradlow, 1993).

There is also real concern that fundholders receive more generous funding than non-fundholders. Since the implementation of the reforms, there have been press reports towards the end of each financial year of hospitals refusing elective admissions from non-fundholding practices because the DHA contract targets have been met and allocations spent (British Medical Journal, 1993). When the fundholding scheme was introduced, budgets were based on past patterns of service use, an unsatisfactory method of allocating resources for several reasons (Coulter, 1992). It was extremely difficult to determine the extent of past activity because of inadequate routine data. Partly for this reason and partly because hospital prices varied widely, budgets allocated to fundholders varied by a factor of three (Day and Klein, 1991). To counteract these problems the Department of Health is now anxious to move towards formula based funding. Nevertheless, there is an underlying and inequitable disparity between fundholding and non-fundholding patients' access to non-emergency care. As fundholders do not have responsibility for paying for accident and emergency care (A&E), they can be sure that their budget for elective surgery will be unaffected by A&E use. By contrast, health authorities are required to pay for all A&E admissions regardless of whether patients are registered with a fundholding or non-fundholding practice. As A&E

admissions have been rising, health authorities have had to reduce the volume of elective work in order to stay within their budgets.

'Cream-skimming' is also a danger. Cream-skimming involves GP fundholders not accepting patients on to their list who are likely to require expensive treatments because they would place additional demands on their budget. Although there has been no systematic research indicating whether patient selection by GPs is or is not happening, it is clearly a real possibility. Unless fundholders are funded on a basis that is adjusted for more costly patients, cream-skimming by fundholding practices could become widespread. There are also indications that patients of fundholding GPs receive preferential treatment. Whitehead refers to growing evidence that a two-tier service is developing with hospitals and consultants offering services to patients of fundholders that are denied to patients of non-fundholders (Whitehead, 1994).

## Accountability of purchasers

Very few members of the public are aware of what health commissioning is supposed to be about, and recently the accountability of fundholding GPs and health authorities has become an issue. This partly reflects growing public disquiet about the membership and activities of 'quangos', but it also reflects specific concerns regarding decisions taken by health authorities, particularly regarding the future of well-known acute hospitals. Yet despite the concerns arising from such decisions, health authorities are still often viewed as having greater legitimacy than GP fundholders.

The debate about the appropriate balance of accountability to the centre and local discretion has existed since the formation of the NHS. The health service is a *national* service that is centrally financed through general taxation; this requires the Secretary of State for Health to be accountable to Parliament for the performance and financing of the NHS. As strict accountability is impossible within such a large and complex organisation, the Secretary of State delegates responsibility to health authorities and Trusts to act as her, or his, agent in managing expenditure on health services. Each authority is directly accountable to the Secretary of State for Health through the new regional offices that have replaced regional health authorities (see also Chapter 12 on devolution). The nature of the relationship between the centre and the periphery has changed over time and reflects growing tensions within the service as finances have become tighter and the political pressures to treat more patients have increased. The NHS had previously been accused of being centralised, monolithic and bureaucratic (Department of Health and Social Security, 1979) and yet also decentralised, fragmented and insufficiently accountable (Public Accounts Committee, 1981). Increasingly as the 1980s progressed, health authorities came to act more as the agents of central government than as the representatives of their local communities (Klein, 1989). As greater operational responsibility was devolved to local managers, so government assumed a tighter control over the strategies, structures and resources within which they could work.

Improvements in accountability can be achieved by demonstrating that public views are sought and taken into account and by working more closely with bodies with a greater legitimacy amongst the population, such as local councils, local residents' associations, as well as directly with the population concerned (Perry, 1994). The removal of local authority representation from health authority boards was seen by some as weakening the links with local communities and as a means of reducing dissent. Health authorities are formally accountable to the Secretary of State for Health, but they are required to consult and take account of the views of their local population in making major decisions regarding the organisation of services - and they should do so.

### Future policy options for health care purchasing

Although the configuration of purchasing organisations will continue to evolve in response to local circumstances, a future Secretary of State for Health may be under pressure to introduce more fundamental changes in order to facilitate greater *local* democratic accountability and to ensure more equitable access to health services. Possible options, some of which could be complementary, are shown in Box 7.2; all involve retaining the purchaser-provider structure.

### Box 7.2  The future of health care purchasing: different organisational structures

| | |
|---|---|
| **Option A:** | Transfer the responsibility for health care purchasing to local government. |
| **Option B:** | GP fundholders and single-tier purchasing authorities are made accountable to a directly elected regional tier of government, which would appoint health authority members. |
| **Option C:** | Abolish GP fundholding and transfer the responsibility for purchasing health care to single-tier purchasing authorities. |
| **Option D:** | Make appointments to health authorities more open by advertising appointments and the selection procedure. |
| **Option E:** | Create directly elected health authority boards. |
| **Option F:** | Replace single practice fundholding by area - based primary care commissioning groups, with health authorities having responsibility for strategic development and performance monitoring. |
| **Option G:** | All GPs would become fundholders with some GPs forming purchasing consortia; health authorities would wither away and regional health authorities would monitor performance of GP fundholders. |

The most far reaching change would involve transferring the responsibility for health care purchasing to local government (option A). The idea of greater local authority involvement in health care is not a new one (Regan and Stewart, 1982), and recently the proposal has been revived by Harrison *et al*

(1991) and Wistow (1993). In principle, the local government option offers three important benefits to health policy. First, it provides a direct democratic input and a democratic legitimacy for rationing decisions. Second, it offers, but does not *guarantee* (Mays, 1993), full integration of health and social care planning and purchasing, ending the present artificial division between the two and the incentives for cost shifting generated by it. The division of responsibility is most problematic for priority care groups such as people with learning difficulties and mental health problems who require an integrated package of services including health care, supported housing and day care. All too often the needs of these groups are not met because of a lack of co-ordination. Third, it brings health policy into a service delivery structure which includes important determinants of health: environmental health, transport systems, public housing and social services, all of which are still substantially regulated by local authorities.

However, integrating the health authority functions with local government has been strongly opposed. The National Association of Health Authorities and Trusts (NAHAT) has argued against transferring purchasing to local authorities on the grounds that local government is not really democratic at all, being both over-politicised and over-bureaucratised with important decisions being made by ill-informed councillors and a correspondingly reduced role for managers (National Association of Health Authorities and Trusts, 1993, p.14). This is a weak argument; local government does have its faults, but these could (and should) be addressed in their own right. For example, the functioning of local authorities could be improved by paying members higher allowances to enable people with business and managerial skills to commit the time required. At least councillors, unlike health authority members, are elected by, and formally accountable to, local residents and can be removed from office if the public feel that they have not represented its interests appropriately. NAHAT has also advocated the status quo because local government control would undermine the national character of the NHS by introducing local variation in the range of services provided. To some extent this already happens, but safeguards do need to be built into the system to ensure that there is equitable access to treatment across the country. For example, a national package of health care rights could be set out that would require all health purchasers to provide a minimum range of services. The NHS Executive could continue to set national priorities and local authorities could be made accountable to the Executive on strategic issues (Harrison and Hunter, 1994). The major difficulty in transferring the purchasing function to local authorities is that it is highly unlikely that central government (both ministers and civil servants) would wish to transfer the control of such a large budget to local government. One option is to raise a much greater proportion of health care finance through local taxation. Local taxation has both advantages and drawbacks. On the positive side, a local tax based service offers the opportunity to increase funding for the health service as residents could decide to pay higher taxes to fund service improvements. It would be possible to incorporate fundholding practices into such a structure, with the practices being accountable to local Health and Social Services Committees for how they spend their budget and implement local health plans. Community Health Councils could take on responsibility for providing advocacy and advice for users of social services. On the negative side, the quality of a health service based largely on local taxes might come to vary widely according to the wealth of the area concerned. Also, of course, there tends to be strong resistance to high levels of local taxation.

There are a range of other options which would increase accountability without requiring a major reorganisation of health service functions. Single tier health authorities (integrated district and family health service authorities) could be made accountable to a directly elected regional tier of government (Option B). Health authority boundaries could be made coterminous with such regional local authorities to facilitate joint working and accountability. Regional government would be responsible for appointing health authority and Trust members. In addition, there could be a requirement to advertise positions on health authority and Trust boards and to ensure a balance of skills, interests and political views (option D). GP fundholders could be made accountable to area health authorities or direct to the region (option G). Regions would also then be responsible for overseeing the performance of Trust boards.

Option C would involve the abolition of GP fundholding and the transferring of the responsibility for purchasing to single-tier purchasing authorities. These health authorities could be directly elected (option E) or part of local government (option A). Although there is great opposition to fundholding, ending single practice fundholding could potentially be a protracted and difficult process and could even result in some GPs withdrawing from the NHS (Glennerster, 1994). An alternative approach would be to correct the real deficiencies of fundholding to ensure greater accountability and prevent the development of a two-tier system. For example, fundholding practices could be required to publish an annual service plan which would be made available to patients at the practice. The rights of patients to be able to change from a fundholding practice to a non-fundholding practice should be strengthened and patients should be able to appeal if they are removed from a list or not accepted by a practice. In addition, a funding formula needs to be devised to ensure that both types of general practice are financed on an equitable basis.

Access to health authority appointments could be opened up through advertising or appointed boards could be replaced by directly elected boards (option E). While direct elections to health authorities may promote local interest in health issues, the evidence from local elections suggests that the turnout will be low (the turnout is presently around 40 per cent for local elections). With elections focused on health issues, there is a greater danger that candidates will campaign to promote health care for some groups rather than others. If elections to health boards were to be introduced it would be necessary to develop advocacy services for people who are traditionally under-represented in decision-making structures. Issues about professional and user representation would also have to be clarified. Under a system of direct elections, doctors and other health care professionals could seek election which could frustrate or delay changes that are in the interests of patients. Parallel structures for professional representation and advice for elected members would need to be developed.

Many authorities have devolved purchasing to localities in order to reflect more fully the needs of individual areas but also to involve GPs in commissioning. Budgets could be devolved to localities and commissioning teams would be required to account to the health authority for the management of the budget; localities would also have to publish their commissioning intentions and show how they intended to meet health targets (option F). The advantages of primary care commissioning groups are that: their administrative overheads are likely to be lower than single practice fundholders as there are economies of scale in purchasing for a larger population; a wider range of health care professionals such as health visitors and district nurses could be involved in purchasing and developing a public health agenda; and smaller purchasing groups have more potential to facilitate the involvement of local residents in health issues than commissions which cover two or three local authorities. Health authorities would then concentrate on broad population health needs analysis, strategy development, resource allocation and performance monitoring to achieve the health strategy (Perry, 1994).

Option G would involve all GPs becoming fundholders, with some practices choosing to form purchasing consortia. The recent Executive Letter, *Developing NHS Purchasing and GP Fundholding - Towards a Primary Care-led NHS* (DoH, 1994) announced an extension of GP fundholding and a reduction in the list size for the standard fundholding scheme and pilot sites for total fundholding. Total fundholding will involve GPs purchasing the whole range of health care for their patients, including accident and emergency services. Health authorities would have a leading role in the development and implementation of a local health strategy, working in collaboration with GPs, NHS trusts, local agencies and residents. The difficulty with this model is that it is based on the belief that fundholding has improved patient care whereas the research findings are mixed. In addition, there are likely to be problems in implementing the strategy because many GPs who decided not to become fundholders are unlikely to enter the scheme voluntarily. Finally, it is doubtful whether there would be continued support within the health service for retaining health authorities that have an essentially advisory role rather than an operational function. The disappearance of health authorities is likely to further weaken local accountability and alternative structures would need to be developed.

In sum, there are a range of policy options for the future organisation of the NHS. We can safely predict that the organisation, or reorganisation, of the NHS will continue to be a focus of heated debate. However, the evidence suggests that such reorganisations tend to have relatively little effect on the delivery of patient care. It would certainly be desirable to revise or refine the system so as to increase the Service's accountability and responsiveness to patients, and also to address specific issues such as risk selection through 'cream-skimming' by parts of the Service. Some policy options to achieve these ends have been described above. However, for the most part, perhaps we should ask, 'Is another reorganisation really necessary?' Perhaps, instead, it is time for us to examine some wider and more strategic issues about health policy.

## Wider issues in health policy

It would be very easy for a future Secretary of State for Health to focus most of their time and energies on the internal workings of the NHS. But there are clearly other pressing issues which need to be addressed. These include: the financing of the NHS and the allocation of resources within the service, access and entitlement to long-term care, and the widening and entrenched inequalities in the health of the population. The responses to these issues will need to form a major part of our strategic health policies in the years to come, and it is to these issues that we now turn.

### Rationing and priority setting: difficult choices ahead

Health care delivery systems across the world are having to find ways of tackling the insoluble problem of rising demand and finite resources. Medical technology and medical science are going through a period of rapid development that is throwing up a whole range of new possibilities in prevention, diagnosis and treatment. Technological developments in every decade since the 1940s have led to the introduction of new procedures and treatments such as effective drug therapy for tuberculosis, the development of coronary care units, and latterly the use of streptokinase for the care and treatment of acute myocardial infarction (heart attack) and the use of lasers for surgical procedures.

Technological developments and an ageing population have led to increasing pressure on the budgets of welfare programmes in all industrialised countries. Since 1973, NHS spending has doubled in real terms, but waiting lists have grown longer (Box 7.1). The increased numbers of very elderly people, together with the fact that NHS costs have tended to rise faster than prices generally (as in education, see Chapter 6), help to explain the discrepancy. Once these factors are taken into account, NHS resources are about one-third higher than what they were twenty years ago (Hills, 1993). Resources have always been rationed within the NHS and the need to make choices has not suddenly appeared since the introduction of a market structure. The purchaser-provider structure has simply made those choices more transparent, as some authorities have sought to restrict the availability of some treatments such as IVF (In Vitro Fertilisation), judging them to be less important than others.

It is now self-evident that the NHS cannot provide everything for everyone and that the demands on the Health Service are increasing all the time. Some difficult choices will need to be made and the relationship between the NHS and private health care carefully considered. Politicians have to be prepared to openly acknowledge that there is a limit to what the NHS can provide. At present the fundamental dilemma for the Government, as the funder of the NHS, is that, while the 'bottomless pit' syndrome is readily acknowledged in private, the public posture is compromised by the pressures of party politics (Chapter 1). The political party in power might wish to open up a dialogue with the public about the inevitability of making choices, and therefore of choosing not to provide some services either at the volume or quality level that might be desired under ideal circumstances. However, to do so can be to present easy political advantage to the Opposition. For the community and for the patients, the tensions derive from the frustrations of experiencing or observing unmet needs and low quality of provision (Knowles, 1993). What is required is for politicians of *all* parties to accept that rationing is inevitable and to enter into a process of dialogue with patients, health care professionals and members of the public about which areas to prioritise.

So far, purchasing authorities have preferred either to urge government to publish guidelines on priorities or to leave matters largely in the hands of clinicians employed by provider institutions (Harrison and Wistow, 1992; Salter, 1993; Redmayne *et al*, 1993). However, leaving such decisions in the hands of clinicians is not a satisfactory response, for there can be a conflict between the needs of the individual patient and those of the community as a whole. By culture and training, doctors are biased towards the individual. They also tend to have a bias towards their own speciality and towards medical treatment in general rather than non-clinical preventive measures (McGuire, 1986, pp.1167-68).

**Figure 7.2  Hospital and community health services:
gross current expenditure by sector 1990-91
(estimate; £ million)**

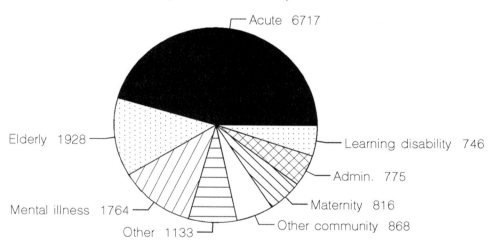

Note:     'Other community' services include health visits, immunisation, screening, health promotion and community dental services. 'Other' services include ambulances, the blood transfusion service, mass radiography and the Service Increment for Teaching and Research (SIFTR).

Source:     Central Office of Information (1995)

There are many ways of rationing medical treatment, including waiting lists, charges or co-payments, or the substitution of cheaper for more expensive treatments (Harrison and Hunter, 1994). Resources can be allocated in different ways, with greater or lesser priority being given to sectors of the population or to forms of treatment. Providing patients with better information about the possible risks of treatment and the alternatives to drugs or surgery is also a way of reducing demand for expensive interventions. The public need to be involved in decisions about health care resources through qualitative opinion research and community consultation at a local level. To combat the risk that this process will simply ignore the needs of people with learning difficulties, mental health problems, and the poor and inarticulate, it is essential to develop advocacy services for these groups, such as through self-help and voluntary organisations (Social Justice Commission, 1994).


*Access to long-term care*

The issue of access to health care is often perceived to be about acute interventions whereas, increasingly, the difficult public policy issues are regarding access to *care*, particularly long-term care. There is an urgent need to clarify the responsibilities of the NHS in providing and purchasing continuing care for elderly people, both in terms of the rights of the people who are already frail and elderly, and also in terms of what future generations can expect to receive. Policy on long-term care has developed in a piecemeal and uncoordinated way, and has resulted in an inequitable pattern of care. Some elderly people are cared for in NHS facilities, such as continuing care beds or community hospitals; these vary in quality from the excellent to the mediocre, but patients are not charged for their care. Other elderly patients, who do not necessarily differ in clinical terms from the first group, find themselves paying all or some of the costs of their care in a private nursing home. Their security of tenure in such accommodation is not guaranteed, and if they become unable to meet the fees, or are judged too dependent for the home to cope with, they may be asked to leave or to move into a shared room. Another group of elderly people are in private care as local authority funded (previously social security funded) residents. They may find few homes which will accept them (and may therefore have to go further afield), or they may receive poorer quality care than fellow residents who are self-financing (Henwood, 1992).

The division of responsibility for the continuing care of elderly people has been shared between the NHS and local government since the creation of the National Health Service in 1948. The National Assistance Act (1948) stated that the provision for long-term care of elderly people who were 'sick' or 'infirm' was the responsibility of the NHS, while care of the 'frail' and 'old' rested with local government (Laing, 1993). The former was free while the latter was means-tested. The boundaries between free health and means-tested social care have been redefined over the last decade. Developments in acute medical care, combined with the financial pressures which many hospitals are increasingly facing, have resulted in falling lengths of stay and early discharge to nursing and residential homes. Until April 1993, residential and nursing home care was funded through open ended social security budgets from central government. However, since the introduction of community care, the responsibility for funding long-term care has been transferred to local authorities, who have cash-limited budgets. Local authority funded long-term care is means-tested regardless of whether or not an elderly person is placed in a private home or a home managed by the social services. If an elderly person has a house and savings worth more than £3,000 then they have to make a contribution towards the cost of their care. If their savings and home are worth more than £8,000 then they are required to pay the full costs of their care. Their house is excluded from the assessment if it is occupied by a non-earning spouse. These means-tested arrangements, apart from being very unpopular among those obliged to pay, can lead to perverse effects such as working partners being forced to give up work in order to avoid the costs of their partner's care.

The funding arrangements for continuing care have encouraged cost-shifting between health and social care. Hospitals have increasingly reduced their number of long stay beds because it is in their interest to pass the responsibility on to the social security budget and to local authorities. It is therefore not surprising that there has been a rapid decline in institutional provision of rehabilitation and convalescent care, and that the availability of GP managed beds, whether in general or community hospitals, varies across the country. Although the quality of continuing care provision in hospitals has been strongly criticised (Health Advisory Service, 1986; Age Concern, 1990), it was, nevertheless, free health care provided by the NHS.

In the ten years between 1976 and 1986 the number of residential places in the private sector grew by more than 260 per cent, and between 1980 and 1990 by over 400 per cent (Henwood, 1992). A proportion of this growth resulted from the transfer of local authority homes into the private sector: in 1983 less than a quarter of the approximately 200,000 elderly and physically disabled residents in homes and hostels in England were in private sector homes, but by 1993 this had risen to nearly three fifths of the 272,000 residents then in homes (CSO, 1995). The extent of local authority provision varies between different localities, and is framed by local priorities, resources and demands. This guarantees, at the very least, a degree of inequity from district to district. Research has already demonstrated geographical variation in the provision of local authority services (Harding, 1992) and this now extends to the provision of what was formerly considered to fall within the province of the NHS (Marks, 1994). In a recent case in Leeds, the Health Service Ombudsman criticised the transfer of a brain-damaged patient from a hospital to a nursing home (Health Service Commissioner's Second Report, 1994). Such cases have forced the Department of Health to publish new guidance on continuing health care needs (DoH, 1995). The new guidelines require all health authorities and GP fundholders to review current plans for delivering and funding continuing health care services and to draft local policies and eligibility criteria. Hospital consultants will ultimately decide whether a patient needs continuing inpatient care; if the patient disagrees with the assessment, he or she will have the right to ask the health authority to review the decision. The health authority will be able to seek guidance from an independent panel.

The new guidelines do not address the fundamental issues of entitlement to, and funding of, long-term nursing care, and the introduction of local eligibility criteria is likely to increase further geographical inequity in access and provision of care. A national debate is therefore urgently required in order to develop a strategy for the funding and support of long-term care, both in institutional and community settings, and for both current and future generations of elderly and disabled people.  This debate will need to involve health and social care professionals, elderly and disabled people and their carers, and service managers and voluntary organisations.  The framework developed must be supported by politicians of *all* parties - there is little value in developing a long-term strategy if it is rewritten every time there is a change of government or a new Secretary of State for Health is appointed.

The task of meeting present and future needs for long-term care is substantial. The Institute of Actuaries has estimated that the number of disabled adults could grow from 6.4 million in 1991 to 8.5 million by 2031.  Of the total number in 2031, 6.8 million are expected to be over the age of 60, and more than a third - 3.2 million - would need either regular or continuous care (Institute of Actuaries, 1994).  Many elderly and disabled people do not receive residential care but are looked after at home by relatives.  There is a pressing need for policy makers to focus on the needs of carers, many of whom are elderly people themselves.  The informal care provided by Britain's 7 million carers is valued at £33 billion (Laing, 1993), representing an enormous saving to statutory agencies.  Apart from Invalid Care Allowance, which is only available for carers who are under the age of 65 when they first claim and whose income does not exceed certain specified limits, the state provides no special assistance or compensation for carers.  Although carers are now entitled to an assessment of their needs under the 1990 NHS and Community Care Act, co-resident carers usually receive little local authority support because of 'informal selectivism' which concentrates social services' resources on disabled and elderly people who live alone (Laing, 1993).  Of all the inadequacies of the welfare state's arrangements for covering long-term care risks, this appears to merit being given priority on grounds of equity.  A review of financial support for carers is also necessary because at the very time when the number of people requiring continuing care is rising the numbers of people who have traditionally undertaken the caring role is falling.  Changes in family structures and the rise in the number of women in employment call into question the capacity of the family to care for elderly and dependent members (see also Chapter 8).  Even on public expenditure grounds, there is a case for increasing financial support to carers, at least in certain circumstances.  Additional support for home-based care can delay or prevent admission to residential care, which is significantly more expensive.  If families withdrew their informal care services the impact on health and social care budgets would be catastrophic (Laing, 1993).

Universal state funding for long-term care is clearly an option but it would undoubtedly be an expensive one.  Whether it is affordable is a political decision.  If there was support for universal state funding then a secondary set of questions would have to be asked about how the money should be raised, such as through general taxation, National Insurance contributions or a hypothecated tax specifically for long-term care.  One alternative that has been suggested would be to require all citizens to take out private insurance for continuing care.  However, private insurance has a number of drawbacks.  It is difficult to predict long-term care needs and therefore to calculate premium levels, and people who have suffered from a disability or chronic illness since they were very young would be unlikely to be eligible for insurance or the premiums would be prohibitively high.  Also, if average premiums are set too low then the State will still have to pay for the shortfall, while if they are set too high, the State will not receive the profit. Social or public insurance, such as through a hypothecated tax, would therefore appear to be the most efficient solution. It would enable the risks of long-term care to be pooled, in effect redistributing resources from families in the fortunate position of not needing such care to those who will require significant support, and it would avoid the uncertainties, inefficiencies and possible injustices of using a private market to solve the problem.

*Widening inequalities in health*

Although Britain today does not experience the severe destitution and poverty of the 1930s, there is mounting public disquiet that an increasing number of people are living in disadvantaged circumstances. The findings of the Commission on Social Justice and the Joseph Rowntree Inquiry into Income and Wealth provide conclusive evidence of widening inequalities in living standards (see Chapter 4).

Social circumstances and health are inter-related. Disadvantaged groups experience higher levels of illness and disability, and at every age the probability of premature death is enormously increased by adverse social circumstances (Fox and Benzeval, 1995). A small selection of the key facts about the extent and nature of social inequalities in Britain is shown in Box 7.3.

### Box 7.3  Inequalities in health

- There would be 42,000 fewer deaths each year for people aged 16-74, if the death rate of manual workers were the same as for non-manual (Jacobson *et al*, 1991).

- Premature deaths amongst unskilled workers cause the loss of nearly three times as many years of potential life amongst men, and twice as many amongst women, as they do amongst professionals (Blane *et al*, 1990).

- A child from an unskilled manual family is twice as likely to die before the age of 15 as a child with a professional father (Woodroffe *et al*, 1993).

- Individuals in social classes IV and V are 60 per cent more likely to report a limiting long-term illness and 40 per cent more likely to have consulted their GP about a serious illness than those in social classes I and II (King's Fund Institute analysis of OPCS Omnibus Survey; McCormick and Rosenbaum,

The links between family poverty, homelessness, long-term unemployment and poor housing are well documented (Eardley, 1989; Wilcox, 1994a). Very few lone parents in Britain are able to combine full-time work with childcare responsibilities and so around three-quarters of all lone parents are in receipt of Income Support - around one and a half million children of lone parents are in households below half the national average income (see also Chapters 5 and

8). Cohen and Fraser (1991) have estimated that half of children under five living on low incomes could be brought out of poverty if childcare enabled their mothers to work. Bad housing also contributes to poor health due to the effects of inadequate heating and dampness. A survey of housing in Glasgow, Edinburgh and London, found higher levels of a whole range of symptoms for both children and adults in damp and mouldy houses against dry dwellings (Platt *et al*, 1989). Unemployment results in a considerable decline in living standards. For example, the income of a single person or married couple without children who are not working is approximately 48 per cent of the income of a single person or married couple in work. Low income is closely associated with poor health, so it is unsurprising that there is a strong association between unemployment and poor health (Smith, 1987; Bartley, 1994). Although people suffering from ill-health are more likely to become unemployed or to retire early, unemployment has been shown to have a direct effect on people's health; unemployed people also have a higher risk of depression, anxiety, poor self-esteem, neurotic disorders and disturbed sleep.

Widening inequalities in health are not inevitable, but if the differences in health status between affluent members of society and the growing number of people living in poverty are not to increase still further, there needs to be a comprehensive strategy to tackle the causes of this ill-health. Such a strategy should be orientated towards tackling the causes of poverty rather than merely alleviating the consequences of deprivation. In this respect, many of the policy options discussed in other chapters in this volume should be of direct interest to those working on health issues. A focus on *health* rather than *health care* has major implications for the allocation of resources to the NHS and other areas of public expenditure such as housing and education. If the main public policy objective is to improve public health, then there is arguably a case for *not* increasing the resources available to the NHS in real terms, but for instead directing such additional resources as become available towards programmes that will indirectly improve people's health such as enabling the long-term unemployed to return to work, increasing the provision of affordable childcare and upgrading the quality and availability of affordable housing.

Achieving broad-based political support for such a strategy will be far from easy (Chapter 1). The political pressures for increased NHS expenditure are intense, immediate and unrelenting. Every MP will be lobbied hard on hospital closures, but few will receive letters, for example, about the poor health of lone parents. Improvements in the health of populations are largely invisible, but hospital closures are ingrained in the memories of local communities. What is required is for politicians to engender widespread public support for a strategy to tackle unemployment and poverty, which interlinks economic *and* social regeneration, and that sets out clear public policy goals and public expenditure priorities.

## Conclusion

As the National Health Service approaches its fiftieth anniversary some difficult choices will have to be made about the future direction of health policy in Britain. Public support for a free health service is as strong today as it was in 1948 and the popularity of the NHS among members of the public is far greater than for other public services. The dilemma for politicians is that there is strong public pressure to safeguard the status quo, yet the nature of health care is changing steadily and decisions will need to be made on what is to be provided, for whom, and how it will be paid for. Unless these issues are discussed openly, problems such as waiting lists and inadequate provision for long-term care will only get worse.

Any future Secretary of State for Health will be under enormous pressure to channel more resources into acute health care and to reorganise the NHS. Yet there is very little evidence that reorganisations actually improve the delivery of patient care (Plamping, 1993; Hastings, 1993; James, 1994), though modest future reorganisations may be justified in order to achieve other benefits such as improved accountability and the elimination of 'cream-skimming'. What is required is greater collaboration and co-operation between professionals, managers and users in order to deliver more appropriate, accessible and cost-effective services, an important part of which should involve the provision of better information to patients. In the last 20 years the NHS has been through three major reorganisations. It does not need another one.

Yet the major policy question which will confront an incoming Government is what priority should be given to health care in relation to other public services such as education, housing and transport. All have pressing claims for additional resources. If the fundamental objective of health policy is to improve the long-term health of the population, then the priority should be to target the causes of ill-health rather than the consequences. Not least of these causes is poverty. This suggests that, alongside a strengthening of more conventional preventative medicine, we should look to incorporate other wider policies in our strategies to improve health, such as reducing poverty, improving education and training, and attempting to facilitate employment. In political terms, this strategic re-focusing will not be easy to achieve, but this does not mean that we should not try.

## References

Age Concern (1990), *Left Behind? Continuing Care for Elderly People in NHS Hospitals. A Review of Health Advisory Service Reports*, England: Age Concern.

Bain, J. (1994), 'Fundholding: a two tier system?' *British Medical Journal*, Vol. **309**, pp.396-9.

Bartley, M. (1994), 'Unemployment and ill-health: understanding the relationship', *Journal of Epidemiology and Community Health*, **48**, pp.333-7.

Benzeval, M., Judge, K. and Whitehead, M. (1995), *Tackling Inequalities in Health - An Agenda for Action*, London: King's Fund.

Blane, D., Davey Smith, G. and Bartley, M. (1990), 'Social class differences in years of potential life lost: size, trends and principal causes', *British Medical Journal*, **301**, pp.429-32.

British Medical Journal (1993), *Hospitals Slow Down as the Money Runs Out*, London: British Medical Journal.

Butler, J. (1992), *Patients, Policies and Politics - Before and After Working for Patients*, Oxford: Oxford University Press.

Butler, J. (1994), 'Origins and early developments', in Robinson, R. and Le Grand, J. (eds.), *Evaluating the NHS Reforms*, London: King's Fund Institute, Policy Journals.

Central Office of Information (1995), *Britain 1995: an Official Handbook*, London: HMSO.

Central Statistical Office (1994), *Social Trends 24*, London: HMSO.

Central Statistical Office (1995a), *Social Trends 25*, London: HMSO.

Central Statistical Office (1995b), *Annual Abstract of Statistics* , London: HMSO.

Cohen, B. and Fraser, N. (1991), *Childcare in a Modern Welfare System: Towards a New National Policy*, London: Institute of Public Policy Research.

Coulter, A. (1992), 'Fundholding general practices', *British Medical Journal*, **304**, pp.397-8.

Coulter, A. and Bradlow, J. (1993), 'Effect of NHS reforms on general practitioners' referral patterns', *British Medical Journal*, **306**, pp.433-7.

Day, P. and Klein, R. (1990), 'Variations in budgets of fundholding practices', *British Medical Journal*, **303**, pp.168-70.

Corney, R. (1994), 'Experiences of first wave general practice fundholders in South East Thames Regional Health Authority', *British Journal of General Practice*, **44**, pp.34-7.

Department of Health and Social Security (1976a), *The NHS Planning System*, London: HMSO.

Department of Health and Social Security (1976b), *Priorities for Health and Personal Social Services in England*, London: HMSO.

Department of Health and Social Security (1979), *Patients First*, London: HMSO.

Department of Health (1993), *Managing the New NHS*, London: HMSO.

Department of Health (1994), 'Developing NHS purchasing and GP fundholding', *Executive Letter* (94) p.79.

Department of Health (1995), *NHS Responsibilities for Meeting Continuing Health Care Needs*, HSG (95)8, LAC (95)5.

Eardley, T. (1989), *Move-On Housing*, London: Single Homeless in London; National Federation of Housing Associations.

Fox, J. and Benzeval, M. (1995), 'Perspectives on social variations in health', in Benzeval, M., Judge, K. and Whitehead, M. (eds.), *Tackling Inequalities in Health - An Agenda for Action*, London: King's Fund.

Grafty, J. and Williams, J. (1994), 'Purchasing for all: an alternative to fundholding', *British Medical Journal*, 308, pp.391-4.

Glennerster, H., Matsaganis, M. and Owens, P. (1994), *Implementing GP Fundholding: Wild Card or Winning Hand?* Oxford: Oxford University Press.

Harding, T. (1992), *Great Expectations...and Spending on Social Services*, London: National Institute for Social Work.

Hastings, F. (1993), *Beyond Provider Dominance - Managing Transition and Change*, London: King's Fund.

Harrison, S. and Hunter, D. (1994), *Rationing Health Care*, London: Institute of Public Policy Research.

Harrison, S. and Wistow, G. (1992), 'The purchaser/provider split in English health care: towards explicit rationing?' *Policy and Politics*, 20 (2).

Harrison, S., Hunter, D.J., Johnston, I.H., Nicholson, N., Thunhurst, C. and Wistow, G. (1991), 'Health before health care', *Social Policy Paper*, No.4, London: Institute of Public Policy Research.

Health Service Commissioner's Second Report for 1993-94 (1994), *Failure to Provide Long-term Care for a Brain Damaged Patient*, London: HMSO.

Henwood, M. (1992), *Through a Glass Darkly - Community Care and Elderly People*. Research Report 14, London: King's Fund Institute.

Hills, J. (1993), *The Future of Welfare*, York: Joseph Rowntree Foundation.

House of Commons (1983), *Hansard*, Vol. 47, col. 1094, London: HMSO.

House of Commons Committee of Public Accounts (1988), *Fifth Report, 1987-88. Use of Operating Theatres in the National Health Services*, HC 348, London: HMSO.

Le Grand, J. and Bartlett, W. (1993), *Quasi-Markets and Social Policy*, London: Macmillan.

Le Grand, J. and Robinson, R. (eds.) (1993), *Evaluating the NHS Reforms*, London: King's Fund Institute, Policy Journals.

Le Grand, J. (1993), 'For better or worse?' *New Statesman and Society*, 19 November.

Jacobson, B., Smith, A. and Whitehead, M. (eds.), (1991), *The Nation's Health: A Strategy for the 1990s*, London: King's Fund.

James, A. (1994), *Managing to Care - Public Service and the Market*, Harlow: Longman.

King's Fund Institute's analysis of OPCS Omnibus Survey, used with the permission of the Controller of HMSO.

Klein, R. (1989), *The Politics of the NHS*, 2nd edition, Harlow: Longman.

Knowles, D. (1993), 'Guidance-delivery tension: an approach to management and organisational development', in Hastings, F. (ed.), *Beyond Provider Dominance - Managing Transition and Change*, London: King's Fund.

Laing, W. (1993), *Financing Long-Term Care - The Crucial Debate*, London: Age Concern.

Marks, L. (1994), *Seamless Care or Patchwork Quilt? Discharging Patients from Acute Hospital Care*, Research Report No. **17**, London: King's Fund Institute.

Mays, N. (1993), 'What are the effects of integration in the Northern Ireland health and personal social services?' *Critical Public Health*, **4**, (2), pp.43-8.

McCormick, A. and Rosenbaum, M. (1990), *Morbidity Statistics from General Practice: Third National Study: Socio-economic Analysis*, OPCS series MSS No. **2**, London: HMSO.

McGuire, A. (1986), 'Ethics and resource allocation: an economist's view', *Social Science and Medicine*, **22**, (11), pp.1167-74.

National Association of Health Authorities and Trusts (1993), *Securing Effective Public Accountability in the NHS: A Discussion Paper*, Birmingham.

Newton, J., Fraser, M., Robinson, J. and Wainwright, D. (1993), 'Fundholding in Northern region: the first year', *British Medical Journal*, **306**, pp.375-8.

Nuttall, S., Blackwood, R., Bussell, B., Cliff, J., Cornall, M., Cowley, A., Gatenby, P. and Webber, J. (1994), 'Financing Long-term Care in Great Britain', *Journal of the Institute of Actuaries*, **121**, (1), pp.1-68.

Ovretveit, J. (1995), *Purchasing for Health*, Oxford: Oxford University Press.

Perry, C. (1994), 'Purchasing for Change', *Speaking Up - Policy and Change in the NHS*, No. **2**, Birmingham: National Association of Health Authorities and Trusts.

Platt, S., Martin, C., Hunt, S. and Lewis, C. (1989), 'Damp housing, mould growth and symptomatic health state', *British Medical Journal*, **298**, pp.1673-8.

Plamping, D. (1993), *Redrawing the Boundaries*, paper given to a conference on 'A Future for District General Hospitals?', 17 November.

Redmayne, S., Klein, R. and Day, P. (1993), *Sharing Out Resources: Purchasing and Priority Setting in the NHS*, Birmingham: National Association of Health Authorities and Trusts.

Regan, D. and Stewart, J. (1982), 'An essay in the local government of health: the case for local authority control', *Social Policy and Administration*, **16** (1), pp.19-43.

Salter, B. (1992), 'The politics of purchasing in the National Health Service', *Policy and Politics*, **21** (3), pp.171-84.

Smith, P. (March, 1994), *Institutional Impediments to Improved UK Housing*, paper presented at Health in Cities conference, Liverpool.

The Commission on Social Justice (1994), *Social Justice: Strategies for National Renewal*, London: Vintage.

Whitehead, M. (1994), 'Is it fair? Evaluating the equity implications of the NHS reforms', in Le Grand, J. and Robinson, R. (eds.), *Evaluating the NHS Reforms*, London: Kings Fund Institute, Policy Journals.

Wilcox, S. (ed.) (1994a), *Housing Finance Review 1994-95*, York: Joseph Rowntree Foundation.

Willis, A. (1992), Who needs fundholding? *Health Service Journal*, 30 April, pp.24-6.

Wistow, G. (1993), Democratic Deficit. *Community Care*, 30 September, p.29.

Woodroffe, C., Glickman, M., Barker, M. and Power, C. (1993), *Children, Teenagers and Health: The Key Data*, Milton Keynes: Open University Press.

# 8 Family change: parenthood, partnership and policy

*Kathleen E. Kiernan* [*]

There is an intriguing contrast between the debate in Britain concerning the family and that in other Western countries. The concern elsewhere is on how the government can do more to help or support families, or at least do less to hurt them, whereas in Britain the family is on the one hand blamed for a range of societal ills and, on the other, asked to take on the disbursement of the welfare state. There is reluctance amongst opinion formers in Britain to state whether the family should be supported or not. The debate on the family has not moved to centre stage and is only just beginning to move beyond generalities and to confront difficult policy choices. The issue of children growing up in the poverty that stems from unemployment and partnership breakdown is, for example, not a central concern. The debate, if anything, seems to be stuck in a moral mire. The current government's policy places most family matters in the private realm even though family trends and issues are increasingly impacting on the public realm.

The predominant family form in Britain remains the married couple with whom children reside until they grow-up, and ends when one of the partners die. Most men and women still marry and have children. However, since the 1970s people have been marrying later and divorcing more. They have also been cohabiting to a greater extent: as a prelude to marriage, instead of marrying, or between marriages. Lone parent families have become more prevalent arising from divorce, the break-up of cohabiting unions, and the increased tendency for young women to have children on their own. Partnerships between men and women have become more varied in type and fragile whilst in recent times parenthood is being postponed, avoided by a

[*]   Reader in Social Policy and Demography at the London School of Economics and Political Science.

growing minority, and occurring more often outside marriage (Hobcraft and Kiernan, 1995; Utting, 1995). The two main trends discussed here relate to family formation and family disruption.

## Family formation patterns

The two major themes in British family formation behaviour in recent times have been (a) the postponement of parenthood and (b) the dramatic rise in extra-marital childbearing. Let us take a closer look at these two developments because, as we will see, these two trends, together with the rise in divorce, have indirectly or directly contributed to the widely debated increase in lone-parent families.

### Postponement of parenthood

Married couples have been delaying the start of their families.[1] The average age at first birth amongst married women has increased by nearly four years over the past two decades, having increased from age 24 years during the early 1970s to 27.8 years in 1992 (OPCS, 1995a). Much of this increase occured during the 1980s. The present average age at becoming a mother is higher than any recorded in the post-war era. There is also evidence that there has been a growth in childlessness: amongst the most recent generations of women reaching their mid-thirties, those born during the mid to late 1950s, around 20 per cent have not had a child, as compared with 10 per cent of those born in the 1940s (OPCS, 1994).

These developments could be viewed either positively or negatively. On the positive side, a later start to parenthood gives young people the increased opportunity to obtain educational qualifications, occupational training and higher savings and incomes. These investments may provide the foundations for a more stable and productive life. Women, in particular, may have had more difficulty in accumulating their own 'human capital' when they had children at a younger age. Spending longer as a couple with two incomes prior to becoming parents is also likely to improve the couple's well-being in terms of housing, consumer goods and leisure activities. Couples may develop life patterns, including mortgage commitments, predicated on two incomes and may, more explicitly than in the past, equate a child with foregone income. Men and women may be having children later or not at all because they have more choices in their lives combined with effective means of controlling their fertility. These choices may reduce men and women's reproductive contribution to society but may expand their overall contribution as citizens and workers. Later ages at marriage and parenthood are also associated with lower risks of marital breakdown. Additionally, later childbearing is associated with a greater attachment of women to the labour market which is likely to lessen the poverty typically associated with the occurrence of family disruption, if this was to occur.

As well as these positive elements there may be negative aspects to the postponement of parenthood and the growth in childlessness. Lower rates of family formation may indicate a generally unsupportive ethos for families and children in our society. Raising children is expensive and many families now feel that they need two employed adults to provide a decent standard of living for themselves and their children. Moreover, women have become increasingly committed to the labour force and dropping out of the labour force for extended periods has become less popular (McRae, 1991). Faced with such dilemmas and other economic stresses such as the potential difficulty of re-entering the labour market, uncertain job prospects and low incomes, some couples may postpone having children to later than they would wish, have fewer children or have none at all. Moreover, changing fertility patterns are the main engine driving the age distribution of the population. The average age of the population is rising and, more significantly, the ratio of workers to elderly dependents is falling. This raises questions about how future pensions and health care will be paid for (see Chapters 4, 5 and 7).

*Youthful parenthood*

Delayed childbearing is a major theme in recent family formation patterns in Europe. However, there is a sub-theme in the timing of parenthood which is peculiar to Britain. In Figure 8.1 we see that, compared with other Western European nations, we have a high rate of teenage fertility and that, unlike any other European country, our rate has not declined over the last decade or so. The United Kingdom rate is around three times that of France and Sweden, over twice that of West Germany and almost four times that of Italy, six times that of the Netherlands and ten times that of Switzerland. The USA is now one of the few industrialised nations with a higher rate of teenage fertility than the UK, with a teenage fertility rate at over 50 per 1000 in 1990 (substantially higher than the rate observed in European countries). The extent of teenage childbearing in the United Kingdom is revealed by the fact that in 1989, the most recent date for which we have data, the UK contributed only 20 per cent of total births within the European Community but contributed 37 per cent of all teenage births (Eurostat, 1994).

As well as a high teenage fertility rate, the United Kingdom has a relatively high rate of childbearing in the early twenties as compared to many other European nations. For example, in 1991 the fertility rate amongst women aged 20-24 years was 56 per 1000 in West Germany, 71 per 1000 in France and 89 per 1000 in the United Kingdom. Undoubtedly, compared with the early 1980s, our level of childbearing in the early twenties has declined, but compared to other major countries in Western Europe we still have a high rate of childbearing at these young ages.

**Figure 8.1  Teenage fertility rates**
**(per 1,000 births)**

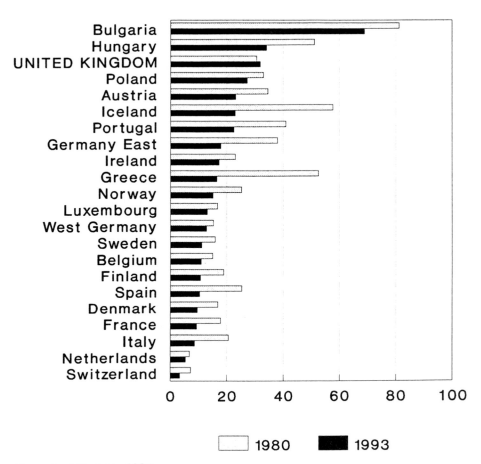

Council of Europe, 1994
1993 rates or latest available

*Why does Britain have a pattern of young parenthood?*

This youthful pattern of childbearing may in part be a by-product of our educational system and youth labour market: an educational system and labour market that encouraged early school leaving may also have encouraged young parenthood.   Until the 1970s, England and Wales in particular, had what sociologists refer to as an elitist education system which invested heavily in a small minority of academically inclined children (see also Chapter 6).  Prior to 1974, the majority of children left school at age 15 with few or no qualifications.  The school leaving age was raised to age 16 in 1973, since when, and particularly during the 1980s, we have seen more children staying on in school and attaining qualifications.  Nevertheless, Britain still has a relatively low proportion of 16-plus year olds in full-time education and invests a smaller proportion of GNP in education than do most comparable developed countries (see also Chapter 2).

In the recent past, full employment and an economy that could support large numbers of young people in relatively well-paid manual and unskilled jobs allowed young people to marry and to start a family within a few years of leaving school. Many other European countries had an education system with either a later school leaving age or more intensive post-school vocational training schemes that may have dampened the possibilities for early family formation.

This pattern of early family formation may have been a contributory factor to Britain's high divorce rate. One of the most consistent and robust findings in divorce research is that the earlier a partnership is formed the more prone it is to breakdown. The socio-economic disadvantage associated with divorce may well indirectly stem from the lack of educational and training investment that has created a workforce with a disproportionately large number of low-skill, low-paid workers. These workers are less able to support themselves and their children when a divorce occurs, and consequently are more likely to become a charge on the state. This long-standing lack of investment in education alongside changing economic structures may well have created a vulnerable group of less skilled men and women that is proportionately larger than in many other European societies (Chapters 2, 3 and 6).

The industrial economy that permitted an early transition to adulthood has, to some extent, now given way to a service economy that either pays low wages or requires qualifications and training for better paid employment. The period of dependency of young people is extending into their twenties. The transition to adulthood including leaving education, entering the labour market, marrying and becoming parents has become more protracted compared with the previous two generations of young people. On the one hand, we have evidence that the majority of young people are adapting to this upward revision in their socio-economic and demographic timetable. This is reflected in later ages at completion of education and entering the labour market, and at entry into marriage and parenthood. On the other hand, the pace of adaptation appears to be lagging behind in particular social groups, and especially among the approximately 30 per cent of children who have benefited least from the enhanced educational opportunities of the last decade and as a consequence are more prone to experience unemployment (see Chapter 3).

Becoming a parent at a young age is less sustainable in today's educational and labour market conditions, and hence it is not surprising that young parents are increasingly having to rely on state benefits for basic living requirements. As mentioned above, young parents are also more likely to become or to be lone parents. Analysis of the 1991 General Household Survey data (Table 8.1) shows that amongst women who were lone parents at the time of the survey, 42 per cent had had their first baby in their teens and a further 28 per cent had had their first child in their very early twenties. Never-married lone-mothers were one and half times more likely to have been a teenage mother than separated and divorced lone-mothers and three times more likely than married mothers.

**Table 8.1 Age at first birth according to current marital status in 1991 - women under age 45**

| Age at first birth | Single | Separated/ divorced | All lone mothers | Married mothers |
|---|---|---|---|---|
| | % | % | % | % |
| 16-19 years | 52 | 34 | 42 | 17 |
| 20-22 years | 25 | 30 | 28 | 24 |
| 23-24 years | 8 | 14 | 12 | 17 |
| 25 and older | 14 | 22 | 19 | 42 |
| N = 100% | 208 | 317 | 525 | 2182 |

Source: General Household Survey Data 1991

*Who become young parents?*

So we have seen that young parents are more likely to become or to be lone parents, but do we know anything else about who becomes a young parent in the first place? A link has been suggested, at a macro-level, between the UK's high teenage fertility rates and the UK's educational system. Similar evidence has been found at the micro or individual level. A recent study (Kiernan, 1995) showed that young parents differ substantially in their childhood and adolescent experiences from their peers who delay parenthood to later ages. Generally speaking young parents had less propitious backgrounds than their peers who had children at older ages. Factors that were implicated in the backgrounds of young parents included the replication of parental behaviour (teenage mothers' own mothers were more likely to have been teenage mothers), poverty, poor educational investment and early school leaving. A particularly noteworthy finding was that young women whose reading and mathematics test scores declined between childhood (age 7) and adolescence (age 16) were even more likely to become young mothers than those who had low scores at both ages. Young women whose educational test scores improved over time had low probabilities of becoming young mothers. Thus, women who underachieve relative to their ability are more prone to becoming teenage mothers. Several other studies have also shown that educational attainment is the most important factor associated with early parenthood. This evidence strongly reinforces the hypothesis that education is of importance to variations in the rates of early parenthood.

Hence, young parents are disproportionately educationally disadvantaged, with all that this implies for their subsequent work careers and level of financial remuneration. Young parents are likely to have fewer resources than older parents to invest in themselves and their children. If parents separate, women who became mothers at young ages are less likely to possess the skills and qualifications necessary for obtaining jobs which would enable them to support themselves and their children. Their ex-partners are also the least likely to be able to make a substantial contribution to the support of their children.   This suggests that the children of young parents are themselves disproportionately likely to suffer from the same disadvantages as their parents.

Young parenthood can pose significant risks to young people's life chances, with drawbacks including poor housing, homelessness, unemployment and reliance on state benefits.  Undoubtedly, there will always be men and women who want and have children at a young age and many will be satisfied and successful parents: the issues are to do with choice and opportunity.  With the currently evolving labour market it is increasingly important to provide and encourage young men and women to equip themselves with the qualifications and skills needed for satisfactory work within and without the labour market.  This conclusion coincides with those of several of the other chapters in this volume and reinforces the impression that education and training should have a central position in current and future strategic policy in the UK.

## Extra-marital childbearing and cohabitation

As well as changes in the timing of fertility, the other major theme in fertility behaviour in recent times has been the rise in extra-marital childbearing, which in turn is intimately related to the rise of cohabitation.  Since the beginning of the 1980s, we have seen an increasing separation between marriage and childbearing.  In 1993, 32 per cent of babies were born outside marriage, as compared with 12 per cent in 1980 and eight per cent in 1970.  However, of these children, a rising proportion have been born to cohabiting parents.  Of the 32 per cent of babies born outside of marriage in 1993, 50 per cent were born to parents who were living at the same address at the time of the birth.  About 20 per cent of the births outside marriage are to teenage mothers and altogether 50 per cent occur to women under 25 (OPCS, 1994).  The younger the mother the less likely she is to be cohabiting at the time of the birth.

## The European experience

The rise in extra-marital childbearing is not confined to Britain (Figure 8.2).  In many Northern and Western European countries there have been noticeable increases in the proportions of births outside marriage (Council of Europe, 1994).  The extent of extra-marital childbearing as measured by the proportion of all births that are born out of wedlock is very large.  At one extreme are Iceland and Sweden where over 50 per cent of children are born outside marriage, with high proportions of over 40 per cent also evident in Denmark, Norway and East Germany.  At the other extreme are countries such as Greece, Switzerland, Poland and Italy where six per cent or less of children are born outside of marriage.  The UK, along with countries such as France, has a middling level of extra-marital childbearing of around one in three children born outside of marriage.

## Figure 8.2 Extra-marital births
### (per 100 births)

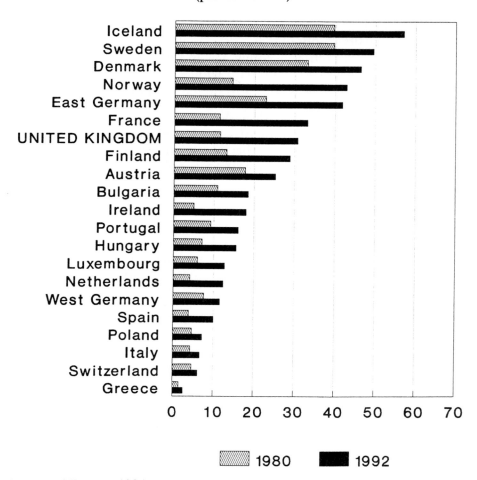

Council of Europe, 1994

There is also a good deal of variation between (and within) European countries in the extent and nature of cohabitation (Kiernan, 1993). In countries where cohabitation is relatively well-established - Sweden, Denmark and Iceland - around one in two children are born outside marriage but the majority are born to cohabiting couples. In these countries, marriage is losing its monopoly on partnerships, but this is not necessarily an outright rejection of marriage, since marriage frequently occurs at later ages.

Britain is part of a middle group of countries, in terms of cohabitation, which includes Austria, Finland, France, the Netherlands, Norway, Switzerland and West Germany. In these countries cohabitation emerged during the 1970s, primarily as a child-free, transitional phase preceding marriage, and has risen inexorably since. This group of countries falls into two distinct clusters: those where extra-marital births are a significant minority of all births and those where extra-marital childbearing is still relatively rare. As we saw in Figure

8.2, the extent of extra-marital childbearing is relatively high in Britain, Austria, Finland, France, and Norway (more than 20 per cent) but it is much less common in West Germany, the Netherlands and Switzerland (11 per cent or less). This suggests that in the former cluster of countries, women are increasingly having their children within cohabiting unions but that in the latter cluster, cohabitation is primarily a childless phase and marriage is still the pre-eminent context for having children. As yet cohabitation is rarer in Southern and Eastern European countries.

## Cohabitation in Britain

In Britain cohabitation is becoming increasingly widespread and is popularly recommended as a pre-marital living arrangement, though there is more ambivalence amongst the public about cohabitation as a permanent living arrangement and the increased tendency to have children outside marriage. Younger people are more permissive about cohabiting and childbearing outside marriage, which suggests that cohabiting and extra-marital childbearing is not likely to diminish in the near future. Analyses of General Household Survey data (Kiernan and Estaugh, 1993) show that, as yet, cohabitants tend to have a youthful profile: seven out of ten are under age 35. Teenage cohabitation and cohabitation beyond age 45 are relatively rare occurrences. Two out of three cohabitants have never been married and the one in three who have been previously married are mainly divorcees. A minority, 27 per cent, of the never-married cohabitants had never had a child, whereas the majority, 84 per cent, of the separated and divorced cohabitants had had a child - most of these children were products of a prior marriage. Cohabitations still tend to be short-lived: in 1989 one third of cohabiting couples had been living together for less than one year and only 16 per cent had lived with their partner for longer than five years.

## Types of cohabitants

Cohabitation encompasses a range of situations and living arrangements. However, cohabitants can be allocated to three main groups (Kiernan and Estaugh, 1993). In order of size these are: young never-married childless couples, post-marital cohabitants (divorced and separated) and never-married couples with children. The circumstances, requirements and needs of these three groups are likely to differ, as are policy responses to them.

Young never-married childless couples constitute about half of all cohabiting couples and are perhaps the least problematic from a policy perspective. In the main these unions are short-lived; they either convert into marriages or break-up. On the break-up of such unions, the main issues to be resolved relate to property and possessions acquired during the relationship.

Post-marital cohabitants, about one-third of the cohabiting couples, are on average older and have been cohabiting for longer. The majority had had children whilst married and many were in effect reconstituted families with all the attending complexities that that entails: one half of the post-marital cohabitants had dependent children. Our comparisons of remarried families and these cohabiting families showed them to be very similar with respect to income, employment status, educational qualifications and so on. The most noteworthy difference was that cohabiting women in step-family settings were more likely to be in receipt of maintenance than their remarried counterparts. Whereas 33 per cent of cohabiting separated and divorced women were in receipt of maintenance for their children, only 17 per cent of the remarried women received maintenance. This suggests that, for the purposes of child support, cohabitations and remarriage are not viewed in the same way by ex-spouses.

The smallest group of cohabitants, about one-sixth, were never-married couples with dependent children. The findings in relation to this group were the most striking. These families were relatively disadvantaged compared with married couple families. These cohabiting couple families, on average, had significantly lower household incomes, were more likely to be in receipt of income support and housing benefit, were more likely to be in local authority accommodation, and the male partner was more likely to be unemployed or to be in semi-skilled and unskilled occupations than was the case in married couple families. Amongst families with two parents, these cohabiting families are likely to be amongst the most disadvantaged.

Institutions, both public and private, will need to address the implications of rising levels of cohabitation, particularly if these unions become more long standing and children are increasingly born and reared within them. Generally, countries with longer experiences of cohabitation, such as Sweden and Denmark, have opted for legislative solutions that compensate cohabitants for drawbacks arising from being outside the legal framework, but mainly on an *ad hoc* basis.[2]

Although there are strong parallels across most other European countries with respect to cohabitation and extra-marital childbearing, there appear to be some differences between these countries and Britain. In most countries there is a high association between the level of extra-marital childbearing and the level of cohabitation, but in Britain there is less of an association. In other words, Britain has a higher level of births outside marriage than would be expected from our level of cohabitation (Prinz, 1995). This suggests that having a child on one's own or in a non-residential partnership is more common in Britain than in most other Western European countries. There is also evidence that cohabiting families in France are no more or less disadvantaged than their married counterparts, which is in sharp contrast to the situation in Britain (Kiernan and Lelievre, 1995).

In sum, developments in cohabitation and childbearing outside marriage have multiple impetuses and that may differ across groups. On the one hand these developments may be responses to insecurity, unemployment and socio-economic disadvantage. On the other hand, they may be responses to more progressive influences such as rising educational participation amongst young women, greater female autonomy in the labour market and domestic spheres, along with higher expectations of relationships and marriage. Generalisations about the causes or consequences of cohabitation and childbearing outside of marriage cannot be assumed across all groups or across time. However, there are particular concerns about the relatively small but disadvantaged group of never-married cohabitants with children, and also about the unusually large number of children born outside of any kind of live-in partnership in the UK.

## Family disruption

There are currently around 1.6 million lone parent families with dependent children in the UK (1993 data; CSO, 1995). Increases in divorce, the dissolution of cohabiting unions and women bearing children outside marriage, have all directly contributed to the growth in lone-parent families.

### Divorce

It can be seen from Figure 8.3 that, in 1991, the United Kingdom and Sweden headed the league table of divorce rates.[3] These data suggest that in most European countries, on present trends, one in three or more marriages will end in divorce. If present divorce rates continue, around one in four children will experience divorce in their family by age 16 (CSO, 1995).

The rise in divorce that has occurred over the last few decades has brought to the fore fundamental issues about the roles of men and women in society and the care and support of children. Divorce legislation has increasingly moved to the 'clean break principle' with greater emphasis put on post-divorce financial independence for the partners. Such changes imply that both spouses should maintain their labour market position throughout marriage to mitigate against the effects of divorce. However, if a mother takes time out of the labour market to care for their children, should she not be recompensed for the opportunity costs of motherhood? Divorce is frequently followed by re-partnering, more so amongst men than women, and this creates problems if there are insufficient resources to support two families. If this is the case, one of the families is likely to have to rely on state support.

Issues surrounding the financial support of children when parents live apart have been high on the political agenda in recent years. The view that is manifested in the 1991 Child Support Act and the Child Support Agency (CSA) is that fathers should not be allowed to escape their responsibilities. Amongst the British public, as expressed in the 1991 British Social Attitudes Survey (Kiernan, 1992), there is almost unanimous agreement that following separation (regardless of whether couples are legally married or not) a father should be made to support his child, and there is a similar level of agreement that the amount of support should depend on the father's income. Attitudes to the continuation of child maintenance on remarriage were less unanimous: four out of ten thought that it should depend on the new husband's income. The implication is that the role of the biological father is not seen by everyone as entailing a life-time commitment to the financial support of dependent children. Step-fathers are also expected to contribute to the maintenance of their step-children.

However, under existing legislation, it is the biological parents only who are liable to maintain their dependent children regardless of family circumstances. Child Support legislation has moved biological fatherhood explicitly to centre stage and the role of social fatherhood performed by step-fathers has been de-emphasised even though such fathers frequently support their wife's children from a previous marriage. The effect of this major change on inter-family relations remains to be assessed, but tensions in the current position and the problems experienced by the CSA suggest that this is a policy area that is likely to require further attention.

**Figure 8.3 Total divorce rates**
**(estimated life-time probability)**

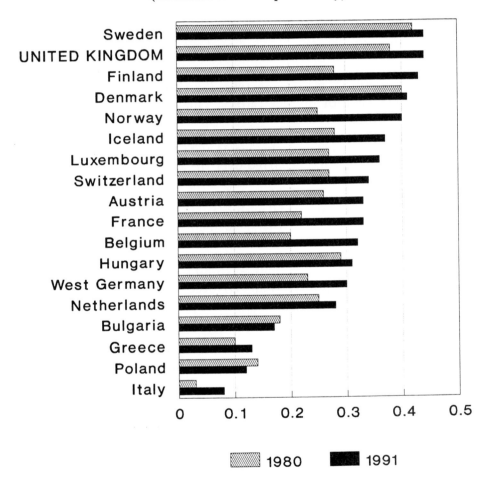

Council of Europe, 1994

*Divorced and separated lone parents*

Not all British couples who divorce have dependent children. As we see in Table 8.2, in 1991 just over one in two divorced couples had children under age 16, a somewhat lower proportion than that observed at the beginning of the 1980s. The numbers of children involved in the divorce of their parents was very similar in 1981 and 1991, at around 160,000.  The number of divorcing couples with dependent children hardly changed over the decade. Thus, divorce *per se* is unlikely to have made a major contribution to the growth in lone-parent families over the last decade.

However, there are aspects of the divorcing population that may have contributed to the growth of lone-parents *on benefits*.  The age distribution of dependent children of divorcees has changed over the last decade.  The proportion of divorcing couples with children under age 4 rose from 36 per cent in 1981, to 47 per cent in 1991.  Mothers with young children are less likely to be in the labour market and therefore are more likely to have to rely on maintenance or state benefits to support themselves and their children. Over the 1980s, we have also had a growth in unemployment (Chapter 3). Unemployed men run a higher risk of divorce (Haskey, 1984) and unemployed fathers who are separated and divorced are the least likely to be able to provide financial assistance for their wives and children.  Such trends, together with the tendency for lone mothers to have accumulated less human capital on their passage to adulthood, are in part likely to account for the low incomes of divorced and separated mothers.  In 1993, two out of three of these mothers had a gross household income of £150 a week or less compared with 12 per cent of married couples with dependent children (OPCS, 1995b).

**Table 8.2  Characteristics of divorcing couples - England and Wales**

|  | Year | |
| --- | --- | --- |
| **Divorcing couples** | **1981** | **1991** |
|  | % | % |
| Children under 16 | 60 | 56 |
| Children 16 or over | 11 | 14 |
| No child stated | 29 | 30 |
| Number of couples | 148,201 | 159,000 |
| **Divorcing couples with dependent children** | **1981** | **1991** |
|  | % | % |
| Age:    0-4 years | 36 | 47 |
| 5-9 years | 42 | 36 |
| 10-15 years | 21 | 18 |
| Number of couples | 88,202 | 88,346 |
| Number of children | 159,403 | 160,684 |
| Divorce rate per 1000 married population | 11.9 | 13.5 |

Source: OPCS (1993a) Marriage and Divorce Statistics

*Never-married lone mothers*

Never-married lone mothers are typically younger, poorer, less likely to be working, more likely to be in receipt of income support and less likely to be in receipt of maintenance than divorced and separated lone mothers.

Since the mid-80s there has been a growth in the proportion of lone-parent families headed by never-married, though not necessarily never-partnered, mothers from three per cent of all families with dependent children in 1986 to eight per cent in 1993. It is likely that some of the recent increase in the proportion of never-married lone mother families is being driven by the breakdown of cohabiting unions. The proportion of separated and divorced lone mothers has increased more slowly, from nine per cent in 1986 to 11 per cent in 1993 (OPCS, 1993b and 1995b).

We noted earlier that cohabiting couples with children were economically disadvantaged compared with their married counter-parts. Thus when these unions terminate it is not surprising that these mothers tend to be relatively disadvantaged compared with previously married mothers. Whatever the mechanism driving the rise in lone-parenthood, there is no doubt that the average never-married lone-mother and her young children are living in poverty with little available money for investment in herself or her children.

### A final look at lone-parent families

The headline data show that lone-parent families, as a proportion of all families with dependent children, increased from 13 per cent in 1981 to 22 per cent in 1993 (OPCS, 1995b). Similarly, the proportion of all children living in lone-parent families almost doubled between 1981 and 1993 from 10 per cent to 18 per cent.

What are the factors that directly determine the number of children in lone-parent families? The numbers of lone parents depends on two factors: the total number of women of childbearing age and the proportion of these that become lone parents. An increase in the proportion of children with lone parents occurs either if the number of children in lone parent families goes up or if the number of children in two-parent families goes down. During the 1980s and on in to the 1990s, both changes have occurred and both are contributing to the large increase in the proportion of children in lone-parent families. The reduction in married couple families with children, emanating from the postponement or avoidance of parenthood, has in effect magnified the increase in the lone parent population and the proportions of children living in lone-parent families.

Policy-makers might want to understand and interpret both trends. Both developments might suggest a society that is lacking in its support of families and children. Declining marriage and fertility rates suggest a society that is not organised around or concerned with families and children. At the same time, an increasing proportion of lone-parent families indicates a climate in which it is difficult to hold families together.

### Policy choices

It is unlikely that any set of government policies can alter some of the fundamental changes in family life that have occurred in recent decades. However, government policies can make it easier to form and support families, can reinforce the fundamental notion that a society should care for and be concerned about children and the families that rear them, and can alleviate some of the hardships of disadvantaged families.

*Work and family life*

It is axiomatic that an essential part of such a strategy is the creation and maintenance of an economy in which families can earn an adequate income from work.    In this respect, close attention should be paid to the recommendations of Steve Nickell concerning unemployment (Chapter 3). Employment is the main source of economic support for families and plays a pivotal role in the lives of both men and women. However, work can also constrain family life by limiting the time available for family tasks and interaction between family members, and conversely the obligations and responsibilities of family life may act as a constraint on labour force participation. Moreover, competing pressures of work and family obligations may make for inefficiencies both in parenting and employment.

Nowadays, most mothers are employed outside the home, a long term trend that is unlikely to go into reverse or be reversible.    Whether a mother continues in paid work or returns to the labour market after time out to care for children partly depends on the balance between the income that employment brings and the financial costs of childcare.  The decision of a mother to work also depends on social and psychic costs and benefits related to her own needs, the needs of her children and the needs of the family unit. For a lone mother with no alternative source of income, the financial factor may be of critical importance (Bradshaw and Millar, 1991).

Research on the effects of maternal employment on children has largely examined the impact on children's academic performance and achievements. The findings in relation to this issue tend to be ambiguous, contradictory and weak.  There is no robust evidence that maternal employment negatively or positively affects a child's educational achievement.  In the USA, where this issue has received more attention, the general consensus among those who maintain that maternal employment affects the child's performance in school is that subgroups of children must be considered separately because employment has different meanings for a child depending on their home environment (Heyns and Catsambis, 1986).

Recognising that the worlds of work and family are interdependent implies the fostering and development of policies that ease the tensions between the two domains.  Such policies are well rehearsed and include: maternity and parental leave; flexible hours of work including part-time employment; family leave to care for sick children; affordable quality child-care, including the provision of nursery schools and after school care; tax concessions and child benefits and allowances (see Chapters 5 and 6).  These policies directly and explicitly support families with children and give recognition to some of the costs in rearing the next generation of citizens (see Figure 8.4). We should also ensure that the tax and benefit systems do not introduce incentives for family break-up.  In particular, some benefits may need to be restructured to ensure that the benefits or earnings of one partner do not count against the benefits or earnings of the other in such a way as to financially encourage partners to live apart (Chapter 5).

*Investment in children*

Much passion and prejudice surrounds the political debate on the family in Britain. An explicit emphasis on the need to invest in children might temper the debate as well as providing a useful guiding principle for family policies. This guiding principle should be to ensure that resources are targeted on the child.

There are three main partners involved in child investment: the government, the major societal investor in children; the parents; and the children themselves. Official or government strategies for targeting investment on children should include high quality effective education from pre-school into early adulthood, health and welfare provision as well as work-family policies. These are all policies which underscore society's fundamental interest in educating and nurturing the next generation. Moreover, universal policies avoid the dilemma of how to assist children in lone-parent families without setting them apart or sending messages that families are more likely to receive help if they live apart. Child benefit is explicitly intended to assist parents with the costs of children. However, it should be stressed that even under the most basic of budgets, present government benefits do not appear to cover the full cost of the child and parents must invest some of their own resources in order to cover the shortfall (see, for example, Oldfield and Autumm, 1993; Figure 8.4).

The investments made by parents in their children depend on the resources they are able and choose to devote to their children - financial resources, but also time and support. However, these may also be affected by government policies. For example, unemployment reduces parents financial resources, so policies aimed at reducing unemployment will obviously help the children of these parents. A more specific example concerns the Child Support Agency (CSA). Policy could be altered so that the state benefits received by single mothers are not reduced so drastically as at present in proportion to the payments collected by the CSA from absent fathers. This minor reform would give single mothers more incentive to help locate absent fathers and would increase the resources going to the children in these relatively needy households.

Then there are the choices that children themselves make about how they spend their time - in education, leisure and so on. One of the objectives of the educational system, above and beyond the provision of high quality education in the early years, should be to ensure that children achieve the cognitive skills and knowledge to make well-informed and considered life-choices. Children should be able to consider wisely the long-term consequences of their educational, occupational and personal choices.

## Figure 8.4  The cost of a child in a low budget household[4]

### Basket of goods and services for the children, and the budgets for a child in the 2 adult/2 child family, £ per week, April 1993 prices

| | Basket of goods and services for the two children | Average cost of a child under 11 (£) |
|---|---|---|
| Housing* | 2 extra bedrooms plus hall and large back garden | 5.14 |
| Fuel | Fuel use for the extra space heating and longer heating time because the house is occupied by the non-working mother and the young children | 3.84 |
| Food | Food for children | 10.21 |
| Clothing | Clothing and footwear for children | 4.12 |
| Household goods and services | Extra cleaning material, shorter lifetime of household furniture, and soft furnishings such as bedclothes and furniture for children's bedrooms | 3.95 |
| Personal care | Extra toiletries and individual personal care items for children, such as tooth brush, hair brush, and a hair cut kit for children | 0.45 |
| Transport | Bus fares for children | 0.27 |
| Leisure goods and services | Children's bikes, toys, games, books and individual leisure expenses for children including going to the movies and a day trip to Blackpool | 2.38 |
| **Total**\*\* | | **30.37** |
| **Total less housing** | | **25.23** |
| **Total less rent** | | **25.62** |

\* Housing costs include rent, water and sewerage charges, internal maintenance and contents insurance
\*\* Due to rounding, totals may not add up to the sum of their component parts

### Low cost budgets for a child aged under 11 and aged 16, April 1993 prices, £ per week

| Age of child | Including housing* | Excluding housing* |
|---|---|---|
| Under 11 | £30.37 | £25.23 |
| 16 | £41.71 | £36.57 |

\* Housing costs for a child aged under 11 and aged 16 are £5.14 per week

Source: Oldfield and Autumn, Child Poverty Action Group, 1993, p.46.

Overall, the present level of investment in children may be too small but it does not follow that all children have too few resources devoted to their development. Many children are doing well: they come from families with adequate incomes, attend quality schools and have high expectations for the future. However, there is evidence that the situation of many British children has deteriorated in recent times: more children are living in lone-parent families, more children are living with unemployed parents and consequently greater proportions of children are living in poverty - around 30 per cent in recent estimates (Hills, 1995). Family instability, unemployed parents, and poverty all work to the disadvantage of children. Hence, a large part of the problem of the current status of children lies in *differences* among children, rather than in the status of the average child: the socio-economic gaps between children in the early 1990s are far larger than they were during the 1970s. Increasing income inequality and unemployment has led to a growth in low income families (see also Chapter 4). These changes, together with polar shifts towards double income families where both parents maintain a high commitment to the labour market, and towards lone parenthood with its associated vulnerabilities, have resulted in problems becoming more concentrated at the bottom of the income distribution. Such families have the least financial resources to invest in their children and these parents, other things being equal, are the least likely to have accumulated educational and training capital on their own passage to adulthood.

That is not to say that lone mothers, unemployed parents and those on low incomes do not value their children's education, do not have high educational expectations for their children, or give less time and support to their children. There is little evidence to suggest that these disadvantaged families differ from better-off families on these measures. Yet, these children do under-achieve. What is needed to support these families is not rhetoric, condemnation or disinvestment, but high quality pedagogic and educational investment from the earliest age for children alongside opportunities for parents to redress any shortcomings or opportunities foregone in their own education and training careers. There is a case for providing additional training and education for parents as extra increments in education have a strong association with the educational success of children. Furthermore, the returns to children of such increments may be greatest at the bottom end of the parental educational distribution than at the top.

As the National Commission on Education (1994) noted:

> Educational achievement is strongly associated with family background. Parental education, particularly the level of education achieved by the mother, has a powerful influence on children's educational progress. When the mother herself has not had the benefit of a good education or learned to recognise its value, there is a risk that her child's early learning experience will be impoverished unless there is outside help (p.112).

Giving children pre-school provision and an educational 'head start' that encourages school success, thereby enhancing opportunities and the possibilities for a wider range of careers, may reduce the chances of early family formation or at least temper the exigencies frequently associated with early parenthood.

## Conclusion

Is there a tendency in our complex societies to overlook what is the ultimate purpose of an economy? It is certainly not to sustain itself for its own sake. One could argue that, at the most fundamental level, the economy is there to maintain its population. Families, in times past, present and into the foreseeable future have been, and are likely to continue to be, the primary loci of reproduction and the rearing of children. The welfare of families is therefore crucial to the effective rearing of the next generation of citizens and workers. Family conditions are also strongly implicated in major social concerns such as crime and educational achievement (Chapters 6 and 9). In advanced societies children have to compete as individuals in the labour market and what they have to sell will depend largely on the level of parental investment alongside the level and quality of educational and training provision. They must also acquire the cognitive skills and motivation at an early age in order to be able to make well-informed life-choices about education, occupation and personal decisions (including early parenthood).

Above all a concerted educational investment is crucial in Britain to reduce the effects of prior neglect. Specific proposals are discussed elsewhere in this volume (Chapter 6). Here it is sufficient to conclude that such an investment seems likely to be the best way forward for breaking the nexus of early family formation and its wide ranging negative implications for the future lives of men, women and children and the State.

## Notes

1. Registration data only permit the computation of average age at first birth for legitimate births since parity is not recorded on the birth certificate for babies born outside marriage. Given that women who have children outside marriage are on average younger than their married counterparts the figure for married couples is likely to be higher than the average for all births.
2. One of the issues that the increase in cohabitation has thrown up is what term should be used to refer to 'partners' or cohabitants, especially given that partners are sometimes same-sex. Given that the term 'partner' has other commonly used meanings, and is also widely disliked, the best alternative may be the wider adoption of the specialist term 'domate' (adapted from 'domestic mate' or cohabiting sexual partner).
3. In Figure 8.3 we have graphed total divorce rates given in Table 2.5 of Recent Developments in Europe 1994, Council of Europe, 1994. A total divorce rate is the probability of divorce for a married person if they were to pass through their marriage years experiencing the duration-specific divorce rates occurring in a given year. It is a synthetic measure and is computed by summing the divorce rates by duration of marriage (generally up to 30 years) observed in a given year.
4. This study calculated that the total (low) budget for such a 2 adult/2 child household was £142.56 per week, compared with a total income support (including

child benefit of £10.00 for the first child and £8.10 for the second) of £108.75, indicating a shortfall of £33.81 per week. At the time of writing (November 1995), child benefit is £10.40 per week for a first child and £8.45 for a second child.

# References

Bradshaw, J. and Millar, J. (1991), *Lone Parent Families in the UK*, Department of Social Security Report, No. **6**, London: HMSO.

Central Statistical Office (1995), *Social Trends 25*, London: HMSO.

Council of Europe (1994), *Recent Demographic Developments in Europe, 1994*, Strasbourg: Council of Europe Press.

Eurostat (1994), *Demographic Statistics 1994*, Luxembourg.

Haskey, J. (1984), 'Social class and socio-economic differentials in divorce in England and Wales', *Population Studies*, Vol. **38**, No. **3**.

Heyns, B. and Catsambis, S. (1986), 'Mothers' employment and children's achievement: a critique', *Sociology of Education*, **59**, pp. 140-51.

Hills, J. (1995), *Income and Wealth: Volume 2*, Joseph Rowntree Foundation.

Hobcraft, J. and Kiernan, K. (1995), 'Becoming a parent in Europe', *Plenary Paper in Proceedings of the 1995 European Population Conference*, Milan.

Kiernan, K. (1992), 'Men and women at work and home', in Jowell, R., Brook, L. and Prior, G. (eds.), *British Social Attitudes: the 9th Report*, Aldershot: Dartmouth.

Kiernan, K. (1993), 'The future of partnership and fertility in Europe', in Cliquet, R. (ed.), *The Future of Europe's Population*, Strasbourg: Council of Europe Press.

Kiernan, K. (1995), 'Transition to parenthood: young mothers, young fathers: associated factors and later life experiences', *STICERD Discussion Paper*, No. **113**, London School of Economics.

Kiernan, K. and Estaugh, V. (1993), 'Cohabitation, extra-marital childbearing and social policy', *Family Policy Studies Centre, Occasional Paper*, No. **17**.

Kiernan, K. and Lelievre, E. (1995), 'Devenir parent hors mariage en France et Grande-Bretagne: les differentes facettes d'un statut particulier', *Population*, Vol. **3**.

McRae, S. (1991), *Maternity Rights in Britain: the PSI Report on the Experience of Women and Employers*, London: Policy Studies Institute.

National Commission on Education (1993), *Learning to Succeed: A Radical Look at Education Today and a Strategy for the Future*, London: Heinemann.

Office of Population Censuses and Surveys (1993a), *Marriage and Divorce Statistics 1991* Series FM2, London: HMSO.

Office of Population Censuses and Surveys (1993b), *General Household Survey Report 1991*, London: HMSO.

Office of Population Censuses and Surveys (1994), *Birth Statistics 1992*, Series FM1, London: HMSO.

Office of Population Censuses and Surveys (1995a), *Population Trends*, No. **79**, London: HMSO.

Office of Population Censuses and Surveys (1995b), *General Household Survey Report 1993*, London: HMSO.

Oldfield, N. and Autumn, C.S. (1993), *The Cost of a Child: Living Standards for the 1990s*, London: Child Poverty Action Group.

Prinz, C. (1995), *Cohabitation or Marriage? New Living Arrangements in the Changing Societies of Europe*, Aldershot: Avebury Press.

Utting, D. (1995), *Family and Parenthood: Supporting Families, Preventing Breakdown*, London: Joseph Rowntree Foundation.

## Acknowledgments

The Economic and Social Research Council funded the preparation of this paper through Grant No L315 25 3015. The research on which it draws has been funded by the ESRC and the Joseph Rowntree Foundation. Material from the General Household Survey was made available through the OPCS and the ESRC Data Archive and has been used by permission of the Controller of H.M. Stationery Office. The paper has benefited from discussions at the 'Options for Britain' meeting at Nuffield College, Oxford and with colleagues in the department of Social Policy and Administration at the LSE.

# 9 Crime and criminal justice

*David Faulkner, Michael Hough and David Halpern* *

Crime is inescapably, and rightly, a political issue. Crime and the fear of crime can cause immense suffering to individuals and damage to communities. When a crime has been committed, the victim and the public expect it to be dealt with firmly and fairly. They expect justice to be done. No government can admit that there is little it can do about crime, or that it is not actively trying to reduce or control it.

Public expenditure on law and order in the United Kingdom currently stands at £14.5 billion per year.[1] This represents over five per cent of public expenditure or 2.3 per cent of the Gross National Product. Over half of this expenditure is on the police (£7.7 billion), and the remainder finances the other elements of the criminal justice system (CJS) including the courts (£2.5 billion), the prisons (£1.6 billion), legal aid (£1.2 billion) and the probation services (£0.4 billion; Central Statistical Office, 1995). However, despite these huge sums of money and the approximate doubling (in real terms) of spending on law and order since 1979, recorded crime has substantially increased over the same period.[2]

As well as involving substantial public expenditure, the criminal justice system exercises authority and coercive powers on behalf of the state. The integrity, efficiency and effectiveness of the organisations that comprise this

* David Faulkner is Fellow of St John's College and Senior Research Associate at the Centre for Criminological Research, University of Oxford; Michael Hough is Professor of Social Policy at South Bank University; and David Halpern is a Prize Research Fellow at Nuffield College, Oxford. This chapter also draws on an outline paper by Anthony Bottoms, Professor of the Institute of Criminology, Cambridge, presented at the Options for Britain Conference 1-3 December, 1994 at Nuffield College, Oxford.

system are rightly matters of political and public interest. Their efficiency, in managerial terms, can in principle be measured relatively easily (though at some cost), but their effectiveness in the sense of longer term outcomes and wider national interests are harder to assess and depend on the view taken of the organisation's purpose. This purpose is not always self-evident or generally agreed except in the broadest terms. Today's successes may be seen tomorrow as failures, and vice versa, as seen, for example, in the abrupt change of attitude and reversal of many of the government's criminal justice policies reflected in the enactment of the Criminal Justice Act of 1993 and the Criminal Justice and Public Order Act of 1994.

Confidence in the criminal justice system has become an increasingly prominent issue during the last fifteen years. This may partly reflect increases in recorded crime and some high profile miscarriages of justice, but confidence is also affected by different factors in different groups. For the general public, confidence is affected if the police appear uninterested or unresponsive, if crime appears to be 'out of control' or if offenders seem to be 'getting away with it', the latter implying that too few offenders are seen to be caught or punished, and that punishments are seen as too 'soft'. For policy-makers and politicians, confidence is affected by perceptions that the criminal justice system is poorly managed and inefficient and that, in some instances, its professionals have too great or too 'liberal' an influence. For professionals themselves, confidence is affected if they feel short of resources or constantly subject to new legislation and incessant demands for change. For victims of crime, confidence is affected if they feel that the system denies them the recognition or respect they believe they deserve or that they have been humiliated and betrayed by it. In addition, reformers continue to campaign for improvements or reforms to the system to address issues such as miscarriages of justice, discrimination against racial and cultural minorities (and sometimes against women) and degrading conditions in prisons.

This chapter considers the issues of crime, the administration of justice, and the management of the criminal justice services which will face any administration during the next five to ten years. It considers the options for reducing crime, improving the quality of justice and increasing the efficiency of, and confidence in, the criminal justice services. The opening sections draw on statistics and research to examine the nature of crime, who commits it, and the causes or reasons for its apparently continuous growth. The next section considers some of the issues and options which present themselves on a conventional analysis of the present situation, and the final sections indicate some more radical options for addressing the position of victims, changing the functioning and structure of the system and for adopting a broader approach to the reduction of crime and criminality.

## The nature of crime

Crime is a complex phenomenon. Like the objective of higher economic growth, reducing crime is not susceptible to simplistic solutions. Unfortunately, as in other politically charged areas, populist explanations often tend to ignore this complexity.

There are substantial variations in the situations, people and outcomes associated with crime. The effects of some forms of crime may scarcely be noticed at all (for example, certain types of fraud); some will only have an effect over a long period of time (for example, some offences involving pollution or drugs); and some will have an immediate and devastating impact. Most crimes bring relatively limited financial gains to those who commit them and most require little in the way of effort, planning or skill (Gottfredson and Hirschi, 1990).

The incidents that reach official attention are not necessarily a good guide to the real extent and nature of crime. Most crimes go unreported to the police, and the majority of those which are reported and recorded go undetected (Mayhew *et al*, 1993, 1994; Home Office, 1994a). The proportion of crimes that are reported to the police also varies according to the offence. For example, comparisons between survey data and police statistics show that although over 90 per cent of motor vehicle thefts are reported, less than 20 per cent of thefts from the person or incidents of vandalism are reported. The British Crime Survey (BCS) therefore offers a better guide than police statistics to the extent and nature of crimes committed against individuals.

As Figure 9.1 shows, only six per cent of BCS incidents are crimes of violence. Most of these are woundings, and a small minority involve sexual offences. The majority of crimes revealed by the BCS are offences of theft, of which vehicle-related thefts account for over a third.

### Figure 9.1  Profile of crimes against individuals

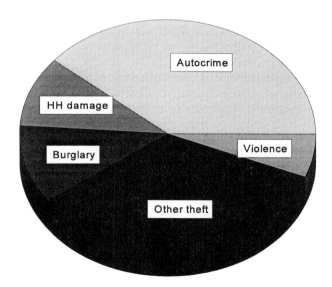

HH  =  Household
Note:   violence excludes common assaults, which involve no injury
Source: British Crime Survey, 1994

The BCS shows that the total net losses arising from the theft of property from individuals are more than £2 billion, the greater part of which is accounted for by car theft (£750 million) and burglary (almost £700 million).[3] However, the BCS measures only those crimes committed against individuals and their personal property.[4]  In crude financial terms, the business sector carries a larger burden: it has been estimated that shoplifting, burglary and other types of property crime cost retailers £2.15 billion (in 1993/94), reducing potential profits by a sixth (Speed et al, 1995).  It is hard to provide firm estimates of the extent and financial costs of the white collar crimes of fraud and forgery but these could be as high, if not higher, than those of theft.  As for breaches of environmental legislation, there is very little information on prevalence, and the social and financial costs are, for the present at least, an imponderable (though see Chapter 10 for a discussion of the costs of 'legal' damage).

Finally, there are so-called 'victimless' crimes, a category dominated by illicit drug use.  Drug taking is commonplace amongst the young: survey estimates suggest that at least a third, and possibly more than half, of people under thirty have taken illicit drugs (Leitner et al, 1993; Mott and Mirrlees Black, 1993, 1995).

The costs of crime are not only financial.  The emotional impact on victims can sometimes be devastating.  Surprisingly, the criminal justice system paid little heed to victims until the 1980s, and the consistent disregard of victims' needs and wishes led commentators to refer to processes of 'secondary victimisation' at the hands of the police and the courts (Fattah, 1991).  There have been changes since then, partly reflecting the general impact of consumerism on the public sector, but more particularly reflecting the specific advocacy of victims groups such as Victim Support and the greater availability of information about victims such as that provided by the British Crime Survey.

Crime also carries broader social costs in terms of the anxiety it generates and the impact that fear of crime has on civil life.  For example, anxiety about street crime may gradually lead to the desertion of public space in cities, and the risk of robbery or burglary may cause businesses to move.  The resultant vacuum provides an environment even more conducive to offending and can lead to a vicious circle of decline.

## Who commits crime?

Those who commit crime do not constitute a small, separately identifiable group of 'criminals'.  Around a third of young men have acquired at least one conviction, usually in their teens, for a relatively serious (broadly speaking, indictable) offence by the time they reach their thirties (Home Office, 1995). Almost half of all the crime that is traced to an offender is committed by young men under 21, and about a quarter of it by young men under 17.  The peak age for offending is in the late-teens.

Most young men stop offending after one or two convictions but a few go on to commit quite a lot of crime.  About five per cent of men seem to be responsible for about two-thirds of attributed crime, with most serious or persistent offenders having started offending at an early age. There is clear evidence (Farrington, 1994; Hagell and Newburn, 1994) that, with the obvious exception of white-collar crimes, such persistent offending is commonly associated with:

- low family income;
- poor housing;
- an unstable job record (the offender's or their parents');
- failure or exclusion from school;
- delinquent family or friends;
- a remote father (though not necessarily an absent father);
- harsh and erratic discipline (at home or at school);
- abuse of drugs;
- mental disturbance and
- previous experience of violence or abuse.

Some of these factors, such as failure or exclusion from school and having an unstable job record, are probably as much symptoms as causes of offending behaviour. However, other factors, such as having a remote father or the experience of harsh and erratic discipline, appear likely to be genuine causal influences on later persistent offending.

## The growth in crime

There can be little doubt that Britain is a safer place today than it was, for example, in the 18th and early 19th centuries. Whatever impression early police statistics may give, the locks, bolts and bars on Victorian buildings are eloquent testimony to the threat of property crime at that time. As for the present century, actual crime levels were probably at their lowest in the period immediately after the First World War, though this is only a 'best guess'. Since then, there appears to have been a progressive increase in crime. One of the fastest rates of annual growth (in percentage, rather than absolute terms) seems to have been between 1929 and 1932 and there was also a rapid rate of increase during the Second World War. Though recorded crime was fairly stable during the 1950s, it has since risen by around ten-fold. However, although the average annual increase in recorded crime since 1970 has been about five per cent, there have been small falls in some years, notably in 1973, 1988, 1993 and 1994. The rate of increase has been roughly comparable with those of many other industrialised nations, though with notable exceptions (such as Japan, which has reported almost no change in its recorded crime rate since the 1950s). The rate of increase has been higher in England and Wales than in Scotland and Northern Ireland.

However, trends in recorded crime can be misleading. There appear to have been long-term shifts in the readiness of victims to notify the police and in the ability and preparedness of the police to record the offences reported to them. For example, police statistics overstated the rate of increase in crime in the 1980s (Mayhew et al, 1994) because of increases in reporting rates. These increases are thought to have been a function of the growth of telephone ownership and household insurance. Another possible contribution to increased reporting is that public tolerance of some types of crime may have declined and especially of those types of crime associated with 'macho' working class culture, such as domestic assaults, pub fights, sexual attacks and racial harassment (Mayhew *et al*, 1993; Aye Maung and Mirrlees Black, 1994; FitzGerald, 1994).

Since 1991, the small fall in recorded crime has not so far been matched by trends in the BCS, which are still rising. This change could be because the new 'performance culture' in police management may be exerting a deflationary pressure on crime statistics. Another possibility is that people are no longer reporting crimes which they would have reported in the past. This in turn may indicate shifts towards a higher tolerance of certain offences or, alternatively, that people have increasingly come to doubt the value of reporting certain offences to the police.[5]

In sum, although the rate of increase in crime may have been overstated by official statistics in the 1980s (and understated in recent figures), we can be fairly certain that there has been a substantial increase in the underlying crime rate in the UK since the 1950s. This trend is parallel to those experienced by many other, though not all, industrialised nations.


*Causal factors behind the growth in crime*

Given that a third of the male population acquire convictions, and that an inevitably larger proportion actually engage in law-breaking, almost every conceivable 'cause' will have some truth in it. Three broad sets of factors can, however, be identified. First, the shift towards a consumer society - which has occurred over a period of centuries - has simultaneously created the opportunities for crime and the motivation for it. Second, there are factors and theories relating to the erosion of systems of informal social control, which translates into tabloid English as a lack of respect for parents, teachers, employers, the church and other authority figures. Finally, there are the links between crime and socio-economic factors - unemployment, poverty, poor housing and other facets of social deprivation.

The evidence and arguments are relatively clear concerning the increased opportunities for crime. Henry Fielding (1751, republished 1988) identified the 'increase in luxury' as a causal factor in the growth in crime, and commentators have since then intermittently observed that levels of consumer goods vary over time, as does the level of motivation to acquire them. Without the motor car, for example, there would be some 6 million fewer crimes per year.

At the same time, it is scarcely less obvious that the post-war period has seen a progressive weakening of those institutions which transmit and enforce moral and civic values, though it is not easy to measure or quantify the significance of this trend (Halpern, 1995). Britain has moved rapidly since the war from a moderately religious to a largely secular society; divorce has increased six-fold since the 1960s, and one in five dependent children now lives with a lone parent; the extended family has become a marginal feature of many people's lives; guaranteed and permanent employment has become a rarity in the space of a single generation of employees; and mobility and telecommunications have tended to undermine place-based local communities. Simultaneous with these developments have been other processes which have both extended the duration of late adolescence and isolated youth culture from the rest of society (Rutter and Smith, 1995). Some commentators have suggested that the range and pace of these changes have generated qualitatively different social arrangements which contain an inexorable dynamic for rising crime (Bottoms and Wiles, 1994).

The third set of explanatory factors have arguably been the most controversial. A variety of mediating processes between social deprivation and crime have been suggested, ranging from absolute and coercive need (for food, clothing, or shelter), through the relative lack of legitimate opportunities to acquire possessions and status, to the tedium facing those with scant resources for filling a jobless existence. The evidence that relative or absolute deprivation has some causal role in occurrence of crime is clear beyond doubt. Shifts in economic activity can certainly explain short-run oscillations around the long-run upward trend (Dickinson, 1994; Field, 1990); economic downturns appear either to draw more people into property crime, or to increase the level of activity of those already engaged in crime. It is also clear that whatever the causal factors are which draw people into property crime, those who are drawn in carry, by and large, all the predictable stigmata of social deprivation (Farrington, 1994).

Populist imperatives have reduced political debate about the causes of crime to the crudest Punch and Judy tussle between moral breakdown and social deprivation, in which only one type of cause can 'win'. Thus, for example, the low (but nevertheless rising) crime rates of the 1930s are seen as 'proof' that social deprivation is irrelevant to crime. Yet only the naive and disingenuous could deny the likelihood of causal interactions between informal social control and economic factors whereby those societies with weak systems of informal social control are able to weather only a small degree of economic turmoil before they experience the problem of rising crime. In our view, all three of the broad sets of factors described above are relevant to the explanation of the growth in crime in Britain (as elsewhere), though none of these factors operates in isolation or in a simple manner.

A more specific causal factor also needs mentioning - the role that the use of illicit drugs may play in fuelling crime. An association between drug abuse and crime is well established, but the notion that people experiment with drugs, get 'hooked' and then turn to crime is an oversimplification. Illicit drug use and other forms of crime often stem from similar causal factors, with the latter often predating the former. However, a proportion of dependent drug users are heavily involved in crime, and the evidence suggests that they may account for a significant minority of crime. Estimates range from single-figure percentages to 50 per cent (see Hough, in press, for a discussion).

## Solutions to crime

It is inevitable and unsurprising that people should look to the formal criminal justice system for ways of containing crime. Large majorities consistently favour more police on the beat and heavier sentences.[6] The belief is widespread that crime can be tackled via the procedures of detection, arrest, prosecution, conviction and formal punishment. In other words, the way to stop crime is seen as being to catch more criminals, to see that more of them are convicted, to send more of them to prison, and to treat them more harshly when they get there. This belief appeals to common sense and seems intuitively correct.

This popular belief makes sense from the perspective of those who have settled lives and living conditions, who have the opportunity and are used to making rational choices, and who have something to lose - status, position and the respect of others. Rigorous enforcement may be an effective way of dealing with overloaded lorries or polluted rivers (Chapter 10). It may well have contributed to the improvement in road safety which has been one of the country's successes over the last twenty years. It may even succeed against organised crime. However, there are very clear limits to what can be achieved by tackling persistent offending through deterrent strategies based on formal enforcement.

Conventionally, penologists distinguish between general and specific (or individual) deterrence (Walker, 1985; Ashworth, 1994). General deterrence is the effect achieved on the population at large of a threat to dispossess (of money or liberty) those who disregard a legal requirement; specific deterrence is the effect of carrying out the threat on those who choose to ignore it. The general deterrent effects of the criminal justice system are palpable - if almost impossible to quantify. However, research has shown that individual or specific deterrence is subject to progressively diminishing returns. The majority of offenders who are caught and punished never reappear before the criminal courts. The minority who have been punished once but reappear before the courts are more likely to reappear again. Those who have several convictions - and who typically receive the heaviest penalties - are especially likely to be reconvicted yet again. Thus on average eight out of ten young male offenders with six or more convictions reappear before the courts (Lloyd et al, 1995). One explanation for this is that progressive dispossession through punishment confers on the punished the freedom of having nothing to lose.

Deterrence is not the only mechanism by which the criminal justice system achieves its impact. Those who are sent to prison are unable to commit further crimes (except within the prison) for the duration of their sentence. Certainly 'prison works' in this sense. However, there is only limited scope for reducing crime through the greater use of imprisonment. Only a small proportion of offenders come before the courts. Figure 9.2 shows that the purchase that the criminal justice system has on crime problems is small: currently only two per cent of offences covered by the BCS result in a conviction in court, and only 0.3 per cent of offences result in a prison sentence. This implies that even substantial increases in imprisonment would therefore have only a marginal effect on the overall level of crime.

Figure 9.2    Attrition within the criminal justice system: outcomes
as a proportion of offences committed

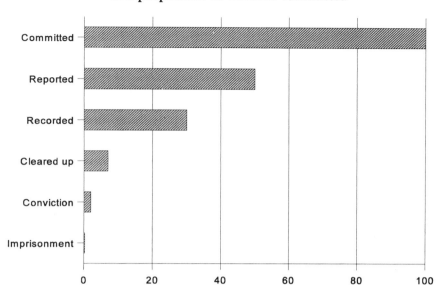

To say that neither formal nor informal systems of social control can be easily manipulated to yield reductions in crime is simply to restate the obvious point that crime has proved an intractable problem in most developed countries throughout the post-war period. There are nevertheless a range of policy options to consider, including a number of which deserve more attention than they currently receive.

## Policy options and issues - conventional approaches

The following list of options is not comprehensive, but aims to identify the key policy issues within the criminal justice system which are generally acknowledged to need attention over the next five years. Some wider ranging and possibly more radical options are identified later in the chapter.

### Policing policy

In Britain, public confidence in the police has tended to be high relative to many institutions and to the police in other countries, with around 70 to 80 per cent of people expressing 'a great deal' or 'a lot' of confidence, though this has fallen slightly in recent years (Timms, 1992). However, the role and activities of the police are not without controversy. For example, there are long-standing debates about the appropriate balance between preventive work and law enforcement, between police accountability to central government and accountability to local communities, and between 'core' and other police responsibilities (Loveday, 1995; Reiner and Spencer, 1995).

For uniformed policing, the central issue is the style, rather than the level, of patrol coverage. Currently favoured innovations include: decentralised operations that assign teams on a long-term basis to defined geographic areas; responsiveness to the public's priorities; maximising contact between the public and the police; and the 'problem-oriented' approach to police work. These strategies have been shown to increase public ratings of the police and sometimes to reduce fear (Bennett, 1991; Goldstein, 1990). However, with the exception of the successes of the problem-oriented approach, the ability of these strategies to reduce crime in the short to medium term remains an open question. Nonetheless, in as far as these strategies support the perceived legitimacy of the police they may lead in the longer term to reductions (or slower increases) in crime and fear through a strengthening of the public support on which effective policing ultimately depends.

The terminology used to discuss uniformed police work - problem-solving, responsiveness to community priorities, tackling problems of disorder and so on - tends to mask the political dimension inherent in police work about the tolerance of social diversity. One person's crime or disorder is often another's recreation. When local police are asked to identify and tackle what the 'local community' perceive as problems, there is always a risk that they will be improperly co-opted by one part of the community in their disputes with another. When this occurs, increased regard for 'the law' amongst the former may be more than offset by decreased regard amongst the latter. It follows that the police mandate must be restricted to functions which are both grounded in law and command broad popular consent.

For detective work, the central issue must be to find ways of halting the decline in detection rates. One of the few things on which deterrence theorists have agreed is that *certainty* of punishment is a stronger deterrent than the *type* of punishment. The fall in clear-up rates from 35 per cent in 1985 to 25 per cent in 1995 must therefore be a source of concern (cf. Farrington *et al*, 1994). Some of the operations targeting specific types of offender, such as Operation Bumblebee, seem to have had promising results (Stockdale and Gresham, 1995).[7] Other changes designed to increase clear-up rates, and especially conviction rates, are more controversial. They include the proposals in the Home Office consultation document on disclosure (Cm 2864) and the change in the defendant's right of silence, enacted in the Criminal Justice and Public Order Act 1994. Concerning the latter, the impact is still to emerge, and it is certainly a policy that should be kept under review. On one view, more serious criminals will be convicted and innocent or vulnerable defendants will have nothing to fear. On another view, argued for example by many lawyers and by the law reform group 'JUSTICE', the innocent and vulnerable are more likely to be intimidated, with the risk of more miscarriages of justice, while experienced criminals will have a new line of defence based on attacking the integrity of the police.

*Prosecution and punishment*

Throughout the 1970s and 1980s considerable emphasis was placed on avoiding or deferring young offenders' contact with the formal criminal justice system, using a variety of diversionary strategies - through informal warnings, cautions and the discontinuance of cases.  On one interpretation, the policy has been strikingly successful, with progressively fewer young offenders coming to official notice.  Against this, this apparent reduction does not necessarily imply that there has been a fall-off in the number of young people engaged in crime. Dealing with young offenders informally means, by definition, that no records are maintained.

The key issue here is how offenders who have not been brought before the courts, their victims and local communities perceive the process.  Are cautions and informal warnings seen as empty threats or gestures, or are they recognised as having a genuine effect in preventing further offending?  The statistics are encouraging.  Table 9.1 shows, for a sample of 3,000 offenders cautioned in 1988, the percentages reconvicted within a two year period.  These indicate that the vast majority of people (over 80 per cent) who are cautioned are not reconvicted within a two year period.  These figures compare favourably with those for community and prison sentences, although adjustments need to be made for offender characteristics.

**Table 9.1  Per cent of offenders cautioned in 1988
reconvicted within a two-year period**

| Age at caution | Reconviction Rate |
|---|---|
| 10-14 | 13% |
| 14-16 | 17% |
| 17-20 | 20% |
| 21 or over | 9% |
| **TOTAL** | 17% |

Source: Home Office, 1994b

Similar issues arise for offenders suffering from mental disorder and for those involved in the possession of small quantities of cannabis.  The use of cautions for such individuals and for relatively minor offences therefore may prove a success, though firmer conclusions must await the publication of further statistics.

The increased use of cautions and informal warnings has not applied to all offences.  For example, reflecting changing perceptions of the seriousness of the issue, there has been an increasing emphasis on arrest and prosecution in cases of domestic violence.  More controversially, certain forms of conduct associated with public protest or public nuisance have become criminalised in the Criminal Justice and Public Order Act 1994.

*Community penalties*

The 1970s and 1980s were a period of considerable pessimism about the scope for achieving any constructive outcome through the use of sentencing. It was widely believed that nothing could be done, either through the form or content of sentences, to reduce the chances of an individual reoffending. However, the evidence to support such pessimistic beliefs was less firm than was recognised at the time. Researchers using the statistical technique of 'meta-analysis' have re-evaluated the studies and come up with more positive results.

Meta-analysis is a technique of standardising and combining the results of large numbers of studies which individually may be too small-scale to show statistically significant results. The technique is not without its own critics, but the results suggest that there are consistently positive trends behind the individually non-significant results of the evaluations of the last thirty years. Together with more recent evaluations, these analyses suggest that some types of court disposal can significantly reduce the risk of reoffending. The emergent consensus (cf. Andrews *et al,* 1990; Gendreau and Ross, 1987; Lipsey, 1991; Lösel, 1993; Hood, 1995) is that rehabilitative gains are largest when programmes:

- target high risk offenders,
- focus on offending behaviour and the factors underlying it,
- are clearly-structured and properly implemented and
- staff are motivated and well-trained.

Even when community penalties are compared *en bloc* to imprisonment, the statistics are encouraging. Having controlled for the age and criminal history of the offender and the nature of the offence, Lloyd *et al* (1995) found that community penalties have reconviction rates no lower than prison sentences, and at a fraction of the cost (Home Office, 1992).

Some community-based programmes aim to achieve the equivalent of prison's incapacitative effect, reducing or eliminating offending for the duration of the treatment. Electronic monitoring is one example. Some treatment programmes for drug-dependent offenders are, in effect, another example. American research suggests that the latter are very cost-effective, and that the benefits (preventing abuse and offending) accrue mainly during the period of treatment, rather like prison but again at a fraction of the cost (Rydell and Everingham, 1994).

The Green Paper 'Strengthening Punishment in the Community' (Home Office, 1995) contains several proposals designed to increase the confidence of sentencers and the public in community sentences. It can be read as a 'marketing strategy' for selling community penalties to sentencers. It can also be read as a political manifesto designed to emphasise to the public the punishment aspects of community penalties (compliance with 'tough' and intrusive conditions) rather than rehabilitation or reform, and to recommend the substitution of judicial for professional judgement on the form that the conditions should take. The Green Paper proposes integrating the existing range of probation orders, supervision orders, attendance centre orders, community service orders and curfew orders into a single 'community sentence', allowing sentencers considerable freedom in specifying the precise elements of supervision, reparation and restriction of liberty in the sentence. The outcome is intended to be closer co-operation between probation and social services and the courts, more rigorous professional practice, and greater use of community sentences rather than imprisonment. All of these are to be welcomed. However, some difficulties can be anticipated. In the first place, there is greater scope for tension and conflict between the sentencer and probation staff over the type of judgement that each is required to make and their accountability for the outcome. Secondly, tough conditions may result in high failure rates, with significant proportions of offenders ending up in prison for offences which would not, in themselves, be thought to justify sentences of imprisonment (Tonry, 1995).

## *The greater use of imprisonment*

Public debate about the effectiveness of imprisonment has been as one-dimensional as that about the causes of crime, with debate typically being reduced to the issue of whether there are any incapacitative gains from imprisoning offenders. The statistic favoured by proponents of incapacitation is that sending a burglar to prison for a year rather than passing a community penalty will prevent between three to thirteen crimes. Opponents cite another Home Office statistic, that increasing the prison population by 25 per cent would yield only a one per cent fall in recorded crime (Tarling, 1993).

The two statistics turn out to be mutually compatible, both being derived from the Home Office Offenders Index. They need to be interpreted in the light of Figure 9.2, showing that under one per cent of crimes result in a custodial sentence. The key question is not whether 'prison works' in preventing crime, but whether this is the best use of the money available to the criminal justice system. Sending an opiate-addicted burglar to prison for six months, for example, will certainly put a stop to his offences during that time; but, as suggested above, a probation order involving a year's methadone maintenance programme might be almost as effective in doing so and at a tenth of the cost.

American criminologists, as distinct from politicians, tend not to argue that the 300 per cent increase in imprisonment rates there have had anything to do with the static or declining crime rates which most states have enjoyed over the last 15 years. Other policies to reduce crime should have had some effect, but it seems implausible that use of imprisonment on the American scale would be without impact. More probably, a reduction in crime *has* been bought, but at an enormous fiscal cost. Also, the long-term social costs of this policy have yet to be addressed seriously.

The American experience demonstrates that popular demand for punishment can be a political phenomenon that has to be taken seriously, though it is an open question as to whether politicians there have fuelled rather than responded to this popular punitiveness. Some survey evidence, albeit from the 1980s, suggested that on both sides of the Atlantic public opinion on sentencing was more diverse, less outrightly punitive and more tolerant of sentencing of varying severity than had previously been supposed (Walker and Hough, 1988).  This evidence suggests that politicians may have underrated or understated their scope for innovative policy-making in this area.


## Mitigating the effects of crime

Policies for mitigating the effects of crime need to focus mainly on the victim. A great deal has been achieved for victims in recent years, but the extent of that achievement is itself raising questions about the nature and extent of victims' legitimate expectations from the state, from the criminal justice system and from society more generally, and about the means (and cost) of satisfying those expectations.

Compensation for the victims of violent crime has been available for over thirty years, but the Criminal Injuries Compensation Scheme has been progressively and restrictively modified during this period and, recently, the government concluded that the scheme could no longer be afforded in its original form.  At the same time, the scheme came under increasing criticism for the extent to which victims were effectively excluded from its scope (Victim Support, 1993).   Attempts to introduce a new and even more restrictive scheme were successfully challenged in the courts.  Legislation for a new scheme has now been enacted by Parliament, but many of the earlier criticisms remain.

A more significant achievement of recent decades has been the establishment and expansion of victim support schemes throughout the country, including schemes to support victims and other witnesses in court.  They have come about largely through the efforts of Victim Support and other, more specialised, voluntary bodies.  This development has been accompanied by a greater awareness of victims' issues and a greater sensitivity to their feelings and situations.  A statement of what victims are entitled to expect was set out in the Victim's Charter - the forerunner of the Citizen's Charter - in 1990. However, there are still concerns that many of those entitlements are not being met in practice and that other needs are scarcely being addressed at all.  There are also concerns that a number of recent initiatives have been too hastily introduced and not fully thought out, such as the requirement for pre-sentence reports to include a reference to the impact on the victim and the 'help line' to enable victims to express opinions about the arrangements for a prisoner's release or home leave.  More radical demands are being made that the victim should have a right to express views on matters such as bail, the choice of charge, the acceptance of a plea and the sentence.

These various issues and the problems associated with the existing arrangements suggest that the time is coming for a more comprehensive and systematic re-appraisal of how victims are supported.  This re-appraisal will need to recognise the acute sense of frustration, exploitation and sometimes humiliation and betrayal which many victims feel at present.  It will also need to recognise the genuine limitations of what is feasible and affordable in providing for compensation, whether by the state or by offenders, or in according 'rights' to victims in an adversarial system of justice where the parties are the offender and the state.  Finally, it will need to accommodate the fact that victims and offenders are not separate classes of people: they are often members of the same communities and many victims have previously been offenders and vice versa.

This re-appraisal should cover three main areas. First, the arrangements for compensation should be reviewed. Second, the services (information, facilities, advice, support) to which victims and witnesses should be entitled, and the means of providing them, should be reviewed. Third, the position of the victim in the criminal justice process and their involvement in decisions relating to the suspect or offender should be reviewed. These three sets of issues should be examined as an interrelated whole.

## Organisational issues and the criminal justice system

As well as the immediate, practical, but for the most part familiar issues discussed in the previous section, a number of underlying longer-term concerns will continue to present themselves with respect to the delivery of justice and the organisation of the criminal justice system.

### Efficiency and fairness

Efficiency and fairness in the organisation and operation of the criminal justice system have been objectives of government policy for many years. However, the meaning of these terms or objectives has changed over time to match changing political situations and public expectations and, sometimes, increased understanding and knowledge. During the 1980s efficiency was seen in terms of improved financial information and financial management, clear definitions of objectives and the cost-effective use of resources including the moderate use of imprisonment. Fairness was seen in terms of equal opportunities, a better understanding of issues of race and gender, consistency in sentencing and a greater transparency in decision-making including the giving of reasons for decisions. More recently, the emphasis has been on 'changing the balance' away from the offender in favour of the victim, on achieving a greater number of convictions and on re-structuring organisations in accordance with market principles.

Looking to the next few years, the pressure to improve the efficiency of the agencies of the criminal justice system is certain to continue. There will be pressures to make better use of new technology, improve detection rates, minimise delays, raise standards, measure performance and control costs. However, we should also expect to see this more strongly tempered by concerns about fairness, with greater attention given to the avoidance of miscarriages of justice, increased sensitivity to race and gender, consistent and principled sentencing, explanations of decisions, and arrangements for hearing grievances and putting them right.

*The management of the service*

Another area of current concern is the practical and often unintended effects of political or management pressures on the agencies of the criminal justice system. These pressures tend to stem from constraints on the use of resources, the operation of performance indicators and standards, and the culture of risk management and risk avoidance. The main concern is that many so-called 'managerial' reforms may actually transform or pervert the basic operation of the system rather than just its management. Similarly, many reforms intended to have a very specific impact on the implementation of the law actually result in very widespread effects on the system.

For example, there are concerns that the use of certain types of performance indicators inside the police force will inadvertently and negatively transform the culture and style of policing. Some senior police officers have pointed to the highly 'efficient' but deeply unpopular Los Angeles police force and have queried whether this is the type of force that the public really want. Another more subtle example within the police concerns the relative priority that the police give to different types of activity. If, for example, the police are led towards giving a lower priority to the service of warrants, then this may have adverse effects on fine enforcement and on the efficacy of community sentences. Similarly, the extent to which the police exercise their new public order powers under the Criminal Justice and Public Order Act 1994 may have considerable consequences for the resources available for other aspects of their work, and for the climate of local opinion in which they have to operate.

The prison service also offers many examples of managerial reforms having much wider effects than intended. New tasks and priorities have been imposed in quick succession to meet political objectives with little regard for their collective impact or their relationship with existing policies or operational requirements. Another example is the introduction of the probation service's performance indicators which have led to a greater emphasis on easily measured short-term outcomes such as the attendance and tracking of offenders with community sentences rather than on their longer term outcomes and eventual progress. Similarly, there is often a tension between demands for the better management and security of offenders and wider and longer term goals such as the rehabilitation and retraining of offenders as emphasised by the Woolf Report after the prison disturbances of 1990.

The point behind raising these issues is not to take a final position on them, but is to highlight the unintended consequences that frequently follow inadequately considered policies. Policies need to be established on a basis of complete information and an accurate understanding of the facts, costs, implications and likely consequences. Policy-making should therefore be based on more effective consultation than has characterised recent years and, where possible, on the informed consent both of those who will be involved in implementing the policy and of those who will be affected by it. This is also because successful policy depends not just on the technical quality of the legislation but on the spirit with which it is implemented.

*The structure and accountability of the system*

For the longer term, attention needs to be given to the structure and accountability of the criminal justice system, and particularly concerning the system's management at local level and the case for continuing to maintain the Prison and Crown Prosecution services as centrally directed, national bureaucracies.

In the Prison Service, the balance between local discretion, the service's own traditions and external political control has troubled successive administrations for 50 years and continues to do so. Despite the transition to agency status, the Prison Service remains a centralised, monolithic bureaucracy under detailed ministerial supervision. Similarly, the Crown Prosecution Service was formed as a centralised, national service. This was despite the recommendation of a Royal Commission that the prosecution service should be locally based though still independent of the police. The structure as implemented has not worked well and has already been partially reorganised several times. The police, probation and magistrates' courts services are locally based but have been subject to increasing direction from the centre.

At the operational level, the absence of common boundaries between different parts of the criminal justice system leads to a lack of coordination across the system, a lack of flexibility in redeploying resources to activities where they would be better used, and many obstacles to providing facilities at the margin of different services' responsibilities. In addition, not only do the boundaries used by the different parts of the criminal justice system not relate to one another, these boundaries are unrelated to the boundaries used by other related services such as Local Authorities and District Health Authorities (Chapter 12). Uncoordinated boundaries and the associated problems are a constant source of frustration and should be reorganised.

*The making of policy*

There is a more general argument to made about the making of policy in relation to crime and criminal justice. There is a need to identify and anticipate better the full consequences and costs of possible criminal justice policies and the reorganisations of the system. There are too many examples where events have not turned out as intended or expected, or have had unwelcome side-effects. The comments above provide some examples. Others include the introduction of unit fines, hastily abandoned after only a few months of operation, and the failed policy of 'tough' regimes in detention centres (YOPU, 1984).

These problems suggest that we may need improvements to the policy-making process itself (see Chapter 1 for a fuller discussion). Such reforms should extend beyond the confines of the Home Office. They should also be designed to encourage the setting of criminal justice policy in a wider context, as discussed further below.

## Preventing crime and reducing criminality

Ultimately, the best way of dealing with crime must be through prevention or 'tackling its causes'. After all, in some sense, once a crime has been committed the criminal justice system has already failed.

Programmes for preventing crime and reducing criminality have been of two broad kinds. One consists of measures targeted at the *immediate circumstances* in which crimes are committed. This 'situational' approach aims to increase the difficulty of committing crimes, and to increase the risks and reduce the pay-offs to the offender. The approach operates though improved environmental design, security and surveillance. The other approach attempts to influence the broader *social circumstances* of actual or potential offenders by fostering alternatives to crime, increasing the employment capabilities of potential offenders and strengthening the informal social constraints on their behaviour. The former approach is generally more straightforward, conceptually and operationally, than the latter. It is also easier to justify and evaluate in terms of quantified results.

### *Situational measures to reduce crime*

Situational measures include stronger or more sophisticated security for buildings, vehicles and processes, improved lighting, neighbourhood watch and related schemes, exploiting the potential for supervision by 'place managers', improving the design and construction of housing estates and shopping areas and land-use planning to 'design out' criminogenic environments. The success or failure of these measures turns on the extent to which they simply displace offenders to other less protected targets. Current thinking is that displacement is rarely total and that it is minimal in relation to opportunistic crimes. In other words, these measures *do* reduce the absolute level of crime, though there is also evidence that they may have relatively limited and short-term effects if not accompanied by measures that address the broader social context (Osborn and Shaftoe, 1995). Focusing such preventive efforts on repeat victims is emerging as a particularly efficient way of putting action in the right place (Farrell and Pease, 1993).

In developing situational prevention, the problem is not in generating new ideas, or even in paying for them, for many situational measures are cost-free. Rather, it is in identifying promising schemes or programmes and sustaining their development and success. There have been weaknesses in the evaluation of these schemes and in integrating their successes into main programmes and normal patterns of provision. Promising schemes have too often been abandoned for lack of continuous support or have not been properly implemented, and therefore not tested, because the external conditions of their success have never been fulfilled (such as coordination with policing or housing policies). Local partnerships and projects such as those promoted by the Safer Cities Initiative can make a useful contribution, but they generally operate at a practical rather than a strategic level. Since crime prevention became a serious issue in the early 1980s, responsibility at the local level has been awkwardly divided between local government and the police (see Loveday,

1994, for a fuller discussion). For both, it has often been of marginal importance, and the resources devoted to preventive work have always been trivial in relation to expenditure on other programmes (about two per cent of total spending on criminal justice).

An important review of policy in this area was carried out by an independent Working Group of the Home Office Standing Conference on Crime Prevention under the chairmanship of James Morgan. Its report (Morgan Report, 1991) was warmly welcomed by local authorities, the police and others. It has stimulated several initiatives at local level. However, it received a half-hearted response from central government and no action has been taken on one of its central recommendations, that '... local authorities, working in conjunction with the police, should have clear statutory responsibility for the development and stimulation of community safety and crime prevention programmes, and for progressing at local level a multi-agency approach to community safety'.

The recommendations in the Morgan Report should be revived, up-dated and implemented, and especially including its recommendations on the statutory responsibility of local authorities.

### Wider programmes: can criminality be reduced?

In theory, the ultimate solution to the problem of crime must be to reduce the general propensity to commit crime, rather than trying to make it more difficult to conduct or its punishments more severe. This is easy to say, but it raises difficult and complex issues, and ones that are different to those raised by situational measures. Local projects and working arrangements of the kind that provided the principal focus for the Morgan Report can make a contribution, but wider questions of social conditions, moral and civic values, and social and economic policies, are also involved.

A recent report by NACRO (1995) explored many of these questions and the links between crime and wider issues of social policy such as training, education, employment, social security and housing. In each of these areas, the report made recommendations which deserve serious attention, and many of which are congruent with those which appear elsewhere in this volume. For the purpose of this review, we have divided this wider approach into three areas: adjusting incentives, promoting capabilities and encouraging informal constraints on behaviour.

### Adjusting the incentives

Part of the effectiveness of the situational approach is that it alters the incentives to commit particular crimes by making them more difficult to commit and by reducing the potential pay-off. However, it is clear that the incentives framework within which a potential offender operates involves far more than the specifics of a given physical situation. Whether an individual commits a crime or is influenced by a given sanction must also depend, at least to some extent, on the socio-economic alternatives that are available to them.

As already indicated, the effect of wider social and economic policies on individual behaviour, and on the general level of crime, are difficult to measure or predict accurately, but they cannot be dismissed or ignored. Wider policies aimed at reducing inequality, poverty or unemployment should assist efforts to reduce crime, but their impact on crime cannot be expected to be straightforward or free from interactions with other factors.

In recent years, many people (including academics) have tended to be relatively pessimistic, even fatalistic, about our ability as a society to influence such wider social issues. However, as we have seen from the other chapters of this volume, although external pressures such as from the globalisation of markets do impose some limitations on nation states and governments, there is still considerable scope for action if there is political will behind the policy (see, for example, Chapters 3, 4, 5, 8 and 11).

Given the age profile of offenders, policy must pay particularly close attention to the opportunities and temptations available to young people making the transition to adult life (both before and after leaving school). An especially important group are those vulnerable young people leaving local authority care. We must seek to provide a sense of hope and progress for these young people. Where possible this should be through further education, training and a realistic prospect of employment. In the cases where this is not a realistic prospect, this sense of hope and progress must be supplied through structured and challenging activities which can provide their own sense of achievement and reward. Concerning the latter, there may be opportunities for the development of outdoor adventure activities (Greenaway and Barrett, 1995) and for voluntary community service, as recommended by the Commission on Social Justice and for which the government has introduced a limited programme of funding.

### Promoting the capabilities of individuals

Closely related to policies intended to influence the incentive structure presented to individuals are polices intended to boost their capabilities. This has been a recurrent theme throughout the present report and it is unsurprising that it is echoed in this chapter. Crime may be one of the few opportunities available to the unskilled and poorly educated, and especially in the context of an economy that has increasingly little need for unskilled workers (Chapter 3). Long-term policies to strengthen the education and hence employment prospects of the population must therefore be relevant to attempts to reduce crime.

In addition to the varied skills that individuals need to acquire for later employment, they must also acquire the specific capability to analyse and comprehend the implications of any given activity both for others and for themselves. A notable characteristic of much criminal offending is that the individual concerned fails to consider or appropriately weight the consequences of their actions either for others or, in the longer term, for themselves. Even if the incentives and punishments presented by the society or a particular situation are such that offending behaviour would be an 'irrational' choice, if the individual lacks the cognitive capabilities to judge the implications of their actions, then they may still engage in such behaviour no matter what. Of course, such skills have a far wider value than simply helping people avoid offending and punishment. Individuals are presented with choices throughout their lives that require them to judge the relative merits of short-term rewards and penalties against longer-term outcomes in educational, employment and personal decisions. This is a skill that everyone would benefit from learning from an early age.

The evidence suggests that effective interventions should focus on childhood experience and should start relatively early. This provides a strong argument in favour of good quality pre-school education and suggests something about its content. A programme to reduce criminality among young people would focus on the means by which children learn to respect the feelings and property of others as well as explicitly teaching the cognitive skills required to make well-informed decisions which avoid the discounting of longer-term consequences. Such a programme might also usefully provide guidance and practical support for parents in dealing with difficult and challenging behaviour (see also Chapter 8).

*Informal constraints and 'belief' in the law*

Most people, most of the time, comply with the law not because of the formal sanctions of the criminal justice system, but because of internalised values and informal social constraints (Halpern, 1995). There are two conditions that are important to the effectiveness of these informal constraints but that have tended to have been undermined by 'the condition of modernity' and the nature of modern life. The first is that individuals need to be committed and attached to strong social networks that will apply informal sanctions, both positive and negative, to guide behaviour. The second is that there needs to be a general consensus and respect for the same set of values or laws: the relativism of modern life is a difficult foundation for a system of justice that needs to assume certain absolute or universal values as the basis of its legitimacy. It is noteworthy that the unusual strength of these two social factors in Japan is widely believed to explain that country's exceptionally low crime rate (Braithwaite, 1990), and it is possible that variations in these factors may also explain some of the large regional differences in the growth of crime within the United Kingdom.

In terms of the first condition, policies aimed at supporting the social institutions which provide informal social control - particularly families and schools - could facilitate longer term reductions in criminality and crime by increasing the availability and effectiveness of informal sanctions. Without strong institutions of this type, individuals will not learn and internalise the sense of duty and responsibility that is the best guarantee of a law abiding and cohesive society. This conclusion is reinforced by what is known about the backgrounds of persistent offenders (see above). Although there are limitations to what the state can, and should, do in this area, its policies are certainly not without impact on the strength and quality of social institutions (see Chapters 6 and 8). For example, welfare and employment policies are not always 'family friendly', but reforms to make them so are clearly possible (Chapter 5) and should be of direct interest to those seeking long-term reductions in crime.

A respect and awareness of the needs of other people has to be learned from the example of others and from the experience of seeing the positive reactions of others to acts of considerate behaviour. Such experiences are normally gained from informal acts of helping behaviour, but might also be stimulated by state sponsored volunteering schemes. Individuals are in turn entitled to expect respect and consideration from others in return. This principle of reciprocity and shared understanding could also be reinforced and legitimated through the use of a formal language of citizenship, rights and responsibilities by the state (Chapter 15).

Rather more specifically, we recommend that a systematic and comprehensive review should be conducted of the arrangements for the care of those at-risk young people who, for whatever reason, are unable to remain with their own families during childhood. The structure of these arrangements is at present confused, with no consistent pattern between different parts of the country. The arrangements to be made in particular cases depend as much on what is locally available and the state of the local authority's budget as on the situation and needs of disturbed children concerned. The proposed secure training centres will add to the confusion, especially as the attraction of central funding will provide an incentive for professionals to recommend the use of these centres in preference to their own local authorities' accommodation. Some extra secure provision is certainly needed, but it needs a much more coherent structure of standards and accountability, and a more systematic integration with services in the community. In terms of schooling, the prevention of bullying and identification and support of children at risk should be a high priority. Wherever possible, exclusion should be avoided, and when occasionally exclusion becomes inevitable, alternative provision for education, discipline and informal support should be available.

Concerning the second condition, it is clear that informal and internalised constraints on behaviour will only operate successfully if there is a general consensus about what is, and is not, appropriate and acceptable behaviour. Translating this into everyday terms, this means having a respect for the law and the agencies responsible for its enforcement, but a respect based primarily on reason not force. Children, and adults, need to grow up with the knowledge that society, regardless of the idiosyncratic values of any particular individual or household, fixes certain boundaries and is prepared to enforce them. They need to respect those boundaries and the process of enforcement, and to believe that the forces of the state stand ultimately for values of fairness and justice which they can accept and 'believe in'. They will not have that respect if they believe the law to be irrelevant to their own situations or perceive it to be arbitrarily, capriciously or oppressively enforced. It is principally for this reason that we have sought to stress throughout this chapter the issues of fairness, justice and accountability. It is our contention that, however efficient the criminal justice system becomes in terms of detection rates, prosecutions and so on, if the system loses public support and respect then it is doomed to failure. In this sense, perhaps we should think more readily of the state as shadowing informal processes of control rather than the other way around.

## Conclusion

The evidence suggests that crime has risen substantially since the 1950s. This has been driven by multiple factors, most of which are closely associated with the nature of modern life, such as increases in affluence and goods to steal, changes in the nature and strength of informal constraints and, when combined with other factors, socio-economic and aspirational factors.

Crime and criminal justice are highly charged political issues, and unfortunately, policy responses to them have too often been based on 'knee-jerk' reactions rather than careful analysis. This situation has been worsened by a general pessimism on the part of many practitioners and academics that, in terms of criminal correction and reducing crime, 'nothing works'. However, we agree with more recent analyses suggesting that this increasingly traditional view is too pessimistic. For example, there is encouraging evidence about the effectiveness of the wider use of police cautions, community penalties and treatment programmes for drug-dependent offenders. In terms of prison, the main issue is not whether it works but how cost effective it is. Prison clearly incapacitates criminals, but as the total number of offenders that are imprisoned is extremely small, even a massive increase in the prison population would have only a very modest impact on the crime rate. Given that the alternatives, such as community penalties and drug treatment programmes, lead to reconviction rates no worse than those following prison (offence and offender having been controlled for) and at a fraction of the cost, increasing the imprisonment rate looks like a very inefficient way of addressing crime.

The organisation of the criminal justice system also requires attention. Many so-called 'managerial changes' have actually led to, or threaten to lead to, many unintended consequences. In addition, the current structure of the system, whereby different services are organised into geographical and organisational units with almost no correspondence across the services, reduces both efficiency and accountability. These boundaries and chains of responsibility should be reorganised along more rational lines. Attention should also be given to the needs of victims, and a comprehensive review of their relationship to the criminal justice system is needed.

In terms of the current volume, one of our most important conclusions is that longer term policies to reduce crime will require much broader policies than those currently pursued. Situational approaches to crime offer considerable promise and should be extended, and the recommendations of the Morgan Report concerning these should be revived. Second, attention should be paid to the incentives framework presented to potential offenders, and the Home Office should take a more active interest in the policies of other departments that act as barriers or disincentives to legitimate work activity. Third, capability promoting policies are also worth pursuing in as far as they increase the likelihood of legitimate employment and, more specifically, all young people should be given the cognitive skills required to make decisions fully aware of the consequences of their acts both for others and, in the longer term, for themselves. Fourth, policies need to recognise and strengthen the informal social institutions that constrain offending behaviour. This latter approach will be most effective if the formal processes of the criminal justice system are seen as just and accountable.

Finally, our review suggests that, with respect to criminal justice and crime reduction policy, the policy-making process itself needs attention. Policy-making needs to pay closer attention to the empirical evidence and rather less to political fashion. It is also important that those who have to implement policy are listened to in the drafting of legislation, not least because the outcome of policy is strongly affected by the spirit in which it is implemented. The goals and policies of the Home Office and the criminal justice system must be better coordinated with other government departments and agencies so that a coherent purpose and message is achieved across policy areas (see Chapter 1). For as we have seen, successful attempts to reduce crime are likely to require policies that extend beyond the remit of a single government department or the formal criminal justice system.

## Notes

1. This figure does not include the cost of social work staff employed in Scotland on aspects related to the criminal justice system which are undertaken by the probation service in England and Wales.
2. This combination of trends has been associated with the unusual occurrence of opinion polls in 1994 showing that the Conservative Party - traditionally seen as the party of law and order - is no longer seen as the party most able to handle the issue. This loss of public confidence also occurred despite the announcement by Michael Howard, the Home Secretary, of 27 'get tough' measures at the 1993 party conference.

   The traditional position of the parties on law and order is reflected in the relatively large amount of space that their manifestos have given to the issue. On average seven per cent of Conservative party manifesto policies over the last four elections have been about law and order, compared to three per cent of Labour's and 4.5 per cent of Liberal's (Topf, 1994).
3. These are figures for 1991 from Mayhew et al, 1993, uprated to take account of inflation and increases in crime between 1991 and 1993.
4. And even then, it is unable to cover some types of crime, such as fraud.
5. The 1996 BCS should help us to answer some of these questions and to separate between these possible explanations.
6. Precisely what public opinion favours is heavily dependent on the way that surveys and polls elicit this opinion. Public opinion is neither one-dimensional nor does it see the criminal justice system as providing the only solutions to crime. An OPCS omnibus survey in November 1990 asked what people thought was the single best way of reducing crime. Responses were:

   | | |
   |---|---|
   | Increase discipline in the family | 30% |
   | Make sentences harsher | 20% |
   | Reduce levels of unemployment | 19% |
   | Increase discipline in schools | 11% |
   | Increase number of police | 9% |
   | Increase use of community penalties | 7% |

7. Stockdale and Gresham (1995) conclude that the improvement in burglary clear-up rates in the MPS areas covered by Operation Bumblebee arose from a combination of a decrease in burglaries and an increase in clear-ups, particularly secondary

detections achieved, for example, through interviews with convicted offenders in prison. They suggest that the well-managed publicity relating to Operation Bumblebee was central to its success.

# References

Andrews, D. A., Zinger, I., Hoge, R. D., Bonta, J., Gendreau, P. and Cullen, F. T. (1990), 'Does correctional treatment work? A criminologically relevant and psychologically informed meta-analysis', *Criminology 28*, **3**, pp.369-403.

Ashworth, A. (1994), 'Sentencing', in Maguire, M., Morgan, R. and Reiner, R. (eds.), *The Oxford Handbook of Criminology*, Oxford: Clarendon Press.

Aye Maung, N. and Mirrlees-Black, C. (1994), 'Racially motivated crime: a British crime survey analysis, *Research and Planning Unit Paper*, No. **82**, London: Home Office.

Bennett, T. (1991), 'The effectiveness of a police-initiated fear reducing strategy', *British Journal of Criminology*, **31, 1**, pp.1-14.

Blair, A. (1994), 'Drugs: the need for action', *News Release*, Labour party.

Bottoms, T. and Wiles, P. (1994), *Crime and Insecurity in the City*, Paper presented at the International Society of Criminology International Course on Changes in Society Crime and Social Justice in Europe, Leuven, Belgium.

Braithwaite, J. (1989), *Crime, Shame and Reintegration*, Cambridge: Cambridge University Press.

Central Statistical Office (1995), *Social Trends*, **25**, London: HMSO.

Dickinson, D. (1994), *Crime and Unemployment*, Cambridge: Cambridge University Press.

Field, S. (1990), 'Trends in crime and their interpretation: a study of post war crime in England and Wales', *Home Office Research Study*, No. **119**, London: HMSO.

Farrell, G. and Pease, K. (1993), 'Once bitten, twice bitten: repeat victimisation and its implications for crime prevention', *Crime Prevention Unit Series*, No. **46**, London: Home Office.

Farrington, D. (1994), 'Human development and criminal careers', in Maguire, M., Morgan, R. and Reiner, R. (eds.), *The Oxford Handbook of Criminology*, Oxford: Oxford University Press.

Farrington, D., Langan, P. and Wikström, P. O. (1994), 'Changes in crime and punishment in America, England and Sweden between the 1980s and the 1990s', *Studies on Crime and Crime Prevention*, Vol. 3, pp.104-31.

Fattah, E. A. (1991), *Understanding Criminal Victimisation: An Introduction to Theoretical Victimology*, Scarborough, Ontario: Prentice Hall.

Fielding, H. (1988 [1751]), *An enquiry into the Causes of the Late Increases of Robbers ... and Other Related Writings,* Zircar, M. R. (ed.), Oxford: Oxford University Press.

FitzGerald, M. (1993), *Ethnic Minorities and the Criminal Justice System: Royal Commission on Criminal Justice Research Study,* No. 20, London: HMSO.

Gendreau, P. and Ross, R. (1987), 'Revivification of rehabilitation: evidence from the 1980s', *Justice Quarterly,* **4**, pp.349-408.

Goldstein, H. (1990), *Problem Oriented Policing,* Philadelphia: Temple University Press.

Gottfredson, M. and Hirschi, T. (1990), *A General Theory of Crime,* Stanford: Stanford University Press.

Greenaway, R. and Barrett, J. (1995) *Why adventure? A review of research literature relating to outdoor adventure, young people and their personal and social development.* Coventry: Foundation for Outdoor Adventure.

Hagell, A. and Newburn, T. (1994), *Persistent Young Offenders,* London: Policy Studies Institute.

Halpern, D. (1995), 'Morals, values and modernity', in Rutter, M. and Smith, D. (eds.), *Psychosocial Disorders in Young People,* London: John Wiley.

Home Office (1995), 'Criminal careers of those born between 1953 and 1973', *Home Office Statistical Bulletin,* **14**/95, London: HMSO.

Home Office (1995), *Stengthening Punishment in the Community: A Consultation Document,* Cm 2780, London: HMSO.

Home Office (1994a), *Criminal Statistics England and Wales 1993,* Cm 2680, London: HMSO.

Home Office (1994b), 'The criminal histories of those cautioned in 1985, 1988 and 1991', *Home Office Statistical Bulletin,* **8**/94, London: HMSO.

Home Office (1993), *Information on the Criminal Justice System in England and Wales: Digest 2,* London: HMSO.

Home Office (1992), *The Costs of the Criminal Justice System, 1992,* London: HMSO.

Hood, R. (1995), 'Psychosocial interventions in the Criminal Justice System: introductory report', in *Psychosocial Interventions in the Criminal Justice System: Proceedings of 20th Criminological Research Conference, 1993,* Strasbourg: Council of Europe.

Hough, M. (in press), 'Problem drug use and criminal justice: a review of the literature', *Home Office Drugs Prevention Initiative Paper,* London: HMSO.

Leitner, M., Shapland, J. and Wiles, P. (1993), *Drugs Usage and Drug Prevention: The Views and Habits of the General Public,* London: HMSO.

Lipsey, M. W. (1991), 'Juvenile delinquency treatment: a meta-analytic inquiry into the variability of effects', in Cook, T. D., Cooper, H., Cordray, D. S., Hartmann, H., Hedges, L.V., Louis, T.A. and Mosteller, F. (eds.), *Meta-analysis for Explanation: a casebook*, New York: Russell Sage.

Lloyd, C., Mair, G. and Hough, M. (1994), 'Explaining reconviction rates: a critical analysis', *Home Office Research Study*, No. **136**, London: HMSO.

Lösel, F. (1993), 'The effectiveness of treatment in institutional and community setting', *Criminal Behaviour and Mental Health*, **3**, pp.416-37.

Loveday, B. (1995), 'Reforming the police: from local service to state police?' *Political Quarterly*, **66** (2).

Loveday, B. (1994), 'Government strategies for community crime prevention programmes in England and Wales: a study on failure', *International Journal of the Sociology of Law, 1994*, Vol. **22**, pp.181-202.

Mayhew, P., Aye Maung, N. and Mirrlees-Black, C. (1993), 'The 1992 British Crime Survey', *Home Office Research Study*, No. **132**, London: HMSO.

Mayhew, P., Mirrlees-Black, C. and Aye Maung, N. (1994), 'Trends in crime: findings from the 1994 British Crime Survey', *Research Findings*, No. **14,** London: HMSO.

Mayhew, P., Elliot, D. and Dowds, L. (1989), 'The 1988 British Crime Survey', *Home Office Research Study*, No. **111**, London: HMSO.

Mirrlees-Black, C. and Aye Maung, N. (1994), 'Fear of crime: findings from the 1992 British Crime Survey', *Home Office Research and Statistics Department Research Findings*, No. **9**, London: HMSO.

Morgan Report (1992), 'Safer communities: the local delivery of crime prevention through the partnership approach', *Report of the Standing Conference on Crime Prevention*, London: HMSO.

Mott, J. and Mirrlees-Black, C. (1993), 'Self-reported drug misuse in England and Wales: main findings from the 1992 British Crime Survey, *Research Findings*, No. **7,** London: HMSO.

Mott, J. and Mirrlees-Black, C. (1995), 'Self-reported drug misuse in England and Wales: findings from the 1992 British Crime Survey', *Home Office Research Study*, No. **89**, London: HMSO.

National Association for the Care and Resettlement of Offenders (NACRO) (1995), *Crime and Social Policy* London: NACRO.

Osborn, S. and Shaftoe, H. (1995), *Safer Neighbourhoods? Successes and failures in Crime Prevention*, London: Safe Neighbourhoods Unit.

Reiner, R. and Spencer, S. (eds.) (1995), *Accountable Policing*, London: Institute for Public and Policy Research.

Rutter, M. and Smith, D. (1995), *Psychosocial Disorders in Young People*, London: John Wiley.

Rydell, C. P. and Everingham, S. S. (1994), *Controlling Cocaine: Supply versus demand programs*, Santa Monica, CA: RAND Drug Policy Research Centre.

Speed, M., Burrows J. and Bamfield, J. (1995), *Retail Crime Costs: 1993/94 Survey - the Impact of Crime and the Retail Response*, Northampton: Nene College.

Stockdale, J. E. and Gresham, P. (1995), 'Combating burglary: an evaluation of three strategies', *Police Research Group Crime Prevention and Detection Series*, London: HMSO.

Tarling, R. (1993), *Analysing Offending: Data, Models and Interpretations*, London: HMSO.

Timms, N. (1992), *Family and Citizenship: Values in Contemporary Britain*, Aldershot: Dartmouth.

Tonry, M. (1995), *Intermediate Sanctions in Overcrowded Times*, Boston: Northeastern University Press.

Victim Support (1993) *Compensating the victim of crime: report of an independent working party*, London: Victim Support

Walker, N. (1985), *Sentencing: Theory, Law and Practice*, London: Butterworth.

Walker, N. and Hough, M. (eds.) (1988), *Public Attitudes to Sentencing: Surveys from Five Countries*, Aldershot: Gower.

YOPU (1984), *Tougher Regimes in Detention Centres: Report of an Evaluation by the Young Offender Psychology Unit*, London: HMSO.

# 10 Transport and the environment

*Stuart R. Taylor and Bridget Taylor* *

Across the world, concern about damage to the natural environment has increased substantially in recent years. Reports about 'a hole in the ozone layer', 'loss of the rain-forests', 'acid rain', and 'global warming', including the possible 'melting of the polar ice-caps', have become headline stories. Through the 1980s, these concerns appeared to be translated into a widespread political movement across Europe which saw the 'green' political parties attracting a significant share of the vote in local, national and even European elections. This development was especially dramatic in Germany where the Greens attracted more than the five per cent of the vote necessary to secure representation at a national level. Pressure groups and voluntary organisations concerned with environmental issues expanded at a spectacular rate. In the UK, membership of Friends of the Earth, grew from around a thousand in 1971, to 18,000 in 1981 and to 111,000 in 1991; Greenpeace grew from around 30,000 in 1981, to 408,000 in 1991; and the National Trust grew from 278,000 in 1971, to over a million in 1981 and over two million by 1991. After many years on the fringes of policy, environmental issues seemed finally to have made it onto the mainstream agenda.

In the early 1990s, the green movement appeared to lose some of its momentum. Though global environment issues continued to attract press attention, the electoral success of the Green parties waned. Part of this loss may have reflected some 'greening' of the mainstream political parties, though

* Stuart Taylor is Gwilym Gibbon Fellow 1994-95 at Nuffield College, Oxford. Bridget Taylor is Research Officer of the ESRC Centre for Research into Elections and Social Trends (CREST) at Nuffield College, Oxford. The views expressed are the authors' own and should not be taken to reflect those of any particular institution.

part may have reflected some fragmentation inside the green movement as well as the de-prioritising of environmental issues in the minds of the electorate during a time of economic recession. Concerning the latter, as we shall see, although the electorate likes the idea of 'environmentally friendly' policy, it is rather less keen on paying for it.

More recently, environmental issues again seem to be firmly back on the political agenda, as witnessed by survey evidence, recent press coverage, the report of the Royal Commission on Environmental Pollution (RCEP, 1994) and the relatively warm political response to that report. Partly this reflects, as before, concerns about global threats such as from ozone depletion, climate change and acid rain, but it also reflects growing concerns about very localised problems such as air and water quality, loss of habitat and 'biodiversity', and the issues of suburban sprawl and rural change. However, the public continue to display the same ambivalence towards environmental issues and the costs associated with addressing them.

Nowhere is this clearer than in the area of transport, the main focus of this chapter. In the UK, travel by car and van has increased since the early 1950s by ten-fold, from 58 billion passenger kilometres (bpk) in 1952 to 577 bpk in 1993 (an average annual growth rate of five per cent). That growth saw the car and van move from a 27 per cent share of the domestic passenger market to an 86 per cent share.[1] Such growth reflects the major benefits that individuals and business derive from the motor vehicle: flexibility, door to door speed, comfort, reliability and so on. At the same time, there is strong opposition to the many and varied ways in which road transport damages the environment: pollution and damage to human and animal health, destruction of countryside and wildlife, suburban sprawl, land use change, community damage, acid rain and global climate change. This opposition has been illustrated, for example, by high profile demonstrations against new road building (as, for example, with the tree based 'village in the sky' at the M65 bypass of Blackburn) and by legal actions by residents to force the closure of roads during periods of high pollution. Despite this opposition, most people are reluctant to reduce their own use of cars - though simultaneously expressing a desire for others to leave the roads free for their own use and benefit. These tensions indicate that if environmental problems are to be addressed further, and especially those associated with road transport, potentially unpopular decisions will need to be taken.

The chapter begins with a review of the state of the environment and environmental policy in the United Kingdom. We go on to examine a wide range of policy options and conclude by offering some thoughts and advice on how policy options might be most effectively combined.

## The state of the environment in the UK and the focus of current policy

Concern among the British public about the range of environmental problems is both widespread and rising. Road traffic in particular is emerging in the public's view as a major environmental problem. For example, half (51 per cent) of all respondents to the 1993 British Social Attitudes Survey (see Stokes and Taylor, 1994) regard air pollution caused by cars as 'extremely' or 'very' dangerous to the environment - a slightly *higher* proportion than those who say this about nuclear power stations (46 per cent). Over half of respondents (58 per cent) were willing to endorse the prediction that, within about 20 years, traffic noise would be 'one of the most serious problems for Britain', a similar proportion to those endorsing shortages of fossil fuels and global warming. As many as 77 per cent endorsed the statement that 'the amount of traffic on the roads is one of the most serious problems for Britain'.

While expressions of concern are costless, when it comes to policy options which might incur increased personal spending or a change in individual behaviour, the public are more guarded. At a general level, they increasingly endorse a shift in policy towards a priority for public transport over roads. Fewer than one in five endorses the principle that 'People should be allowed to use their cars as much as they like, even if it causes damage to the environment'. However, support is more limited for the specific measures that might be required to put these principles into practice. One explanation for these apparent differences of emphasis lies in the incentive that individuals have to 'free ride': they may judge that travel and environmental conditions will be improved if they express sufficient concern, but that others will bear the cost of the policy, leaving themselves free to travel as they will.

Below we list the main environmental concerns in the UK at present, though with special emphasis on transport related damage. The review is not intended to be exhaustive, rather it illustrates the range of environmental effects currently causing particular concern. The discussion leaves aside road traffic congestion and road accident damage. While these involve individuals imposing costs on society, and can have health and financial implications, they have been discussed at some length in the transport literature and, in any case, there is considerable overlap in terms of their nature and the possible policy responses.

Probably the most important factor responsible for increasing environmental damage is growth of the economy. Rising average incomes, over time, tends to mean more demand for some goods and services, less for others, but generally more consumption overall. New production, service and residential accommodation will be required, adding to and extending existing levels of damage to the environment. New road, rail and air services may be needed to cater for the changing demands. These may themselves encourage new travel patterns as well as adding directly to environmental problems from infrastructure construction. In addition, as economies grow and product types change, more of some fuels and raw materials will be used and less of others, changing the environmental implications.

The concept of sustainable development has become quite widely accepted over recent years. Sustainable development is concerned with economic development such that any environmental damage should meet '...the needs of the present without compromising the ability of future generations to meet their needs' (WCED, 1987; see also Pearce, 1993). The Royal Commission (1994), in its wide ranging report on transport and the environment, endorsed the UK government's general starting point when applying the sustainability concept in the field of transport (Cm. 2426, HMSO, 1994). This policy framework has four main elements. First, to strike the 'right' balance between the ability of transport to serve economic development and the ability to protect the environment and sustain future quality of life. Second, to provide for the economic and social needs for access with less need for travel. Third, to take measures which reduce the environmental impact of transport and influence the rate of traffic growth. Finally, to ensure that users pay the full social and environmental cost of their transport decisions, so improving the overall efficiency of those decisions for the economy as a whole and bringing environmental benefits.

Those sustainability criteria are quite widely accepted as forming the general policy goalposts, but the main debate concerns their translation into actual policy measures. The Royal Commission outlined various policy ideas, including a doubling of fuel price by 2000 and the setting of targets, primarily for increased market share of modes other than private road travel. We return to these issues at various points below. However, we must emphasise the underlying strength of demand for road travel that currently exists. Over the last ten years, expenditure on motoring as a share of total household expenditure has remained fairly constant at around 13-14 per cent (Department of Transport, 1994) while real incomes have grown strongly. As real incomes rise with economic growth, the absolute amount spent on road transport - and almost always travel itself - will increase more or less 'automatically' (as more is spent on leisure activities, more shopping trips are made, people move to live further from their place of work and so on). Of course, such a relationship may not hold if some of the main parameters - fuel price, regulations on vehicle design and use, land use controls - are changed significantly. The same overall picture holds for commercial traffic.

### Air pollution: local effects

Air pollution is a major and renewed source of public concern within the UK, partly from observed smog episodes but more particularly from the suggestion of serious health implications (see, for example, the report of the *Royal Commission on Environmental Pollution*, 1994). Air pollution can also lead to further indirect regional effects such as acid rain (see below). Industrial plant, especially for production of chemicals and plastics, is an important source in some areas, while road transport has a significant effect across large, densely populated urban areas. Table 10.1 shows UK emissions from road traffic relative to those from other sources.

Regulation of industrial plant, power stations, road vehicles (both at the design stage and in use) and so on, has been the main policy response to this problem. Economic instruments have been used to a limited extent - for example, a duty differential on unleaded petrol was used in conjunction with regulation of the lead content of petrol, to reduce the incidence of air-borne lead.[3]

As traffic has grown over past decades, pollution levels in urban areas have increased significantly. Most projections for the next ten years or so show declining levels for most pollutants, mainly as a result of European Union (EU) regulations for the design of new vehicles. The most significant impact so far has been for petrol vehicles: the three-way catalytic converter has needed to be fitted to new petrol cars since 1 January 1993 (under directive 91/441/EEC).

This can reduce emissions of carbon monoxide, hydro-carbons and nitrogen oxides by around three-quarters, once the catalyst is fully warmed.[4] The financial cost of the catalyst and associated technological improvements is around £500-£1000 per car, most of which will be borne by the motorist. Work is underway, by both government and manufacturers, to try to resolve the 'cold start' problem, which can undermine catalyst performance during short journeys such as early morning trips to work or school.

### Table 10.1  Air pollution by source

|  | Carbon monoxide | Sulphur dioxide | Nitrogen oxides | Hydro-carbons | Black Smoke | Carbon dioxide |
|---|---|---|---|---|---|---|
| *Per cent* | | | | | | |
| Road traffic | 90 | 2 | 51 | 37 | 47 | 19 [2] |
| Electricity supply | 1 | 69 | 25 | - | 5 | 33 |
| Domestic | 4 | 3 | 3 | 1 | 28 | 15 |
| Other (including direct industrial) | 5 | 26 | 21 | 62 | 20 | 33 |
| *Million tonnes* | | | | | | |
| Total | 6.7 | 3.5 | 2.8 | 2.6 | 0.5 | 155.0 |
| Road traffic | 6.0 | 0.07 | 1.4 | 1.0 | 0.2 | 29.5 |

Source:  1992, data from National Environmental Technology Centre, quoted in CSO, 1995

So far, EU legislation has been less stringent for diesel vehicles, partly because the technology has been more difficult to improve. Some significant tightening of nitrogen oxide limits for new diesel cars and HGVs (Heavy Goods Vehicles) will come into force from 1996, taking diesel car nitrogen oxide emissions per kilometre close to those for catalyst petrol cars. In the case of black smoke or carbon particulate matter, particulate traps are being developed. At present these are capable of cutting particulate matter by around 70 per cent, at a cost of about £1000 for cars, £3500 for buses and up to £10000 for HGVs. Evidence on the health effects of carbon particles in general - and of different size particles in particular - is far from being clear cut, but some further scientific research is underway.

*Water quality*

Legislation agreed at the EU level has required the water supply companies to implement major capital investment projects to improve the quality of drinking water. The EU is also pressing for improvements to the quality of many

British beaches. Further afield, there are mounting concerns about damage to seas and oceans (with implications, amongst others, for the food chain), not least owing to discharge and leakage from shipping. It was these concerns that led to the public outcry over the sinking of the Brent Spar oil rig and that eventually forced the company concerned to reverse its policy in July 1995.

### Noise and vibration disturbance

Noise from business premises is held within regulated limits. Most complaints concern more occasional noise sources, such as from neighbours, street-works or new construction. Within the UK, planning guidelines recommend noise limits for new sites intended for residential use. Transport noise is experienced across many localities, varying in intensity and duration. As with gaseous emissions, noise is regulated at the EU level to help achieve 'economies of scale' in vehicle production and to ensure consistency of approach to regional environmental problems, within the single European market for new road vehicles.

### Land use and 'urban sprawl'

The spread of activity to suburban and rural areas has resulted from a combination of the 'just-in-time' method of production and distribution, 'out-of-town' shopping and residential dispersion. This has put significant environmental pressures on rural and semi-rural communities and landscapes (see below for more detail). All such developments have been dependent on flexible and fast transport facilities, as offered by motorways, improvements to other trunk roads and to local roads. By often involving longer trips or a greater number of trips, such developments have contributed to high traffic growth rates - both as part of a growing and changing composition of gross national product (GNP) and from traffic inducement by new infrastructure. A problem facing alternative modes of travel is that such dispersed and varied travel patterns are those that tend to be quite unsuited to travel by fixed track or semi-fixed route public transport.

In recent years, new planning guidance to local and residential authorities has aimed to limit the impact of commercial development, especially that on the edge of urban areas which can impinge directly on rural areas. The government issued new guidance to local authorities on land use planning and its relation to transport (*Planning Policy Guidance Note 13*, 1992). In July 1995, consultation began on revisions to PPG6, covering location of new shopping development. This sought to encourage local authorities to restrain development in out-of-town areas and to favour land use development which would 'reduce the need to travel'. Use of land for landfill sites and quarries also has been a significant concern. The problem of landfill led to a new tax on waste being proposed in the 1994 Budget.

*Local community damage*

This phenomenon can result from a variety of sources, including the design of buildings and the level of crime in an area, but here we focus on road transport. As traffic has grown over the last forty years, communities have experienced varying types and degrees of environmental disruption. The density and frequency of vehicles moving along a given road can discourage contact between people and facilities on each side of the road (the 'barrier effect'). Traffic levels, speed of movement, and the concentration of emissions and noise have been shown to reduce outdoor activities, reduce neighbour friendliness and contribute to mental health problems (Halpern, 1995).

For many countries, one policy response to traffic growth has been to build more and better roads. This can, however, introduce additional damage in new areas. For example, a bypass aimed at reducing severance in a town or village may impinge directly on other villages, partly through the barrier effect from construction of the new road and partly from the effect of traffic in new localities.

Of course, traffic results in community severance mainly when it is concentrated near to human settlements. Measures which target emissions in urban and suburban areas are therefore likely to be more effective at addressing community severance than are measures aimed at traffic operating at any time or place. Measures such as the charging of traffic in urban centres would help to reduce community severance endured by people in and around the urban core. However, to the extent that such measures encourage more travel around the periphery of the urban area or in the suburban and rural fringes, significant impacts may be faced by new groups of people. This points to the need for urban measures to be part of a carefully designed package, which tackles central urban problems without creating or exacerbating problems elsewhere.

An important aim of PPG13 (see above) is to reduce community damage effects from urban dispersion, particularly in rural and suburban areas. The aim of reducing the need to travel was part and parcel of this but also reflected the need to reduce carbon dioxide emissions. While PPG13 is merely advisory in nature, it points to a fairly wide package of land use planning and transport measures that might be deployed to achieve its objectives (see Matthew, 1993, for an outline and assessment of PPG13). Note, however, that potential conflicts may arise as development shifts back to urban areas and urban authorities try to address pollution and other problems that may be associated with higher levels of mixed land use.

*Damage effects of new infrastructure*

Construction of new infrastructure tends to involve a wide range of adverse impacts on the environment, together with some improvements where traffic is taken away from existing areas of damage. The present UK practice is for all road schemes costing over £1 million to be subjected to an environmental assessment, the results of which are presented in an 'Appraisal Framework' at a Public Consultation and in more detail at a Public Inquiry. The environmental assessment can cover: visual intrusion, traffic noise, air pollution, carbon dioxide and other gaseous emissions, community severance, pedestrian amenity, and effects on agriculture, heritage and conservation areas, and ecology. The Appraisal Framework is a matrix of information in which all the significant environmental effects are analysed and shown for consideration alongside the elements of the scheme expressed in financial terms.

Reduction of existing levels of environmental damage caused by traffic in many towns and villages is one of the stated objectives of the present UK roads programme. This involves the construction of bypasses and relief roads. If far fewer such roads were built in future, through-traffic would need to be kept out of village and town centres by other means such as traffic bans or road user charges - themselves subject to practical implementation problems and potential opposition. Another objective of the UK road building programme is to relieve congestion on motorways, mainly through the addition of extra lanes. If that policy was reduced considerably, problems of congestion and unstable flow would need to be addressed by, for example, the management of traffic flow and, perhaps, by assigning higher priority to certain types of vehicle.

In 1992, the Standing Advisory Committee on Trunk Road Assessment (SACTRA) recommended that the Department of Transport (DoT) move toward the use of money values to enable some, possibly most, environmental effects to be assessed in the monetary part of the appraisal. In the same report, SACTRA also recommended the appraisal of road schemes at a strategic level. At present, short stretches of road (of a few kilometres in length) are appraised individually, mainly for operational reasons including the availability and timing of capital expenditure. With a strategic assessment, which considered a longer length of road in the context of the travel requirements within a corridor or region, alternatives to road building (including the use of different modes, less travel and new travel patterns) should be more easily assessed on a consistent basis (for further analysis, see Therivel *et al*, 1992).

*Global climate change*

Evidence of the effect of greenhouse gas emissions in causing global climate change has attracted much concern and research in recent years. The majority of the global greenhouse effect, around 60-65 per cent, is attributable to carbon dioxide. The first Assessment Report of the Intergovernmental Panel on Climate Change concluded that without intervention an increase in temperature of around 0.3 degrees celsius per decade is likely to occur (CSO, 1995). Of around 7,500 million tonnes of carbon dioxide produced annually from man-made sources around the world, just over two per cent comes from sources within the UK. Power stations and industry are the major sources of carbon dioxide in the UK (see Table 10.1) and in most Northern countries,although their output has actually fallen over the past twenty years. Between 1971 and 1992, UK emissions from power stations fell by over 10 per cent and carbon dioxide from industry fell by almost two fifths. This largely reflected structural changes in the economy, with large scale closure of heavy industry and shifts away from the burning of coal and oil. Over the same twenty year period, carbon dioxide emissions from road transport almost doubled as rising real average incomes and social changes encouraged growth in car ownership per household, and numbers of trips made and their length. During the first part of the 1990s, however, road traffic emissions remained flat as economic recession induced a variety of changes to consumer and business behaviour. More recently, there has been some resumption of traffic growth, and predictions remain for more or less a doubling of traffic by around 2025, assuming no major change of policy.

Such traffic growth is the main reason why carbon dioxide emissions from road transport are expected to rise by almost 50 per cent from 1995 to 2020 (under central assumptions about economic growth and 'low' fuel prices - together referred to henceforth as 'central' assumptions - in the latest projections of the Department for Trade and Industry (Energy Paper 65, DTI, 1994)). Over the same period, power stations are expected to show an initial decline as gas powered plant continues to replace coal. From 2000 to 2020, however, the electricity supply industry is forecast to have growth in carbon dioxide emissions of around 45 per cent, mainly as a result of the phasing out of nuclear capacity. By 2020, both road transport and power stations are each expected, on central assumptions, to account for 50 million tonnes of carbon (MtC).

At the Rio Conference in 1992, Northern countries (the 'developed countries') agreed to return their output of greenhouse gases to the 1990 level by the year 2000. This was taken as an initial step, prior to the establishment of firmer knowledge about global climate change. While appearing to be a modest step, recent estimates suggest that the UK and Germany are among the few Northern countries that are on course to meet the 2000 target (*The Economist*, 1 April, 1995).

The road sector currently accounts for around 19 per cent of UK carbon dioxide emissions (Table 10.1). However, the latest UK projections (DTI, 1994) indicate that this share is likely to rise to around 24 per cent of the total by 2020 (using central assumptions) if demand for road use continues to increase in line with economic growth. The present UK policy of five per cent per annum real increases in fuel duty will slow the growth in carbon dioxide emissions to around eight per cent below the level that would otherwise be expected in 2000. Some of this saving will result from slower traffic growth (around three to five per cent less than otherwise), more fuel efficient and smaller new vehicles, better driver technique, improved vehicle maintenance and reduced speeds (Virley, 1992). Overall, the five per cent p.a. strategy is expected to save around 3 million tonnes of carbon (MtC) in 2000, a figure which forms 40 per cent of UK's total carbon saving measures of 7.5 MtC.

*Acid rain*

As coal and oil burn, they release a mixture of gases. When some of those gases combine with water vapour, oxygen and sunlight, sulphuric and nitric acid are formed, and fall back to earth as acid rain. Across Europe, acid rain is destroying millions of hectares of forest (more than 60 per cent of Britain's forest being affected) and is undermining some soils, particularly where the soil is already poor in quality. Emission standards for new vehicles have been set that can only be met at present through the fitting of catalytic converters to all new petrol cars (see above). Other standards require flues or 'scrubbers' to be fitted to fossil fuel power stations. These regulations will bring significant improvements over the next ten to twenty years.

### Stratospheric ozone depletion

The use of chloroflorocarbons (CFCs) and halons has been shown to contribute to degradation of the ozone layer in the stratosphere, so that more harmful ultraviolet radiation can reach the earth's surface, posing a health risk both to humans and other organisms. The Montreal Protocol (1987), strengthened in 1990 and again in 1992, brought in regulatory measures for most Northern countries to reduce substantially the main ozone destroying substances, used mainly in refrigerators, fire extinguishers, household aerosols and some industrial processes. By 1993, the sales of CFCs in the EU had fallen to less than two-fifths of sales in 1976 (CSO, 1995). CFCs and halons are presently due to be phased out by 1996 and hydrocarbons by 2030.

## The policy priorities

Before we can decide which policy options to pursue or extend, we must make a strategic assessment of the scale and urgency of each aspect of transport related damage. The later sections of this chapter are based on this assessment of potential damage problems. Some readers might wish to weight the importance of environmental issues in different ways; depending on how this is done, slightly different policy conclusions will result. However, we feel that the following assessment is a reasonable one, and should attract widespread support.

*Reducing urban air pollution* is recommended to have a *high* priority because of the scale of the potential health threats, and despite the costs of further policy intervention. Looking ten to twenty years ahead, significant problems in urban areas are likely to remain (with the costs of extra damage often likely to exceed the costs of additional policy action in the most dense urban areas) if the policy response is restricted to a continuation of existing measures. Urban air pollution is also rapidly becoming a major local political issue and has the potential to mobilise increasingly large sections of the electorate, especially if increasing numbers of motorists are persuaded of the need for major change.

*Reducing local community damage* is recommended to have a *medium to high* priority. The problem is significant, widespread and growing. However, there is relatively little information about the ways in which the costs of policy action compare with the extra costs from inaction. A first priority, therefore, is further research to determine the costs and benefits of measures directed at road transport and at other elements of the modern economy and society. The passage of much time will be required before new measures can have significant effects, and there are potential problems of conflict with other elements of current policy which need to be resolved (for example, the finding of Halpern (1995) that mixed land use may be associated with worsened mental health problems). This issue is also important because of its relationship with wider non-environmental policy, such as crime (see Chapter 9).

*Reviewing and reducing the need for new roads* is recommended to have a *high* priority. This reflects pressure from multiple environmental concerns. In the UK policy no longer seeks to accommodate traffic growth through the building of major new road capacity within urban areas. While many local authorities are putting in place various elements of traffic restraint and management, bus priority, pedestrianisation, cycling measures and some new public transport services, current pollution and congestion problems point to the need for more substantial and comprehensive policy packages. In the interim, the 1995 Environment Act provides local authorities with the powers to close heavily polluted roads. In many cases, the costs associated with continuing with a piecemeal approach are likely to exceed considerably the costs that would result from more substantial and comprehensive policy packages in dense urban areas.

We also assign a *high priority* to the issue of *inter-urban traffic growth*. It is important that inter-urban and urban interactions be reviewed, and especially concerning the building of cross-country bypasses primarily aimed at removing traffic from urban areas. This review should feed into decisions about the extent to which existing plans for motorway widening should be implemented, and should include allowance for 'induced traffic growth' (SACTRA, 1994). A related question concerns whether responsibility for 'trunk' road maintenance and new construction should be transferred from the Department of Transport to local authorities.

*Reducing emissions of greenhouse gases* is recommended to have a medium to high priority. Potentially, global climate change is an enormous problem for every country in the world, and for some it could literally be disastrous. This is a problem that can only be addressed through international cooperation, yet the international community still has to decide on emission targets for the years beyond 2000. In terms of policy inside the UK, the government has already decided that road transport should carry 40 per cent of the UK carbon dioxide target savings for 2000, despite there being some energy efficiency options for the industrial and domestic sectors that could deliver savings at significantly lower cost per tonne and which are only being required to deliver a relatively small part of the 2000 target. Set against such arguments, and partly justifying the 40 per cent share, is the fact that road traffic shows the highest expected rate of demand growth across the economy.

From the above, we can see that *traffic growth* lies at the heart of many of our (and others') more pressing environmental concerns. In most Northern countries, both passenger and freight traffic have grown by an average of around three to five per cent per annum for the last forty or so years, and similar, if not faster, rates are now occurring in Southern ('developing') countries as their economies expand. The present UK forecasts for traffic growth (Department of Transport, 1989) imply mid-point growth (between 'high' and 'low' forecasts) of over two per cent per annum to 2025, for both cars and lorries.

*Setting targets*

While we have indicated above how we see the balance of priorities, there remains the question of what scale of action to take in each area of damage. If we had robust and widely accepted money values for each element of additional environmental damage, we could derive the implied price changes, and use the consequent price and activity levels to guide policy change. In the absence of such values, and with strong arguments for some use of regulation as well as pricing, we recommend that quantitative targets be set for some aspects of road transport environmental damage.

The use of targets was one of the recommendations of the Royal Commission (RCEP, 1994). Table 10.2 summarises the main targets suggested by the Commission. The aim of the Commission was to build on its main policy 'stick' of doubling fuel prices by the year 2000 by encouraging improvements to the main alternatives to private road travel. As we argue later, it is often vital to combine policy 'carrots' with the main policy stick(s). However, given the present dominance of the car and lorry and their past strong rates of growth (closely tied to rising real incomes) we consider that the targets set by the Royal Commission for future shares of the travel market will not address the issue of traffic growth to any significant extent. A doubling of fuel price by 2000 would slow traffic growth, but perhaps only from two per cent to something around 1.5 per cent per annum. In that context, market share targets for other modes will be extremely difficult to achieve: a very much tougher stick than a doubling of fuel prices would be required.

Instead of the Commission's targets for modal shares of travel markets, we see some merit in the setting of upper limits on road traffic growth by local authorities. National targets would be difficult to implement in a way that related to policy objectives. This is because total traffic comprises a mix of trips for widely differing purposes, whether of short, medium or long length, and whether classified as local, regional or cross country. Agreement on appropriate financial compensation of certain areas (for example, the rural parts of much of Scotland, Wales and Northern England) may be very difficult to achieve, with endless debate over the costs imposed, including the permanent loss of economic development by some areas. However, individual local authorities (and perhaps neighbouring groups of, or regional, authorities) might find the setting of traffic targets at the local level to be a valuable focal point for policy development. By underpinning virtually all environmental damage effects, traffic growth targets would serve as a 'catch-all' central objective of local policy. Local authorities should be left to decide whether limits on traffic growth in their localities would prove sufficiently useful: some will instead prefer local targets for pollution and community damage.

To assemble targets that are as appropriate and equitable as possible, the local policy maker will need to make some assessment of how the costs and benefits of reducing environmental damage by a certain amount compare with the costs and benefits of not doing so. Such targets also need to reflect the scale of existing policy measures and planned developments, and the scale of traffic growth that would be expected on that basis.

**Table 10.2 Policy targets of the Royal Commission on Environmental Pollution, 1994**

| Policy area | RCEP targets |
| --- | --- |
| fuel price | double 1994 price by 2000 |
| urban journeys by car | reduce from 50% in London to 45% by 2000 and 35% by 2020; reduce from 65% in other urban areas to 60% by 2000 and 50% by 2020 |
| cycle use for urban journeys | increase from 2.5% in 1993 to 10% by 2005, with government setting further targets thereafter |
| total passenger kilometres by public transport | from 12% in 1993 to 20% by 2005 and 30% by 2020 |
| freight tonne-kms by rail | from 6.5% in 1993 to 10% by 2000 and 20% by 2010 |
| freight tonne-kms by water | from 25% in 1993 to 30% by 2000 and at least 30% thereafter |
| carbon dioxide emissions | return to 1990 level (30 MtC) by 2000 (saving 6.5 MtC) and bring to 20% below 1990 level by 2020 |
| local air quality | full compliance by 2005 with WHO health-based guidelines |
| noise | reduce daytime and night-time exposure to road and rail noise by specified degrees |
| non-renewable materials | increase proportions recycled of scrapped vehicles, tyres and road construction materials |

For the derivation of local targets each authority will need to decide why, and how far, it is going to discourage car and lorry travel, at what times of day and for what sorts of traveller. How far should there be priority for certain road users, such as the emergency services, the disabled, the elderly, the commuter dropping off children at school, the central area shopper travelling at off-peak times, business service vehicles and so on? Other relevant considerations include: the present level of rail facilities and the scope for new light railways; the scope for bus-only lanes and dedicated cycleways; the present vitality of the urban core and the degree of competition from neighbouring towns and out-of-town facilities; the average incomes of inhabitants and workers, and the distribution of those incomes; and other special local circumstances. Local people, assisted by local politicians and others, should choose targets that reflect the wide range of local circumstances, while also taking account of the potential implications for future generations. Already, some authorities have consulted the public and others are following, and some have already proposed upper limits on local traffic growth. Whether it is necessary to have *national* targets for traffic growth is a separate issue that we return to in the conclusions.

There remains the issue of national targets for global warming emissions, in particular for carbon dioxide. At Rio, most countries agreed national targets for each greenhouse gas by the year 2000. The principle of continued use of national targets is generally accepted, but the international community has yet to decide precise targets for years beyond 2000. Once a national target is agreed, the UK government will need to decide how to allocate the burden between each sector of the economy. As we saw earlier, while road transport's share of carbon dioxide emissions is expected to rise from the present 19 per cent to 24 per cent by 2020 (assuming expected rates of traffic growth occur), its share of the 2000 target of a 7.5 MtC saving is already 40 per cent (at 3 MtC).

The Royal Commission (1994) recommended that, by 2000, road transport carbon emissions should be returned to the 1990 level. By 2020, RCEP wanted road transport emissions to be 20 per cent below their 1990 level. However, RCEP provides little if any rationale for these transport-only targets. The target for 2000 would entail savings of over 7 MtC, more than twice as much as the current plan and over 90 per cent of the carbon savings for all the UK's Rio measures (7.5 MtC). Whereas the five per cent annual duty increase will leave real prices at the pump in 2000 about 30 per cent above their 1994 level (after inclusion of a small effect from world oil market pressures), a phased doubling of fuel price by 2000 would require annual duty increases averaging 14 per cent instead of five per cent.

In selecting its targets for road transport, RCEP paid little if any heed to the likely outcome of international negotiations, nor to the range of costs per tonne of carbon saved that underlies the international negotiations. Nor does it seem to have considered whether any particular UK target might be met at less overall cost to society and the economy through more measures aimed at industry, electricity generation, domestic energy efficiency, or agriculture. While we are in favour of long term targets in the climate change context, we prefer not to recommend new targets for transport before ongoing negotiations about post-2000 targets for all countries are concluded - not least because that would tie the negotiating hand of any UK government relative to the rest of the world, undermining UK living standards and jobs. In the interim, our working assumption is for road transport's share of UK carbon savings to be kept at 40 per cent, itself a figure higher than cost effectiveness estimates alone might justify.

## General comments on the approach to environmental policy

Before turning to the 'pros and cons' of particular policy instruments, it is worth reflecting on the framework or general approach within which these policies are placed. This will also help to set our own conclusions in context.

### International coordination and the Rio Conference

The first point is simply to emphasise that some major environmental issues, if not most, are truly global in their scope. This means that the full implications of possible targets must be assessed within international negotiations. That was the intention of the 1992 Rio Convention of the United Nations Conference on Environment and Development (UNCED), which brought together heads of government from over 150 states. The final declarations and agreements from the Convention covered four areas: 'Agenda 21' addressing action for sustainable development into the twenty first century (with some emphasis on local issues), global climate change, biological diversity and forest principles. The 'Rio Declaration' itself covers twenty-seven principles to guide action on environment and development (for a good summary see Grubb *et al*, 1993).

The UNCED Agreements set some targets for the international community (for example, an initial target for greenhouse gas emissions by the year 2000) and indicated the direction of future policy but without prescribing particular policy instruments. There was general agreement on the application, wherever feasible and appropriate, of the 'polluter pays principle'. There was also agreement that pursuit of major environmental objectives should not be allowed to undermine unfairly the living standards and future economic growth of Southern (so-called 'developing') countries.

The notion of 'sustainable development' also featured prominently at Rio. This tries to indicate how economic growth, and hence material standards of living, and other wider improvements in the quality of life - such as access to education, health care, cultural diversity and security (themselves closely related to economic growth) - can be achieved while simultaneously protecting the environment. One of the greatest challenges at the end of the twentieth century is to reconcile these two goals - economic growth and environmental sustainability - a challenge that exists at both global and local levels.

### Environmental costs and benefits: the winners and losers

It is a characteristic of environmental damage that it almost always falls on agents other than those who create the damage. This is what economists term an 'externality effect' or an 'externality'. The classic textbook example is of smoke from a factory chimney that soils the clothing of those who live nearby. The costs are borne by households in the form of extra washing which results in higher energy, detergent and water costs, and more labour to carry out the washing process. The extra use of detergent can add to downstream water purification costs, some further externality damage, and so on. These costs are real, but are not incurred by the owner of the factory, nor even those purchasing its output. Indeed, the factory owner may be oblivious to the existence of such costs, and has no incentive to change behaviour so as to reduce the damage.

Similar examples apply in the case of road vehicles. Individual motorists may fail to appreciate much of the environmental damage that their travel is causing. For example, such damage can worsen the health of some people, causing personal suffering, reducing their activity and earnings, and contributing to health care costs. Similarly, by damaging the natural habitat or by contributing to global warming, the motorists' activity may result in many wider and longer term costs. As with the smoky factory, those causing the damage may have no clear financial incentive to consider their contribution to others' costs. (For a fuller discussion of the way environmental costs are borne by people and business, see Goodwin, 1992.)

In essence, people derive a range of benefits from various types of activities and also from undamaged environmental assets to which most individuals attach a positive value. Yet because the costs and benefits often fall on different individuals and society generally, and can be widely spread across time and space, the prices faced by any given individual will often fail to reflect the full marginal costs of a particular activity. The value placed on each environmental benefit or cost also varies according to other factors, including the income of individuals and their particular preferences (Pearce and Turner, 1990). Road transport is a case in point. The spectacular growth in the amount of travel by road is a reflection of the scale of benefits that individuals and business derive relative to the costs they face for each trip, combined with the rising ability of travellers to pay existing charges or meet the costs of existing regulations as their incomes have risen. Policy solutions need to consider ways of giving incentives to polluters to reduce their activity to 'efficient' levels.[5]

*Regulation or economic instruments?*

The traditional approach to environment policy in the UK and elsewhere has been to use regulation or standards to require industry to reduce pollution damage. Similarly, planning controls have operated to limit damage from new industrial and domestic uses of land. However, with the white paper, *This Common Inheritance* (1990), the UK government pointed to a greater use of market or economic instruments, wherever feasible. Market instruments operate by providing signals to polluters about the wider damage being caused by their activities, thereby giving incentives to reduce emissions. If, for example, we wanted to reduce the use of a given fuel (say petrol), we could simply ration the amount of fuel that people are allowed to purchase - that would be a regulatory instrument. Alternatively, we could increase the price that is charged for the fuel by raising of taxes so that demand for the fuel will fall - that would be an economic instrument.

Benefits from the use of economic instruments to address some environmental problems are now recognised quite widely (von Weizäcker and Jesinghaus, 1992; Kågeson, 1993; Andersen, 1994; Porritt, 1995; Fergusson and Wade,

1995). Furthermore, for sectors such as transport where there is considerable interaction between different modes, the overall effectiveness of policy can be improved by using the revenues raised from one mode to invest in alternative modes. By providing incentives to change behaviour, rather than constraining behaviour to a pre-determined level through regulation, economic instruments tend to be able to achieve any given environmental improvement at a substantially lower cost than can regulation. For example, Leone and Parkinson (1990) have estimated that the costs of regulating new motor car fuel efficiency in the United States to be around two to four times greater than the cost of achieving the same fuel saving through increased fuel prices.

However, despite this strong argument, there are several important reasons why regulation may be preferred in practice (see, for example, Baumol and Oates, 1988). First, the simple application of an economic signal to make the 'polluter pay' may not work if other market failures are present. The classic example is a polluting monopolist who may simply raise prices in response to a tax and do little about the pollution. However, that example is not all that appropriate in the case of road transport: many individuals will reduce fuel consumption by varying amounts in response to a fuel tax, and have several means of doing so; a differential tax on vehicle producers will encourage some shifting to different types of vehicle. A second, more convincing point, is that there may be scientific or technical reasons why an economic instrument will be impractical. In the case of non-carbon dioxide emissions, for example, price signals that reflected the variation in emission levels during any trip would change considerably over a short space of time. It might be extremely difficult for motorists to respond to such signals. Also, the sophisticated technology that would be required to implement such a system of charging would impose large cost barriers and potential concern about civil liberties. Third, there may be political factors that weigh against the use of economic instruments such as problematic distributional or equity effects, although these can always be overcome through appropriate, targeted compensation. Equally, regulation may be preferred because the costs can seem to be 'hidden'. Fourth, environmental and economies of scale concerns within the EU tend to point to the use of regulation. Several member states of the EU are firm defenders of the right to determine tax rates at a national level. At the same time, there is a well-established history of vehicle design being set at the EU level and such standards can be agreed under qualified majority voting, whereas unanimity is required for taxation measures.[6]

In conclusion, while the recent move towards a greater use of economic instruments is justified in terms of efficiency, there remain several strong practical reasons why regulation will continue to be preferred in various situations. The reality, at least in the short to medium term, is that both regulation and economic instruments will need to be used to address the UK's and world's various environmental problems.

## The policy options: individual policy instruments

Policy instruments to address environmental damage from road travel can be divided into those targeted directly at the road vehicle, fuel or infrastructure (policy 'sticks'), and those directed at alternatives to road travel (policy 'carrots'). A range of such instruments is presented below. The list is not intended to be exhaustive, but aims to cover conventional options together with some further possibilities. Against each policy, we indicate the situation in which the instrument may be most useful in addressing environmental damage. Table 10.3 summarises the main characteristics of each instrument. A wider assessment of various policy options is contained in Wade (1995) and Taylor (1996, forthcoming).

Anticipating later sections, we want to emphasise that most, if not all, environmental policy objectives will be better achieved if major policy instruments ('sticks') are accompanied by wider policy 'carrots' (and when policies work in the same direction). Recent modelling work has shown that significant transfers from car to public transport will only be achieved if a carrot of, say, better public transport or lower fares is combined with a policy stick to discourage use of the car.[7]

*Direct policy instruments, or policy 'sticks'*

*Rationing could be introduced.* This could be of fuel supply, vehicle use, infrastructure capacity, or parking space. Such a tough measure is best used when a rapid reduction of environmental damage is required, perhaps lasting only for a short period of time. For example, controls could be introduced on vehicle use in some dense urban areas during summer periods when atmospheric conditions combine with exhaust emissions to produce smog and considerably increased health risks. In fact, the 1995 Environment Act provides scope for local authorities to apply for powers to close urban roads at times of chronic pollution levels. Rationing performs well in reducing environmental damage to any given target, while avoiding incentives to increase travel (see Table 10.3). Its drawbacks are almost entirely on the cost side, with large costs to individual motorists, industry, and for administration and enforcement. Some form of cost-benefit comparison would be particularly helpful to the policy maker, in judging the scale of costs and benefits from new policy action compared with the costs and benefits from no further action. If there is scope for the trading of individuals' pollution rights or quotas (whether through legal or illegal trading), rationing may converge on the pricing solution, except that transaction costs will normally be very much higher in the case of rationing and particularly when compared with fuel charging.

*Regulation of vehicle design could be extended.* Such a policy is most appropriate where a major change in damage is possible with low to medium costs, spread across all polluters. Examples of this include EU emission standards, or where significant 'no regrets' technological developments can be identified. (A 'no regrets' policy refers to situations where individual consumers would financially benefit from a measure but might fail to implement it for some reason, such as inconvenience, short-sightedness, or a lack of information.)[8] Again, as for rationing, the main drawback is cost. Regulation of vehicle design involves somewhat lower costs to the motorist when compared to rationing, mainly because travel itself is not directly constrained. However, the 'resource' cost of new technology may be considerable; and the scale of environmental improvement will be limited by the potential pace of technological development at any one time and, if fuel economy is to be improved, more travel will be encouraged as the marginal fuel cost is reduced. The regulatory approach also suffers by not providing incentives for manufacturers to do better than the given standard. In contrast, the 'tradeable credits' form of standard setting incorporates dynamic incentives to exceed the targets together with several other advantages over straight regulation (see Taylor, 1992; Kågeson, 1992; and Cointe *et al* 1994). The costs to buyers of new vehicles will be reflected in the second-hand market, generally in a regressive manner. For example, demand may shift from large new cars to large nearly-new cars, with a ripple effect throughout the second hand market which is likely to push up the price of vehicles bought at the bottom end of the market by poorer motorists.

*In-service vehicle emission standards could be tightened.* The existing standards for in-service vehicles cover carbon monoxide and black smoke. These limits could be tightened and extended. More vehicles would fail the MoT test, and more would need to be scrapped earlier than otherwise. Again this would be quite regressive as it would disproportionately affect the cars of the less affluent. To have even a small but significant impact on air quality, existing and future standards would need to be enforced more aggressively, with penalties and charges needing to be considerable to cover enforcement costs. Greater enforcement would best be used to target the most severe concentrations of carbon monoxide and black smoke emissions in dense urban areas. To deliver significant improvements while containing costs, enforcement resources could be shifted between localities according to the quality of ambient air at any one time. The US federal government has taken enforcement further than most other governments by establishing an 'environmental police force'.

*Regulation could be introduced to require the fitting of speed limiters to new cars.* While this would impose time costs on individual motorists, when considering the speed limiter as a policy tool, there is a case for ignoring time benefits gained from travelling at speed in excess of existing laws. In this respect, it is noteworthy that over half (56 per cent) of motorway drivers recorded at free-flow sites were exceeding the national speed limit (Transport Statistics of Great Britain, 1994). Retrospective fitting of a speed limiter to cars already in use would be very costly and administratively difficult, whereas applying a speed limiter to new cars only would entail minimal production costs. Compulsory fitting of the speed limiter to new cars would be most appropriate where long-distance road building or widening were to be reduced but no significant 'stick' policies were to be introduced. The speed limiter would help, to some extent, to make motorway traffic flows more stable. Primarily, the measure is one aimed at improving road safety, but by saving fuel it would yield a small but significant reduction in carbon dioxide emissions. After around ten years, such a limiter could save around 1 MtC annually (about three per cent of 1990 road transport carbon dioxide emissions). As motorists would perceive the impact of the policy quite quickly (with some perverse effects as older cars of any size sped past new big cars!) the policy might prove quite unpopular, especially in the shorter term. Even so, any government faced with fast rising inter-urban traffic levels and increasingly unstable traffic flows might want to pursue this relatively simple and cost effective means for enforcing existing legislation, itself rooted in road safety policy. For some years, new lorries and coaches have been required to have speed limiters fitted.

*Land use planning policy could be tightened.* In the medium to longer term, the environmental benefits of such a policy could be substantial. Costs to motorists and business would be incurred but these would tend to impinge on a small number of people and companies, at least in the early years. Particularly careful policy design would be necessary to ensure that different aspects of policy did not conflict; for example, to ensure that the shifting of development into urban areas did not add to pollution, congestion and safety problems; and that mixed residential-commercial development did not occur in such a way as to affect adversely the quality of communities, neighbouring behaviour or increase crime or fear of crime (Halpern, 1995). Another potential problem is competition - for jobs and residents - between local authorities, whether primarily urban or rural. For these and other reasons, land use-transport planning along the lines of PPG13 (see above) may well need to be made compulsory, as advocated by the Royal Commission (1994). While at present PPG13 is advisory, it must by statute be taken into account in local authority plans. Alternatively, financial incentives to business and grant allocations to local authorities could be made dependent on the overall balance of policy, much as the 'package approach' (which enables local authorities to transfer expenditure away from local roads) has required.

*Bans on Heavy Goods Vehicles, at certain times and places, could be introduced.* For example, HGVs could be banned from central urban areas between the hours of, say, 8am to 7pm. This option would help to complement a measure such as parking restraint. Significant costs to business would result, some of which would be passed on to consumers. To the extent that prices of goods in shops are affected, this might lead to adverse distributional consequences. A second, more localised option would be to ban HGVs from exclusively residential areas. In many localities, both in small and large towns, HGV drivers may seek to save time by 'rat-running' through residential areas. Bans on access coupled with significant penalties for the driver for non-compliance would probably be very effective at addressing this particular problem. However, the potential scale of policing or enforcement costs might be considerable, even with camera technology.

## Table 10.3 Individual policy instruments compared

| | Environmental impact | Causes extra travel | Costs to motorist | Costs to industry | Flexibility | Time to implement | Equity | Public expenditure |
|---|---|---|---|---|---|---|---|---|
| **Direct policy instruments - 'sticks'** | | | | | | | | |
| Rationing | ☺☺☺ | ☺☺ | XX | XX | XX | XX | ☺☺ | X |
| Regulation of vehicle design | ☺☺ | XX | XX | XX | XX | XX | X | x |
| Emissions enforcement | ☺☺ | ☺ | X | X | — | X | XX | XX |
| Car speed limiter | ☺ | X | XX | ☺ | — | X | ☺ | ☺ |
| Land use planning policy | ☺☺☺ | ☺☺ | X | X | — | XXX | ☺ | X |
| Bans on HGVs | ☺☺ | ? | ☺ | XX | X | X | — | X |
| Traffic management | ☺ | ? | X | X | XX | X | — | X |
| Increase fuel price | ☺☺☺ | ☺☺ | XX | X | ☺☺ | ☺☺ | X→☺ | ☺☺ |
| Congestion charging | ☺☺☺ | ☺☺ | ☺/X | ☺ | ☺☺ | XX | X→☺ | ☺☺ |
| Differential vehicle taxes | ☺ | XX | X | X | ☺ | X | X | ? |
| Voluntary agreements | ☺/— | XX | — | — | ☺ | X | — | — |
| **Indirect policy instruments - 'carrots'** | | | | | | | | |
| Bus passenger subsidies | ☺☺ | X | ☺ | ☺ | ☺ | X | ☺ | XX |
| New urban light rail | ☺☺ | X | ☺ | ☺ | ☺☺ | XX | ? | XX |
| Rail freight subsidies | ☺☺ | X | ☺ | ☺ | ☺☺ | X | X | XX |
| Fund public transport information | ☺ | ☺ | ☺ | ☺ | ☺☺ | X | ☺ | X |
| Improve local facilities | ☺ | ☺ | ☺ | ☺ | ☺ | X | ☺ | XX |
| Fund cycleways, park & cycle, rail cycle subsidy | ☺☺☺ | ☺☺ | ☺ | ☺ | ☺☺ | X | ☺ | X |
| Build bypasses | ☺/XX | XX | ☺ | ☺ | ☺☺ | XX | X | XX |
| Commercialise road costs/charges | ☺☺ | ? | X | ☺ | ☺ | XX | X→☺ | ☺ |

'☺' = good; '—' = neutral; 'X' = bad; '→' = revenues fund compensation;
'?' = effect depends on specific circumstances

*Traffic management schemes could be extended.*  Traffic management covers a wide range of smaller measures, including speed humps, traffic diversion, parking restrictions, chicanes, pedestrianisation and so on.  Such measures are best used to ensure that through-traffic uses a bypass or ring-road, or to intervene at specific locations suffering from severe environmental damage or accident risks.  Transport 2000 (Transport Retort, 1995) has drawn attention to an approach developed by the Scottish Office - 'route action plans' (RAPs). This combines various forms of management with some limited improvements to the infrastructure.  Traffic calming measures cover various regulatory or management devices, including traffic light controlled entry to the road, speed limit variations, lorry only lanes and so on.  The main costs are likely to result from operation of the system and enforcement (and some individual motorists may suffer considerable inconvenience and delay); the benefits will be very specific to each locality.

*Fuel prices could be increased.*  Increases in fuel prices are best used to target damage that varies in direct proportion to the amount of fuel consumed or travel undertaken.  That will be of particular benefit to carbon dioxide emissions and some aspects of community damage.  As table 10.3 indicates, this option offers significant benefits, especially if some of the revenue raised is used to offset the potentially adverse distributional effects.  There are various ways of targeting distributional compensation, for example: via reductions in other forms of taxation, increases in benefits or though increased local authority grant allocations, leaving authorities to choose appropriate forms of compensation.[9]  Fears that people will pay the prices and not change behaviour are ill-founded: if a target level of damage is to be achieved, prices can be raised by whatever amount is necessary; if a particular price signal is to be given, social and economic efficiency will be achieved if distributional compensation is accompanied by the charging of prices that properly and fully reflect marginal damage effects.

*Congestion charging could be introduced in dense urban areas.*  Urban congestion charging[10] is a 'second best' means of pricing emissions, not being directly targeted on emission variations *per se*.  With more sophisticated congestion charging systems, however, charges can vary according to traffic speed and flow, providing a reasonable proxy for emission variations.  Using advanced equipment, it should be possible to target separately (initially at large technological cost) diesel and petrol vehicles; HGVs, LGVs, buses and cars; and older vehicles (associated with higher emissions).  Price signals would be much better targeted than, say, is possible with parking charges.  In fact, Goodwin (1992) points to the 'green-gold' scenario that can result from use of congestion charging as a proxy for emission charging: environmental benefits will be secured at the same time as scarce urban road space is used more efficiently. However, the potential distributional effects of urban charging could be considerable.  These might adversely affect motorists resident within the charging zone and workers carrying out relatively low paid jobs in the urban core, though these problems might be partly or wholly offset by the increased reliability and reduced average journey times of buses.  Another distributional aspect concerns urban areas with charging compared to rural or urban areas without charging.    For most forms of distributional compensation, the individual local authority - assuming that it is allowed to keep the revenues raised by charging - should be well placed to determine appropriate measures.

*Differential taxes on vehicles could be introduced with taxes set according to relative emission rates.*  Such taxes could apply both at the point of purchase (on new vehicles) or at the point of registration (vehicle excise duty, VED). These measures could, for example, be used as a means of encouraging improved fuel economy per kilometre, thereby reducing carbon dioxide emissions.  They could also be used to provide incentives for vehicle purchasers to opt for a particular piece of technology, possibly bringing reductions in some non-carbon dioxide emissions.   However, the benefits of differential vehicle taxes may be relatively small, and will be reduced to the extent that extra travel is stimulated when motorists purchase more fuel efficient vehicles, making travel cheaper per kilometre.

*Voluntary agreements with manufacturers could be pursued.*  In our judgement, there is little point in pursuing voluntary agreements as manufacturers will have an incentive to propose small changes that they were planning to introduce in any event as part of their normal production cycles, in response to market forces.

*Indirect policy instruments or 'carrots'*

*Subsidies to public transport could be increased or extended.*  Subsidies are best used in dense urban areas, especially when targeted on particular corridors or services, and in conjunction with a policy stick.[11]   Although there are potentially large public expenditure implications, subsidies to public transport bring significant positive benefits, albeit relatively modest in the absence of a policy 'stick' to discourage the use of private transport.  A general subsidy to reduce fares or improve overall quality of service will entail large 'deadweight losses': many people already using public transport do not require an inducement to persuade them to continue using the service.  There is also a problem when large subsidies to rail or bus services generate additional travel (for example by encouraging rail commuters to live still further from their place of work) or encourage switching from other modes such as walking or cycling (Hughes, 1993).  Such effects reduce the overall impact of subsidies on emissions and other environmental damage, and support the need for targeted subsidy, geared to new or extended services, or new users.

General increases in subsidy to public transport on long distance or inter-urban routes will again be most effective when combined with a significant policy stick such as a substantial increase in fuel prices.  Recent evidence from studies of public transport projects that enhanced the existing service (for example, the Midland Main Line and the Trans-Pennine corridor studies) shows that although these projects increased the patronage of the service, they did little to reduce the use of road transport in the particular inter-urban corridor. Some of the trips were newly generated, others simply involved transfers from coach.

*Rail freight operations could be further subsidised.* Grants already exist to link business into the rail and waterway networks, and to help attract certain types of traffic to rail. The example given in Table 10.3 is intended to reflect a subsidy designed to attract small units of freight to rail. The main cost would be in terms of public expenditure, although there may also be adverse distributional effects if financial benefits accrue to business (all be it to secure the desired environmental gain) and are funded by general taxpayers or by private motorists.

*Local facilities could be improved.* Alongside better public transport services and the various policy sticks described earlier, local facilities may need to be enhanced in order to offset some of the possible negative outcomes and to act as a 'sweetener'. Improvements to the quality of the inner-cities would increase their attractiveness to residents and should thereby reduce commuter travel. Without such improvements, the restraint or price effect of sticks aimed at, say, urban pollution and congestion may serve to push people and businesses out of town, causing new environmental damage in rural and suburban areas. Local improvements might include: new leisure facilities, pedestrianisation, cycleways, cycle parks, park and cycle facilities, street furniture, the planting of trees and other such measures, literally to 'green' the city. These projects could be funded out of the revenues generated by the price-based policy sticks or would need to be raised from local or national taxes.

*Cycling could be encouraged.* First, public expenditure could be used to construct dedicated cycleways both within and between urban areas (see, for example, Shayler *et al*, 1993). Cycle lanes marked on road carriageways offer some protection for cyclists, but fail to convince many that safety is really improved. They also leave the cyclist exposed to high concentrations of vehicle emissions, though other policy instruments may help to ease this. Dedicated cycleways are being developed in some urban areas, and Sustrans[12] has drawn up plans for 8000 kilometres of cycleway across the United Kingdom, some of which are already in use (with 60 per cent of users being pedestrians). Public sector support for such developments, which often utilise disused railway lines, canal tow-paths and derelict land, can prove very cost effective, with the main costs arising from the initial financial outlay.

Second, start-up grants could be used to encourage bicycle hire services at rail and bus stations, and at out-of-town or near-town car parks. This latter option would represent an extension of the 'park and ride' and bus services that have begun to develop on the periphery of towns. To guard against loss or theft of hired bicycles, a one-off deposit could be made with the hire company, either in cash or using the individual's credit card as a guarantor. The scale of subsidy could prove relatively low, being required initially to overcome potential concerns about the loss of cycles, even when deposits are taken. Subsidies could also be used to fund town centre cycle racks.

Third, supplementary subsidies could be given to rail operators in proportion to the number of cycles carried. Again, this measure would best be used alongside a policy stick, especially when targeting dense urban areas both for urban and long distance travel. At present, many trains are only capable of

be obstacles in the way of fully monetised CBA and particularly the lack of widely accepted values with which to express both costs and benefits in money terms (Adams, 1995). These obstacles must not be allowed to prevent a comparison of cost and benefit information, even when some is in physical units and some in money units. The policy maker will need to make judgements both about the absolute scale of costs and benefits that society and individual groups 'should' face (together with the scale of any compensation) and about the relative balance of costs and benefits arising from one policy option compared to another.

When it comes to choosing between specific policy tools in a particular context, it is important for policy-makers not to assume that what worked in one area is necessarily the best policy in another, even if the problem to be addressed looks similar. For example, while congestion pricing or rationing might be appropriate to address pollution or congestion problems in a given urban area, such measures might be quite inappropriate, too unfocused and costly for specific problems associated with long-distance traffic or travel in rural areas. The difficulty for policy-makers is that the policy solutions to specific environmental problems must be tailored to the local context, and yet they must also fit well into the overall strategic policy framework. Consideration must also be given to the scale of costs to particular groups, businesses and regions, and to the need for compensation of some groups or areas, and the source from which compensation will be funded. Similarly, it is important to investigate how far the individual motorist or polluter will receive a clear signal and how far a change in behaviour is realistically possible, be it through incentives, force or rationing.

There is also quite a long list of what *not* to do. First, the obvious but important point should be made that doing nothing or very little in response to an issue where overall, net costs appear high is a very poor policy option. For example, the costs of dealing with global warming may seem very high, but several studies indicate that the costs of not dealing with the issue are likely to be considerably higher. The second general warning, following on from the earlier comments, is that it will normally be a mistake to expect to find single or blanket solutions to most environmental problems. The classic, and oft suggested, 'solution' to many transport problems is simply to subsidise public transport. However, in the absence of rather less popular policy 'sticks', these subsidies are likely to be relatively ineffective, especially if paid on a blanket basis and not targeted at particular corridors or services. It is a similar mistake to think that it is possible to deal with a localised, micro-level environmental problem using a macro-level tool without severe costs and considerable public opposition. For example, it would be inefficient and unpopular to attempt to tackle the specific problem of localised urban pollution through a large national increase in fuel prices (though such a policy might help ease other environmental problems).

A related 'no-go' area concerns the need to avoid overlooking possible perverse effects of policy in one area versus another. For example, improvements to the fuel efficiency of the internal combustion engine (yielding lower carbon dioxide emissions per kilometre) may well result in higher emission of nitrogen oxides. Equally, removal of lead from petrol results in some deterioration in engine fuel efficiency. Perhaps one of the most fundamental trade-off problems at present concerns relative damage effects in urban and out-of-town localities.  Growing concern about pollution and community damage points to the need for less traffic in urban areas.  At the same time, pressure for less damage to the countryside points to new business, leisure and residential development occurring only in and on the fringes of urban areas, where it may add to pollution, congestion and community damage problems.

The bottom line is that no policy measure will entail zero costs, though it may sometimes be possible to 'conceal' them.  Some commentators consider that regulation and land use planning are costless options.  In fact, these will almost always be the more costly options, but the costs are not always immediately apparent.  For example, while the three-way catalyst and associated technology adds £500-£1000 to the cost of producing a petrol car, this may not be identifiable in the shorter term to the new car buyer for whom price paid will be affected by other factors such as the strength of demand (and thus scale of dealer discount), productivity trends and so on. Environmental and transport issues cannot be conveniently sub-divided, as the problems to be addressed, and the likely solutions, are highly interrelated in their form.  On the other hand, for solutions to be politically acceptable and reasonably efficient, they have to be carefully tailored to the local context. Clearly, if any area of policy must be handled in a strategic framework, it is transport and the environment!.

## Policy conclusions

Policy-makers, and indeed most of the public, are now generally aware that something extra will have to be done about the environmental problems presented by our growing, almost insatiable demand for transport, and that the present situation is 'unsustainable', at least in urban areas and on some stretches of inter-urban road.  However, as we have seen, none of the potential policies that are likely to be effective are without costs (at least in the short term) and whatever action is taken is likely to be deeply unpopular with certain sections of the community.

From our review we have identified · a number of transport related environmental issues which we believe must be given a high policy priority. These include the need to reduce urban air pollution, local community damage and emissions of greenhouse gases.  We also strongly recommend the reviewing of new road-building proposals in a strategic context and against a scenario for policy levers which reflects 'heightened' environmental concern.  This may well result in the abandonment of some bypass and road-widening schemes. The reduced scale of new build will depend on the combined effect of strategic assessment and actual new policy (see below).

*Two broad policy packages*

In Table 10.4 we present two alternative policy packages that a government might consider when addressing the main environmental damage effects of transport. One package gives more preference to regulatory solutions while the other places a greater emphasis on economic instruments. Neither excludes use of instruments traditionally associated with the 'other school of thought'.

Despite the differences of emphasis, the two packages are broadly similar. One major difference lies in the way the policy stick operates in urban areas. In the absence of significant local sources of revenue, the regulatory-inclined approach will need to raise substantial revenues from fuel duty or from general Exchequer sources. Arguably, this use of general revenues is inequitable compared to finance that derives from charges for road use or environmental damage. Roads commercialisation is consistent with either of the two main approaches.

Both policy approaches will impose significant costs on society. However, it should be stressed that environmental damage is already imposing costs on society and also that, at present, these costs are typically not borne by those who create them.


*Some concluding thoughts for a future policy package*

For a policy package to be effective and efficient, it will often require both policy 'carrots' and 'sticks', and probably will utilise both economic and regulatory approaches. Each environmental problem requires a different set of solutions, but it is essential that these policies are coordinated and implemented as a coherent whole. This may require extended dialogue between national and local government and interested groups within society.

A government of any mainstream political party should be able to take one or other of the broad policy packages contained in Table 10.4 as the heart of its policy approach. We emphasise the need for strategic policy assessment. We stress that a 'mixed' approach will often be necessary, with neither regulation nor economic instruments serving as the only policy approach. We accept that for many years to come, policy-makers will be unable, for one reason or another, to target each area of environmental damage at the appropriate marginal level of individual decision making. Those considerations lead us to encourage local authorities to adopt explicit targets for pollution and community damage effects, or for 'acceptable' local rates of traffic growth. Whatever their form, limits should be tailored to reflect the severity of local damage and the costs of change, specific local priorities, existing rail and cycle facilities, and so on (see above). We also recommend the establishment of a Transport Anti-Pollution Unit (TAPU). The unit's main work could be to sponsor the testing of new policy ideas ('best practice' possibilities) in real life situations, and it would also be responsible for a new 'environmental police force'.

## Table 10.4  Possible policy packages

| | Emphasis on regulation | Emphasis on economic instruments |
|---|---|---|
| Urban air pollution | Quotas or permits for car use; control of parking space and higher parking charges; or selective vehicle bans. | Congestion charging or increase parking charges; possibly use selective vehicle bans during chronic pollution episodes in some localities. |
| | Resources to fund public transport, cycling measures and urban area improvements from:<br>• extension of 'package approach' to enable planned road expenditure to be spent more widely on local facilities;<br>• increased parking charges for commuters, low charges for shoppers travelling outside peak flows to encourage use of town centre facilities<br>• earmarking of revenue from fuel duty increases<br>• cycling measures to include: dedicated cycleways, secure cycle parks, cycle hire, park & cycle, and rail subsidy for cycle carriage<br>• public transport support focused on certain bus routes and new light rail or trolleybus | Resources to fund public transport, cycling measures and urban area improvements from:<br>• congestion charging revenues and increased parking charges for commuters, low charges for shoppers travelling outside peak flows to encourage use of town centre facilities<br>• cycling measures including: dedicated cycleways, secure cycle parks, cycle hire, park & cycle, and rail subsidy for cycle carriage<br>• public transport support focused on certain bus routes and new light rail or trolleybus |
| | Continuing tightening of vehicle emission standards for CO, $NO_x$, HCs and black smoke for new and in service vehicles. | Some further tightening of vehicle emission standards; occasional vehicle tax incentives where significant new technology available. |
| | Local authority to decide whether targets to be used: levels of pollution/community damage; limits on future traffic growth. | In the absence of robust money values for marginal environmental damage and inability to charge at point of damage, targets might be used. |
| | Establish Transport Anti-Pollution Unit (TAPU). Main work to fund 'best practice' real life experiments: environment friendly city, extensive cycleways & other cycle support, electric bus, congestion charging or traffic bans. Perhaps create environmental police force to enforce in-service vehicle emission standards. | Establish Transport Anti-Pollution Unit (TAPU), possibly funded by special levy on road fuel. Main work to fund 'best practice' real life experiments: environment friendly city, extensive cycleways & other cycle support, electric bus, congestion charging or traffic bans. |
| Local community damage | Degree PPG13 applied tied to central government finance or specific grants; urban damage reduced by urban traffic bans; requirements for sensitive design of residential, business and mixed developments; localised traffic bans; speed chicanes, pedestrianisation. | Incentives via grants for Local Authorities to apply PPG13; urban damage reduced by congestion charging; requirements for sensitive design of residential, business and mixed developments; speed chicanes, pedestrianisation; localised traffic bans where severe damage. |
| Global climate change | Depending on carbon dioxide target post 2000, continue with at least five per cent p.a. real duty increases, perhaps plus differential vehicle taxes or 'tradeable credits' system. | Depending on carbon dioxide target post 2000, continue with at least five per cent p.a. real duty increases, perhaps plus differential vehicle taxes or 'tradeable credits' system. |
| Traffic growth | If seen as an overall problem, use fuel rationing or increases in fuel duty; if a localised problem, ban cars and lorries entirely, 8am-7pm, use local trip quotas or control parking spaces; also use traffic management and sensitive design of the built environment. | If seen as an overall problem, increase fuel duty further; if a localised problem, use congestion charging or parking charges; also use traffic management and sensitive design of the built environment; plus lorry bans, 8am-7pm if necessary. |
| Road building | Conduct strategic assessments, including of alternative modes and options for corridors/regions. Minimise new bypasses and motorway widening; use car speed limiters, traffic lights and traffic management to smooth speed-flow. | Conduct strategic assessments, including of alternative modes and options. Continue some road improvements, as fit within overall strategy. More traffic management on motorways unless strong case for widening. |

Given the advantages and drawbacks associated with both traffic bans and congestion charging, we do not wish to come down in favour of one or the other, not least because circumstances differ so much between localities. We do, however, encourage local authorities to consider seriously both main options, noting the evidence that people may regard traffic bans as 'fairer' while also noting that it is only the economic instrument that will generate revenues that could be spent on improved local infrastructure and other carrot or compensatory measures. Such decisions are best made locally, with local people and policy-makers coming together to decide the appropriate way forward.

If daytime traffic bans are used, a particular problem to address will be the difficulty of carrying heavy and bulky items by public transport, cycle or foot. The problem will be compounded as development switches back into urban areas. One option would be for local authorities to provide individuals with vouchers to secure reduced fares on a given number of taxi trips each year. Another possibility would be to encourage evening and Sunday shopping by car.

We have refrained from endorsing the Royal Commission's call for a doubling of road fuel prices by 2000. That seems an unreasonably drastic action in the context of carbon dioxide emissions, given existing international targets, the cost effectiveness of measures for other areas of the economy, and the fact that road transport is already being required to carry 40 per cent of the 2000 target savings when it accounts for only a fifth of the economy's emissions of carbon dioxide. In short, there are better alternatives, not least being improvements in energy conservation in other sectors. As a means of slowing traffic growth, a doubling of fuel prices by 2000 would have relatively little impact when compared to underlying traffic growth of two per cent per annum and would fail to target traffic growth in areas of maximum damage.

We do not, however, rule out very substantial fuel price increases as a long term strategy. Unless the world community chooses extremely radical carbon targets for 2010 and 2020, we propose that the five per cent annual fuel duty increases be continued to 2020. That judgement assumes that road transport should make a major contribution to carbon savings and that policy should address the wider concerns about traffic growth. With five per cent annual duty increases the pump price of fuel would be roughly double the 1994 level by 2010 and roughly treble the 1994 level by 2020. Instead of growing from 33 MtC in 1990 to 53 MtC in 2020 (as under present mid-range forecasts) road transport emissions would be held back to 34 MtC at most, and more likely cut to 27 MtC, 20 per cent below the 1990 level and one half the projected 2020 level. By coincidence, economy wide emissions in 2020 would have been returned to the 1990 level of 158 MtC instead of the projected 184 MtC.

Given our preference for traffic bans and charging measures in towns and cities, and the five per cent per annum increase in fuel duty, we favour a major scaling back of bypass construction so as to minimise the damage effects of new infrastructure.

An issue for society to ponder concerns whether or not we should adopt explicit upper limits for total traffic in the UK, not just encourage local authorities to adopt localised limits, as we do above. The economist would tell us that it is the individual damage effects with which we need be concerned, not traffic *per se*. That is all very well in logic, but we have pointed to problems of valuing individual effects and targeting measures at the appropriate margin of behaviour. Also, we must recognise that we start from our present position of having a host of regulations governing the design of infrastructure and vehicles or rolling stock for private and public travel; and we have a number of different tax signals. Such parameters already influence expectations of future traffic growth. That said, the case for national traffic growth targets will revolve around the issue of whether the totality of damage effects is greater than the sum of the individual parts - and, as a result, whether more and more people are becoming disillusioned by the prospects of further traffic growth, despite the benefits that they derive when in the car. The growth of existing pressure groups, such as the Pedestrians' Association, and new, sometimes militant, pressure groups points to mounting concern. Perhaps electoral popularity will lie with the bold, despite the undoubted costs the majority of the population - as motorists - will have to bear.

Finally, it is essential that transport policy be developed in a strategic framework. The assessment of major infrastructure projects - appraising projects in a wide context which embraces other modes of travel, land use patterns and so on - is already a requirement of EU Directive 85/337. The recommendations of the Standing Advisory Committee on Trunk Road Assessment (SACTRA, 1992), that whole stretches of road be assessed in a strategic context, alongside other travel and land use possibilities, should be developed as far as feasible. All transport and environmental policy, while showing sensitivity to the local context, should be conducted within a strategic framework which includes costing, or at least detailed consideration, of *all* likely costs and benefits. It is also important that these costs are reflected, and preferably signalled, in the 'price' that the end consumer or traveller pays. Given railway privatisation, it may be worth considering the parallel commercialisation (in a firm and clear regulatory framework) of the road system as well.

In conclusion, we can see that the environmental issues generated by contemporary transport are real, growing and need to be further addressed. Although the costs of policy action can be considerable, the costs borne by society if no further action is taken may be very much larger. In various ways, there are conflicts between the rights of the individual to enjoy the benefits of private, flexible travel and the rights of society and future generations to enjoy a clean and sophisticated environment. As more economic prosperity brings rising average incomes, more people will want the right to drive more often and over longer distances. Already, policy is trying to reduce the need to travel, but some of the pressures are long term in nature, not least land use patterns and the expectation of rising real incomes. Some future policies may be unpopular among many sections of the population, at least in the short term. Policy-makers need to square up to these difficulties and must be frank about what needs to be done. It may be that, given the likely unpopularity of many of the measures, cross-party cooperation will be needed to develop and implement the necessary policies. We must look both to informational campaigns among the general public and to the foresight of party leaders to hope that this consensus is achieved.

## Notes

1.  The biggest decline in modal share was seen by the pedal cycle, which fell from 23 per cent of the market in 1952 to one per cent in 1993 (from 23 bpk to 5 bpk). The market shares of bus and rail fell to 14 per cent and 28 per cent respectively of their 1952 shares. That meant a halving of bus patronage (to 42 bpk), whereas rail passenger travel remains almost unchanged in absolute terms at 39 bpk (albeit with numbers in the mid 1960s to the mid 1980s roughly 10% below the beginning and end points of the period).
2.  This figure excludes the emissions from oil refineries to produce fuel. The inclusion of this would increase road traffic's share of carbon dioxide emissions to around 21 per cent.
3.  Lead concentrations in Central London are now approximately one sixth of those measured in the early 1980s (CSO, 1995), and by 2005 very few petrol-engined vehicles will be running on unleaded petrol.
4.  Note that the three-way catalyst tends to result in a marginal worsening of fuel economy, thereby increasing $CO_2$ emissions per kilometre to a small degree. This effect, however, does tend to be offset by the engine management and fuel injection systems that are necessary for catalyst operation.
5.  The economically efficient level is that at which the full marginal costs of an activity are equated to the marginal benefits of the activity (i.e. 'Pigouvian pricing'). Where regulation is used instead of pricing, efficiency in a pure sense will not be achieved. However, as we show, regulation can prove to be an attractive means of bringing environmental costs to the attention of polluters, all be it without the incentives to change behaviour in the ways offered by price signals.
6.  For further details on the merits of economic versus regulatory instruments, see Taylor (1996).
7.  See, for example, Transport Research Laboratory (1994), as reported in Royal Commission on Environmental Pollution 1994, Chapter 11.
8.  A non-transport example of this phenomenon occurs with the non-insulation of housing: people would save money if they insulated but often fail to do so.
9.  Stokes (1995) has pointed to the possible use of 'swipe card' technology to enable rural, or all, adults to buy a given amount of road fuel at a substantially discounted price, guaranteeing particular groups, or all travellers (if also applied to public transport fares), a basic amount of travel at low prices, with additional trips at the prevailing market price.
10. Urban congestion charging provides a price signal to each motorist to indicate the scale of delay their journey is imposing on other motorists. The price signal serves as an incentive to reassess the benefits derived from each trip relative to the extra social costs imposed. In its more sophisticated form, electronic charging would be used, with roadside beacons interacting with on-board meters. Crude versions include a flat-rate charge for crossing one or more boundaries. With the former, billing might be on a monthly or quarterly basis. With the latter, pre-paid tokens or window stickers might be purchased from local shops prior to entry to the charge zone. Revenue collection, treatment of urban centre residents, and accommodation of visitors from another area, town or country are just three of several practical and administrative problems. The idea of congestion charging is not a new one, having been advocated by Smeed in the early 1960s and considered in the Buchanan Report (1963). So far, few places have introduced the policy: Bergen, Oslo and Singapore being the main places to have tried a form of congestion charging. In the last year or two, the Dutch government and Cambridge County Council have backed away from initial plans, mainly because

of the complexities involved and the feared scale of public opposition.  Even so, we think that the potential scale of benefits make this policy one worth trying to sell to the public in certain dense urban areas, particularly if revenues are retained in the local area.

11.  See, for example, Transport Research Laboratory (TRL) work reported in Royal Commission on Environmental Pollution 1994, Chapter 11.

12.  Sustrans is a civil engineering charity which designs and builds traffic-free routes for cyclists, walkers and people with disabilities.  Sustrans aims to build at least one traffic-free route into every urban area in Britain, and to create a national route network.  So far, only about 400 kilometres of cycleway has been built.

## References

Adams, J. (1995), *Beyond Cost Benefit Analysis*, Oxford: Green College Centre.

Andersen, M. (1994), *Governance by Green Taxes: Making Pollution Prevention Pay*, Manchester: Manchester University Press.

Baumol, W. and Oates, W. (1988), *The Theory of Environmental Policy*, Cambridge: Cambridge University Press.

Central Statistical Office (1995), *Social Trends*, London: HMSO.

Cointe, R., Foray, J-P., Taylor, S. R. and Tinch, R. (1994), *Tradeable Credits to Reduce Carbon Dioxide Emissions from Cars*, European Union official discussion paper (unpublished).

Cm 1200 (1990), *This Common Inheritance*, London: HMSO.

Cm 2674 (1994), 'Transport and the environment', *Royal Commission on Environmental Pollution, 18th Report*, London: HMSO.

Department of the Environment and Department of Transport (1993), *Planning Policy Guidance: Transport (PPG13)*, London: HMSO.

Department of Trade and Industry (1994), *Energy Paper* **65**, London: HMSO.

Department of Transport (1989) ,*National Road Traffic Forecasts 1989*, London: HMSO.

Department of Transport (1994), *Transport Statistics Great Britain 1994*, London: HMSO.

Dixon, J. A., Scura, L. F., Carpenter, R. A. and Sherman, P. B. (1994), *Economic Analysis of Environmental Impacts*, London: Asian Development Bank and The World Bank, Earthscan.

The Economist (1 April 1995), *Global Warming and Cooling Enthusiasm*, pp.67-68.

The Economist (17 June 1995), *The Great Transport Cop-Out: a Sensible Transport Policy Must Include Road-Pricing*, p.20.

Fergusson, M. and Wade, J. (1995), *Sustainable or Mobile? A Critique of UK Transport Policy and Carbon Dioxide Emissions*, London: Institute for European Environmental Policy.

Goodwin, P. (1992), 'Efficiency and the environment: possibilities of a Green-Gold Coalition', in Banister, D. and Button, K. (eds.), *Transport, the Environment and Sustainable Development*, London: Spon.

Goodwin, P. (1994), *Traffic Growth and the Dynamics of Sustainable Transport Policies*, Oxford: Linacre Lecture, Transport Studies Unit Report No. **811**.

Grubb, M., Koch, M., Thomson, K., Munson, A. and Sullivan, F. (1993), *The 'Earth Summit' Agreements: a Guide and Assessment*, London: The Royal Institute of International Affairs, Earthscan.

Halpern, D. S. (1995), *Mental Health and the Built Environment*, Basingstoke: Taylor and Francis.

Hughes, P. (1993), *Personal Transport and the Greenhouse Effect: A Strategy for Sustainability*, London: Earthscan.

Kågeson, P. (1992), *Making Fuel Go Further: A Critical Evaluation of Different Policy Instruments for Improving the Fuel Efficiency of New Cars and Other Light Vehicles*, Brussels: European Federation for Transport and Environment (T & E) 92/6.

Kågeson, P. (1993), *Getting the Prices Right*, Brussels: T & E 93/7.

Leone, R. and Parkinson T. (1990), *Conserving Energy: Is There a Better Way? A Study of Corporate Average Fuel Economy Regulation*, Putnam, USA: Hayes and Bartlett Inc.

Linton, M. (1995), 'Majority back ban on cars in city centres' and 'Drivers would avoid tolls', *The Guardian,* 9 August.

Matthew, D. (1994), *Lucky Number? PPG13 Briefing*, Transport Retort, **17**/4., London: Transport 2000.

O'Neill, J. (1993), *Ecology, Policy and Politics: Human Well-Being and the Natural World*, London: Routledge.

Peake, S. (1994), *Transport in Transition: Lessons from the History of Energy*, Royal Institute of International Affairs - Energy and Environmental Programme, London: Earthscan.

Pearce, D. W. (1993), *Blueprint 3: Measuring Sustainable Development*, London: Earthscan.

Pearce, D. W. and Turner, R. K. (1990), *Economics of Natural Resources and the Environment*, Hemel Hempstead: Harvester Wheatsheaf.

Porritt, J. (1995), 'Sleepy green world of Rip van Wilfred', *The Guardian,* 29 May.

Shayler, M., Fergusson, M. and Rowell, A. (1993), *Costing the Benefits: The Value of Cycling*, Godalming: Cyclists' Touring Club.

Standing Advisory Committee on Trunk Road Assessment (1992), *Assessing the Environmental Impact of Road Schemes*, London: HMSO.

Standing Advisory Committee on Trunk Road Assessment (1994), *Trunk Roads and the Generation of Traffic*, London: HMSO.

Stokes, G. (forthcoming, 1995), *Assessing the Effects of New Transport Policies on Rural Residents*, Transport Studies Unit Report No. **836**, Oxford.

Stokes, G. and Taylor, B. J. (1994), 'Where next for Transport Policy?', in Jowell, R., Curtice, J., Brook, L. and Ahrendt, D. (eds.), *British Social Attitudes: the 11th Report*, Aldershot: Dartmouth.

Taylor, S. R. (1992), 'Tradeable credits: variants for the transport sector, in *Climate Change: Designing a Tradeable Permit System*, Paris: OECD.

Taylor, S. R. (1996, forthcoming), *Pathways to Greener Transport*.

The specially shortened version of the Buchanan Report (1963), *Traffic in Towns*, Penguin Books, 1964.

Therivel, R., Wilson, E., Thompson, S., Heaney, D. and Pritchard, D. (1992), *Strategic Environmental Assessment*, London: Earthscan.

Transport Report (July/August 1995), *Route Action Plans - the Way Forward?*, Vol. **18**, No. **4**.

Virley, S. J. (1993), *The Effect of Fuel Price Increases on Road Transport $CO_2$ Emissions*, Transport Policy, Vol. **1**, No. **1**, Oxford: Butterworth-Heinemann.

Wade, J. (1995), *European Community Personal Transport: the Need for a More Integrated Approach*, Environmental Change Unit, University of Oxford, paper presented to ECEEE 1995 Summer Study, Latitudes, Mandelieu, France.

von Weizsäcker, E. U. and Jesinghaus, J. (1992), *Ecological Tax Reform: a Policy Proposal for Sustainable Development*, London: Zed Books.

World Commission on Environment and Development (WCED) (1987), *Our Common Future*, Oxford: Oxford University Press.

# 11 The role of housing

*Richard Best* [*]

## Introduction

Housing - housing policy, housing investment and housing management - has been blamed for many of Britain's economic and social ills. Housing policies are accused of stoking inflation in the 1980s and deepening recession in the 1990s. Fiscal policies for housing have boosted owner-occupation, at a substantial cost to the Treasury, and created an uneven playing field for the rented sector: these policies are blamed for encouraging unsustainable levels of home ownership with consequent problems of arrears and possessions, creating difficulties for people who need to move for job reasons, and shortages of rented housing (leading ultimately to homelessness). The ways we subsidise housing provision - increasingly through personal, not 'bricks-and-mortar', subsidies - have led to higher rents that are said to be creating dependency on Housing Benefit and fierce disincentives to work. Finally, housing management practices are accused of increasingly concentrating and segregating poor and disadvantaged households on council estates, with consequences for levels of crime, ill health and low educational attainment.

This chapter argues that there are policies for housing - for investment, taxation, subsidies and housing management - that can be the solutions to, instead of the causes of, economic and social problems.

---

[*] Director of the Joseph Rowntree Foundation, York

## Housing and the wider economy

A programme of research by the Joseph Rowntree Foundation (JRF), co-ordinated by Professor Duncan Maclennan and involving academics from 12 universities, concluded in June 1994 that changes in housing policy were critical to support the labour market flexibility which is essential to Britain's economic future (Maclennan, 1993). This body of work built on an earlier analysis by John Muellbauer that had demonstrated the role of the UK housing market in stimulating the boom and then aggravating the recession of the late 1980s (Muellbauer, 1990).

### Why housing affects the economy

With the benefit of hindsight, it now seems clear that although the UK housing market might not have caused the boom-bust cycle, it substantially affected it.

Stimulated by mortgage interest tax relief and exemption from capital gains tax, a very high proportion of the UK population - more than two-thirds of households - are owner-occupiers. The largest section of their personal wealth (excluding pension rights) is in their homes; its value is about £800bn net of outstanding mortgage debts. Changes in house prices, therefore, affect the wealth - and the associated 'feel-good' factor - of the great majority of consumers. In addition, about two-thirds of home-owners (over 10 million households) have mortgages; their total mortgage debt is now about £300bn (up from £75bn at the beginning of the 1980s). In contrast to many other countries, these mortgages are borrowed mostly at variable interest rates so fluctuations in rates have a deep effect upon the spending power of a large number of households. Government policies over recent years have tended to make particular use of interest rates as a regulator of the economy. Wide fluctuations in interest rates therefore create highly significant changes in the fortunes of mortgage-holders (who comprise the majority of those with average and above average earnings) and this volatility has a significant impact upon consumer spending and confidence.

Despite this volatility, no safety net exists for those in employment who find themselves unable to maintain their mortgage repayments (often due to one partner ceasing to work). Inevitably, this leads to mortgage arrears and repossessions, which have the consequence of further depressing the market. Currently there are over 350,000 home-owners with mortgage arrears of more than six months. Although the number of repossessed homes has fallen slightly from its level of 75,000 homes in 1992, this overhang of debtors could jeopardise recovery in the market if lenders decided the time was right to take possession of their homes (Ford and Wilcox, 1995). Reductions in State support to cover mortgage repayments during times of unemployment, to be introduced in 1995, will increase these insecurities.

Britain has the weakest private rented sector in Europe (the private rented stock in Germany, for example, is four times as big; McCrone and Stephens, 1995). So there is little alternative to owner-occupation for the majority of home seekers, and those in trouble who want to sell out and rent, may not be able to do so. Without an active private rented sector there are no other purchasers in the housing market when owner-occupiers are unable or unwilling to move home. Unlike many other countries, Britain gives no special incentives to first-time buyers. There are no counter-cyclical measures, therefore, to offset problems facing existing owners by stimulating the entry of new purchasers.

For these reasons, the swings of the house-price pendulum in the UK tend to be more exaggerated - and to affect far more people - than in competitor countries.

*The impact of fluctuating property prices*

Changes in property prices have a widespread impact upon the economy. When the property market is *booming*, we now know that there is heavy equity withdrawal and a pronounced increase in spending on consumer goods. People save less, or spend savings, if the value of their main asset is rising rapidly. Others borrow against the increased equity in their homes. In the boom year of 1988, mortgage equity withdrawal represented over seven per cent of personal disposable income (£20.4bn - exceeding the amount of consumer borrowing which was lent explicitly for consumption purposes). But in 1992, in recessionary times, this flow of funds to households had all but disappeared (Westerway, 1994).

**Figure 11.1**
**No equity withdrawal in 1993**

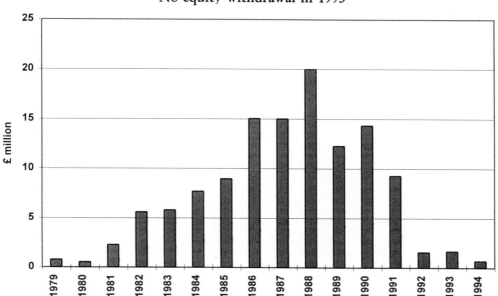

Sources: Financial Statistics (AAPR); Housing and Construction Statistics;
UK National Accounts (DFDF and CTCS)

Higher house prices also encourage a greater volume of transactions, and this creates a further stimulus to spending (particularly on white goods, furniture and fittings) resulting from the number of house moves. Since the costs of moving are lower in the UK than in other European countries - where transaction taxes alone are over 10 per cent in many cases - it is easier in the UK to 'trade up' to extract equity in boom periods (Maclennan, 1993).

In addition, surges in house prices can lead to over-heating in the building industry, which responds slowly to changes in the market: this has inflationary consequences for house prices and wages. In particular, construction responds more to a fall in price than to a rise: this asymmetric response is one reason why the recent recession in construction has been so severe (Maclennan, 1994).

In a depressed or *falling* property market, consumer spending is markedly reduced. Negative equity - unsecured mortgage debt - depresses confidence and dampens spending. Also, by making it more difficult for people to move, it leads to a reduction in transactions and a consequent additional drop in associated spending; 1995 estimates indicate that negative equity was still affecting over a million households (with the highest proportion in the south east; Dorling and Cornford, 1995). Lack of demand for new homes also compounds problems in the building industry, helping to raise unemployment - with up to 500,000 jobs lost over the last 15 years - and further hampers economic recovery.

### Figure 11.2
### The Declining costs of MIRAS and Income Support for home buyers

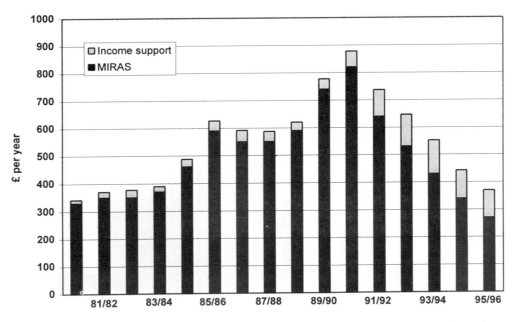

Sources:  Inland Revenue Statistics;  Parliamentary Questions 09/03/3, 25/03/93 and
          02/11/93;  Annual Statistical Enquiries;  Income Support Statistics Quarterly
          Enquiries, May 1993 and 1994

**Figure 11.3**
**The growth of means-tested help with housing costs**

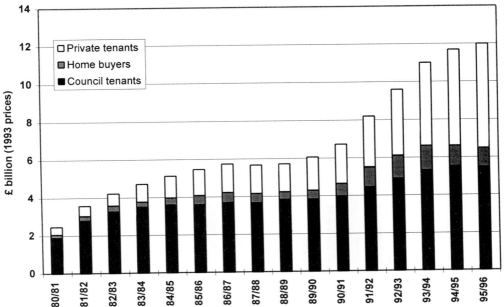

Sources:   Answer to Parliamentary Questions 09/07/91, 17/03/93, 29/11/93; Inland
Revenue Statistics; Income Support Statistics Quarterly Enquiries, May 1993
and 1994; Social Security Departmental Reports Cms 1914, 2215,2515,2813

This is why the private rented sector - charging market rents for relatively short-term lets - has one role to play, and the social rented sector - charging below-market rents for permanent lettings - has a different role. It is why, in the autumn Budget of 1994, the Government announced measures to stop the rapid escalation of council rents; and why, in its June 1995 White Paper, the Government announced that the Housing Corporation would be placing new conditions on housing associations in relation to their rent levels. This reverses a trend for rents to increase at about twice the rate for incomes: rents for housing association tenancies rose by 84 per cent between the beginning of 1989 and March 1995, while incomes for those in work rose by 37 per cent over the same period (National Federation of Housing Associations, 1995).

*Finding the money*

The machinery is in place to expand the social housing sector, alongside measures to revive private renting. The main providers of subsidised homes are now the housing associations, not least because all the borrowing by these non-statutory organisations falls outside constraints on public expenditure. Since around half the cost of providing a new home is found by means of borrowing that is repaid out of rents, the public expenditure implications of housing associations building homes are much more favourable than for local authorities continuing to do so. However, constraints on all forms of public spending have led to a severe curtailment of the output of housing associations. Severe reductions over previously published figures emerged from the autumn Statement and Budget in both 1993 and 1994. The position today can be summarised as follows:

**Figure 11.4**
**Public spending on housing 1980/82-1996/97**

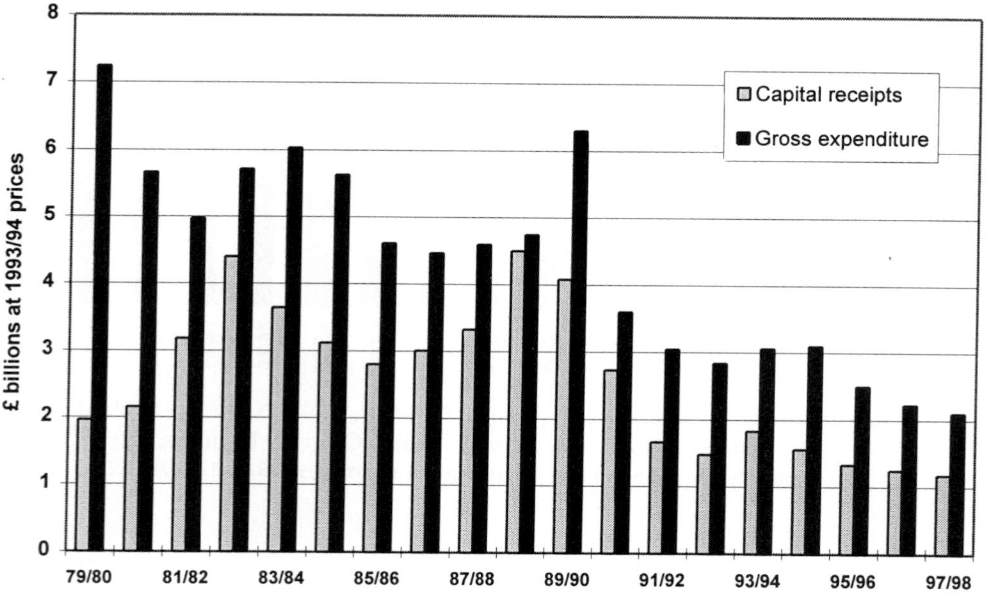

Source:  Department of the Environment

Council housing investment is now set to fall, in real terms, to below one third of its 1979/80 level (Wilcox, 1995). But continuing restrictions on public spending make it unlikely that sufficient amounts of 'new money' will be available to provide the extra homes needed or to renovate all the rundown council estates where so many social problems are now concentrated.

A Joseph Rowntree Foundation report in 1993 advocated an acceleration of the transfer of housing stock out of the ownership of local authorities and into the hands of non-public sector bodies (Wilcox et al, 1993), noting that local housing companies and housing associations fall outside government capital spending controls. While debts on council housing stand at around £20 billion, the value of this stock - assessed, very modestly, at about £10,000 per council home - exceed £40 billion. This gives the margin for borrowing that could generate huge new resources to inject into wholesale renovations.

To March 1995, some 180,000 homes had been transferred into the ownership of newly created bodies; some £2.65 billion had been raised in private finance, not simply to purchase this stock from the councils, but also to undertake substantial programmes of 'catch-up' repairs and improvements that are the envy of local authorities who remain within the grip of public spending limitations. To date, the transfers have been limited to councils where the value of their stock was greater than the outstanding debt (enabling a surplus to be made from the sale). But the Joseph Rowntree Foundation report showed how the system could work well even where the residual debt could not be fully covered by the sale price. Because all future borrowing by the landlord body will not count against the government budget deficit, there can be savings for the Treasury for many years to come.

In other European countries, since direct ownership by municipalities along the lines of UK council housing is so rare, social sector housing landlords are free to raise private finance without the kind of government borrowing controls that apply in this country. With over four million properties still in the hands of local authorities, and with further expenditure on them still severely curtailed, the transfer route - through local housing companies or similar bodies - offers an important opportunity for raising the capital for tomorrow's housing investment.

## The wider benefits of housing investment

To persuade policy-makers of the value of enhanced investment in social housing, it may be necessary to highlight the wider social benefits which accrue from this kind of spending.

### Jobs

At its most simple, investment in construction creates employment, particularly for men in manual jobs where problems of rising unemployment are concentrated. Since it is through work that much of the nation's wealth is redistributed, the creation of employment opportunities in the construction industry combats growing inequalities and helps to forge a more cohesive society. Households disconnected from the labour market are likely to confront, and sometimes to cause, wider social problems - crime, ill health, family breakdown - that are disturbing and expensive for the rest of Society to remedy (Commission on Social Justice, 1994; Hills, 1995; and Chapters 4, 7, 8 and 9).

An extra £100 million of investment in housing would create 1,000 jobs in the construction industry in the first year. In addition, it is estimated that a further 540 jobs would follow as a result of the extra spending by construction workers. Over two years, some 3,000 extra jobs would be generated (Meen, 1992).

Because nearly half of the cost of providing social housing through housing associations is funded through private sector borrowing, extra investment in construction of £1 billion can be secured for less than £550 million of public investment. Furthermore, of this public spending, government will directly recoup between a third and a half in the form of taxes on the income and spending of those who take the jobs, and in the reduction in welfare payments

(Meen, 1993).   This suggests that £500m net per annum of government spending on construction would lead to 30,000 jobs over two years.

Would such investment be inflationary?  There are a number of reasons for thinking not.  Total employment in the construction industry has fallen by half a million (25 per cent) from its level in 1990.  So there is a huge supply of potential workers.  Second, uncertainties that continue to face the private sector building for sale mean that the 1994 level of completions - 155,000 homes - seems unlikely to be increased over the next few years.  Third, training schemes exist that are dependent on on-site opportunities in the construction industry: new recruits, therefore, can be drawn in quite readily to cope with the prospect (at present remote) of any excess demand for labour. Finally, public investment in housing can be concentrated in particular areas where it contributes to wider urban regeneration: it can thereby increase the growth potential of the local economy.

These arguments lead to the conclusion that greater investment in housing can be achieved without a worrying increase in inflation.  The £500m input by government, leading to a total investment of £1 billion, would increase the Retail Price Index by some 0.1 per cent by 1997 (Clapham, 1995).

### Health

There is an impressive array of evidence to explain how housing and *health* interact (Burridge and Ormand, 1993; Arblaster and Hawtin, 1993).  Together, these studies add up to a compelling case for accepting that investment in housing is likely to prevent a range of health problems.

The extreme conditions of street homelessness clearly have a profound effect on health: in-patient hospital stays, and problems with bronchitis, tuberculosis, arthritis, skin diseases and infections as well as psychiatric difficulties are all more prevalent among single people who are homeless (Bines, 1994).  Families living in temporary accommodation of the bed-and-breakfast kind also face a range of hazards, such as resulting from overcrowding, inadequate facilities for preparing food, high rates of accidents and so on.  Inadequate heating and dampness contribute to or exacerbate respiratory disease, heart disease and strokes.  Condensation is bad for asthma and (unsurprisingly) surveys show higher levels of wheezing and chesty coughs for those in homes affected by damp and mould (and this relationship was found to be independent of smoking and socio-economic factors; Arblaster and Hawtin, 1993).

When investment provides homes for homeless households, reduces or eradicates damp and cold conditions through better heating and insulation, or relieves the stresses that contribute to mental illness, there is a pay-back in savings to the National Health Service (Arblaster, 1993; see also Chapter 7).

### Wider social ills

In addition to easing problems for the individual, investment in housing can have an impact on the health and well-being of whole communities.

A side effect of the housing policies which encouraged owner-occupation and confined subsidised rented housing to those in the poorest circumstances, has been the physical concentration of those on the lowest income in particular places - usually council estates. People in these neighbourhoods frequently face 'social exclusion', become labelled as an 'underclass' and find themselves cut off from the wider economy. Recent research has documented how poverty is now increasingly a *geographical* phenomenon (Green, 1994; Noble *et al*, 1994).

Housing policies at both the national and the local level may have helped create the concentrations of deprivation which now exist in inner city areas and on the peripheral estates around them. These policies have led, in turn, to an overload on the communities' ability to provide a satisfactory and safe environment. High child densities, often created by a heavy proportion of single parent households, make it more difficult for children to be socialised and disciplined in ways that have been regarded, in the past, as the norm (Page, 1993). A concentration of deprived households in one place can also overwhelm the social services and the capacities of the police. The consequences of segregating poorer people, marginalising them from mainstream society and creating 'benefits ghettos' of welfare housing, are well documented by researchers in the US (Kasarda, 1993).

However, housing also provides the key to combating these problems. Local authority housing departments, and housing associations, are the points of contact between the wider society, these deprived neighbourhoods and the individuals within them. Housing provides, therefore, the chance to understand the key issues on estates, to act as the intermediaries with local authority departments and other agencies to secure extra resources, and - through their own substantial budgets for repairs, maintenance, cleaning, management and security - to make creative use of the resources spent in the area (Best, 1995). Similarly, housing investment can trigger the building of skills by residents: the activity on the estate can help the community build up its own strengths. The involvement of residents in the management of housing - through estate management boards, management co-operatives and tenant managed organisations - can build up the capacities and confidence of tenants (Watson, 1994; Gibson, 1993).

Ideally, the housing investment which leads to more jobs would directly help those in the poorest areas to get back to work. However, it is unrealistic to expect that there will be many immediate, permanent jobs as a result of public spending on the physical regeneration of disadvantaged urban areas. Research indicates that the potential for job creation is less than is generally imagined: skills are needed and training may not produce these in time; most of the jobs will come through subcontractors, and arrangements with the main contractors - often household names - will be of limited value. Nonetheless, opportunities do exist to provide a more but continuous source of employment for those living on estates and these could be exploited more fully, particularly in relation to repair and maintenance work and the training opportunities that go with this (McGregor, 1995).

Housing providers also have a range of other opportunities to engage the local community in economic activity. Although housing associations find shortages of money make progress slow, there is a growing interest among housing associations in acting as catalysts to build links and develop relationships between neighbourhoods and a range of other agencies. This broader role of housing in community development and in wider economic regeneration seems likely to characterise the future activity of many inner city housing associations (McArthur, 1995). Indeed, through the encouragement and support of 'community enterprise agencies' that can handle area renewal through a partnership between the communities themselves and the public and private sectors, housing associations and local authority housing departments may prove to be key players (Thake, 1993).

## Conclusion

This chapter has argued that housing policies have, in the recent past, had large-scale undesirable consequences on the wider economy. It suggests there has been an over-dependency on an expansion of home ownership, and that greater attention should be given to the revival of private renting.

Despite its recent history, housing policy has the potential to have a very large part to play in healing a number of expensive and unsettling social divisions. The polarisation of society between home-owners and tenants, between the better-off and those on the lowest incomes, between those in work and those without jobs, may have been unintentionally generated by past housing policies and practices, but it is through investment in housing, and through the actions of those engaged in housing work, that the remedies may lie.

In addition to suggesting policies for encouraging investment into the private rented sector (policies which government is already showing an interest in), a substantial enhancement in public spending on social housing is also recommended. This would have wider positive economic and social impacts, not least in generating employment among relatively unskilled, male manual workers, and in reversing the decline of some neighbourhoods where social exclusion is proving costly and disturbing for the rest of society. Housing policies based on market rents and extensive (means-tested) personal subsidies are *not* recommended - such policies result in substantial disincentive to work effects, administrative inefficiencies and the risk of inflation. A better option is to target spending on 'bricks and mortor' subsidies.

A growth in the transfer of council housing into the ownership of local housing companies or newly-formed housing associations is recommended in order to unlock the capital resources required to pay for large-scale renovation. This approach also has the added advantage of encouraging housing associations and local authority housing departments to act as intermediaries between local communities and other agencies in efforts to build up the capacities and confidence of local communities. Such efforts will help to create a stronger social fabric and will assist efforts to address other wider social ills.

# 12 Devolution

*Vernon Bogdanor* [*]

## Introduction

Devolution in Britain is in large part the history of something that has not happened (Rose, 1982). Of six devolution or Home Rule bills since 1886 - the four Irish Home Rule bills of 1886, 1893, 1914 and 1920, and the Scotland and Wales Acts of 1978 - only one, the Irish Home Rule Act of 1920 actually came into effect; but it came into effect in only one part of Ireland, the six counties of north-eastern Ulster which came to form Northern Ireland; the other twenty six counties repudiated Home Rule and broke away entirely from the United Kingdom. Northern Ireland, however, had, paradoxically, been the one part of Ireland which had *not* sought devolution; she had wished simply to retain her membership of the United Kingdom on the same basis as every other part of the country. So it is that the experience of Northern Ireland between 1921 and 1972 evades the central problem associated with dispersing power to one part of the country in a unitary state. For devolution is normally undertaken in order to contain ethnic nationalism; the pressures which it is designed to meet are centrifugal. In Northern Ireland, however, the pressures were not centrifugal but centripetal, the majority in the province seeking to remain within the United Kingdom, not to break away from it. For Northern Ireland, devolution was, in the words of her first Prime Minister, Sir James Craig, in 1921, 'a *final settlement* and supreme sacrifice in the interests of peace, although not asked for by her representatives' (my italics; see Bogdanor, 1979, p.47)[1].

---

[*] Reader in Government, Oxford University and Fellow of Brasenose College, Oxford.

Why has the history of devolution in Britain been so largely one of failure? The answer lies deep in our constitutional principles, themselves the product of a combination of institutional practice, conventions and 'tacit understandings' (see Low, 1904, p.12). Perhaps the most important of these principles is the unitary nature of the British state. Unlike countries such as Germany and the United States, Britain's government is not based on the principle of the division or separation of powers.

Our fundamental - perhaps our only - constitutional principle is that of the supremacy of Parliament. Yet the idea of the supremacy of Parliament creates difficulties for us when we seek to come to terms with a territorial division of powers, whether with Europe or with Scotland. For it leads us to believe that in every political community there must be one supreme political authority. Thus policy-makers and citizens alike find it difficult to understand how, in our relationship with Europe, there could be any alternative to a Europe of states other than a Europe centralised in Brussels, a Europe that, as Hugh Gaitskell once said, would mean the end of a thousand years of history. We tend therefore to see Westminster and Brussels, not as complementary powers, but as engaged in a zero-sum game, a duel which only one side can win. Similarly, we find it difficult to conceive of a Scottish parliament as anything other than a half-way house to the separation of Scotland from the rest of the kingdom. Yet in each case, there is a third alternative, a genuine division and sharing of powers within which each layer of government is able to perform the tasks most suited to it so that it complements rather than dominates the others. That indeed is the rationale of European Union, the idea that power can be shared and sovereignty divided so as to create a political entity capable of carrying out common policies without compromising the identity of the component units. It is no coincidence, therefore, that those who are most sympathetic to European Union tend also to be sensitive to the needs of the non-English parts of the United Kingdom; while it is those hostile to European Union who tend to be rather sceptical of proposals to devolve power from Westminster. For them subsidiarity stops at Whitehall.

Yet, although our notion of the supremacy of Parliament lends itself to a conception of a uniform and homogeneous state, we have, fortunately, rarely taken the doctrine to its logical conclusion. The spirit in which Britain is administered helps to counteract its logic. For, until recently at least, Britain has been able, with Ireland remaining the one glaring exception, to accommodate identities, such as that of the Scots or the Welsh, within the framework of a unitary state. Thus it has been possible for those living in Scotland or in Wales to see themselves both as Scots or Welsh *and* as British without these identities conflicting. It has never been necessary to buttress the unitary state with an ideology of uniformity. The British state, unlike, for example, the French, has never needed to see itself as the guardian of the nation. So it is that the United Kingdom has been able to accommodate a considerable diversity of relationships - devolution in Northern Ireland between 1921 and 1972, looser constitutional relationships with the Channel Islands and the Isle of Man, and a considerable degree of administrative devolution to Scotland and Wales - relationships which have proved perfectly compatible with the unity of the British state.

The traditional relationship between Westminster and Scotland - a relationship that might be described as one of centralisation tempered by goodwill - was, however, put under severe strain by the centralising measures of the Conservative governments of the 1980s and 1990s. The centralisation of power did not, of course, begin with the government first elected in 1979. But the reaction to it had a special colouring in Scotland where a government representing a minority of Scottish voters nevertheless sought to impose its own ideological prescriptions upon the Scottish people. It is true that on occasions when Labour wins a large majority, such as 1945 and 1966, there is the possibility of legislation affecting England being passed against the wishes of the majority of English MPs. But England could never find herself in the position that Scotland has faced since 1987 when Scottish legislation has been regularly passed with the support of no more than the 10 or 11 Conservative MPs out of 72 from Scotland. Such a situation undermines the unwritten contract according to which Scotland has been governed since the Union which requires that a United Kingdom majority treat Scotland with respect and sensitivity to her particular needs.

It is this sense of a national identity under threat that gives rise to the demand for devolution, for a parliament in Edinburgh. Devolution, however, has a dual dynamic. For not only can it re-establish the terms of the contract with Scotland; it can also, in dispersing power from Westminster and Whitehall, offer an example to be followed by other parts of the United Kingdom, by Wales and the English regions. The crucial question, however, is whether a future government can avoid the pitfalls which have dogged Home Rule and devolution in the past by devising a policy which can serve both aims - accommodation of the Scottish desire for autonomy and the dispersal of power from Westminster and Whitehall to the regions and localities of the United Kingdom.

Table 12.1 Scottish opinion on desired political status of Scotland (% response)

|  | Sep 1985 | Mar 1986 | Aug 1988 | Mar 1989 | Nov 1990 | Nov 1991 | May 1993 | Jan 1995 |
|---|---|---|---|---|---|---|---|---|
| An independent Scottish Parliament, separate from England | 29 | 34 | 33 | 33 | 33 | 35 | 31 | 29 |
| A Scottish Parliament with substantial powers, but within the framework of British government system | 44 | 46 | 42 | 46 | 44 | 43 | 50 | 47 |
| No change from present | 21 | 15 | 20 | 17 | 18 | 18 | 16 | 20 |
| Don't know | 6 | 8 | 6 | 3 | 4 | 4 | 2 | 3 |

Source: *System Three Scotland* (polls since 1985)

The fundamental argument of this chapter is that these two aims can be reconciled through the principle of 'rolling devolution', devolution to the nations and regions of the United Kingdom in accordance with popular demand.   The premise must be that any nation or region which seeks devolution is entitled to it; the corollary must be that any nation or region which does not seek devolution should not be allowed to prevent it being introduced elsewhere.

## Box 12.1  Arguments for and against devolution

### Arguments for devolution

Why consider devolution of powers in a unitary state such as the UK?  Various arguments are heard, which may be summarised as follows:

1. *The Scots will not settle for less.*  The evidence is that Scottish opinion has hardened in favour of devolution since it was narrowly carried in the 1979 referendum there (see Table 12.1).  The proportion of Scots who say they want independence is steady, and considerably smaller than the proportion who say that they want some form of Scottish Chamber within the UK.  Proponents of Scottish devolution inside Scotland simply say that it is what the Scots demand after over 15 years of being governed by a party which commands only a quarter of the votes and a seventh of the parliamentary seats in Scotland.  Proponents of devolution outside Scotland add that it is more likely to preserve the Union than either the status quo or - obviously - independence.  They argue that Scottish support for autonomy is broad but not deep.  It is likely to be satisfied by the sort of distinctive provision that has been made in minority areas in other European states, such as the cases of Greenland, the Aaland and Faeroe Islands mentioned in this chapter.  Non-Scottish proponents of Scottish devolution, therefore, see it as a way to save the Union.

2. *There already is a substantial degree of devolved government in the UK that exists without direct democratic control.*  For many years, the Scottish, Welsh, and Northern Irish Offices have controlled most internal functions of government within those areas.  These include responsibility for health, transport, education, land-use planning, and industrial promotion.  Many, but not all, of these functions are actually carried out by local authorities, which get most of their funding from central government.  In the regions of England, many territorial functions of central government have similarly been devolved to regional offices since the 1970s.  Until recently, there was a Babel of boundaries in England.  Although there were Standard Regions, which have been used for reporting statistical data, by no means all departments used them as their regional boundaries.  However, in 1992, the UK government united the regional functions of several different departments to form unitary Regional Offices.  London has no elected authority, as explained in this chapter, but it has a London-wide police force (the Metropolitan Police) which is an agency of a central government department.  Other London-wide services are overseen by a minister with special responsibility for London.

   Furthermore, the movement of many central government functions to agencies since 1979 has led some to complain about 'quangocracy'.  The complaints are particularly vehement in Wales, after scandals at the Welsh Development Agency and elsewhere.  There are not many active Conservatives in Wales, but disproportionately many of them seem to have been involved in running quangos.  Some of the quangos have had a poor financial record.  All this has led to a demand for democratic control of these executive agencies, by means of Welsh and regional English assemblies.

*contd./*

**Box 12.1** (contd.)

3. *The UK state is overcentralised, even as traditionally centralist states such as France are introducing a regional tier of government.* There is no objective measure of centralisation, therefore no grounds on which one can say for sure that one state is too centralised and another one not centralised enough. But those who make this argument buttress it in a number of ways. One, mentioned in this chapter, is the enhanced role given to a Committee of the Regions in the Maastricht Treaty. This in itself proves nothing: there is no evidence so far that the Committee on the Regions will have any influence on the distribution of EC resources. What is probably more important is that large amounts of EC money, from the Regional Fund and the Structural Fund, are distributed in the UK through the relevant territorial ministry - which takes us back to the previous argument. Another argument under this heading refers to James Madison and the American Federalists, who defended the proposed Federal constitution of the USA in 1787 on the grounds that it would limit abuses of power. One local majority might behave tyrannically in one place and another in another. But the division of powers between Federal and state authorities would ensure that there was no overall majority (or, worse, minority), which could override freedom throughout the Union.

**Arguments against devolution**

1. *Outside Scotland, there is no demand for it.* The proposed Welsh Assembly was defeated by a 4 to 1 margin in the 1979 referendum. Although Welsh opinion, like Scottish, has probably been moving in a pro-devolution direction since 1979, it has a long way to go to make up for that overwhelming rejection. In London, as stated in this chapter, the abolition of the GLC in 1986 was unpopular, but it is far from clear that Londoners want it back. And in the rest of England, nobody except local political elites has ever shown any interest in a regional assembly.

2. *Devolution would put further strains on already anomalous features of the constitution,* especially the overrepresentation of Scotland and Wales in the House of Commons, and the presence of Secretaries of State for the three territorial departments in the Cabinet. Measures to rectify these imbalances are recommended in the chapter.

3. *How would the jurisdictional boundaries between devolved and central government be maintained?* Arguments about whether a proposal was within the powers of a devolved assembly would have to be settled somehow. This could only be by a constitutional court, whatever the body was actually called. In particular, which court system would settle disputes between the Scottish Assembly and the UK Parliament about the powers of the former? It could not be either the Scottish or the English court system. The only all-UK courts at present are the House of Lords in its judicial function, and the Judicial Committee of the Privy Council.

4. *It is difficult to define the areas of competence of a devolved legislature or executive.* As explained in the chapter, the distinction between primary and secondary legislation is highly problematic for this purpose, at least as regards legislation already in force. Enumerating functions in a long list, as in the Scotland and Wales Acts in the 1970s, is also problematic. New functions arise and old ones become obsolete. How would the list be kept up-to-date?

5. Some people would say that the introduction of regionally elected Chambers will lead to overgovernment, with five tiers of government in parts of England (two-tier local government, a regional assembly, Westminster, and Europe), and four tiers in the rest of the UK. Administratively this is a weak argument but it may have some political appeal. At the least this argument would suggest that a genuine effort to devolve power should be accompanied by some re-thinking about the functions of government at all levels.

*Iain McLean, Stewart Wood*

## Scottish devolution

The Labour Party is committed to establishing a parliament in Edinburgh and a parliament or 'senedd' in Cardiff, while the Liberal Democrats and their predecessors, the Liberals, have long been committed to Home Rule for Scotland and Wales as part of their programme for a federal system of government for the whole of the United Kingdom. Both parties propose, in the light of Scotland's separate legal system, legislative devolution for Scotland but executive devolution for other parts of the United Kingdom. But legislative devolution for just one part of the country would create a constitutional imbalance between Scotland and the rest of the country - or rather it would accentuate, unacceptably, an already existing imbalance.

For Scotland, like Wales and Northern Ireland, already has a Secretary of State who can argue her case in the Cabinet. Like Wales she is over-represented in the House of Commons, there being 72 MPs from Scotland as compared with the 57 to which she would be entitled if the same criteria were applied to Scotland as are applied to England. With devolution, Scotland would enjoy the additional advantage of a directly elected parliament able to press her claims upon Westminster. The extra political weight which a parliament would give to Scotland would mean that she would probably be able to attract public funds which would otherwise go to the more deprived regions of England, especially perhaps the north of England. It was indeed a revolt from Labour MPs primarily from northern constituencies that was largely responsible for undermining the devolution bills in the 1970s (see Guthrie and McLean, 1978).

The most striking anomaly to which legislative devolution in Scotland would give rise is the 'West Lothian Question', so named in honour of the then MP for West Lothian, Tam Dalyell, MP for Linlithgow since 1983, who pressed it with such pertinacity in the 1970s. Dalyell asked what justification there could be for the fact that, after devolution, English, Welsh and Northern Irish MPs would no longer be able to vote on Scottish domestic matters, but Scottish MPs would still be able to vote on English, Welsh and Northern Irish domestic matters. What justification was there for the fact that Scottish MPs would still be able to vote on health and education in West Bromwich, while English MPs would no longer be able to vote on health and education in West Lothian?

'West Lothian' problems surfaced during the experience of Stormont. In May 1965, the 12 Northern Ireland MPs, then all Ulster Unionists who almost always supported the Conservatives, voted against the Labour government's Manchester Corporation bill and Rent bill, the provisions of which did not apply to Northern Ireland. The government then enjoyed a majority of only three, and the Prime Minister, Harold Wilson, gave the Ulster Unionists a veiled warning. 'I would hope that Northern Ireland Members who are here, and who are welcomed here, for the duties they have to perform on behalf of the United Kingdom in many matters affecting Northern Ireland, would consider their position in matters where we have no equivalent right in Northern Ireland' (House of Commons Debates, 6 May 1965, col. 1561).

The 'West Lothian question' is, as a matter of pure logic, unanswerable short of establishing a full-scale federal state for which there is certainly no demand in England. It would be constitutionally impossible entirely to exclude

Scottish MPs from Westminster while Scotland continued to remain part of the United Kingdom; and the so-called 'in and out' solution, championed by Gladstone at one time during the proceedings on the 1893 Home Rule Bill, offers the worst of all possible worlds (see Chapter 2 in Bogdanor, 1979). According to the 'in and out' solution, Scottish MPs would only be allowed to vote at Westminster on non-devolved issues. But this could mean that there would be two different majorities at Westminster, according to whether domestic or non-domestic issues were being discussed. Thus, on education and health, it might be that there was a Conservative majority able to sustain a Conservative government, since Scottish MPs would be excluded from voting, while on foreign affairs and defence, when Scottish MPs would be readmitted, there might be a Labour majority able to sustain a Labour government. It would hardly be possible to govern a modern industrial state on such a basis.

The West Lothian question draws attention to an anomaly inherent in devolving legislative power to just one part of a country. There is no inherent reason, however, why an anomaly of this kind should disrupt devolution. In the European Parliament, there is an analogous anomaly. For British MEPs currently vote on matters connected with the Social Chapter, even though Britain, under the Maastricht Treaty, has opted out of it. There are also Continental examples showing that where the will to conciliate is present, special treatment for one part of a country, far from stimulating separatism, can actually help contain it. In Finland, the Aaland Islands with their Swedish population, have long had their own assembly, while in Denmark, the Faeroes and Greenland enjoy such wide autonomy that they have been able to remain outside the European Union while Denmark remains a member.

Thus the question of whether recognition of Scotland's national identity is compatible with the maintenance of the United Kingdom should be decided not on the basis of administrative tidiness or logical symmetry but on the basis of practical judgement. The West Lothian question is worrying, not so much because of the anomaly to which it draws attention, for all constitutions contain anomalies; but because it draws attention to the fact that devolution would unacceptably accentuate an already existing constitutional imbalance, thereby making it intolerable. Without further adjustments, legislative devolution to Scotland would create a lop-sided structure of government in the United Kingdom in which the citizens of England, Wales and Northern Ireland would become second-class citizens, under-represented and without assemblies which could fight for their interests as the Scottish parliament would fight for the interests of Scotland. How can such a constitutional imbalance be mitigated?

If Scotland were to enjoy legislative devolution, there would seem to be no case for retaining the Secretaryship of State. The Scottish Office exists primarily to administer policies where a separate Scottish dimension is possible. After devolution, however, those policy areas will be in the hands of the Scottish parliament. Responsibility for policy areas where no such Scottish dimension is possible ought to be transferred to non-territorial Whitehall departments.

Secondly, there would be no case either for continuing with the over-representation of Scotland after devolution. Northern Ireland, during the years between 1921 and 1972 when she enjoyed devolution, far from being over-represented in Parliament, was actually under-represented, returning only 12 MPs (13 before the abolition of the university seats in 1948) to the House of Commons rather than the 17 to which she would have been entitled on a population basis. Scotland ought at the very least to have her representation reduced from 72 MPs to 57 after devolution; and there is a case for reducing her representation even below that, using Northern Ireland as a precedent. Such a reduction in the number of Scottish MPs would not, of course, be an answer to the West Lothian question. But it would mitigate its effects, since it would become less likely, although still perfectly possible, that Scottish MPs would affect the balance between a Labour and Conservative government. The anomaly might, however, then become one that the English, the Welsh and the Northern Irish would be prepared to accept as a price worth paying to keep Scotland within the United Kingdom.

A devolution package of this type amounts essentially to a renegotiation of the terms under which Scotland is to remain in the United Kingdom. Unlike the 1978 Scotland Act, which provided for the retention of the Secretary of State for Scotland and of Scottish over-representation at Westminster, such a package would impose losses upon Scotland as well as gains. It may indeed be that the Scottish people would not want devolution upon such terms; they might believe that a parliament purchased at the cost of the removal of the Secretary of State and a reduction in Scottish representation at Westminster is too high a price to pay, and that it would be better to maintain the status quo. It is, surely, for the Scottish people to decide which alternative they prefer, and there must, therefore, be a strong case for putting a devolution package of the type outlined to the Scottish people in a referendum.

## Executive devolution

According to current Labour Party proposals, Wales is not to be offered legislative devolution but rather executive devolution, as will any English regions to which devolution is offered. Executive devolution appears at first sight as merely a weaker variant of legislative devolution. Under executive devolution, an assembly would not have the power to pass primary legislation, but only secondary legislation, responsibility for the framework of primary laws remaining with Westminster. Executive devolution, however, is not so much a weaker form of devolution than legislative devolution, but a quite different form which would introduce into Britain a wholly new and as yet untried structure of governmental relationships.

For while legislative devolution involves a *transfer* of powers, executive devolution involves a *division* of powers. It would be possible to ascertain the precise functions of a parliament with legislative powers simply by inspecting the provisions of the devolution legislation and looking at the statute book. With executive devolution, however, the functions which an assembly enjoys would depend not only upon the provisions of the devolution legislation, but also upon the way in which legislation for the devolved areas is drawn up by the government and the degree of discretion which the government thinks it right to confer upon the assemblies. For there is, in Britain at least, no clear dividing line between policy making and administration and no general rule to determine whether a particular matter falls under primary legislation in which case it is to be retained, or secondary legislation in which case it is to be devolved.

Legislative devolution involves a decision as to whether or not to transfer responsibility for a particular function, for example, education. Executive devolution, by contrast, involves the additional decision as to *how much* responsibility should be transferred. This requires an answer to the prior question of how primary legislation ought to be drafted. If primary legislation is drafted loosely, then there will be scope for the assembly; if, on the other hand, it is drafted tightly, the scope for the assembly would be correspondingly reduced. It would thus be possible for a government to limit the autonomy of an assembly by drafting legislation in such a way as to leave it with little scope for independent action. Indeed, a Conservative government in London faced with a Labour assembly in Cardiff or Liverpool might well be tempted to limit the freedom of action of the assemblies to prevent them from frustrating government policy on a policy such as, for example, the continuation of grant maintained schools.

In Britain, legislative and executive powers have in the past been so closely fused that, in the words of the Royal Commission on the Constitution in 1973, the division between them 'is not a precise one, and under the present arrangements they are not clearly separated' (Royal Commission on the Constitution, 1973, para. 828). Past legislation does not seem to have been guided by any very clear principles in this regard. In the past the dividing line has often been drawn simply for convenience, related, perhaps, to considerations of parliamentary time. This is because the distinction between primary and secondary legislation was never intended to provide the basis for a division of powers between different elected bodies. Therefore, with regard to existing legislation, the Welsh and regional assemblies would find that their powers were of uneven scope and depth since there would be no reason why the division between primary and secondary legislation in one policy area, for example health, should match the division in another, for example, education. Thus the initial powers of the assemblies would have no clear rationale. This would make an integrated approach to policy-making extremely difficult. There would be no alternative to accepting this situation at the outset, for any attempt to adjust all relevant statutes to provide a more logical dividing line would simply mean delaying devolution.

Even so, the assemblies would not be the final authorities on the policies for which they were responsible. For Westminster, under the model of executive devolution, would still retain control of all primary legislation. Moreover, the majority of devolved functions will involve the supervision of services delivered by local authorities. This means that policies involving, for example, education or the social services would have to proceed through three layers of government - central government, the assembly and the local authority. It may become more difficult, after devolution, for central government to draw up primary legislation effectively since it would have lost contact with the local authorities actually delivering the services, such contact being mediated by the assemblies. The assemblies will be in a better position to appreciate these needs; but, because they will have no legislative powers, they will have to rely upon close co-operation with the Secretary of State for Wales or the Secretary of State for the Environment to promote legislation for the areas for which they are responsible. Since these ministers, however, may belong to a different party from that of the majority in the assemblies, co-operation cannot by any means be assured. What is clear is that executive devolution, even more than legislative devolution, relies upon co-operation between the assemblies and central government. Devolution is likely to work successfully only if there is a spirit of compromise between government and the assemblies which is able to overcome the practical problems involved.

Executive devolution, then, devolution of a 'horizontal' type, is not just a weaker form of legislative devolution than devolution of a 'vertical' type, but a wholly different kind of animal raising problems which have not hitherto been confronted in the British political system. If executive devolution is to prove effective, two fundamental problems will need to be resolved.

The first is that, since, by contrast with Scotland, there are few specifically Welsh bills, and hardly any bills specifically framed for particular regions, statutes in relevant issue areas will have to be framed differently for those regions of the country with executive devolution from those without it. For, if they were to be framed similarly, then either they would be drawn up too loosely for the regions without devolution in which case ministers would enjoy too wide a discretion and wider delegated powers than Parliament would otherwise have chosen; or, alternatively, legislation would be drawn up too tightly for the areas with assemblies in which case they will have insufficient scope for policy-making.

The second problem is to devise principles which might regulate the dividing line between primary and secondary legislation. This could not, as we have seen, be done immediately, but if executive devolution was to have any rationale at all, it would have to be achieved eventually. Such principles have been developed in the Federal Republic of Germany where the structure of public law 'displays a relatively high degree of coherence and homogeneity' so that 'it is possible ... to achieve a consistency of principles ... which is unattainable within the traditions of pragmatic positivism which have shaped both the common law and the statutory public law in Britain'. To develop similar principles in Britain, therefore, would involve 'the review and re-writing of major slices of public law, and with the express intention of removing numerous powers from the hands of ministers' (Johnson, 1973, paras. 6, 134). What is needed is to make Westminster legislation in relation to Wales 'framework' legislation as is done in Germany, by gradually amending existing statutes and suitably drawing up new ones. In Germany, however, the division of powers in the federal system is buttressed by a constitutional court which ensures that the demarcation lines are observed. In Britain, there is, of course, no such constitutional court and there is no way in which Parliament at Westminster could bind itself to observe principles which happened to be drawn up by a particular government at any one particular time.

Thus, if it is to prove successful, devolution to Wales and to the English regions would require a considerable alteration in British constitutional practice. It would require governments to accept principles which limit their power. It would require government and assemblies alike to be willing to share power, to co-operate rather than indulge in adversarial relationships. It would require, in short, a change in the political practices of British government.

## The Welsh case

What are the merits of the case that devolved power of this kind should be given to Wales now? When, in the 1970s, Labour ministers decided to offer devolution to Scotland, Wales seems almost to have been added on as an afterthought. The presumption seems to have been 'if Scotland, then Wales'. But the configuration of political forces in Wales was very different from that in Scotland. In the October 1974 general election, the SNP, with 30 per cent of the Scottish vote, had become the second largest party in Scotland in terms of votes and clearly threatened Labour's electoral hegemony there. Support for Plaid Cymru, on the other hand, was actually lower in October 1974 in terms of percentage of the vote per opposed candidate than it had been in 1970, having fallen from 11.5 per cent per opposed candidate to 10.7 per cent. This gap in the level of support for the two nationalist parties remains. In the 1992 general election, the SNP gained 21 per cent of the Scottish vote, but won just 3 seats while Plaid Cymru's vote was 8.8 per cent, although it succeeded in winning 4 seats.

Nationalism in Scotland is a political force which unites, but in Wales it is divisive primarily because of the language issue. In Scotland, the institutions of nationhood - the church, the legal system, the universities - elicit wide feelings of sympathy amongst almost all Scots. In Wales, by contrast, the most obvious badge of Welsh identity - the language - incites conflict in a principality in which nearly 80 per cent of the population cannot speak Welsh. If, as the founder and first president of Plaid Cymru, Saunders Lewis, maintained, the language is 'more important than self-government' (see Bogdanor, 1979, p.125), then the electoral prospects of Plaid Cymru cannot be very great. In fact the party's successes in general elections have been confined to Welsh-speaking North and West Wales, while the SNP's vote is fairly evenly spread across Scotland.

The language issue was one of the reasons for the defeat of devolution in Wales by a majority of four to one in the 1979 referendum, despite the fact that three of the four political parties in Wales - excluding only the Conservatives - favoured it. The question is whether Welsh opinion has changed so massively since 1979 that a majority now favours devolution; and whether, in the absence of such evidence, a government claiming allegiance to democratic values could be justified in imposing devolution on Wales against the wishes of its inhabitants. That is the case for a referendum in Wales.

## Devolution in England

Many, although by no means all, of the problems associated with devolution in Britain arise because it is being proposed on an asymmetrical basis. Devolution is being proposed for Scotland, for Wales and perhaps also for some of the English regions, rather than for the United Kingdom as a whole.

A number of the problems could be avoided were 'Home Rule All Round' to be proposed, transforming Britain in one fell swoop from a unitary into a federal system. The strength of the federalist argument lies in the fact that the case for devolution in the English regions and Wales is not wholly dissimilar to the case for devolution in Scotland. That case is based on the need to disperse power from the centre in *every* part of the United Kingdom. For Britain is now by far the most centralised member state of the European Union, and one of the most centralised states in the world. Thus, a policy of 'devolution all round', to relieve the over-concentration of power in Whitehall and diminish the span of control of central government could benefit every part of the United Kingdom, not just Scotland and Wales.

A policy of this kind, moreover, has been carried out in the post-war years by those Continental countries that had hitherto suffered from over-centralisation - France, Italy and Spain. Indeed, the other member states of the European Union of a similar size to Britain - France, Germany, Italy and Spain - all have regional layers of government. The Maastricht Treaty, by creating an advisory Committee of the Regions, explicitly recognised the constitutional role of the regions in building European Union. Since many European projects are planned on a regional basis, and since structural funds are administered on a regional basis also, Britain is likely, in the absence of a regional layer, to suffer in the competition for funds. 'Without effective regional groupings', the Audit Commission declared in 1991, 'the United Kingdom will lose out' (Audit Commission, 1991, p.40). Thus the argument for the dispersal of power from the centre and the creation of a regional layer of government is much strengthened by developments in the European Union.

Nevertheless, the introduction of a federal system of government, through one legislative act, while no doubt logical, is hardly practical politics. It would either condemn parts of the country which did not want devolution to have it because Scotland wanted it; or, alternatively, it would compel Scotland to wait for devolution until every other part of the United Kingdom wanted it, and that could prove a very long time indeed. The proposal to implement a federal scheme in one fell swoop flies in the face of reality.

It is because the demand for regionalism in many parts of England is so insubstantial that the Labour Party faces such difficulty in drawing up a policy on devolution that can both meet the needs of Scotland and yet not arouse a backlash from England. The sensible solution would be to approach federalism in a piece-meal manner, granting devolution to those areas which want it, while not forcing it on those which are opposed to it. The Labour Party could derive considerable benefit from studying the experience of Spain which faced a similar problem after the death of Franco in 1975 when democracy was restored. For, in Spain, there was a strong demand for autonomy in the historic provinces - the Basque country and Catalonia - but much less demand elsewhere. The solution was found through the principle of *rolling devolution*. Autonomy was given to the historic provinces immediately, but at the same time it was announced that any other region of the country which sought autonomy could enjoy it also. Because devolution in the Basque country and Catalonia seemed to be working successfully, it was not long before the demand for devolution made itself felt in the other provinces, so that Spain today is a state of autonomous communities, a quasi-federal state comprising seventeen autonomous regions each with their own government and parliament.

So also in Britain, any future government should lay down two principles governing its devolution policy. The first is that devolution will be given only to those nations and regions of the United Kingdom which seek it; the second is that a nation or region which rejects devolution cannot prevent another nation or region from embracing it.

Is there, however, any region of England which would actually seek devolution? In many parts of England, the regions, it is true, are ghosts, with no reality in popular consciousness. There have been suggestions that there is a demand for devolution in the North of England. In the 1970s, northern opinion was primarily directed towards preventing Scottish devolution which it believed would divert public funds from the north of England to Scotland. This is of course a legitimate reason for demanding regional autonomy, and policy-makers would be ill-advised to confirm or deny claims for devolved chambers based on judgements about motivation. Nevertheless, it does not indicate that the North is a particularly compelling candidate for trying out devolution within England.

There is, perhaps, a stronger latent demand for devolution in London. It is, after all, absurd that London should be one of the very few, if not the only, capital of a democratic country to have no authority or forum of its own. Since the abolition of the GLC in 1986, London has been governed by the 32 London boroughs, by a host of government-appointed quangos, by joint bodies and committees and by central government departments. The creation of a Minister for London by the Conservatives, a junior minister in the Department of the Environment, offers tacit acknowledgement that London, is from the point of view of government, a single entity; and yet, there is no body that is responsible for London as a whole, for its transport system, its health service and its education system.

It would be sensible, then, for a government to begin its devolution policy by creating, together with a Scottish parliament, a regional authority for London. This would not be a revived GLC, for the GLC enjoyed few functional responsibilities of its own and therefore sought to encroach upon the powers of the London boroughs. It came, indeed, to be squashed between the boroughs and central government, and acquired a reputation for political extremism. Even so, if survey evidence in the mid-1980s is to be believed, the majority of Londoners were opposed to the abolition of the GLC. It is likely that there remains a basic London patriotism which would welcome the creation of a London-wide authority with substantial functions of its own, devolved from central government, and which could speak for the city. There are clear London-wide issues, such as transport, the health service and the future of the London hospitals, which could be better resolved by a London authority than by central government and a jumble of assorted quangos.

## Box 12.2  What powers should devolved assemblies have?

Some of the powers to be devolved are easy to describe. For instance, a Scottish Assembly should scrutinise all legislation that would change Scottish law. This might have wider ramifications than it seems, since some quite substantial matters of commercial and property law are handled differently in Scotland from the rest of the UK. But there is no good objection to letting Scots law be determined by the Scots. If anything may be held to have been guaranteed in the Act of Union, that was. Likewise, most policies to do with minority languages can be devolved to the administration of the countries where the languages are spoken.

The powers which in other countries are typically handled by a Ministry of the Interior are also relatively easy to transfer. These include most things done by the Department of the Environment and the Home Office in England, which are already done by the three territorial ministries in the rest of the UK. The recently created Department of National Heritage is an excellent candidate for a similar break-up. Transport is a bit trickier, and education, social services and health are trickier still. In each case there are either network arguments or arguments for national uniformity. For instance, the Department of Transport sees itself as responsible for the national highway network, the management of which has been devolved to a Highways Agency which has <u>not</u> been incorporated into the new regional government structure. Furthermore railway, and airport, privatisations have been designed in ways that do not fit well with regional government. However, they do not fit well either with any national network perspective, so the network argument for keeping transport as a Whitehall function could be overridden by an incoming government.

Education, health, and social services all involve political arguments about national uniformity which cross-cut those about devolution. Social services are the easiest to deal with. An incoming government which believes that social service benefits should vary according to the conditions of regional labour markets would have grounds for transferring them to regional governments and allowing them to vary the level of benefits. One which believed that standards should be nationally uniform would have no reason to transfer their administration. Education policy since 1979 has involved some Jacobin centralism (such as the National Curriculum, and the funding councils for higher education), and some extreme localism, such as the devolution of control over school budgets to individual schools. However, there is no reason why education should not be overseen by regional governments as it is in Germany. Health policy has moved since 1979 from an attempt to iron out regional inequalities from the centre (a policy whose much-delayed culmination was the decision by Health Secretary Virginia Bottomley to shut several London hospitals in 1995) to an attempt to mimic the market within a uniform service. An incoming government of any complexion has to decide whether to keep, modify, or scrap the NHS internal market (see Chapter 7). Only when it has made that decision can it decide whether there are any health functions that can be devolved.

The proliferation of 'Next Steps Agencies' poses a problem for devolution. Next Steps Agencies are divisions of the civil service which are responsible for the delivery of a service, and which are run as near as possible on commercial lines, complete with a mission statement and a chief executive. A government which wished to devolve oversight of, say, prisons or trunk roads to regional bodies would have to either renegotiate the agency agreement, so that the Next Steps Agency was responsible to different bodies for its operations in their regions, or scrap the agency and take the function back into the mainstream civil service.

Devolution of functions entails devolution of funds. Some commentators do not wish devolved assemblies to be given tax-raising powers, except in Scotland. The Scots may or may not be pleased to pay higher taxes in order to support a wider range of services delivered by a devolved assembly. People regularly tell the pollsters, throughout the UK, that they would rather pay more tax for more services than less tax for fewer services. But talk is cheap. Outside Scotland, the amount of money available for devolved services might be fixed centrally. Each region would lobby for itself, which need not be sinister providing that every region has a devolved body, but could be awkward if only some do. But there is also a case for tax-raising powers, based on the principle that an administration responsible for expenditure should also be responsible for raising at least some of the revenue to pay for it.

*Iain McLean*

Indeed it could be argued that the condition of, for example, the London hospitals, the underground system or indeed transport planning as a whole in London would be improved if London enjoyed an authority which represented the wishes of the users of these services. If the authority were to be elected, like the Scottish parliament, by proportional representation, there would be little danger of extremists coming to control it, as occurred with the GLC. Moreover, it would be far easier to implement devolution in London than in the north of England, since London, like Scotland and Wales, already enjoys a unitary structure of local government, while much of the north of England does not. An elected assembly inserted upon a two-tier structure of local government would, as the Welsh Council of Labour said of a similar proposal in the 1970s, be 'like a jellyfish on a bed of nails' (see Bogdanor, 1979, p.143). Devolution in other parts of England would seem to require a reform of local government to create new unitary authorities, a problem which does not arise in London. If devolution worked well in the capital, however, it could be expected to give rise to a demand for devolution in other regions of England. Thus an effective regional authority in London could prove an excellent advertisement for a policy of rolling devolution, the only feasible way in which a quasi-federal Britain could ever in practice come about.

## Government in a devolved state

### Regions and Local Authorities

A prime purpose of devolution is to disperse power in an over-centralised state. Yet this is not to be achieved simply by establishing new parliaments and legislatures. Were the Scottish parliament or the regional assemblies to seek to take power from local authorities, the result of devolution would be, not decentralisation, but the centralisation of power, to Edinburgh, Cardiff, Liverpool and Newcastle, and away from local authorities within Scotland, Wales and the regions.

There is undoubtedly a real danger that a devolved parliament and assemblies would encroach upon the prerogatives of local government. For the Scottish parliament and the regional assemblies would, presumably, be responsible for distributing grants to local authorities. The amount of grant which local authorities received would largely determine the extent of the autonomy which they enjoyed. The parliament and the assemblies, however, will be composed of elected members with their own distinctive views as to the proper shape of local government spending; they will have their own geographical and functional concerns, and they may well seek to press these concerns upon local authorities and to use their control of grants to ensure that their views are taken into account. Were that to happen, local authorities could become little more than executants of the policy of the parliament and assemblies, and local choice would be drastically reduced if not eliminated.

When Scottish local authorities, for example, come to negotiate with a Scottish parliament for funds, the local authorities will be competing with the parliament itself which may wish to earmark a certain proportion of central government grant for its own purposes. If the Scottish parliament wishes, as is quite likely, to determine priorities for Scotland, then it will wish to have influence over how available moneys are spent. It would be perfectly possible for the Scottish parliament to retain grant which central government believes is better distributed to local authorities. Or, alternatively, it could decide to spend more than it has been allocated, making up the shortfall by forcing Scottish local authorities to raise their rates of council tax in order to maintain the existing level of services. There seems, therefore, to be some possibility of a built-in conflict between the Scottish parliament and local authorities in Scotland.

But devolution need not necessarily lead to so malign a scenario. It could be avoided if central government were to earmark that portion of the funds which it pays to the Scottish parliament and the assemblies for distribution to the local authorities. Moreover, it could be argued that, after devolution, local authorities would be in a stronger position negotiating with a parliament or with an assembly than they are at present negotiating with central government. For such consultation as local authorities at present enjoy with central government over the distribution of grant does not in practice give them any significant influence over either its size or its distribution which remain primarily matters for the Cabinet to decide. A Scottish parliament, by contrast, or a London assembly, will be more familiar with, and more sympathetic to, Scottish and London local authorities respectively; the parliament and the assembly will have more information about local problems than central government can ever hope to have. Thus local authorities might well find it easier to make their wishes known and to secure attention to these wishes when negotiating with a directly elected parliament and assemblies than they can achieve at present when negotiating in Whitehall. Moreover, the Scottish Parliament and regional assemblies will be able to take over the running of many bodies and quangos which are at present appointed by central government. That would lead to greater democratic control over an already existing layer of administration and perhaps better and more cost effective control. Devolution could, therefore, lead to improvements in public administration and to services that are more responsive to those who use them.

### Devolution and equality

The commitment to devolution poses a particular problem for a government which is dedicated to the principle of equality of treatment in the provision of public services. The Left has often under-estimated the importance of local and national allegiances. European socialist parties have historically subscribed to the view 'that large centralised states were progressive and small regional autonomies reactionary' (Seton-Watson, 1977, p.445). In the 1880s, Joseph Chamberlain opposed Home Rule to Ireland in part because he believed that the problems of the Irish peasant were no different in kind from those of the Welsh agricultural labourer or the Scottish crofter. These problems would be remedied not by a parliament in Dublin but by a powerful radical government at Westminster. So, also, in the 1970s, left-wingers like Eric Heffer and Neil Kinnock opposed devolution because they believed that the problems of the Scottish and the Welsh working-class were no different in kind from the problems of the English working-class. The problems would be remedied not by devolved assemblies but by a powerful socialist government at Westminster. Arguments of this type proved crucial in defeating devolution both in the 1880s and in the 1970s.

The development of the welfare state has made it more difficult to promulgate an effective devolution policy. For one fundamental principle of the welfare state is that benefits should depend upon need and not upon geography. A deprived child in Glasgow should not receive better benefits than a similarly deprived child in Liverpool, simply because Glasgow happens to enjoy an assembly while Liverpool does not. There is, therefore, an inherent tension between devolution which involves a dispersal of powers, and equality of treatment. A government committed to devolving power, therefore, must define the proper scope of diversity very carefully. Would, for example, a government of the Left be prepared to allow every secondary school in a Conservative region to become grant-maintained? Would a government of the Left allow a regional authority to privatise the National Health Service within its region - and if not, by what principles could the regional authority be denied such a power? To create an elected parliament and assemblies is to hand a weapon to those who will run them. It would be unrealistic to assume that the weapon will be used only for the purposes which governments in Westminster think desirable.

*Jurisdictional boundaries*

Devolution will only prove successful if there is a genuine will to disperse power and the spirit of co-operation that makes it possible. It would have to be accompanied by what the Royal Commission on the Constitution called 'a new style of thinking, positively favourable to devolution and based on co-operation rather than the exercise of central authority' (Royal Commission on the Constitution, 1973, para. 282). But how is such a 'new style of thinking' to be achieved?

It will be essential, after devolution, to limit the danger of confrontation between the Scottish parliament, the Welsh and regional assemblies, and central government. The best way of achieving this is by minimising the role of ministers in resolving disputes and giving that role to the courts. In the 1978 Scotland Act, in addition to the role of the courts in reviewing the *vires* of Acts of the proposed Scottish Assembly, the Secretary of State was given the power to override the Assembly if it used its powers in a manner contrary to the public interest or in such a way as to affect a non-devolved matter. Thus, if the Scottish Assembly had sought to use its planning powers to prevent the construction of military airfields, the Secretary of State would have been able to use the override, since defence would have been a reserved matter.

The experience of Northern Ireland, however, on the very rare occasions when the Northern Ireland Parliament sought to use its powers in a manner displeasing to the British government, shows how difficult it is in practice for the government to exercise its reserve powers. In 1922, for example, the Northern Ireland government proposed to abolish proportional representation in local government elections, a measure which lay within its legislative competence, but which, the British government believed, went against the spirit of devolution because it would be seen by the Catholic minority as a measure hostile to it. Winston Churchill, the Colonial Secretary, wrote that the measure was 'inopportune' but the Northern Ireland government declared that if the abolition of proportional representation was vetoed, it would resign. The British government was forced to give way (Bogdanor, 1979; pp.52-3). It is a mistake, therefore, to believe that the presence and threatened use of reserve powers by the central government will necessarily prevail when central government policies conflict with the wishes of a directly elected devolved body. Thus, policy override powers would be risky to use in practice since they would put the British government in direct conflict with a majority in one part of the kingdom. The Scottish parliament or the assembly in question would claim that it, rather than the government, represented the feeling of the nation or region that it was responsible for, and there could be a damaging confrontation with the government.

Therefore disputes between the British government and the Scottish Parliament should be resolved, so far as possible, not by the government, but by the courts, as is often the case in federal systems. The Judicial Committee of the Privy Council would, no doubt, be the body whose function it was to determine the *vires* of legislation emanating from the Scottish parliament. If that were to happen, the Judicial Committee would become in effect an embryonic constitutional court. Admittedly, the Judicial Committee would be able to pronounce only on Scottish and not on Westminster legislation. Nevertheless, if it were to decide a dispute over the division of powers in Scotland's favour, it would be difficult to imagine Westminster deliberately choosing to legislate for Scotland on a matter which the Judicial Committee had ruled was devolved. In practice, therefore, the Judicial Committee might well come to assume something like the role of a constitutional court with respect to Scottish legislation. To this extent, devolution would provide a powerful impetus to a codified constitution for Britain as a whole. For it would be proposing a quasi-federal system of government with a politically sanctified division of powers and a court to act as arbiter of that division.

We have seen, moreover, that there are other areas where constitutional definition is likely to be required if devolution is to prove successful. If executive devolution, a category hitherto unknown in the United Kingdom, were to work, there would have to be a process of definition of the proper sphere of primary and secondary legislation such as occurs in the German constitutional system. Moreover, if the Scottish parliament and assemblies are not to encroach upon local authorities, principles would need to be worked out to ensure that devolution strengthens local autonomy rather than encroaching upon it. There would have to be a defence of the rights of local authorities, a Charter of Rights perhaps for local government so that it could secure its autonomy not only against central government, but also against a Scottish parliament or regional assembly.

The purpose of devolution is to destroy the omni-competence of Parliament. If it succeeds in doing so, it will force us to develop a corpus of explicitly constitutional thought. Devolution will work best if it is implemented not in isolation but as part of a larger constitutional settlement, involving the judicial protection of rights and a juridically guaranteed division of powers between different layers of government. Thus devolution involves nothing less than a commitment to a new kind of constitutional relationship in Britain, a relationship based on power-sharing. That would be a reaction against the trends of over three hundred years. For it was the Glorious Revolution of 1689 which emphasised the principle of the supremacy of Parliament. The time has now come to de-emphasise it.

## Notes

1. This book gives a history of earlier Home Rule and devolution measures.

2. See unpublished paper by Iain McLean (1995), *The Representation of Scotland and Wales in the House of Commons.*

## References

Audit Commission (1991), *A Rough Guide to Europe: Local Authorities and the European Community*, London: HMSO.

Bogdanor, V. (1979), *Devolution*, Oxford: Oxford University Press.

Guthrie, R. and McLean, I. (1978), 'Another part of the periphery', *Parliamentary Affairs*.

Johnson, N. (1973), *Federalism and Decentralisation in Germany*, Royal Commission on the Constitution, Research Paper I, London: HMSO.

Low, S. (1904), *The Governance of England*, London: T. Fisher Unwin.

Rose, R. (1982), *Understanding the United Kingdom: The Territorial Dimension in Government*, Harlow: Longman.

Seton-Watson, H. (1977), *Nations and States*, London: Methuen.

# 13 Britain in Europe

*George Brock* *

## Introduction: Britain's position in Europe

Napoleon said of Germany that it was a country that never reached a fixed state of being but was always on the way to becoming something. The same could be said of the European Union (EU). Many politicians dream of a day when the Union's hiccuping, staccato sequence of constitutional conferences decides a blueprint which will not need altering almost as soon as the signatures are dry. They will be disappointed. The issues facing the leaders of the European Union between 1996 and the end of the century, the legacy of the Cold War's end, are sufficiently difficult to guarantee that the deals which must be struck will not be set in stone. The shape and scope of European integration will divide and preoccupy the continent's states for the next decade and beyond.

British governments face a unique combination of difficulties in the EU not confronted by any other member state. Firstly, Britain's economy and welfare state evolved separately from those of its Continental counterparts. Britain's economic and political systems are structurally different from those of other member states of the European Union (examples include: its first-past-the-post electoral system, the degree of centralisation of political power, and historical economic peculiarities derived from early industrialisation such as the dependence on mass production manufacturing industries and imperial markets). Secondly, thanks to misjudgement of the EEC's potential and to General de Gaulle's hostility, Britain joined the Community late. Its ex-imperial and transatlantic economy has adapted slowly to European markets.

---

* European Editor of The Times

Thirdly, belief in the benevolence of European integration has never taken hold in Britain while faith in the ideal has been, at least until recently, a public religion in several continental states. The experience of World War in continental Europe prompted the founding six members of the EC to integrate in order to avert future conflict. In Britain, however, the War left a sense of distance and distinctness from mainland Europe and its emerging political forms. Consequently, the idea of national sovereignty and the continuity of political institutions is stronger in the UK than in other EU nations. Proposals to diminish the powers of these institutions arouse strong fears.

Britain also faces special difficulties in formulating a policy for the EU. 'European Policy' is a moving target. A government must develop consistent positions (simultaneously defensible to the House of Commons and attractive to allies on the continent) on everything from cooperation treaties with Russia to nitrate norms for lettuce. The task of hammering out positions which attract support in Brussels or Strasbourg while satisfying voters at home has proved testing for British politicians accustomed to adversarial politics. The negotiating politics of the EU require skills not normally sharpened at Westminster. The two-party system engenders a culture of adversarialism that encourages ambitious politicians to avoid conciliatory rhetoric (see Chapter 1). In addition, each position adopted by government is a compromise between Whitehall departments, long-range national interests and domestic lobbies. Governments are faced with unceasing demands that Britain's body language towards its partners be either nastier or nicer, and consistency evades even the best-intentioned governments. Britain campaigns for 'subsidiarity' and less interference from Brussels while insisting at the same time on heavy and detailed pan-European laws on protecting the welfare of animals being transported across borders. The first is a piece of a strategy, the second a response to a powerful lobby.

Consistency of policy is further hindered by the emerging contradictions within the structure of the union. Policy and legislation are made in a system based squarely on nation-states, but the states link themselves by a treaty (Maastricht) whose spirit and letter assume that nation states will gradually melt into an 'ever closer union'. National welfare states with extensive powers survive despite the fact that transnational communications, economic developments and supra-national powers like the EU are altering and reducing their scope for action. Economic integration has always moved faster and further than political. Recent opinion surveys suggest that the 'permissive consensus' which allowed political elites to pursue integration without accounting to their electorates in detail may have evaporated after the Single European Act (Reif, 1993).

By setting in motion an 'irreversible' programme for economic and monetary union (EMU), the Maastricht Treaty embarked on the most ambitious attempt yet made to resolve the tensions between nation states and supra-national integration. Maastricht lays down that EMU should start in January 1999 with no minimum number of participating states unless a majority of the EU has decided to move earlier. It is extremely unlikely that a majority of member states will have satisfied the convergence criteria before the political decision to start EMU in January 1999 is taken, probably in early 1998 (see Box 13.1 for details on these criteria). The choices facing a British government equipped with the right to stand aside from a single currency dwarf all other European issues. The decision to set a binding timetable for the start of monetary union was a victory for the EU's 1991 majority which saw EMU as a political project which would not work unless a vanguard was encouraged to force the pace. Governments are only now coming to terms with the real implications of the treaty for the cohesion of the Union and for individual economies.

The Maastricht decisions of 1991 triggered off reflection on what degree of 'political union' was needed to underpin EMU. Most states likely to qualify believe that this must involve greater consistency and effectiveness in joint action on foreign policy, immigration and transnational crime. Yet as they broach these exceptionally sensitive areas, countries like France and Germany are markedly more cautious both in their rhetoric and prescriptions than they were in 1990 and 1991 during the preparation of Maastricht. They are heading in the direction mapped out by the founding fathers of the EEC but doing so with less verve and conviction than in the past. The Franco-German political axis that has been at the heart of the Union and of the drive towards closer integration is undermined by discord over the future of the nation state. French politicians and policy-makers believe that the nation state remains the basic political unit of political life; they argue for a strong Europe with weak central institutions. Their German equivalents believe that the state is too small to face the challenges of the 21st century and needs to be superseded by supra-national powers.

### Box 13.1  The Single European Act (1987) and the Treaty on European Union (The Maastricht Treaty) (1991)

On 1 July 1987, a series of amendments to the Treaty of Rome (the founding document of the European Economic Community) came into effect. The central aim of the Act was to establish 'an area without internal frontiers in which the free movement of goods, persons, services and capital is ensured' by 1992. Other provisions included: co-operation in research and technology development among European states, the improvement of working conditions in member nations, 'economic and social cohesion' (i.e. the reduction of inequalities between regions), environmental protection, and steps towards economic and monetary union. One of its important amendments was to allow decisions in the Council of Ministers to be taken by a qualified majority vote on most issues pertaining to the internal market (previously the Treaty of Rome had predominantly required unanimity of the states). Furthermore, the Act strengthened the ability of the European Parliament to delay and amend legislation, and also stipulated that member states should inform and consult each other on foreign policy.

In September 1988 a committee chaired by Jacques Delors was established to discuss monetary union. The plan that emerged was presented to heads of government in June 1989, and 'Stage 1' of the process towards monetary union was begun in 1990. An Intergovernmental Conference on Economic and Monetary Union worked throughout 1991 on establishing terms and timetables for further monetary integration. In December, a draft Treaty on European Union was agreed at Maastricht (and signed in February 1992). The agreement envisaged three stages of monetary union:

**contd./**

**Box 13.1** (contd.)

***Stage 1*** (already begun in 1989): Member states were to ensure complete liberalisation of capital flows, and to adopt programmes for the convergence of their economies. The criteria for such convergence, which must be fulfilled in order for a nation to be a candidate for inclusion in a monetary union, are fourfold:

a) On inflation: A 'sustainable' price performance and an average rate of inflation observed over a period of one year that does not exceed that of (at most) the three best performers by more than one and a half percentage points.

b) On deficits: A budget deficit that is under three per cent of GDP, and a ratio of outstanding debt to GDP that is no more than 60 per cent.

c) On Exchange Rate Mechanism (ERM) performance: The country should have remained within the 'normal' bands of the ERM without 'severe tensions' for at least two years and should not have instigated a downward realignment of its bilateral exchange rate against any other member country in this period.

d) On interest rates: Long-term interest rates which, on average over the previous year, should not have been more than 2 per cent higher than those of the three best performers.

***Stage 2*** (begun January 1994): A European Monetary Institute (EMI) was set up to review and 'co-ordinate' monetary policies in order to assist in the stabilization of prices. The EMI was also supposed to report to the Council on the progress of member nations in meeting convergence criteria. So far, the EMI has remained largely a research body, though it has been consulted on a number of aspects of domestic legislation. Heads of government were supposed to decide by 31 December 1996 whether a majority of states had fulfilled the conditions necessary for proceeding with the adoption of a single currency. If such a majority existed, a date for the beginning of Stage 3 was to be established, but if no such agreement could be secured, Stage 3 would begin automatically on 1 January 1999. The 1996 deadline was implicitly abandoned at the Cannes Summit in June 1995, where a resolution was passed committing member states to 'prepare the transition to the single currency by January 1st 1999 at the latest'.

***Stage 3*** (to begin by January 1999): This stage will include only those countries that have fulfilled the necessary conditions. Stage 3 will be inaugurated by the replacement of the EMI with a European Central Bank (ECB). Exchange rates will be irrevocably fixed, and a single currency introduced. Most member states will be exempt from participation if they have failed to meet agreed entry criteria. The exceptions are the UK - which is allowed to make a further decision about whether to proceed to Stage 3 - and Denmark, which reserved the right to submit participation in Stage 3 to a referendum.

At present, even the latest target date for Stage 3 (January 1999) seems unrealistic. Britain and Italy remain outside the ERM after their exit in 1992, with no immediate prospects of return. Only a minority of member nations have, at any one time, satisfied the stipulated convergence criteria. Perhaps more importantly, opposition to the introduction of a single currency in the short-medium run is significant in a number of EU states - particularly in Britain, where 60 per cent oppose participation in a single currency (MORI/On-Line telephone poll, conducted in June 1995, reported in 'The Economist' (July 1-7), p.30. See also Box 13.2). Despite these disagreements about the number of states that will participate in EMU, and the timing of its introduction, the Maastricht Treaty requires that the EMI prepare for Stage 3 by the end of 1996. A preliminary decision about how to introduce the single currency should thus be expected by early 1996. This question is itself fraught with disagreement. The European Commission is in favour of establishing a single currency to be used by governments and banks for a three-year trial period before introducing it to the general public. The Bundesbank, on the other hand, supports a 'delayed Big Bang', involving the locking of exchange rates but delayed introduction of a single currency until banks have accustomed themselves to offering services in ECUs (European Currency Units).

The Maastricht Treaty also originally included a chapter on social affairs, which at the UK's insistence was omitted, and now forms a separate protocol. The protocol enabled the other states of the EU to proceed with the implementation of the Social Charter, originally proposed by the Commission in 1989, and covering freedom of movement, fair pay, improvement of working conditions, social security rights, freedom of association, collective wage agreements, workers' participation rights in the workplace, and sexual equality.

*Stewart Wood*

*The key strategic issues*

Against this background, four key issues face European governments between now and the year 2005.

- *Cushioning the shocks of the single currency, if it happens.* Monetary union, in 1999 or soon after, involving half the EU's membership or less will be the largest political fracture since the EEC's creation. Although the Maastricht Treaty purports to provide a comprehensive flight plan for the glide path to monetary union, its text leaves large gaps for national governments to fill. Important questions about political influence on monetary policy, application of the convergence criteria and the inclusion or exclusion of borderline economies will have to be answered in the face of financial market speculation. Politicians have to be sure that governments permanently withstand the political consequences of the unemployment which will occur in the least successful zones of the currency union.

- *Enlargement of the EU.* A long queue of applicants is forming: all 13 east European states due to have 'Europe Agreements' - which explicitly look forward to eventual full membership - will be candidates. A handful of them are among the seven states who already have formal membership bids pending. Pushing the EU frontier eastward remains a basic aim of German policy. Most states reluctantly acknowledge, though almost none except Britain say it out loud, that the absorption of states like Poland into the CAP and the 'structural' and 'cohesion' funds (regional subsidies) will mean the drastic overhaul of both financial transfer systems.

- *The distribution of power in the EU system.* This is the most immediate and painful set of dilemmas facing the British government. Recent and future increases in the number of member states raise three possible changes in the balance of power: between large and small states, reducing or abolishing the power of national veto, or between the EU's own central institutions. Well before the 1996 review of the Maastricht Treaty, solid support has appeared for increased use of majority voting and re-weighting the voting system to give big states greater proportional weight.

- *Foreign policy and defence.* Cooperation and integration in these fields are under permanent discussion in not only the EU but also Nato and the Western European Union (WEU). These debates are driven by the fiasco of half-hearted attempts to influence the outcome of the Bosnian civil war, probable American disengagement from some European security emergencies and the belief expressed in the Maastricht Treaty that a fully-developed Union should have not only a foreign but also a defence policy. Developments in the EU are closely linked to the 1998 renewal of the WEU's Brussels Treaty and the debate inside Nato over the alliance's possible enlargement to the east and its impact on Russia.

A single negotiation such as the 1996 'intergovernmental conference' on Maastricht cannot contain, let alone settle, such sprawling issues. Behind the official agenda of the treaty conference formally due to open in 1996 lie several profound changes which will inform alignments, conditions and attitudes across the Union. Member governments must take account of these shifts as they plan policy. Three important developments should be anticipated.

First, if the 1996 talks deadlock over issues such as the national veto and majority voting, German and Belgian politicians will press for treaty changes allowing a small 'hard core' of states to deepen their bonds, if necessary without the agreement of all the Union's members. Karl Lamers, foreign policy spokesman for the German Christian Democrats in the Bundestag, has suggested that this would involve rewriting Article N of the EU treaty (which specifies that each treaty change must be approved by all states) and that hard core states should be able to exclude other states from their decisions under provisions similar to Article 109, which sets up the inner circle of single currency states (Lamers, 1994). France and Germany would try to set the terms and conditions for an inner group and probably succeed. The Union would split into two, or perhaps more, tiers.

Second, in 1992 only two EU states (Germany and Britain) were net contributors to the EU budget. By the turn of the century, more than half the current 15 members will be net payers. The precise effects of this unregarded and revolutionary change are hard to predict, but two seem certain: national politicians will find their EU strategies and tactics under closer domestic scrutiny and on a tighter rein. Value for money will be a more important factor in formulating national positions. Secondly, tensions between north and south will grow. Both Spain and Italy stand to be heavy losers in the second half of the 1990s. Neither country can expect to qualify for the single currency by the 1997 decision date, and they are scarcely likely to do so by 1999. Both stand to lose substantial EU subsidies as new member states from the east stake their claims. Aside from financial stresses, strains between the large and small states will be heightened by moves towards more credible joint foreign policies. Since the creation of the 5-nation 'contact group', the EU's battered and minimalist Bosnia policy has effectively been run by a 'directoire' of the French, German and British governments. The arrangement suits the big three and irks the rest.

The third development stems from the political events following from the fall of the Berlin Wall, to Maastricht's travails and through to the French presidential election of 1995 that left two earlier assumptions in ruins. Firstly, the automatic presumption that the evolution of the Union would move power to the centre is under sustained challenge. Subsidiarity rather than centralisation has become the popular organisational model for the Union, and has shifted the terms of the debate towards more clear-eyed discrimination about what the Union can or should most usefully do better than states or regions. Secondly, an unquestioned assumption that a federal European constitution was the model to which all aspired is no longer taken for granted. Opinion polls and referendums have not revealed any loss of faith in the idea of European integration but have revealed more suspicious electorates and low levels of support for a federal Europe (MORI, 1994). France, whose fears of German power have fuelled the motor of European integration, endorsed the Maastricht Treaty by a thin 2.09 per cent majority in September 1992. The indifference of many voters is often overlooked. European Commission opinion polls suggest that - in a founding EEC member renowned for its loyalty to European unification - almost half the Belgian respondents would not particularly care if the EU evaporated tomorrow.

Anxieties about the legitimacy of political power underlie these doubts and developments. The European Parliament was a late and awkward addition to the original designs for the Coal and Steel Community and the EEC which relied heavily on executive supra-national powers. MEPs have slowly increased their leverage on the European Commission and Council of Ministers but failed to convince voters that they should become the linchpin of the system. Since direct elections to the Parliament began in 1979, turnout has fallen steadily. Public support for the abstract aim of a European federation is low across Europe - and especially low in Britain (see Box 13.2) - for the simple reason that people see it as having little to do with their basic agenda of seeking or holding jobs and preserving the stability and safety of their societies. National governments enjoy the legitimacy which makes industrial democracies work: a level of public consent high enough to ensure that voters will tolerate decisions by the majority but which they see as against their own interests. The institutions of the EU do not enjoy this consent and the power which people are prepared to give them is correspondingly limited.

As long as the EU is a hybrid system combining intergovernmentalism with federal elements, the option of complete withdrawal will remain before British politicians and be debated outside government if not inside. Ministers and officials accustomed to making European policy for two decades in relative privacy will have to get used to answering the most fundamental question of all: why should Britain stay in the EU? In short, the answer is: to reshape the EU to serve better the country's needs and interests.

Britain's continued membership of the EU should be contingent on the Union adopting an organisational form which is able to promote British interests. This chapter advocates 'variable geometry' within the 'pillars' of the EU, a willingness to envisage European integration as a pluralistic process involving multiple policies and institutional arrangements, to which nations may commit themselves to the degree that their perception of self-interest allows. This approach should then inform a government's stance on two key issues - the degree to which power should be ceded by national governments, and the 'widening' *versus* 'deepening' debate concerning future integration. The terms of current British political debate suggest that government policy should either unquestioningly follow the EU agenda suggested by France and Germany or put up obdurate resistance to all supra-nationalism backed by a willingness to pull out of the Union altogether. A 'cost-benefit' approach to EU laws and policies will be more realistic and effective than either.

In the remainder of the chapter, the key policy challenges facing future British governments are addressed, and specific recommendations in six policy areas are put forward.

### The motivating ideals of membership

The generation of Europe's politicians headed by Francois Mitterrand and Helmut Kohl has been driven towards further integration by fear of the recurrence of war.  Post-war European integration has successfully entangled the economic interests of democracies to ensure that they remain democracies and at peace.  The EU can be described as the most sophisticated balance of power ever achieved or (in more diplomatic language) as 'a radical kind of contract in which states delegate at least some powers of decision to common bodies' (Duchene, 1994).  The difference between the 19th and 20th centuries is that the cross-border entanglements guaranteeing peace are more deeply rooted.  The failure of this experiment would lessen Europe's capacity to save itself from its worst tendencies.  Every state, Britain included, has a responsibility to preserve integration's main achievement so far: maintaining the peace.

But the war is too far in the past to stir and mobilise.  We have marked the 50th anniversary of the last war's end and 'peace' is too diffuse an ideal to solve disputes over fishing net mesh or the ingredient rules for chocolate. 'Peace' has a different resonance depending on where you are.  In states invaded or occupied by Germany during the past century, the need for insurance against the big neighbour is measurable in the experience of people still alive.  In Portugal or Sweden, the wish to bind Germany in a web of trade and political decisions counts for less in the national consciousness.  Belief in Jean Monnet's ideal of pursuing pragmatic political integration by economic integration is probably now strongest among the eastern European and German elites.  Some observers of the EU's current malaise have urged governments to be more brutally explicit about the EU's function as a form of containment of German power.  This is hardly an acceptable nor a feasible motivating ideal - it is understandably very unpopular in Germany (witness the reaction to the French socialist party's Maastricht referendum poster which featured a voter's cross obliterating a cartoon Hitler).  More importantly, it is not a strong motive for people under the age of 35.  Peace makes an integrating organisation a necessity; but memories and aspirations are different in each generation.  It is not axiomatic, or even probable, that what worked in one generation will work in another.  Nor should it be assumed that all forms of integration necessarily promote peace and stability: some may fracture and not bind.  Witness the debates about closer forms of defence cooperation within the EU; the American interpretation of 'deepening' as a strategy for creating a trade block; and Russia's resistance to the eastward creep of both NATO and the European Union.

The gradual expiry of the peace-making ideal which fired the wartime generation has given way to a search for an agreed purpose for the EU.  But voters outside Germany do not appear easy to convince that the preservation of peace requires not merely existing integration but steady progress towards 'deepening'.  Germany's emergence as the chief promoter of 'political union' (a term with no agreed meaning) has prompted reflection in other states on how far the peculiar intensity of Germany's needs to embed herself in a deeply integrated structure match the needs of her partners.  In this context, it is necessary to reconceive the terms and purposes of membership.  Rather than insisting that member states (and prospective member states) be united by a shared progressive ideal of further integration, the states should recognise that the motives moving states inside or closer to the EU vary.  In 1994 Finland enjoyed very free trade already with the EU through the European Economic

Area. EU membership promised access to the political process which sets Europe's economic rules but threatened to reduce the level of agricultural subsidy. Finns were also being offered the opportunity to abandon the neutral status which they had been forced to adopt during the Cold War. Opinion polls suggest that geopolitical factors helped swing referendum voters behind EU membership. A state like Hungary, when and if it faces a similar decision will be balancing economic cost-benefit with security considerations. France sees the EU as the best insurance it has enjoyed since Napoleon that it is, and can remain, a leading European state. The Union offers an opportunity to create a regional power independent of American military might and culture. States shattered by war surrendered carefully calculated pieces of sovereignty in order to win gains in bigger games (see Milward, 1992). France, Belgium and Luxembourg used the external disciplines and subsidies of the Coal and Steel Community to draw the political sting from the run-down of their mines and steel mills. Spain's governing class won support for opening the country's markets to foreign competition by turning EU membership into a symbol of Spanish re-entry to the western family which ended the isolation of the Franco era.

Given the impossibility and undesirability of unified ideals for the Union, Britain's policy in the EU, whether active or reactive, should reflect a similarly *discriminating* and *instrumental* view of continued membership and of further integration - 'discriminating' in the sense of being prepared to endorse some rather than all or none of further forms of integration: 'instrumental' in the sense of evaluating courses of action in terms of detailed studies of practical costs and benefits. A single guideline based on 'pro' or 'anti' Europe positions does not answer the detailed dilemmas which the EU agenda throws up every day of the week. Correspondingly, when British policy-makers contemplate the sort of Union that continued membership will allow them to help shape, they must opt for a general framework that will maximise their latitude to pursue this strategy. British policy need not be wholly self-centred. Much of the obsessive discussion about the EU's constitution obscures the elemental importance of knitting together the two halves of Europe divided by the Cold War. Britain has backed moves to smooth eastern Europe's path to the EU, rightly seeing this aim as the crucial task in the remaining years of this century.

## What sort of Europe?

Three kinds of institutional arrangements could emerge in the next decade as the Union grows in size:

1. A classic federation controlling military, economic (both fiscal and monetary) and political power, led by a vanguard group of states.

2. A highly integrated economic region except for core sovereignty areas of currencies and armies. This would be reached by a more evolutionary and inclusive process, and more probably stress economic rather than political integration.

## Box 13.2  British attitudes towards the European Union

It is widely held, both within the Britain and the EU, that British attitudes towards the European Union are distinctly hostile. Evidence over the past ten years taken from the Eurobarometer Survey (a biannual public opinion survey conducted by the European Commission in all member states) reveals a more mixed picture. Since the mid-1980s, only Danish respondents have been less enthusiastic than the British in positive appraisals of the national benefits of EU membership, support for increased European integration, and support for continued membership. However, in this period the number of British citizens who viewed the common market as bad for Britain has never risen above 20.0 per cent. The number of respondents who think of EU membership as good for the country peaked at 59.0 per cent in 1989, and has since remained consistently above 40.0 per cent. A clear majority of Britons are in favour of continuing the process of European political integration, though the figure has fallen a little since 1988. With regard to impressions of European institutions, the British are more sanguine than their European counterparts. The percentage of those who had received a favourable impression of the European Commission fell from 54.2 per cent in early 1990 to 28.1 per cent in mid-1992, for example. British opinion regarding European integration and European institutions in general became markedly more sceptical in 1992 after the depreciation of Sterling and eventual exit from the European Exchange Rate Mechanism (ERM). Whereas in Spring 1992 44.8 per cent claimed that Britain benefited from EC membership, later in the same year only 30.6 per cent responded similarly. In the same poll, more people (27.9 per cent) stated that they would be relieved if the EC disappeared tomorrow than those that maintained they would be very sorry (25.8 per cent). This anti-EC sentiment seems to have moderated somewhat in the last two years. Nevertheless, an Autumn 1993 poll revealed that the percentage of British people in favour of the Maastricht Treaty (23.0 per cent) was the lowest in all EU states by over ten percentage points (though more Danes than Britons said that they were opposed to the Treaty). Similarly, in June 1995 60.0 per cent of British respondents said that in a referendum they would vote against membership of a single European currency. However, an equally high number opposed the idea of ruling out British membership of a single currency forever. And more importantly there remains little support for taking Britain out of the European Union altogether - 29.0 per cent of respondents support this option at present, while more than double that figure oppose it.

*Stewart Wood*

3.  Common rules, disciplines and policies where useful and possible (e.g. common single market rules, closer defence cooperation) but 'variable geometry' for many policies and particularly for new members from the east.

The present EU is heading towards the second option with a majority of politicians pushing for option 1. Britain's best interests lie in moving as close as possible to option 3 while ensuring that a looser-jointed EU will not run the risk of incoherence or disintegration. The key choice is the scope and power of central institutions in a Union in which states enjoy wide choice to opt in

the weakness of public support fully justify Britain's semi-detached stance, and would not justify entry under present conditions.

*Institutional questions.* The more technical issues such as the rotation of the Union presidency or the numbers of European Commissioners are secondary to the pivotal issue of the veto. Recent experience demonstrates the hard truth that despite the criticism levelled at Britain for use of the veto, a government's room for manoeuvre is greater with a veto to wield. Blocking the nomination of Jean-Luc Dehaene as President of the European Commission used that power to obtain a result which Britain had been unable to achieve in private negotiation beforehand. Other states such as Germany and France had managed to secure allies for their own vetoes of other candidates in private talks before the final showdown.

Britain would be badly advised to abandon the veto on immigration issues, transnational crime, foreign policy and defence, tax, social policy, the EU budget or treaty changes. A limited number of joint foreign policies could be agreed with a single state simply standing to one side. But the use of 'consensus-minus-one' decisions has to be restricted to policies where the dissenting state is not directly involved in the policy concerned. If 11 EU governments had decided to recognise Macedonia by leaving the fiercely opposed Greek government to one side, the decision would have been meaningless. Britain should also revive the idea that new applicants to the EU might not be required to join all three 'pillars' of the EU's structure at the same time. Many, if not all, east European states should be ready to join the second (foreign policy) and third (crime and immigration) councils before their economies and legal systems are braced for the rigours of single market rules, environment policies and the European Court of Justice.

Even dealing with cross-border pollution, successful collective policies need to balance the strategy of the centre against the tactics of the national government. After several years of deadlocked debate over a carbon energy tax, governments have now accepted guidelines for reducing exhaust emissions by whatever fiscal discouragement they choose. But where EU law is a broad framework to deal with a genuinely cross-border issue (such as acid rain or global warming) not among the 'core' sovereignty areas, Britain should seriously consider extending the use of majority voting. There are still areas of economic liberalisation where a shift from unanimity to qualified majority would benefit Britain. Pan-European rules to cut steel subsidies which undercut unsubsidised British firms have been blocked by states exploiting their veto.

*Subsidiarity and social affairs.* The EU's existing economic system can only make sense if states are allowed room to use their comparative advantages. The drive to complete the single market and the advocacy of a matching 'social Europe' by Commission President Jacques Delors began moves to restrict the play of those national advantages by harmonising social and welfare regulation. Political pressures, particularly from a German government attentive to businesses keen to deregulate, have for the moment stemmed the flow of new social directives. There is a fundamental difference between liberalising rules which open movement, trade and opportunities to European citizens and moves to extend social and welfare rules already applying in several states.

Liberalisation increases opportunities for economies to gain by comparative advantage, a freedom diminished by the levelling effects of social legislation across the EU market. There is no axiomatic reason why cross-border market rules must be matched by social rules since the effects produced are of a different kind. Governments of both left and right should think long and hard before surrendering their freedom of choice to shape social policies at a national level. A future British government which wanted to resist, say, a French-driven proposal to shorten the European working week below a 48-hour maximum[1] (see Aubry, 1995) would have to place great faith in political persuasion if the Social Chapter opt-out had been abandoned. On the other hand, a British government committed to such proposals could enact domestic legislation even if the opt-out was still in force. The advantage of forfeiting the opt-out would be that future governments would be more credibly bound to its provisions than would be the case through equivalent domestic legislation. But for this very reason, the decision to engage in such a commitment surely requires a greater degree of consensus over the relevant benefits of the Social Chapter than exists at present.

*Foreign policy and defence.* The EU will only achieve anything worthwhile in these spheres if its leaders rigorously insist on judging by results. Initiatives in external affairs invented to create the illusion of superpower activity undermine the idea that Europe may need to keep its own peace in the near future and, at worst, can kill people. Yet the challenges are there and unanswered. As America disengages from European security (we do not yet know exactly how far), Europe's major powers need to find ways to extinguish ethnic or border disputes which have already destroyed the former Yugoslavia. Politicians have been cowardly and inert in the face of the problem. They have failed not only to confront Serbian aggression but also to sound the alarm which such conflicts pose for neighbouring states. France's search for a (self-sufficient) common European defence is now more realistic than Britain's clinging to outdated ideas of rebuilding or refreshing the transatlantic relationship. Stripped of alphabet soup arguments about the relative merits of the EU or the WEU, British policy should be directed at preparing to take peace-keeping or peace-enforcement decisions in any forum where military command (and thus advice about costs and benefits) is closely integrated with political control.

*Policy towards the European Commission.* The European Commission, target of attack from all quarters since Jacques Delors overplayed his hand in the late 1980s, should be encouraged to be more mobile. The treaty hands the Commission a mixed role: guardian of the EU treaty's spirit, a monopoly right to initiate legislation, and implementation and enforcement duties of a civil service. It is already shifting from being less of a legislator to more of a regulator. But it lacks the ability or encouragement to seek out areas where popular support for a co-ordinating or catalytic role can force governments to acknowledge the need for a supra-national role. The Commission would be better advised to show that it can add value on harmonising and linking information society strategies, educational exchanges or advice on new legal systems in the ex-Soviet Union than to fight trench warfare against governments over its institutional role in a common defence policy.

## Conclusion

This chapter has argued that Britain's orientation towards Europe needs to be 'discriminating' and 'instrumental', meaning that each policy area needs to be considered on its own merit and that no simple 'for' or 'against' stance is appropriate. The most important strategic function served by the European Union has been the prevention of war, though clearly this is not a sufficiently specific principle to assist us in deciding many of the issues now facing the Union. A number of issues are analysed in the chapter, but of these the most important are whether to promote 'widening' *versus* 'deepening' of the Union and whether to seek monetary union. On the former, the view is advanced that, in general, 'widening' is the more important goal, not least because of the need to integrate the emerging eastern European economies. However, this will bring with it politically uncomfortable consequences for many countries, including the reform of the structure of voting (which Britain will find uncomfortable) and reform of the CAP and other transnational capital transfers (which, for example, France, Spain and Portugal will find uncomfortable). On the issue of EMU, an open but sceptical view is advanced. The early timetables of politicians in favour of EMU now look very unrealistic. More importantly, the social, political and economic implications of EMU are complex and the arguements do not overwhelming point in either direction. What is certainly clear is that any route to EMU will be a very bumpy one, and that Britain would be well-advised to hold onto its opt-out clause on this issue in the run-up to 1999.

During the second half of the 1990s, the sour scepticism which has cooled earlier support for European integration will itself give way to more constructive curiosity about how governments are going to cope with the challenges they face. By insisting on old formulas while the continent was turning upside down around them, the EU's leaders and institutions did much to provoke voters to ask whether European integration any longer served a purpose. Lessons were taught by unconvinced voters and learnt by at least some politicians. The challenge of reinventing the ideal of a peaceful Europe lies ahead of them.

## Notes

1.    A major plank of the French Socialist Party's campaign in the Presidential election of April/May 1995 .

## References

Aubry, M. (1995), *Libération*, April 13.

Duchene, F. (1994), *Jean Monnet: The First Statesman of Interdependence*, Norton.

Lamers, K. (Autumn, 1994), Meetings of the Konrad Adenauer Stiftung, Brussels, and the Assemblée National Foreign Affairs Committee, Paris.

Milward, A. (1992), *The European Rescue of the Nation-State*, London: Routledge.

MORI (1994), Poll for 'The European' conducted during the European Parliament elections of 1994, published 13 May-2 June.

Reif, K-H. (December, 1993), 'Introduction', in *Eurobarometer*, No. 40.

communities, fairness in geographical terms (Curtice, 1992). If one emphasises one concept of fairness - for example, to voters - then one might prefer a system such as STV; on the other hand if one aimed for fairness to parties, then one might prefer electoral systems with a list element or plurality systems such as the Alternative Vote. It is easy to say that an electoral system should be fair to voters, but taking that as the sole criterion underestimates the critical importance of parties in a representative democracy. Fairness to minorities might imply a choice of a list system. A concern for regional fragmentation might indicate a preference for an Additional Member System. One cannot therefore invoke the concept of fairness without trying to reach a consensus over the question of to whom one is trying to be fair.

Equally one has to accept that critics of proportional systems do not see fairness as the predominant criterion for an electoral system. In their view, effective government is a more important criterion than a complex and disputed notion of fairness. By 'effective government' here is meant a single-party government elected on a specific political programme (or mandate) which it then tries to implement in government. Majoritarian electoral systems are seen on this view as necessary in order to deliver such clear governmental outcomes. Proponents of this view also emphasise the fact that under a majoritarian system the election of a government is in the hands of the electors, whereas under a more proportional system the government usually emerges from negotiation conducted between political elites within a pluralistic (or 'hung') Parliament.

The Working Party believed that underlying this dispute was a much more fundamental one about the nature of representation. We believed that those who favour a more proportional system of election believe in what we called the *microcosmic view of representation:* that a parliament should as far as possible represent the whole range of political opinion in society. A proportional system of election would produce a more microcosmic form of representation with the likelihood that no single party would have an absolute majority in the legislature. A government would then emerge from such a microcosmic legislature by a process of negotiation and there would therefore have to be a greater degree of consent-seeking by a party which wanted to form the government (or a part of it). This in turn would require seeking support outside the party either for tacit support or for coalition partners.

This conception of the nature of representation is rejected by the majoritarian on several grounds. First of all because the supposed microcosmic nature of representation is defective. The majoritarian prefers what we called the *principal/agent concept of representation.* On this view, a member of a legislature has to act on the basis of the simple plurality view in the constituency which he or she represents and to act as far as possible in their interests. Secondly a proportional system is unfair in its outcomes in that it will give disproportional power to small parties in the process of consent-seeking and coalition-building. Thirdly it is argued that this process of building support detaches the emergence of a government from the choices of the electorate. Under the microcosmic view the central feature of an electoral system is to elect a representative parliament from which government emerges by negotiation. Under a majoritarian view an election is as far as possible about electing a government rather than merely a representative parliament.

Fourthly, a government that emerges by negotiation is not likely to be an effective or strong government.

This last point is particularly disputed by proponents of a more proportional system in that it assumes that effective government means single-party government - that is to say a government able to fulfil its mandate using the votes of only its own supporters in the legislature. The assimilation of effectiveness and single-party government is disputed by supporters of proportional representation (PR) on the grounds that one can have a single-party government with a large majority elected on a minority of the popular vote which is ineffective because it lacks wide-ranging consent for its policies. The 'poll tax' is often cited as an example in which a single-party government pursued its own preferences in a single-minded way which ultimately proved to be unsustainable because of a lack of broad consent for the policy.

One way of putting this contrast between the arguments of the defenders and critics of majoritarian electoral systems is that majoritarians are more concerned with the effectiveness of government outcomes whereas those who favour PR in some form or other are more concerned with the legitimacy or procedural fairness of the composition of a parliament. However, this is a rather tendentious way of pointing up the contrast in that defenders of more proportional systems will invoke the points made in the previous paragraph; namely that strong government does not necessarily mean effective government, and also that there are lots of European countries which have strong and effective governments that emerge from more representative parliaments.

Another central issue concerns constituency representation. It is impossible to have a more proportional system which does not dilute constituency representation because elections have to take place either in large multi member constituencies (as in STV, for example), or using list systems, where accountability of representatives to the electorate is diminished. There are two issues here in the UK context. The first is the undoubted attachment of existing Members of Parliament to the constituency system, a point which has to be taken fully into account in any proposal for reform which would eventually have to be passed by the House of Commons. Secondly the existing system is thought by its defenders to be a more defensible form of political accountability than the kind of accountability under STV which, if the experience of the Republic of Ireland is anything to go by, seems to involve accountability to coalitions of supportive groups within a constituency. Equally it is regarded as more defensible than the form of accountability under a list system or under a more hybrid system such as AMS, under which the majoritarian critic argues that accountability is less to the voters and more to the party hierarchy that has the responsibility for determining the position of a candidate on a list. Although it is possible to have flexible lists in which the voter is able to have an input into the ordering of candidates, this is often thought to be more an apparent than a real virtue within, say, a regional list, where many of the candidates on the list will not be known to electors in a region. However, under AMS it is possible for the list to be composed of party candidates chosen to fight seats in the region. The 'best losers' become the additional members (Linton and Georghiou, 1992).

The final distinction which the Working Party found useful in trying to think its way through these complex issues is the distinction between *legislative* and *deliberative* bodies. Legislative bodies have the power to enact legislation and the executive derives its power from the consent of a majority in a legislative body. A deliberative body is more concerned to articulate the outlook of a community or a region on a set of issues, to give voice to interests in so far as they are affected by legislative bodies and perhaps to oversee the regulation and delivery of public services in an area when a legislative body has determined that these services will be provided. Obviously the House of Commons is primarily a legislative body, as a Scottish Parliament would also be, whereas regional assemblies would be much more deliberative in function. The House of Lords is rather a hybrid: it is a revising chamber so it has an impact on legislation; it can initiate legislation and yet many of its functions have a purely deliberative function. The European Parliament aspires to move from being a deliberative to a legislative body. The Working Party took the view that the question of an appropriate electoral system could not be detached from an account of the broad function of the representative body. Therefore we did not take the view that there had to be a common electoral system for all the bodies about which we were asked to make recommendations.

It is also worth noting that many members of the Working Party took the view that the supposedly beneficial effects of First Past the Post in delivering strong single-party government were highly contingent. It is certainly true that over most of its history First Past the Post has produced a governing majority in the House of Commons, although it is not uniformly the case. However, there is nothing in the logical nature of First Past the Post that makes this inevitable, and it is quite possibly a good deal less likely in the future given the continuation of a strong showing of the Liberal Democrats nationally and of the Scottish National Party in Scotland. If it became clear that the capacity of First Past the Post to produce single-party government were declining, then there would be little left to its rationale, depending as it does on arguments about the link between effectiveness and single-party government.

This, then, is a brief sketch of some of the distinctions which weighed with the Working Party during its deliberations. In the next section I want to explain briefly how these worked out in the specific recommendations that were made.

## Box 14.1 The properties of electoral systems

As Raymond Plant says in this chapter, there can be no perfect electoral system. People want different, indeed incompatible, things from them. The two broad families of voting systems are *majoritarian* systems and *proportional* systems. Each of these derives from a particular concept of representation, as explained in this chapter. A principal-agent view of representation points towards majoritarian systems; a microcosm view of representation points towards proportional systems. Majoritarian voting rules are appropriate when the voters have to choose one person, policy, or course of action, as in the election of a president, the choice of somebody to fill a job, or a referendum. Proportional voting rules are appropriate when the voters have to choose a deliberative body which is to represent their opinions, or physical characteristics, in a microcosm. Which of these conceptions is appropriate for a national legislature is a deeply value-laden question which has no correct answer.

contd./

The main **majoritarian** electoral systems are:

**M1: Alternative Vote (AV).** Used in Australia and often in club and society elections in Britain. Voters rank the candidates in order. First preferences are counted. Any candidate who has obtained over 50 per cent of the votes cast is elected. If there is none, the candidate with the fewest votes is eliminated, and that candidate's ballot papers are redistributed according to the second preferences on them. The process is repeated until a candidate gets over half of the votes.

**M2: Exhaustive ballot.** Common in Labour Party and trade union selection conferences. As AV, except that voters express only a first preference. They re-ballot among the remaining candidates after each elimination.

**M3: Runoff systems.** Used in France and the USA. The election is in two rounds. In the first round, anybody may stand. Any candidate with more than half the votes is elected. If there is none such, a second round is held in which only the top two candidates from the first round may enter. A complicated variant, with both runoff and AV components, and with no bar on new candidates entering at the second stage, is used for the election of a Conservative Party leader.

Systems M1 to M3 all have similar virtues and defects. They are straightforward and familiar, and they all ensure that the majority winner among the last two candidates is elected. But they may fail to elect either the 'Borda candidate' (see M5) or the 'Condorcet candidate' (see M6). Although these are not the same, they are the only two claimants to the title of 'true majority winner' when there are more than two candidates.

**M4: Plurality rule ('First Past the Post').** Voters choose one candidate. The candidate with the largest number of votes is elected, whether or not that number is greater than half of the votes cast.

**M5: The Borda rule.** Often used to select candidates for jobs. Each voter ranks the candidates. The ranks are added up. The candidate with, on average, the highest ranking is elected.

**M6: The Condorcet rule.** Occasionally used to select candidates for jobs. Each voter ranks the candidates. The rankings are used to compare the candidates two at a time. Any candidate who beats all the others in these pairwise comparisons is elected. If there is no such candidate, there must be what is called a 'top cycle' (A beats B, B beats C, and C beats A, all at the same time: cycles may involve three or more candidates). Any Condorcet procedure must bring a tie-breaking rule into play.

Each of these rules (M4 to M6) aims to select the candidate who is the best on average. But there are different kinds of average. What we usually call average, mathematicians call 'the mean', which corresponds to the Borda rule. Two other concepts are 'the mode' and 'the median'. The modal candidate means the candidate most frequently chosen by voters - in other words the First Past the Post winner. The median of any set of people or things arranged in some order, such as size, is the one with exactly as many members on either side. In this context, the median candidate corresponds to the Condorcet winner. Most voting theorists think the Condorcet winner best exemplifies 'majority rule'; a few think the Borda winner does; none think the plurality winner does. Plurality rule is always justified by references to its (supposed) consequences - it tends to deter third parties from 'splitting the vote', and therefore tends to produce two-party contests and hence single-party government. In Britain since 1970, it has produced single-party government although not two-party contests.

**M7: Approval voting.** Each voter casts an unranked ballot for as many of the candidates as the voter finds acceptable. Compared with M4, approval voting is more likely to select the Condorcet winner. A mixture of Alternative Vote and Approval Voting, called by its inventors the *Supplementary Vote*, was proposed in the Plant Committee. It would require each voter to reveal his/her first two preferences only. Second preferences would be brought into play only if no candidate won more than half of first preferences. Unknown to the authors of this scheme, it was proposed by Condorcet in 1793, and used in Geneva with chaotic results.                    contd./

The main **proportional** systems are:

**P1: Party list systems.** Used in most democracies for their legislative elections. Each voter chooses one party in a multi-member constituency. Parties are awarded seats in the constituency in proportion to the votes they get. There are many variants concerning the allocation formula and the opportunity (if any) for voters to change the parties' rankings of their candidates, but the main variable is constituency size: the larger the constituency, the more proportional the outcome. Good at getting proportionality; poor at getting responsiveness of politicians to their voters.

**P2: Additional member systems (AMS).** Used in Germany. A set of legislators is elected in single-member districts. Voters cast a second (party-list) vote which determines the overall party composition of the legislature. Each party is given a number of additional members such that the overall outcome is in proportion to the second votes. AMS could also be operated on the basis of one vote per voter, with parties' entitlements to additional members depending on their aggregate shares of the vote. Good at combining the advantages of proportional representation (PR) and plurality; opponents object to its creation of two classes of legislators.

**P3: Single Transferable Vote (STV).** Used in Ireland and Tasmania; favoured by the Liberal Democrats. In multi-member constituencies, each voter casts a ranked ballot, as in AV (M1 above). A quota sufficient to elect just the right number of candidates is fixed. Candidates with more than one quota of first preferences are elected, and their surpluses distributed until no more candidates can be elected by this route. Whenever this occurs, candidates are eliminated as in AV and their votes transferred. Produces legislators more responsive to their voters than does party-list, but suffers from technical weaknesses and may reject Condorcet winners.

**P4: Single Non-Transferable Vote (SNTV).** Used in Japan until recently. In multi-member constituencies, each voter has just one vote. At first glance this does not appear to be a PR system, but if voters and parties act rationally it functions as one. Parties have an interest in nominating neither too few nor too many candidates in each constituency. The strengths of this system are similar to those of STV; perverse outcomes may occur if parties do nominate too many or too few candidates.

*Iain McLean*

## The Scottish Parliament

Under the Labour Party's proposals the Scottish Parliament would be a legislative body but it would not have responsibilities for foreign and defence policy, macro-economic policy or social security. The Scottish Parliament would therefore be primarily a legislative body, but it would not have the full panoply of powers of the Westminster Parliament. The Working Party was sufficiently impressed by the merits of First Past the Post and the importance of retaining constituency accountability in a legislative body to recommend that a majority of seats should be elected by First Past the Post. However, it was unanimously agreed by the Working Party and by the NEC that there should be a number of additional seats which would be available to create a more proportional outcome overall while retaining the possibility of single-party government. There were three main reasons for this decision.

First, the Scottish Parliament had to be made acceptable to the Scottish people as a whole and this made it important that the electoral system for a Scottish Parliament should be of a sort to allow for a degree of pluralism in its representation and not to create what might for many years be seen as a one-party state. A degree of proportionality was therefore seen by the Party to be necessary to create an overall sense of legitimacy for the Scottish Parliament.

It is interesting to contrast this position with political opinion in Wales over the electoral system for the Welsh Assembly. As I have said the Working Party was suspended before it was able to make recommendations about the Welsh Assembly, so the deliberations of the Party in Wales were not informed by a recommendation from the Working Party or the NEC. In fact the 1995 Labour's Welsh Conference decided that First Past the Post is 'the preferred system' for the Welsh Assembly. This decision has been met with exactly the reaction from its opponents that the Scottish proposals avoided. Critics of the Welsh proposals, particularly the Liberal Democrats (who favour a Welsh Assembly), argue that this decision will turn the Welsh Assembly into a one-party body for the foreseeable future. The difference in outcome here is partly a reflection of the absence of a Welsh equivalent to the Scottish Constitutional Convention.

Second, the Scottish Constitutional Convention played an important role in influencing the decision of the Working Party in favouring a substantial element of proportionality for the Scottish Parliament. The Convention was open to all parties and groups in Scotland. It was boycotted by the SNP because they want complete independence and by the Conservatives who rejected the establishment of a Scottish Parliament. Nevertheless, those who participated in the work of the Convention as a means of trying to create a widespread degree of legitimacy for the Scottish Parliament favoured a degree of proportionality in the electoral system as an essential part of establishing this legitimacy. Even those members of the Working Party who were not particularly sympathetic to PR accepted the need to agree on proposals for an electoral system which was consistent with the aspirations of those within and outside the Labour Party who wanted to see a Scottish Parliament enjoying a wide degree of acceptance in Scotland.

Finally, in addition to the above, it was argued by those who did not favour the extension of PR to the Westminster Parliament that the Scottish Parliament was *sui generis*. First of all there is a difference between recommending an electoral system for a new body without established conventions and traditions, and extrapolating from this new body to the case of the House of Commons. So it was argued that while the Scottish Parliament would be a genuine parliament it should not set a precedent for the House of Commons. These groups also contended that the differences between the powers of the Scottish Parliament and of the House of Commons were sufficiently important to justify the maintenance of First Past the Post for the latter while conceding an Additional Member System for the Scottish Parliament. In particular, it was argued that defence, foreign policy and macro-economic policy (especially in relation to interest rate and monetary policy) required strong single-party government, which First Past the Post (in their view) would produce.

### The Second Chamber

Under the proposals as they emerged from the Policy Review the House of Lords would be replaced by a small (about 300 members) elected chamber which would represent regional interests. The chamber would primarily be a deliberative rather than a legislative body although it would be involved in revising and delaying legislation which might be thought by that chamber to infringe individual rights. The Working Party's first inclination was to choose the Additional Member System for this new chamber partly because, since the Scottish Parliament would be elected by this system, there was something to be said for having a limited number of electoral systems in play at the same time. However, given the regional dimension and the rather limited size of the chamber it seemed impossible to devise an AMS system for this body. It was agreed that the chamber should be elected by a more proportional system partly so that it would be seen not to have the same constituency basis as the Commons. In light of these factors, the Working Party agreed to recommend a regional list system.

As things stand at the moment this is Party policy, but it looks as though the whole basis on which our recommendations were made will be rejected. The Labour Leadership appears to favour a nominated chamber rather than an elected chamber. This means removing the voting rights of hereditary peers and moving towards a nominated chamber consisting of life peers only. If this policy turns out to be acceptable to the party then obviously the Working Party's proposals will become redundant. However, I would like to put on record that I remain strongly committed to our original proposals and the findings of the post 1987 Policy Review. The problem which I, and I think many people, feel about a wholly nominated Second Chamber of Life Peers is that it will look extremely odd, to put it mildly, for a Labour government to come into office committed to a programme of democratic reform (which will also involve an onslaught on what has come to be called the 'quango state') while turning the House of Lords into a wholly nominated body. It has been said with some justice that this will transform the Lords into the biggest quango in the country. If the current proposals are accepted then it seems to me to be vital that they should be seen explicitly as transitional, so that the Party sees a nominated Second Chamber as an interim body until regional electoral boundaries have been set up to facilitate Labour's post-1987 policy of creating a wholly elected Second Chamber.

## The European Parliament

The Treaty of Rome envisages a common electoral procedure among member states of the Union. Certainly this would seem to be a necessary condition for increasing the powers of the European Parliament and its legitimacy. The other members of the Union employ electoral systems which embody the principle of proportionality, although the actual methods differ somewhat between countries. Britain however retains the First Past the Post system. Again the Working Party would have liked to have recommended an Additional Member System for the European Parliament for much the same reasons as obtained in relation to the House of Lords. However, this again proved to be impracticable and the Working Party recommended a list system. Again this was initially accepted by the Party and it remains Party policy.

Nevertheless, press reports recently suggest that many Labour MEPs would like to see this commitment rejected in favour of keeping First Past the Post.


## The House of Commons

The House of Commons was obviously the chief battleground in the Working Party and there were three proposals in play: First Past the Post, the Supplementary Vote (under which voters reveal their first two preferences for candidates in single member constituencies), and the Additional Member System (the proposal being considered was for 500 constituency members with 150 additional members elected regionally on a 'best loser' system in the regions). A clear majority of the Working Party favoured a majoritarian system, but there was a split over the choice between First Past the Post and the Supplementary Vote. The reasons for this were essentially those set out in the second section of this paper. There was a small majority in favour of the Supplementary Vote over the First Past the Post system, but it was clear that the Working Party was split in three ways. In the light of this John Smith announced at the NEC meeting which received the Report of the Working Party that he favoured a referendum on the issue. Although he went no further in public, I know from conversations with him that he had in mind something on the model of the New Zealand referendum.[3]

After John Smith's death, the candidates for the Leadership all committed themselves to retaining the referendum proposal. However, at the time of writing this policy is under severe pressure from the First Past the Post Group in the run up to the 1995 Labour Party Conference.[4] If Labour's referendum policy is overturned, the likelihood is that the issue would not be on the government's agenda during at least the first term of a Labour government.


## Electoral Reform and New Labour

The issue of electoral and representational reform focuses attention on the nature of the 'new' Labour Party's commitment to 'pluralism'. I believe that it is possible to identify three strands of thought at work behind the idea of pluralism, only one of which would favour electoral reform as far as the House of Commons is concerned. The first sense of pluralism has little intrinsically to do with representational reform at all and is concerned much more with opening the Labour Party itself up to a wider range of influences and forms of policy. Instead of having a dominant ideology or overarching big idea, this idea suggests that the aim of the party should be to use a wide range of policies embodying market, state and community/voluntary initiatives to achieve a wide range of ends: economic efficiency, greater fairness, the strengthening of the place of the individual in the community etc. This involves a rejection of the Marxist and a substantial challenge to the post-war social democratic tradition: of the Marxist tradition because of its insistence on common ownership and large scale planning; of the social democratic tradition because it emphasises equality and distributive issues over those of production. This has gone along

## Box 14.2  The Liberal Democrats and Electoral Reform

The Liberal Democrats, and the Liberal Party before them, have long advocated reform of Britain's electoral system. They advocate the operation of the single transferable vote (STV) system in Parliamentary election contests, the same system as is currently used in the Irish Republic. STV is used in conjunction with multi-member constituencies - voters number candidates for three to five elected posts according to their preferences, and candidates are elected when they receive a certain quota of votes, either outright, or after successive redistributions of second preferences. Although the electoral map of Britain would have to change in order for larger constituencies to be created than are at present permitted, MPs would retain a link with their locality, a link which might be lost under the German Additional Member System (AMS), or under a pure party list system of voting.

Support for STV represents a compromise between a desire to attain proportionality of votes cast in parliamentary elections and to retain relatively small constituencies. At the moment, efforts to retain proportionality within the electoral system are based on a geographic interpretation of that concept. The Boundary Commission strives to ensure that electors' votes are of equal weight, wherever they happen to be cast. However, this approach ignores the rise of party identification within the electorate and assumes that electors vote on the basis of which candidate will make the best MP for the locality. Liberal Democrats argue that although the link with local constituencies should not be broken completely, the electoral system should be altered to reflect the rise of the party system, so that the party composition of the House of Commons more accurately reflects electors' votes.

Of course the main problem, Liberal Democrats argue, with the present electoral system is that it under-represents parties which have a small but geographically well-spread share of the national vote. This has obviously affected the Liberal Democrats and their predecessors in Parliament - who have comprised between 1 and 4% of the House of Commons since 1945, regardless of a national vote of as much as 25.4%, in 1983. It has also disenfranchised voters of all the minority parties in 'safe' seats, whose votes are rendered irrelevant and who may be dissuaded from approaching an MP whom they feel does not represent their views and interests. Multi-member constituencies enable a wider spread of representatives to be elected for a district. Furthermore, the need to achieve geographical proportionality in the electoral system provides an incentive for the largest parties to gerrymander constituency boundaries.

In both 1918 and 1931 the House of Commons voted to adopt the alternative vote (AV) system for parliamentary elections; only pressure from the House of Lords prevented a change occurring. The Liberal Democrats do not favour this system as it is majoritarian, rather than proportional. Second preferences expressed under this system are used in a limited fashion, to clarify which party wins a close contest for a single member seat. The Plant Commission recently backed a similar scheme - the supplementary vote. Both that system and AV would have made very little difference to the results of the 1992 general election, had either been adopted for it. The Plant Commission's proposals received a lukewarm backing from the Liberal Democrats; although its existence indicates that the idea of changing the electoral system is back in the political mainstream, the argument over the nature of that change is yet to be won.

*Mark Egan*

with an emphasis in some of Tony Blair's speeches on the many strands which have historically informed the development of the Labour Party, including the impact of the Social or New Liberalism of the late nineteenth century. Pluralism in this sense seeks to make the Labour Party itself a broad church drawing upon a range of traditions and values which can then attract support from a wide range of people who may have felt excluded from support for the Party for a generation. Nevertheless, advocates of this organisational model for the Party in general resist the idea of sharing governmental power with other parties, and thus support the retention of the First Past the Post system.

The second sense of pluralism draws upon a distinction which was drawn in our final report between inter-institutional pluralism and intra-institutional pluralism. Inter-institutional pluralism involves a strong commitment to devolution of power to other bodies such as the Scottish Parliament and Welsh Assembly, strengthening local government and strengthening the House of Lords via democratic reform so that it can be a stronger brake on the power of the House of Commons and on the historically strong executive. These other bodies may be elected by PR and may well have a different political complexion from the Westminster government. In this sense there would exist a genuine division of power between institutions and a greater sense of the executive having to negotiate consent for its policies with other centres of power in the country. The House of Commons on this view would however still be elected by First Past the Post, or at least some form of majoritarian system on the grounds that within a more devolved system it is important to have an executive with a clear set of policies the impact of which can then be negotiated within a devolved system between the representatives of the nations, regions and central government. On this view pluralism within the government itself (i.e. the sharing of power within a coalition government elected by some form of PR) is neither necessary nor desirable. It is not necessary because of the greater pluralism and devolution of power that would come about as a result of these other constitutional changes and undesirable because it is important in such a devolved system to have a clear sense of direction at the centre.

Intra-institutional pluralism is more radical and sees the case for a politics of negotiation and consent-seeking as applying all the way down, including within the House of Commons. Those who support this view argue that the impact of PR for other bodies in a devolved system is bound to have an effect on the legitimacy of the electoral system for the Commons over time and make First Past the Post seem illegitimate. Against those who believe that this is a recipe for very weak government, with parties sharing power at Westminster having to negotiate with other centres of devolved power in the country at large, the point is often made that Germany, which is governed in a not dissimilar way, is capable of running the strongest economy in Europe and absorbing the costs of social and economic adjustment consequent to reunification. Certainly the construction of a 'politics of consensus' to replace the sharp ideological and party political divisions in British politics, a theme emphasised recently by Tony Blair,[5] could certainly be furthered by electoral reform.

The battle for the future and scope of electoral and representational reform within the Labour Party is taking place within the parameters of this debate concerning the three different understandings of pluralism. The last of these understandings is the one which is currently under the greatest challenge, although elements of the second alternative of inter-institutional pluralism are also being challenged (as shown by the vote of the Party in Wales to accept First Past the Post as the preferred system for the Welsh Assembly, and the preference for a nominated rather than a democratically elected Second Chamber).

## Summary of the Plant Commission's recommendations:

1.       An Additional Member System (AMS) for the Scottish Parliament.

2.       A regional list system for the House of Lords together with the exclusion of hereditary and life peers from exercising voting rights.

3.       A regional list system for elections of British representatives to the European Parliament.

4.       Introduction of the Supplementary Vote system for the House of Commons.

## Notes

1.  See Chapter 12 for a discussion of the arguments for constitutional reform regarding regional assemblies in Scotland, Wales and England.
2.  The Working Party consisted of:
    - MPs: Graham Allen (from 1992), Hilary Armstrong (from 1992), Margaret Beckett, Alistair Darling, John Evans, Bryan Gould, Geoff Hoon (from 1992 elected MP), Jo Richardson (until 1992), Jeff Rooker;
    - Peers: Reg Underhill, Patricia Hollis and Raymond Plant (from 1992);
    - MEPs: Geoff Hoon, Gary Titley (from 1992);
    - Trades Union representatives: Tom Burlison, Richard Rosser, Judith Church (from 1992);
    - representatives from the nations: Scotland: Murray Elder (until 1992), Jack McConnell (from 1992); Wales: Ken Hopkins; and
    - Academics: Raymond Plant and Ben Pimlott.
    Although they did not have voting rights, officials from Walworth Road played a full part in the deliberations: Geoff Bish (until 1992), Joyce Gould, Tim Lamport, and Larry Whitty.
      I was asked to Chair the Working Party by Roy Hattersley, and appointed following recommendation first by Neil Kinnock and subsequently by the NEC.
3.  New Zealand held two referenda on electoral reform. The first referendum offered the choice between the 'status quo' (Westminster electoral model) and change to some other form of electoral system. The result was a majority in favour of change. The second referendum presented a list of possibilities for a new electoral system. Of these alternatives, the Mixed Member Proportional system was chosen (a version of AMS). For details on the referenda and the choice of referendum format, see Bowden and Falck, 1996).

4.  However, Jack Straw recently reaffirmed his support for the idea: 'It would be a breach of faith with the party and with the country if we were to overturn the decision to hold a referendum. It would also dishonour the pledge given by John Smith' (*The Guardian*, 24 August).
5.  See, for example, Tony Blair's July 1995 Fabian Lecture.

## References

Bowden, B. and Falck, L. (1996, forthcoming), 'Redistribution and representation: New Zealand's new electoral system and the role of the Political Commissioners', in McLean, I. (ed.), *Fixing the Boundaries*, Aldershot: Dartmouth.

Curtice, J. (1992), 'The British electoral system: a fixture without foundation', in Kavanagh, D. (ed.), *Electoral Politics*, Oxford: Clarendon Press.

Institute for Public Policy Research (IPPR) (1991), *The Constitution of the United Kingdom*, IPPR.

Labour Party (1991), *Democracy, Representation and Elections; First Interim Report of the Labour Party Working Party on Electoral Systems*, Labour Party.

Labour Party (1992), *Second Interim Report of the Working Party on Electoral Systems*, Labour Party.

Labour Party (1993), *Report of the Working Party on Electoral Systems*, Labour Party.

Linton, M. and Georghiou, M. (1992), *A British Additional Member System? Issues That Need to be Decided in an AMS System*, Labour Campaign for Electoral Reform.

Linton, M. and Georghiou, M. (1993), *Labour's Road to Electoral Reform: What's Wrong with First Past the Post?* Labour Campaign for Electoral Reform.

McLean, I. (1991), 'Forms of representation and systems of voting', in Held, D. (ed.), *Political Theory Today*, Cambridge: Polity Press.

# 15 Conclusions

*David Halpern, Stewart Wood, Stuart White and Gavin Cameron*[*]

Before drawing final conclusions about what policies we should pursue, we should ask ourselves what it is that we are trying to achieve. What type of society do we want to live in? What are the major principles or objectives that should guide policy-making? We suggest that there are three basic objectives that policies should aim to promote. These are:

I. *To increase the quality of life.* Economic prosperity, and the generation of material comforts, are an important but not exclusive aspect of this goal. Other factors which may not be adequately captured by simple economic analyses include the quality of our relationships with others, the state of the environment, our health and our perceived security. In addition, we must think of the implications of policies for future lives. Future generations may be able to assess the relative importance of these factors more precisely, but we already know enough to be aware of their importance and should adjust our strategic policies accordingly.

II. *To spread opportunity and to share risks that are beyond the control of individuals.* All individuals should be able to share the opportunities which society can offer and, similarly, the costs of risks that fall unevenly across society should be shared across the members of that society. Hence, for example, two individuals born with the same innate abilities, given similar efforts, should have access to the same opportunities. Similarly, society should seek to ameliorate the effects of

---

[*] The following conclusions have been drawn up by the editors, though they are felt to represent the views of the majority of the authors of this report.

misfortune.  However, it is reasonable, under certain circumstances, to expect individuals who choose to engage in high risk activities to pay a higher premium for the protection they receive from the community.

III.    *To share power (through democracy) and to protect individuals and small groups from tyranny.*  As far as possible, political power should be shared across society.  However, in order to protect individuals and small groups from tyrannies of the majority, certain basic human rights should be protected.[1]

Most people would see these objectives, and especially *I* and *III*, as uncontroversial.  However, some might pause over objective *II*, and particularly issue of 'sharing risks beyond the control of individuals'.  Is this too harsh a principle?  As one contributor asked in discussion, 'Does this imply no wheel-chairs for rock climbers, health care for smokers or ambulances for overtakers?'  The answer is 'no', and in fact we would like to see a reduction in risk selection at the point of service provision.  What is being suggested is that where an individual makes a life-style choice that puts them at a higher but predictable risk of, say, needing expensive treatment paid for by the community, then the community may wish to consider applying an extra levy to that activity or individual equating to the scale and likelihood of the higher costs.  This would also have the added advantage of providing a signal to the individual of the risks involved and giving them the option of avoiding the higher risk and expense.  Hence, in the example above, one could argue that rock-climbing or hill-walking equipment might have some small added tax to pay for the cost of the mountain rescue services.  Similarly, smokers could be expected to pay an additional tax on tobacco (as they already do) to pay for their higher risk of health care, and high risk drivers could be expected to pay higher insurance premiums to pay for their higher probability of needing treatment for an accident.  All these duties should be set at a level such that at the point of service provision (mountain rescue, treatment for cancer, emergency medical treatment) no selection on the basis of lifestyle is necessary.

Generally speaking, the three objectives can be promoted concurrently, but on occasion may be in tension.  In addition, they are by no means specific enough to close down political debate.  For example, what level of compensation should be given to an individual in the event of some misfortune?  It can be argued that if the compensation is too large then it will divert too many resources from the rest of the population and thereby depress the quality of life of the rest of society, but if the compensation is too small it can be argued to be unjust to the individual.  There are no easy answers for such conflicts.  Nonetheless, it does seem of value to attempt to state what our objectives are.  As we shall see, the congruence and overlap between them is sufficient to justify quite broad sweeps of policy.

The ranking and numbering of the recommendations that follow do not indicate an order of priority.

## Generating wealth - the goal of strong and even economic growth

All the major political parties agree that economic growth is a good thing. Economic growth indicates the increased supply of valued goods to society, though some would qualify its value with reference to other factors such as its effects upon the environment. In addition, policy-makers often see economic growth as the route to other positive objectives (such as improved health care through increased tax revenue). Given this, the important question is therefore a technical, though complex one: how can we minimise the fluctuations of the business cycle and secure strong and even long-term economic growth?

In Chapter 2, David Currie summarises what we know. In the short term, the prospects for growth look good in the United Kingdom. However, the long-term growth performance of the United Kingdom gives cause for concern. There are a number of likely reasons for this, such as problems in the labour markets and financial markets, failures in education and training, and failures in the development and application of new technologies. It now seems clear that, in order to improve its growth performance, the United Kingdom will need to solve a complex set of supply-side issues, and that it is not enough to rely upon low inflation and tax cuts to generate growth. While 'demand-side' policies (such as fiscal and monetary policy) may have a role in smoothing the fluctuations over the business cycle, they have a relatively limited role to play in the long-term growth process. The single most important policy for such long-term growth must therefore be the encouragement of shrewd investment in both people and technology. There are many ways in which Government can encourage and engage in this investment, but a useful starting point would be to provide a clear signal to industry to encourage investment. With this in mind, we recommend:

1. **Tax credits should be introduced for research and development.** This tax credit, of around 25 per cent, should be based on changes in the ratio of R&D to sales as in the successful post-1990 system in the United States. Other policies to encourage long-term investment are also to be encouraged.

It is unlikely that the introduction of tax credits for R&D will generate much increased growth without attempts to improve the education and skills of the workforce, and we will return to such issues below. Our analysis suggests that some of the policies that have been presumed in recent years to be of great importance to growth may not be so important after all, the most notable of these being the obsession with maintaining low inflation. Most analysts now agree that, provided hyper-inflation is avoided, the absolute level of inflation has relatively little effect on long-term growth (though it may be of importance to other areas such as wage-bargaining, and hence to questions of income distribution and equality).

Our second objective is to ensure a high level of opportunity for all. All things being equal - in other words, assuming that the same level of growth could be achieved - most people would agree that it would be better to achieve economic growth relatively evenly rather than have it concentrated in small parts of the population or country. But are all things equal? In the Thatcher years, the theory became popular that increased inequality was good in so far as it stimulated a higher rate of overall growth from which everyone would eventually benefit. We now know that the latter part of this 'trickle-down' theory was not true - despite the economic growth of the 1980s, people in the bottom part of the income distribution failed to benefit significantly (Chapter 4 and Chapter 5, Box 5.1). In recent years there have been growing doubts about the first part of the theory as well - increased inequality *per se* does not necessarily increase overall growth.[2] The Social Justice Commission argued for an opposing theory, that economic growth is actually reduced by inequalities and that reducing inequalities could actually stimulate growth. Our own view of the evidence is somewhat more agnostic, but we would certainly agree that there is no *necessary* conflict between economic growth and equality, and that there are definitely strategic policies that could be pursued that would assist us to reach both goals simultaneously.

A striking manifestation and cause of economic inequality is unemployment and, in Chapter 3, Stephen Nickell asks the simple question, can it be reduced? His conclusion is 'yes'. To achieve even but efficient economic growth, and also to reduce unemployment, we believe that two types of policies must simultaneously be employed (see also Chapters 3, 5 and 6). These are incentives-promoting policies and capability-promoting policies (Box 5.4 in Chapter 5).

The aim of incentives-promoting policies is to ensure that work pays adequately to motivate people at all levels of the economy, and not least to motivate welfare recipients to seek and hold work. At the higher level of the income scale, perhaps the most important policy area in relation to incentives is taxation (discussed in Chapter 4). However, John Hills' cross-national analysis of taxation policy suggests that moderate changes to current levels of tax rates are unlikely to affect incentives. It is at the lower end of the income distribution that the incentives to work are most lacking and that policy requires most work. In this respect, attention will also have to be focused on policies for housing (discussed by Richard Best in Chapter 11). The most important incentives-promoting policies are:

2.   **A minimum income should be ensured for those in work.** This could be done through a combination of a minimum wage and 'in-work' benefits. To the extent that we ensure that 'work pays' through benefits, we must take care to extend the coverage of in-work benefits - notably Family Credit - to include childless couples and single persons.

3.   **Further incentives-promoting reforms should be introduced to the benefits system.** These should include (a) higher and more flexible earnings disregards for means-tested benefits such as Income Support, (b) reduced rates of benefit withdrawal, and (c) allowing people to stay on Income Support after entering work while their Family Credit is calculated, and automatically re-entitling people to it if they lose their jobs.

4.   **The housing benefit system should be reformed.** Rather than pursuing a system of market rents and individualised housing benefits for the bottom end of the market, policy should move towards 'bricks and mortar' subsidies and modest incentives (or at least a 'level playing field') for private renting. This will be more efficient and will take us away from the substantial disincentive effects of the present housing benefit system.

In general, as Ruth Lister points out in Chapter 5, there is a strong case for retaining individualised national insurance benefits where they currently exist, rather than trying to phase them out in favour of means-tested benefits in which the benefits received by one family member are reduced in line with the earnings of another, and which therefore tend to reduce the work incentives of the partners of the unemployed. In this respect, the government's job-seeker's allowance legislation is not at all sensible as a welfare-to-work strategy. In terms of reducing the rates of benefit withdrawal, this is as much about adjusting the *speed* of withdrawal as about the amount.

Incentive-promoting policies, if applied in isolation, would probably only have a limited effect on reducing unemployment and stimulating growth. As the analysis in Chapter 3 demonstrated, there has been a decline in the demand for unskilled workers, and without skills these workers will become increasingly unemployable - unless, of course, wages (and living standards) are to fall through the active promotion of a low-skills economy. If this is not what we want, then we must seek to implement a range of capability-promoting policies, the aim of which is to increase (and maintain) the skills and employability of the workforce, and especially those of welfare recipients and low-skilled workers. Of course, capability-promoting policies may also be incentives-promoting in so far as they increase the individual's expected return from work. In addition, capability-promoting policies will expand the opportunities for individuals to enter and change employment as their preferences demand. We believe that the most important capability-promoting policies that should be implemented are the following:

5.   **Better access to child-care should be provided.** This applies especially for lone parents. In the medium- to long-term, we should aim to make free child-care available to all 3 and 4 year old children whose parents wish it, and should facilitate the provision of after-school care for parents who work.

6.   **The receipt of benefit should be integrated with education and training programmes.** Initially this programme should be targeted on those most lacking in skills. The Jobs, Education and Training (JET) programme advocated by the Commission on Social Justice is perhaps the most appropriate working model currently proposed. In general, we must promote the idea that individuals should attend to the updating and re-equipping of their own skills throughout their working lives.

7.     **Programmes need to be developed to prevent potentially productive
       individuals from entrapment in long-term unemployment.** These
       could include wage subsidies to help reconnect the long-term
       unemployed to the labour market. Alternatively, as Stephen Nickell
       prefers, the state could act directly as employer of last resort, offering a
       'job guarantee' for those who have been unemployed for over, say, 18
       months, or by enrolling the long-term unemployed in retraining
       programmes geared to the expressed needs of employers. In practice,
       these options could shade into one, with employers being invited to
       tender for works (for example, environmental improvements), part of the
       explicit conditions of which would involve the employment of a
       proportion of long-term unemployed.

In summary, two central themes of future policy intended to stimulate strong
and even growth must be (a) increasing the skills of the population, and
especially those of the relatively unskilled, and (b) getting our incentives
structure right. In terms of the former, the need to improve the capabilities
of the work-force is a strategic imperative that must inform the goals of the
educational system; more specific priorities for education are discussed below.
Upgrading the capabilities of the work-force is not only the responsibility of
the state - individuals should also take an active interest and responsibility for
their own skill levels.
   The second theme - getting our incentives structure right - is equally
important. Most politicians, and from all parties, would agree with this, but
are reluctant to spell out publicly what it would mean. If we are to remove
the poverty trap by making the transition from welfare to employment more
financially attractive, then this inevitably implies some transfer of resources.
Two alternatives appear open to us. The first is to cut or tighten benefits,
transferring resources from those already on low incomes, and in this way
'pushing' people into work. The second is to reduce benefit withdrawal rates,
as suggested above. Other things being equal, this would imply that higher
taxes would have to be paid by those on moderate to high incomes. In our
view, we should do a bit of both, but primarily the latter. On the one hand,
at the margins of the benefit system, an individual should not expect to receive
something for nothing - someone who has been receiving benefit for an
extended period of time but who refuses re-training or a job of last resort
should expect their benefits to be cut. Similarly, arguments can be made for
the limiting of social security provision for mortgage payments, for tightening
checks on individuals on certain types of extended benefits, and possibly for
adjusting unemployment benefit such that it is more generous at the outset but
is then gradually reduced. On the other hand, the present benefit system
(especially in the short-term) can hardly be described as generous, and it seems
unlikely that much could be humanely cut. This means that the resources that
we wish to target on those low-income people in-work will have to come from
higher taxes on the moderate to well-paid. Hence taxes would probably have
to rise in the short-term, but in the longer-term these policies should lead to
reduced taxes through stronger growth.

## Sharing opportunities and spreading risks

We believe that one of the fundamental objectives of public policy should be to ensure that opportunities are shared according to ability and effort. We believe that this leads to a more efficient, equitable and legitimate society. Some of the policies already suggested would assist in the spreading of such opportunities. However, the application of this principle leads to a number of further policy implications. Competition policy has a role to play not only in encouraging economic growth (through increasing productivity, efficiency and promoting innovation) but also in forcing equality of opportunity. The spread of competition can be used to open up opportunities, threatening privileged interest groups and cartels with change or disappearance. Of course, competition policy should not apply only on the shop floor, but should reach all levels - including the boardroom.

8. **Competition should be sharpened, but where this is not possible, independent regulation should exist.** Despite the rhetoric of the market, many sectors of the economy have managed to avoid any real competition. These sectors require close attention, whether in private or public ownership. We would encourage the provision of greater information for shareholders and other stakeholders and also the development of clearer channels for their influence. The attention of policy-makers should include not only natural monopolies such as the privatised utilities, but also more subtle 'self-regulated' monopolies such as the legal professions and possibly the boardroom. Where competition is impractical, rigorous independent regulation should exist.

If opportunities are to be available to all, then it is essential that the state mitigate structural disadvantages by ensuring that every individual be given the best possible educational opportunities. In effect, the state should strike a deal with every new-born along the lines 'we promise you the opportunity to acquire the skills you will need to succeed, but it is up to you what you make of this opportunity.' In practical terms, this means that in the years prior to the maturity of an individual, the state should undertake to provide a very high quality of educational provision. By the time an individual reaches maturity and higher education, they should be expected to take some of this responsibility for themselves (see Chapter 6).

9. **High quality nursery, primary and secondary education should be available free to all.** The same principle of quality applies to all three levels of education, and if necessary, public resources should be switched from higher education in order to guarantee this, and especially to correct the present resource deficits in primary education.

10. **A new system should be introduced for financing further and higher education.** The discredited present arrangements for handling student loans should be replaced. Nevertheless, it is vitally important, from the standpoints of both equity and economic efficiency, to ensure widespread access to higher education. We believe that an income contingent loan

(switched off when repaid) represents a fair and effective way to increase the resources available for this. Over the longer-term, we should institute a national 'learning bank' along the lines sketched out by the Social Justice Commission, financed by a range of sources including a new graduate tax and a training tax on employers. The long-term aim should be to provide each citizen on maturity, via the learning bank, with access to the equivalent of three years full-time higher education. The learning bank could also be used by people who want to train or re-train themselves - a sort of 'skill mortgage' system.

The educational system is of central importance to many areas of strategic policy - economic growth, reducing unemployment, the family, crime and so on. Some strategic objectives and policies for the educational system have been suggested above. However, the educational system itself requires attention if it is to serve these wider policy objectives, for the educational performance of many of Britain's children continues to lag behind those of our major competitors. Fuller proposals for education are outlined by Josh Hillman in Chapter 6.

11. **There should be an integration and broadening of post-16 qualifications.** There are a number of options for doing this, but the main objective should be to reduce the barriers between the three current 'tracks'. This could be done by encouraging the present system to evolve towards a 'portfolio framework' whereby combinations of qualifications embodying various core skills and abilities could be accredited as a loose overarching diploma. This diploma could then be used for entry into Higher Education and accepted by employers as evidence for starting a skilled job.

12. **Action needs to be taken to accelerate the improvements in school and teacher performance.** Teachers must have access to life-long learning. Their role should become more focused with more extensive use of support staff for administrative and supervisory activities. A new Teacher Training Agency should be established to spearhead the promotion of teaching, but at the same time, procedures for dismissal of poor teachers should be simplified. The training, selection and initial back-up of head-teachers should also be improved. The Reading Recovery Programme should be restored.

Alongside the sharing of opportunities should go the spreading of risks. Many types of risks can be effectively and efficiently spread through private insurance, such as for damage to private property - housing, cars or personal possessions. However, there are a number of risks which the private sector would be reluctant to handle or where efficiency and equity would be in direct conflict. For example, genetic screening can identify individuals who are at particularly high risk of certain types of expensive-to-treat diseases. A private insurance scheme would seek either to avoid covering these at-risk individuals or to charge them very much higher premiums. If it is equity that we are seeking, then an insurance scheme would have to be set up which included all individuals and which avoided risk selection or such weighting of premiums. The police and judicial system, the National Health Service, the state educational system and the welfare state all provide examples of the state intervening to spread risk. However, now that markets have been introduced into public services, and particularly into health care, we must ensure that these new markets do not exclude people on the basis of risks over which they have no control.

13.  **State providers or agencies, within the health service and elsewhere, must not be allowed to 'cream-skim' low risk individuals.**  In particular, the arrangements concerning General Practitioner fundholding should be reformed or adjusted to ensure that there are no incentives for GPs to avoid unhealthy and therefore 'expensive' patients.

14.  **A premium should be added on National Insurance to pay for long-term care in old age.**  This recommendation reflects the need to take action now to cope with long-term demographic changes - population ageing - many of the consequences of which are already with us today. The effects of this trend will be of continuing importance over the coming decades.  The premium should also be levied on pensions.  This system would remove the need for the deeply unpopular current means-tested provision.

Yet, as Sally Prentice argues in Chapter 7, perhaps the most important form of risk spreading, in terms of health, would be to reduce the concentration of disadvantage within particular groups, families and individuals.  The best way to do this is through the spreading of opportunities, especially with education, and through reducing the damaging effects of disadvantage, for example, with suitable housing policies and in-work benefits for the low paid (see above).

## Social and economic partnerships for improving the quality of life for all

As we indicated in our suggested objectives, economic growth is an important component in the drive to increase our quality of life, but it is by no means synonymous with it.  Policy-makers must not lose sight of the relative importance of non-economic factors on the quality of our lives, such as the quality of our relationships with other people, our family lives, our security, and our environment.

A recurrent theme through much of the report and across policy areas is the destructive influence in our society of widening, and cross-generationally stable, patterns of inequality and disadvantage.  For example, in Chapter 8, Kathleen Kiernan demonstrated how teenage pregnancies were associated with, and reinforced by, low educational achievement and poor labour market prospects. Similarly, distinctive patterns of parenting and disadvantage are typically to be found in the backgrounds of low achievers at school and those who go on to get into trouble with the law (Chapter 9).  Our view is that the long-term solution to these problems must be to break the 'cycle of disadvantage' by targeting resources - and especially educational resources - on the children.

Once again, this points to the importance of the educational policies we have suggested earlier, and especially of those designed to increase the educational attainment and subsequent employment opportunities of the approximately 30 per cent of the population with few skills. We would also add that one of the best ways of encouraging parents to improve their basic skills and consequent employment prospects is by involving them in the education of their children. This whole approach implies a partnership between parents, children and the state. The state must fulfil its role by providing high quality education, child care and, as far as possible, the incentive and opportunity to work (see above). Parents also have an important role to play.

15. **Parents - including fathers - should share responsibility for the well-being of their children.** We endorse the activity of the Child Support Agency (CSA), but would wish to see its efficiency improved. The role and activity of the CSA should be advertised among young people as part of their more general sex and parenthood education. However, the state benefits received by single mothers should not be reduced as drastically as at present in proportion to the payments collected by the CSA from absent fathers. This minor reform would give single mothers more incentive to help locate absent fathers and would increase the resources going to benefit the children in these households. Potential parents should also take care to ensure that they have acquired the skills and resources that their role will demand of them, and the possibility of explicitly teaching 'relationship' and 'parenting' skills at school should be seriously considered.

Crime, and fear of crime, have become a major problem for most modern industrialised societies. After reviewing the evidence, David Faulkner, Michael Hough and David Halpern conclude that the solution to this complex problem does not lie in the state issuing ever greater punishments (Chapter 9). Generally speaking, the probability that a sanction will be applied is of greater importance than the severity of the sanction. This indicates that criminal justice policy should be more concerned about detection rates than increasing the severity of punishments. The relative success rates of community penalties and cautioning should be built on, and prison sentences used more sparingly. Prison does 'work' to some extent, but at a huge cost compared to the alternatives, many of which are equally effective.

Tackling crime must be recognised as ultimately involving a wide range of policies including: situational prevention, influencing the economic incentives and alternatives to crime, and strengthening the commitment, or 'embeddedness', of potential offenders to society and thereby the effectiveness of informal sanctions upon them. More specifically, it is important that children learn the basic cognitive skills that will enable them to appreciate the longer term and wider consequences of their actions. An individual who habitually discounts longer term costs and benefits is both less likely to be successful as an individual and more likely to impose costs on the society around them.

16. **The Home Office should be actively encouraging the wider use of non-custodial sentences.** Examples include the more extensive use of community sentences and the treatment of drug-dependent offenders with substitution treatments. These will be more cost effective strategies than continuing to increase the size of the prison population. The extra resources released could then be used for other more important priorities such as improving detection rates and extending situational crime prevention.

17. **The concept of the 'prevention' of crime should be pursued through a strategic re-orientation of policy.** The first stage of this approach is to encourage the Home Office to broaden its vision beyond the narrow, and relatively ineffective confines of the formal criminal justice system. Environmental prevention through improved design should be extended and the recommendations of the Morgan Report (see Chapter 9) should be revived. Pre- and early school education should be used to ensure that children develop a full awareness of the consequences of their actions on others and children must learn the cognitive skills to be able to make effective long-term cost-benefit analyses. Older children should learn parenting skills. Finally, the influence of social and economic policy on the incentive structure presented to potential offenders should be a legitimate concern of the Home Office.

Like the social environment, the physical environment also has major impacts on our quality of life. The concept and goal of 'sustainable development' has moved from the political fringes to being publicly accepted, even embraced, by all the major political parties. Unfortunately, governments and political parties have been slow to act upon their new-found green ideals. This reluctance to act may have stemmed from the popular belief that there is a major tension between environmental protection and economic growth. We believe that this tension has been over-stated: environmental protection typically results from stronger rather than reduced economic growth.

A specific example of this perceived tension, discussed by Stuart Taylor and Bridget Taylor in Chapter 10, has been the perception of a political conflict between the environment and the need of the economy for an efficient transport system. The tension has been exacerbated by the 'Not in my back yard' (NIMBY) syndrome and the overwhelming popularity of cars. But the re-emergence of smog in our cities, delays in our journeys, and respiratory disorders in our children, indicate that current policies are both unsustainable and increasingly expensive in their 'external' consequences. We must, therefore, do something about our transport policy as a matter of some urgency. Any such strategy must balance the needs of the economy with the needs of our environment and the important role it has in the quality of our lives.

18. **The principle should be applied of taxing environmental 'goods' and 'bads' according to the damage that they cause.** The main intention of this principle is *not* to increase overall tax revenues, but to provide meaningful price signals to consumers and clear incentives to reduce

environmental damage. Where this principle leads to substantial price rises, these should be offset by decreases in other taxes and increases in benefit entitlements. For example, increases in the cost of domestic fuel could be partly refunded via reductions in council taxes banded according to the average use in the geographical area (the compensation being larger in colder areas of the country). Tax credits could also be given for the cost of energy saving measures such as insulation.

19. **Fuel duty should be increased at least at the rate of 5 per cent per annum for the foreseeable future, and congestion charging should be considered in urban areas.** The extra revenue generated by these 'stick' measures should be used to fund a number of complementary 'carrots'. These would include improvements in the quality and frequency of public transport, improvements in the road network (through less intrusive methods), and a substantial improvement in cycling facilities. Such revenues could also be used to provide compensation for the higher duties through reductions in other taxes and increases in benefits. Where congestion charging is introduced, such as through systems of day and time-banded resident permits and perhaps eventually through electronic charging, the revenue generated should be kept for use in the local area either for environmental and transport improvements or, at the discretion of the Local Authority, for reduced council taxes.

### Building a modern democracy

It is our belief that power should be shared through the population, but that individuals and small groups should be protected from the 'tyranny of the majority'. The twin purposes of democratic politics are to promote effective administration and to involve citizens in the decision making apparatus of their state. These considerations should prompt us to take seriously the issue of the appropriate level at which political debate should be conducted - the issue of 'subsidiarity'. We should be prepared to ask tough questions about the value-added of all levels of government - not just Europe - and in every policy area. This brings us to the issue of devolution, discussed by Vernon Bogdanor in Chapter 12. Our view is that:

20. **As far as possible, the geographical boundaries of local and regional government agencies should be adjusted to be coterminous.** At present, even very closely related services, such as branches of the criminal justice system (the police, the probation service, the courts, the Crown Prosecution Service and so on; Chapter 9), operate within very different geographical boundaries. These in turn typically have little correspondence with other services such as District Health Authorities or Local Authorities. The boundaries and chains of accountability of these many services should be rationalised to improve their coordination, efficiency and accountability. This should tie in with longer term moves towards regional government.

21.    **A Scottish Parliament and new regional tier of government for London should be created.** The introduction of a Scottish parliament is now a political imperative. However, we believe that the provision of regional government for London is equally urgent, though for different reasons. These new bodies should have limited tax raising powers. Parliamentary legislation should specify an upper limit of their legislative and fiscal powers. These limits would then be clearly signalled to other regions contemplating applications for similar assemblies in England and Wales. It should be a condition of these applications that the administrative body that is established serves to replace existing 'quangos' and in their place secures a greater degree of accountability and transparency in the administration of public policy.

22.    **We should introduce a bill of rights.** The European Convention on Human Rights should be directly incorporated into British law. Given the growing importance of European Law, this is presently occurring by default. However, the importance of such a convention goes beyond its narrow legal function; it is also constructive for people to have a sense of what their rights are - and an awareness of what the rights of others are - on an informal, day-to-day level. We should make the incorporation of the convention explicit, in order to reinforce 'educational' policies (such as in recommendation 17) that are intended to emphasise the nature of the 'social contract' that exists between individuals and between individuals and the state. More generally, given the incorporation of European Law, and also the development of devolution within the United Kingdom, we should consider establishing a judicial review body to examine conflicts between the legislation of different layers of government. This raises difficult issues about Parliamentary sovereignty. However, we would suggest that it is time to consider Parliamentary sovereignty as a means rather than an end. There is no instrumental justification for viewing this sovereignty as sacrosanct, and it is already being undermined, in any event, by our involvement in international treaties, the operation of political parties and cabinet government, the European Union and the world economy more generally.

Concerning our relationship to Europe, discussed by George Brock in Chapter 13, we believe that:

23.    **We should adopt a tough 'value-added' approach to European issues.** We should seek to distinguish more clearly which areas are most fruitfully pursued at the European level and those which we wish to retain at the national level. We should also require a greater degree of transparency in European institutions and European wide decisions. Institutions at the European level must make themselves available to scrutiny by interested groups, and they must improve the dissemination of information about what they actually do.

24.  **Enlargement of the European Union should be a priority.**  If
necessary, depth should be sacrificed for breadth, and variable geometry
should be accepted as a political reality. Having said this, a reduction in
the power of vetoes is inevitable. We should establish a consistent set of
preferences on the areas in which we are prepared to countenance a
majority voting mechanism rather than a unanimity rule in the Council
of Ministers (for example, unanimity to be retained for the border
control of people, but majority voting to be used for health and safety
legislation).

We found it impossible to come to a firm conclusion about the issue of
European Monetary Union (EMU) other than to say that it would certainly
be a mistake to exclude ourselves from the option. Also, if EMU was to go
forward within a core of countries, our judgement is that it would be better
to be in than out. What is certainly needed is a lot more political, social and
economic analysis of the costs and benefits of monetary union - and of
different sorts of monetary union - before any decision is made.

The issue of representational reform - electoral and constitutional - was
considered by Raymond Plant in Chapter 14. There are long-standing
arguments about the strengths and weaknesses of various electoral systems, and
the choice between them is not simple. This is not just because of the
technical complexity of the issues involved or even because of political
differences of view, but because the arguments in favour or against a particular
electoral system are significantly affected by changes in the institutional
context. For example, when political institutions lead to a high concentration
of power, the arguments in favour of some form of proportional
representation are very strong, but if power becomes highly devolved, then the
argument in favour of a more majoritarian system strengthens. In other
words, political institutions work in tandem, so that the 'cherry picking' of
particular constitutional changes is very problematic.

Nonetheless, it is clear that our current electoral system is relatively unusual
compared to other systems in having the effect of encouraging political parties
to concentrate their efforts, and the benefits of their policies, on the floating
voters of marginal constituencies. This means that political parties can largely
ignore the needs of voters in all non-marginal areas - whether they be their
own voters or those of an opposing party. This is especially unsatisfactory
given that voting patterns have shown a growing tendency in recent years to
regional political divisions. Devolution offers a possibility for the wider
introduction of a form of proportional representation using multi-member
constituencies that should be seized. At the centre, however, we believe that
the best option is provided by the reform of the second chamber along the
lines proposed by Raymond Plant.

25.  **Multi-member constituencies should be employed in regional
elections.**  Initially, such constituencies would be used in the new
regional assemblies for Scotland and London. They would then be
introduced into other regions on a rolling basis if and when they are
ready to establish their own assemblies.

**26.  A new second chamber should be created at Westminster elected by proportional representation.** This would replace the role of the present House of Lords. Removing the voting rights of hereditary peers could be done as an intermediate step, but this should only be seen as a transitory arrangement before a fully elected chamber is created.

For reasons already stated, the issue of electoral reform for the House of Commons is left open. This issue will need to be decided, presumably through a referendum, once political agreement has been reached on the interrelated issue of devolution. However, the presence of a more legitimate, democratically elected second chamber is likely to bring considerable pressure on the House of Commons for some sort of reform.

## Improving the policy-making process

In conducting this review, we have been struck by the fact that the policy-making process in Britain is fragmented in a number of ways. Government departments conduct policy research behind closed doors and with poor coordination between departments. Political parties face incentives in the bipolar political system to engage in negative debating, to hoard rather than to share ideas and, once in power, they tend to be primarily concerned with policies that will bring short-term pay-offs in time for the next election.

The weakness of Parliament in the context of a strong two party system undermines both the policy-making powers of our sovereign legislative chamber and its ability to scrutinise the activities of the executive. This, coupled with the high degree of inaccessibility to the workings of Whitehall, serves to remove policy debate and deliberation even further from the forum of public debate. To implement, and see the benefits of, effective policy in areas such as education, employment, pensions, health, crime, the environment and so on, takes many years. Furthermore, as this volume has shown, the links between these issues are complex and important, and compartmentalised approaches to policy-making are inappropriate and ineffective.

Many of these institutional problems are part of the more general tension facing governments in any democracy between the dictates of re-election and those of good governance. However, there are good reasons to believe that the constitutional and electoral system of the United Kingdom accentuates this tension more than in many other European nations, and this is a major factor behind our recommendations for electoral and constitutional reform. The partial devolution of power, the rationalisation of the geographical relationship between government services and the introduction of more proportional electoral systems will improve the coordination of policy on a practical level and foster the search for common ground on the political level.

In addition, we would recommend some more detailed and immediate reforms of the workings of Parliament itself in order to temper the conflictual style of politics with one that encourages better informed and better coordinated debates about strategic and long-term policy issues. These were listed at the start of the report (Chapter 1), but are summarised here.

27. **Future bills should be routinely reviewed by Parliamentary Special Standing Committees.** Parliament should insist that this procedure, provision for which already exists, is actually used. The Committees' role would be to examine the intentions behind a piece of legislation and to consider its likely consequences and effectiveness at an early stage. The Committees should be allowed to call in expert witnesses to advise them. This procedure would lead to a better quality of debate and, ultimately, to better drafted and considered legislation.

28. **The Select Committees should be strengthened and encouraged to explore strategic issues.** They should be encouraged to cooperate, and hold joint sittings, over matters that cut across departmental boundaries, not least to identify conflicts and contradictions between departments' policies. They should be encouraged to enquire about the longer-term objectives of government departments and could provide a suitable forum for the airing of tentative proposals in front of a range of interested parties. In addition, the restrictive 'Osmotherly Rules' governing the behaviour of civil servants giving evidence should be removed, or at least extensively rewritten, to allow the Committees to do their work.

29. **A specialist research unit, attached directly to Parliament, should be created to review the strategic policy options in public policy.** This unit should have direct links with the Central Statistical Office (CSO) and the House of Commons Library. The role of the unit would be to serve Parliament and the Committee system both with information in response to specific enquiries and also with more general ideas and strategic reviews in order to inform and improve debate. The unit, in cooperation with the CSO, should develop a capability to model and predict longer term social, economic and institutional trends. Members of Parliament should be able to refer policy ideas to the unit for further consideration and should be involved in the selection of personnel. However, MPs should not be involved in the day-to-day running of the unit. The unit would be funded directly by Parliament to protect it from absorption by government departments.

There also needs to be a strengthening of the ability of government and the civil service to develop, review and coordinate strategic policy. Explicit in this must be the use of longer time scales, especially by the Treasury: the immediate financial year is an inadequate time-frame for the appraisal of strategic policy.

30. **The structures of the Civil Service should be encouraged to become more flexible and less departmentalised.** This should build on the opportunity presented by the 'Next Steps' initiative, making the smaller and less specialised core functions of the Civil Service more strategically orientated and more cooperative with other departments. This should be reflected at Cabinet level by a greater emphasis on strategic policy objectives and a lesser emphasis on Ministries. In this looser

departmental structure, it should become common for cross-departmental teams to be formed to investigate, and sometimes implement, policy options. For certain phases of policy development, this process might include the use of competing teams to develop alternative ideas, but with team members still drawn from across departments.

31. **The Cabinet Office should be charged with the responsibility of translating the winning party's manifesto into a realistic strategic plan after general elections.** This would ensure that there would be a clear and coordinated understanding across government departments about the overall direction and objectives of government policy over the government's period in office. The Cabinet Office should draft people in from across departments to assist with the process. A deadline should be set for the production of the plan so as to reduce the likelihood of the civil service paralysing the process.

Finally, we feel that there is a strong case in favour of improving the capability of the political parties to develop and refine alternative policies. It is very important that there is an effective 'market' for the generation of policy ideas. Such a market of ideas is necessary in order to stimulate continuous, vibrant public debate and good quality and widely legitimated policies. At present, there are few institutional channels for the development of strategic policy ideas outside of the government in power and their civil service. Even the various so-called 'independent' think-tanks are often highly constrained by their funding arrangements and the funders themselves, many of whom are actually government departments.

Political parties conduct policy research, but behind closed doors rather than through public debate. This process undoubtably falls prey to the complex constraints of political organisations seeking re-election and therefore looking to the preferences of their electorate, their potential electorate, and groups within the parties themselves. Nonetheless, it may be wise to increase the capability of opposition parties to develop and test policy ideas, perhaps through changes in central funding arrangements for policy research activity. This would serve to increase the pool of available ideas while in no way detracting from the autonomy of the elected government and the civil service in choosing between these ideas.

32. **The access of the Opposition to information should be improved, and the possibility should be considered of some state funding of policy research inside the political parties.** At present, the Opposition's policies are typically based on informed guesses about the incumbent government's policy and expenditure commitments, projected revenues, and so on. This means that the Opposition's policies are often artificially unrealistic and their ability to contribute to debate reduced. It is worth seriously considering state funding of Opposition policy development in order to ensure a good supply of alternative, well constructed and fully costed proposals, and to generate an effective 'market' of policy ideas. The National Audit Office should keep track of how this money is spent.

## Conclusion

Britain has many policy options, perhaps more than we tend to assume. Though it may sometimes be politically convenient for the government to emphasise the external constraints on what it can do, such as from the pressures of global trade, these constraints are by no means overwhelming. The main constraints are political, and sometimes psychological. If politicians have the imagination to develop and the courage to champion new ideas, and if the public are prepared to vote and pay for them, then there is a huge amount that can be done.

Complacency, and sometimes pessimism, about government policy often arises because we assume that someone, somewhere in government, must have thought through the options; why else would the current policy be 'X' or 'Y'? After all, policies don't just 'happen', do they? Unfortunately, our conclusion is that, surprisingly often, there isn't anybody who has really thought through the issue, at least not in terms of the 'bigger picture'. When the question is asked, 'who in government is keeping track of the overall direction and results of policy?' the response tends to be an awkward silence. Consider, for example, the issue of the overall incentives to work. The incentives profile across income levels is the net result of many different policies and from many government departments - Social Security, the Treasury, the Department of the Environment, and so on - yet there is no clear body or department keeping track of how these policies all fit together to ensure that the net result is what was intended. In essence, there is no real strategic capability at the heart of government. This is a problem that is not unique to Britain, but it is a fundamental flaw in our political culture and institutions that we must address.

No doubt many readers will disagree with some of the specific proposals offered by the panel of experts in this book, but who could disagree with the underlying purpose? As we enter the Twenty-First century, it is important that we ask ourselves where we are going and what sort of society we want to live in. We *do* have choices, but if we have no plan or direction of where we want to go or what we want to achieve, then the chances are that we will be disappointed with the net result. Ultimately, successful policies take a long time to implement and need the commitment of many individuals and communities of interest. What we must ensure, therefore, is that we have a real public debate about what our longer term objectives and options are, and that we have a government and administration with a capability and preparedness to think long-term, inter-departmentally and strategically.

## Notes

1.   In the language of political philosophy, objective I reflects a commitment to a principle of general welfare; objective II, a commitment to a modestly egalitarian conception of distributive justice; and objective III, a commitment to democratic self-government and the maintenance of basic liberty.

2.   For a recent review of the evidence, see Persson, T. and Tabellini, G. (1994), 'Is inequality harmful for growth?', *American Economic Review*, **84** (3), pp.600-21.

# Index